T0299360

SPORTS
Nation

Contemporary American
Professional Organizations

SPORTS
Nation

Contemporary American
Professional Organizations

Frank P. Jozsa, Jr.
Pfeiffer University, USA

NEW JERSEY · LONDON · SINGAPORE · BEIJING · SHANGHAI · HONG KONG · TAIPEI · CHENNAI · TOKYO

Published by

World Scientific Publishing Co. Pte. Ltd.
5 Toh Tuck Link, Singapore 596224
USA office: 27 Warren Street, Suite 401-402, Hackensack, NJ 07601
UK office: 57 Shelton Street, Covent Garden, London WC2H 9HE

British Library Cataloguing-in-Publication Data
A catalogue record for this book is available from the British Library.

SPORTS NATION
Contemporary American Professional Organizations

ISBN 978-981-3225-51-0

Desk Editor: Sandhya Venkatesh

Typeset by Stallion Press
Email: enquiries@stallionpress.com

Printed in Singapore

To sports fans

PREFACE

The most prominent and successful organizations in American professional team sports emerged, developed, and matured during different but distinct periods of time. When actually named, these different groups — from most to least experienced in each sport as of their 2015 season — include 140-year-old Major League Baseball (MLB) — officially American League (AL) in 1901 and National League (NL) in 1876 — and then the 99-year-old National Hockey League (NHL), 96-year-old National Football League (NFL) — named American Professional Football Association in 1920–1921 — and 69-year-old National Basketball Association (NBA).

Despite internal problems as owners and front-office disputes and players' injuries, and also such external issues as economic recessions and government legislation, teams within these sports performed in regular-season games and then if qualified, competed against each other in playoff series and types of postseason championships. Consequently, they and their parent organizations became important, popular, and unique in American culture, history, and society especially in years of the 20th and early 21st centuries.

To organize and schedule games in each of their regular seasons and postseasons, the four major sports encouraged and promoted their teams to exist for years and even decades within small, midsized, large, or very large metropolitan area and appeal to fans in local, regional, national, and even international markets. Essentially, professional teams perform to provide entertainment for spectators and on television networks by competing in home and away games within new and/or renovated arenas, ballparks, and stadiums while also operating as franchises or commercial enterprises in order to earn maximum profits with sufficient amounts of cash inflows and revenue.

For various reasons, however, some teams previously located in metropolitan areas of America and also others in provinces of Canada ultimately folded because they had financial problems; inferior owners, coaches, managers and/or players; apathetic hometown fans; and/or simply underachieved for periods while playing rivals primarily within their division and/or conference.

PURPOSE

From researching such sport-specific sources as books, journals, newspapers, and websites on the Internet, and studying demographic, economic, and financial data and other information in the literature, *Sports Nation* focuses on, identifies, and analyzes various divisions and conferences and their teams' historical regular-season and postseason performances, and also provides a recent financial profile of them while being competitive, profitable or unprofitable, and well-known enterprises. For sure, this is a newsworthy and significant topic for different audiences because it includes existing sports franchises and reveals how effectively they competed as a group and also individually operated, survived, and prospered or not prospered from a business perspective.

BOOK OVERVIEW

After the front matter, which consists of the Preface, About the Author, Acknowledgements and Abbreviations, *Sports Nation* include eight chapters followed by a Conclusion and then Appendix, Bibliography and Index. As such, the following describes the structure of these chapters and also information about their contents.

While the Acknowledgements and Abbreviations are self-explanatory, each chapter discusses teams within divisions and divisions within conferences. Assigned to major sections — AL and NL in MLB, American and National Football Conferences in the NFL, and Eastern and Western Conferences each in the NBA and NHL — there are several subsections regarding each group. Sequentially, these focus on organizations' history and then market data, team performances, financial information, their ballparks, arenas, or stadiums including amenities and fan cost indexes, and also interesting but important and relevant business and economic news.

More specifically, the chapters denote when, where and how effectively teams in divisions have historically performed and their financial status and significance as members of competitive and popular professional sports organizations. Readers learn, for example, which of them won division and/ or conference titles and championships; the age, construction cost, and economic value of their home-site venues; amounts families spent for tickets and other items to attend teams' home games; franchises' market value, revenue, operating income, gate receipts, and other financial information including their debt-to-value ratios and players expenses; and any current topics and local activities, events, and projects that influence them as business enterprises. The contents also explain why some teams succeeded more than others based on such things as attendances at their home games and also win-loss records, market size, and estimated worth.

Within chapters, franchises are compared to current rivals in their division like the Boston Red Sox and New York Yankees in the AL's East Division, Chicago Bulls and Cleveland Cavaliers in the NBA's Central Division, Atlanta Falcons and Carolina Panthers in the NFL's South Division, and Edmonton Oilers and Vancouver Canucks in the NHL's Pacific Division.

Among its audiences, *Sports Nation* was written and published for current and prospective owners and executives of sports franchises and potential investors in these organizations; MLB, NBA, NFL, and NHL commissioners, executives, and their staffs; practitioners and scholars who research the sports industry; college and university professors who teach undergraduate and graduate students majoring in sports administration, business, economics, history, management, and/or marketing; and also dedicated fans of all ages who support current professional baseball, basketball, American football, and ice hockey teams.

Frank P. Jozsa Jr.

ABOUT THE AUTHOR

A former college and semiprofessional athlete with an undergraduate degree in accounting and a masters' degrees in business administration and economics, and also a doctorate in economics, Frank P. Jozsa Jr. is the author of several books on team sports in professional baseball, basketball and football, another on intercollegiate sports programs at American colleges and universities, and an unpublished manuscript on professional ice hockey. His memoirs, *A Hoosier's Journey: Athlete, Student, Teacher, and Author* were published by Dog Ear Publishing in 2011.

Besides books, Jozsa has written several articles published in journals, magazines, and newspapers. His dissertation — "An Economic Analysis of Franchise Relocation and League Expansion in Professional Team Sports, 1950–1975" — was completed in 1977 at Georgia State University in Atlanta, Georgia. After teaching undergraduate and graduate courses in economics, finance, and statistics for more than three decades, Jozsa retired from Pfeiffer University in 2007.

ACKNOWLEDGEMENTS

While organizing, writing, and editing the manuscript for this book during mid-to-late 2016/early 2017, a few individuals provided information for it and thus helped me in different ways. Most important to my project, Pfeiffer University's library director and assistant professor of library science Lara Little found numerous readings about professional sports organizations from such publications as *Business Week*, *Forbes*, *Fortune*, *SportsBusiness Journal* and the *Wall Street Journal*, and then promptly forwarded them to me. I appreciate Lara's professionalism and her commitment to spend time and obtain articles, reports, and studies for me regarding the business, economics, finance, and operations of teams in the sport. Surely, Lara is a superstar librarian for the University's administration, faculty and staff, and especially for the school's undergraduate and graduate students.

Besides Lara, another contributor was University of Michigan professor of sport management and co-director of the school's Center for Sport Management Rodney D. Fort. He provided me, for example, an update regarding the National Hockey League and its teams' fan cost indexes. The coauthor of *Pay Dirt*, Professor Fort produces business and other historical data on professional sports leagues at https://sites.google.com/site/rodsweb pages/cod.

Former Loras College economics professor Laddie Sula and I have been friends since the early 1970s when doctoral students at Georgia State University in Atlanta. For *Sports Nation*, he offered advice and spoke with me about Major League Baseball including his knowledge and opinion of teams — especially the National League's Chicago Cubs — and their managers and players. While at Loras, Laddie had a great career playing on the school's basketball team. As a result, he was inducted into its Sports Hall of Fame.

Forbes sports editor Kurt Badenhausen directed me to some websites regarding the business and history of professional sports teams and their coaches and players. He told me when *Forbes* publishes its annual financial data and other information about franchises in Major League Baseball and also the National Basketball Association, National Football League, and National Hockey League. For one of my previous books, Kurt answered my questions about financial amounts reported in articles such as the magazine's "The Business of Basketball" and "2016 NHL Valuations." Player's expenses, for example, are altered to account for benefits, costs, and insurance teams get back for injured players, draft picks sold, amnestied players, and other things. Special thanks to Professor Fort, Laddie, and Kurt.

Research analyst Gino Belmonte at thinktv.ca forwarded me demographic data. This included the rank of North American television markets on population and also geographic areas for extended markets in Canada. He sent me maps with estimates of Montreal Anglo and Franco, Toronto, and Ottawa-Gatineau Anglo and Franco. Thanks Gino.

My fiancé and best friend Maureen Fogle allowed me to use her computer to organize and write a manuscript for this book. She understands how important this project was for me to complete and then submit a professional copy of it to World Scientific Publishing Company on or before the due date. Once again, thanks to Maureen for her cooperation and patience particularly since my retirement as a business/economics professor from Pfeiffer University in 2007.

Frank P. Jozsa Jr.

CONTENTS

ABBREVIATIONS

AAFC	All American Football Conference
AA	American Association
ABA	American Basketball Association
ABC	American Broadcasting Corporation
AFC	American Football Conference
AFL	American Football League
AL	American League
ALCS	American League Championship Series
ALDS	American League Division Series
APFA	American Professional Football Association
AD	Atlantic Division
AVGATT	Average Attendance
BAA	Basketball Association of America
CD	Central Division
CMAs	Census Metropolitan Areas
CCC	Clarence Campbell Conference
CBA	Collective Bargaining Agreement
CBS	Columbia Broadcasting System
CL	Continental League
D/V	Debt-to-Value
DH	Designated Hitter
DMA	Designated Market Area
DMATVH	Designated Market Area Television Homes

$	Dollars
ERA	Earned Run Average
EBITDA	Earnings Before Interest, Taxes, Depreciation, Amortization
EC	Eastern Conference
Elo	Elovation App
ESPN	Entertainment Sports Programming Network
FCI	Fan Cost Index
GR	Gate Receipts
HRs	Home Runs
LA	Los Angeles
MSG	Madison Square Garden
MLB	Major League Baseball
MD	Metropolitan Division
MSA	Metropolitan Statistical Area
MSAPOP	Metropolitan Statistical Area Population
MWD	Midwest Division
MVP	Most Valuable Player
NA	National Association
NABBP	National Association of Base Ball Players
NAPBBP	National Association of Professional Base Ball Players
NBA	National Basketball Association
NBL	National Basketball League
NBPA	National Basketball Players Association
NBC	National Broadcasting Corporation
NCAA	National Collegiate Athletic Association
NFC	National Football Conference
NFL	National Football League
NHA	National Hockey Association
NHL	National Hockey League
NL	National League
NLCS	National League Championship Series
NLDS	National League Division Series
NPBL	National Professional Basketball League
NO	New Orleans
NY	New York

NFLPA	NFL Players Association
NHLPA	NHL Players Association
ND	North Division
NED	Northeast Division
NWD	Northwest Division
NA	Not Applicable
OBP	On-Base-Percentage
OI	Operating Income
PCHA	Pacific Coast Hockey Association
PD	Pacific Division
PE	Players Expenses
PL	Players League
PWC	Prince of Wales Conference
R	Rank
RBIs	Runs Batted In
SVS&E	Silicon Valley Sports & Entertainment
SD	South Division
SED	Southeast Division
SWD	Southwest Division
SD	Standard Deviation
SPC	Standard Players Contract
SCup	Stanley Cup
SB	Super Bowl
TMR	Team Marketing Report
TP	Total Performance
UA	Union Association
U.S.	United States
Univ	University
WD	West Division
WC	Western Conference
WL	Western League
W%	Winning Percent
WAR	Wins Above Replacement
WHA	World Hockey Association

Part I
Major League Baseball

Chapter 1

AMERICAN LEAGUE

HISTORY

Founded in 1892 as a minor baseball league, the Western League (WL) ceased operations in July because of financial difficulties. Former sports editor Bancroft 'Ban' Johnson, who supported the Players League in 1890, was given a task to revive the struggling circuit. Appointed president of it in 1894, he accepted his new job with fervor, and quickly the WL became one of the most entertaining, popular, and profitable sports organizations in the nation.[1]

By 1897, some WL teams were outdrawing their counterparts in the National League (NL) that, due to economic and other problems, jettisoned the Baltimore Orioles, Cleveland Spiders, Louisville Colonels, and Washington Senators after its 1899 season. Meanwhile, the former league had teams in Buffalo, New York; Columbus, Ohio; Detroit, Michigan; Indianapolis, Indiana; Kansas City, Missouri; Milwaukee, Wisconsin; and both Minneapolis and St. Paul, Minnesota. Given an opportunity to expand regionally especially into more populated areas of the lower Midwest, Johnson moved a small-market franchise from St. Paul to Chicago and another from Columbus to Cleveland, Ohio.

Reorganizing in 1900, the WL was renamed American League of Professional Baseball Clubs or simply American League (AL) by Johnson but nevertheless, it existed as a minor league that year in the sport. The newly-named organization's mission, however, was to compete for baseball fans and market share against teams within the rival NL.

3

In 1901, the AL declared itself a "major league" and thereby located teams in such very large cities as Boston, Massachusetts and Philadelphia, Pennsylvania while its other clubs played at home in midsized-to-large metropolitan areas of Baltimore, Chicago, Cleveland, Detroit, Milwaukee, and Washington, D.C. Although Boston, Chicago, and Philadelphia were also occupied by NL teams, the AL was successful at recruiting some talented NL players and signing them to contracts. Although the AL Chicago White Stockings and NL Pittsburgh Pirates each won a pennant in 1901 and AL Philadelphia Athletics and Pirates again in 1902, there were no World Series between them.

In 1903, a precarious peace treaty was established through the National Agreement whereby the NL recognized the AL as a "major league" and both agreed to honor the reserve clause in player contracts. During September/ October, the AL champion Boston Americans defeated the NL champion Pirates five-games-to-three in baseball's first World Series. In 1904, however, the World Series was cancelled because New York Giants owner John T. Brush and manager John McGraw refused to play a team from the AL for being a "minor circuit." Shortly thereafter, public pressure forced permanent peace between the two organizations, and therefore, they remained distinct entities with their own officials but compete in World Series.

In fact, the two leagues assigned their own umpiring crews, with the AL home-plate umpires continuing to use outside chest protectors for decades although the NL umpires eliminated them. Despite wearing an outside protector, the AL umpires stood further back from home plate and batters than did those in the NL. Some historians contend that this positional difference, and also umpires perspective on the strike zone, may have caused variations in pitching styles of teams in the two leagues from mid-1900 into the free agency era. In other words, the NL became known as a fastball league in which pitchers 'challenged hitters' whereas the AL was considered a "breaking ball league."

Initiated by Chicago Tribune sports editor Arch Ward to coincide with the celebration of Chicago's Century of Progress Exposition, the AL defeated the NL 4-2 at Comiskey Park and won the sport's first all-star game in 1933. Being titled the "Midsummer Classic", the game usually occurs on either the second or third Tuesday in July which marks a symbolic halfway-point in the Major League Baseball (MLB) season. To provide additional incentive for victory, MLB reached an agreement with the players union to award home-field advantage for the next World Series to the champion of the league that won the all-star game in 2003 and 2004. After being extended to 2005 and 2006, the agreement continued but then dropped after the 2016 season.[2]

Because of expansion in 1969, the AL (and NL) restructured organizationally and established an East Division (ED) and West Division (WD) with six teams each in these divisions. It also added another round to the playoffs in the form of the AL Championship Series (ALCS) with the first place team in each division advancing to the playoffs. Then four years later, the AL but not NL teams introduced a designated hitter (DH) as a part of their regular-season and postseason games. Under this experiment or new rule, each team used a batter in its lineup who was not in the field defensively, replacing any player — usually the pitcher — in the batting order as compared to the old rule that required a pitcher to bat.

After 25 seasons with two divisions, the AL reorganized again by adding a Central Division (CD) with five teams each in the ED and CD but only four in the WD. It also incorporated a third round into the playoffs in the form of the AL Division Series (ALDS), with the best second-place team advancing to the playoffs as a wild-card, in addition to the three divisional champions. However, because of a players strike, MLB owners cancelled the 1994 season during mid-August. This was baseball's eighth work stoppage since 1972.

In 1998, the newly-enfranchised Tampa Bay Devil Rays joined the AL's ED and Arizona Diamondbacks the NL's WD for a total of 14 and 16 teams, respectively, in each group. Because of these different totals, this meant at least one team in each league was idle on any given day, or alternatively, the odd team out had to play an interleague game against its counterpart in the other league. The initial plan was to establish three five-team divisions per league with interleague play year-round — or possibly as many as 30 interleague games per team each year.

From administrative, organizational and scheduling viewpoints, it seemed practical to eventually have an even number of teams in both leagues. Even so, in 1998, the AL Milwaukee Brewers were moved from the CD to the NL's CD while the former league's Detroit Tigers transferred from the ED to its CD, which allowed the Devil Rays to join the New York Yankees, Boston Red Sox, Toronto Blue Jays, and Baltimore Orioles in the ED.

Following the move of the Houston Astros from the NL's CD to AL's WD in 2013, both leagues each consisted of fifteen teams.

Beginning in MLB's 2012 season, a second wild card was incorporated into each league. As a result, the AL's two wild card teams faced each other in a one-game playoff with the winner advancing to meet the number one seed in the ALDS. As of October 2016, the league's ED had produced 18 of 27 wild card teams led by the Red Sox's seven, Yankees' five, Orioles' three, Devil Rays/Rays' two, and Blue Jays' one; the WD six with two from the Oakland Athletics and one each from other teams; and the CD three with one each from the Cleveland Indians, Detroit Tigers, and Kansas City Royals. These results reflect, in part, differences in competitiveness and parity between teams within and across divisions of the league.

From the early 1900s to 2000s, the AL restructured itself by adding several clubs in various metropolitan areas. These included, for example, the Los Angeles Angels and Washington Senators in 1961, Kansas City Royals and Seattle Pilots in 1969, Seattle Mariners and Toronto Blue Jays in 1977, and Tampa Bay Devil Rays in 1998. In other words, the league entered into new baseball markets to expand its operations and fan base across the United States and Canada, and also to generate additional revenue and likely more profit for its franchises.[3]

In contrast to that group, a number of existing AL clubs moved to sites in other cities. Three of these were the Philadelphia Athletics to Kansas City in 1955, Los Angeles Angels to Anaheim in 1966, and Seattle Pilots to Milwaukee in 1970. Several things caused these and other relocations to occur such as lack of local support and declining attendances at a team's home games in regular seasons; an inferior ballpark prior to relocating and construction of a modern one after at a new site; differences in population, growth in population, and household's disposable and per capita income between the current site and a potentially more attractive metropolitan area; significant short-term changes in the ownership and/or financial status of a franchise; deteriorating local or regional economic conditions; and other demographic, financial, social, and sport-specific factors.

As of the AL's 2016 season, a historical overview of the clubs enfranchised in each division was as follows: ED — Baltimore Orioles in 1901 as the Milwaukee Brewers, moved to St. Louis in 1902 and then to Baltimore 52 years later; Boston Americans in 1901 and renamed Red Sox in 1908;

New York Yankees in 1901 as the Baltimore Orioles, moved to New York in 1903 and nicknamed Highlanders (officially adopted alternate nickname Yanks/Yankees in 1913); Tampa Bay Devil Rays in 1998 but renamed Rays 10 years later; and Toronto Blue Jays in 1977.

In the Central Division — Chicago White Stockings enfranchised originally as a member of the WL and named Sioux City Cornhuskers in 1894, moved to St. Paul one year later and then to Chicago in 1900 and renamed White Sox in 1904; Cleveland Indians in 1887 as the Blues of the American Association, played as a minor league franchise in 1900, and joined the AL in 1901; Detroit Tigers in 1894 in the WL and then the AL in 1901; Kansas City Royals in 1969; Minnesota Twins enfranchised in 1894 as the Kansas City Blues, moved to Washington and named Senators in 1901, and relocated to Minneapolis–St. Paul in 1961.

For the league's WD — Houston Astros, originally named the Colt 0.45s, enfranchised in 1962 as a NL team, renamed Astros in 1965, and transferred to the AL in 2013; Los Angeles Angels of Anaheim, originally enfranchised in 1961 and named Los Angeles Angels, renamed California Angels in 1965 and moved to Anaheim 32 years later; Oakland Athletics enfranchised in 1901 in Philadelphia, moved to Kansas City in 1955 and renamed Kansas City Athletics, and then relocated to Oakland in 1968 and renamed Oakland Athletics; Seattle Mariners, an expansion franchise in 1977; Texas Rangers enfranchised in 1961 as the Washington Senators and moved to Arlington in 1972 and renamed Texas Rangers.

Based on information from 1901 to 2016, seven former AL franchises ceased to exist and became extinct operationally because of inferior performances in regular seasons, low attendances and lack of support from fans at their home games, financial problems, and other issues. These were the Baltimore Orioles (1901–1902), Kansas City Athletics (1955–1967), Milwaukee Brewers (1901), Philadelphia Athletics (1901–1954), Seattle Pilots (1969), St. Louis Browns (1902–1953), and Washington Senators (1901–1960) and (1961–1971).[4]

From administrative and leadership perspectives, there has been 10 AL presidents. Chronologically they are Ban Johnson (1901–1927), Frank Navin (acting president 1927), Ernest Barnard (1927–1931), Will Harridge (1931–1959), Joe Cronin (1959–1973), Lee MacPhail (1973–1984), Bobby Brown (1984–1994), Gene Budig (1994–1999), Jackie Autry

(Honorary, 2000–2015), and Frank Robinson (Honorary, 2015–present). Except for Navin, Barnard, Brown, Budig, and Autry, the other presidents are in the Baseball Hall of Fame.[5]

From 1901 to 1903, the AL's eight teams each had a 140-game schedule. Then in 1904, their number of games expanded to 154 as they played each other 22 times. In 1918, the schedule was curtailed during early September on orders from the War Department, and each team played about 125 games. However, when the war ended, the clubs hustled to get some of their players out of a military uniform and into baseball uniform for a 140-game schedule in 1919. One year later, a 154-game schedule was again implemented and continued without a hitch through World War II. But expansion brought about the 10-team, 162-game schedule for the AL in 1961, which marked the first year when the two leagues played schedules of unequal length and with a different number of teams.[6]

In sum, these were highlights but also important and interesting events in the emergence, development, and structure of the AL from 1901 to 2016. Each of them had a major or minor impact on the league and contributed in some way to the popularity, prosperity, and success of MLB and its teams. Although officially younger than the NL by 26 years and despite economic, financial, and social problems affecting many American small, midsized, large, and very large metropolitan areas, the AL continued to improve historically and exists as an organization consisting of 15 geographically-dispersed but competitive and mostly profitable franchises.[7]

TEAMS

Markets

During MLB's 1901 season, eight AL teams existed in different urban places within the United States (US). Based on the population size (in parentheses) of their market, they played home games in Chicago (2), Philadelphia (3), Boston (5), Baltimore (6), Cleveland (7), Detroit (13), Milwaukee (14), and Washington, D.C. (15). Consequently, such midsized to large places as New York (1), San Francisco (9), New Orleans (12), Newark (16), Jersey City (17), Louisville (19), Minneapolis (19), and Providence (20) were either occupied by a NL club, too remote geographically, or simply unattractive and unfamiliar sites to host an existing or new AL team.[8]

From 1902 to 2016, the league changed in different ways. For various demographic, economic and sport-specific reasons, some new teams joined the AL and located in such metropolitan areas as Los Angeles and Washington, D.C. in 1961, Kansas City and Seattle in 1969, Seattle again and also Toronto in 1977, and Tampa Bay in 1998. Among the group, four of these expansion clubs continue to perform at their original home including the Kansas City Royals, Seattle Mariners, Toronto Blue Jays, and Tampa Bay Rays.

Because of a better ballpark, financial problems, inferior performances and other reasons, nine AL teams moved their operation from one place to another after 1901. Their pre-move and post-move sites were, respectively, Milwaukee→St. Louis (1902); Baltimore→New York (1903); St. Louis→ Baltimore (1954); Philadelphia→Kansas City (1955); Washington→ Minneapolis (1961); Los Angeles→Anaheim (1966); Kansas City→Oakland (1968); Seattle→Milwaukee (1970); and Washington→Arlington (1972).

Besides the aforementioned expansions and relocations, the Astros have remained at home in Houston but nevertheless shifted from the NL's CD to AL's WD in 2013. After this change, the AL and NL each contained 15 teams with five each in three divisions. This, in turn, created new rivalries especially among those in the two divisions and also generated other benefits, costs, and opportunities for MLB.

To provide and examine some current, interesting, and relevant data about existing AL teams in order to examine the quality and other elements of their markets, there is information about them in Table A1.1. Within the table, variables researched were each team's Metropolitan Statistical Area Population (MSAPOP), number of Designated Market Area Television Homes (DMATVH), and average attendances (AVGATT) at home games in MLB's 2016 season. These criteria are measured, listed, and ranked to reveal the attributes of such competitors as the ED's Red Sox and Yankees, CD's White Sox and Tigers, and WD's Angels and Athletics.

Based on data in Column 2 of Table A1.1, the average MSAPOP of AL teams was estimated at 6.2 million in 2015. Because of the very large-market Yankees in New York, the ED teams ranked highest on average at 7.3 million while those in the WD placed second at 7.1 million and CD third at 4.3 million. According to their areas' populations, respectively, the Indians and then Royals and Orioles each play in the league's three smallest markets. Although there are differences among them, the ED's Red Sox and Blue Jays, CD's Tigers and Twins, and WD's Athletics and Mariners roughly exist in mid-sized markets.

According to variations within divisions, the populations of ED teams' markets have the highest standard deviation at 7.2 million and thus are the most unequal primarily due to New York being biggest and most dense versus the much smaller areas of Baltimore and Tampa Bay. In contrast to that group, the lowest dispersion in populations exists among clubs in the CD at 3.1 million since Cleveland and Kansas City are very similar in size but not Chicago, Detroit, and Minneapolis.

Among only those in the WD, 9.6 million more people live in Los Angeles–Long Beach–Anaheim statistical area than Seattle–Tacoma–Bellevue while the metropolitan area populations of Houston–The Woodlands–Sugar Land and Dallas–Fort Worth–Arlington are within 500,000 of each other. These gaps in population between divisional teams' areas explain, in part, such things as differences in their attendances at home games, revenues and market values, and even the salaries and contracts of their managers and players.

According to the data in Column 3 of Table A1.1, the league's average among teams is 2.6 million television homes in 2016–2017. While the designated market areas of teams within the ED and WD each averaged about three million television homes, those in the CD had a lower total especially in Kansas City and then Cleveland, Minneapolis, and Detroit. Apparently households in the four latter places had relatively fewer opportunities to view home games of the Royals, Indians, Twins, and Tigers during their regular seasons and any in postseasons. Alternatively, homes in New York, Los Angeles, and Chicago had the most televisions for games being broadcast, respectively, of the Yankees, Angels, and White Sox.

In number of television homes, the largest variation existed in areas of ED teams compared to those in the CD and WD. The differences between the number of them in New York and Baltimore are greater, for example, than Chicago and Kansas City, and Los Angeles and Seattle. Although the league's standard deviation was relatively low at 1.7 million, television homes across the majority of metropolitan areas are well-dispersed except for three outliers. If the New York, Los Angeles, and Chicago areas were excluded in the table, the three divisions would deviate less and thus share television homes more proportionately.

The data in Column 4 denote AL teams' average attendance at home games during MLB's regular season in 2016. Overall, it was 28.8 million per game. Because of their large metropolitan area populations and other demographic and economic advantages, the Yankees and Angels ranked second and third, respectively, yet followed the Blue Jays in average attendance.

The ED teams had the highest average attendance at 31.7 million since the Red Sox, Orioles, and Blue Jays each played well enough to compete for a title throughout most of the regular season. Interestingly, the Indians won the CD but nevertheless placed fifth or last in its division — 13th in the league and 28th in MLB — in attendances at Progressive Field. Within the WD, the Athletics had the smallest audiences at their home games while the mediocre Angels led the division. Thus, market size was a major factor in evaluating availability of regular-season tickets and also ticket sales for each of these teams at their ballparks.

Compared to the league's standard deviation of 7.7 million, the variations in average attendance of ED clubs exceeded those in the CD and WD. In fact, the statistic was 10.4 million for the former division but only 5.4 million and 6.9 million, respectively, for the latter two groups of teams. While the Yankees and Red Sox had similar attendances at their home games in 2016, so did the CD's Tigers and Royals and also WD's Astros and Mariners. Since they had the largest metropolitan area population on average, ED teams had the greatest deviation in home-game attendances especially between the Yankees and Rays.

Given the data and its distribution in Table A1.1, the Yankees, Angels, White Sox, and Rangers each play their home games in relatively large markets; the Red Sox, Blue Jays, Tigers, Twins, Astros, and Mariners in midsized markets; and the Orioles, Rays, Indians, Royals, and Athletics in small markets. Because of their winning percentages and competitiveness, some clubs in small markets were actually more successful than others in large and small areas.

For more about two of these variables and their potential as baseball markets, the most populated places without a MLB team are such Metropolitan Statistical Areas (MSAs) as Riverside–San Bernardino–Ontario (4.48 million), Charlotte–Concord–Gastonia (2.42 million), and Portland–Vancouver–Hillsboro (2.38 million). With respect to DMAs in the top 25, three without a club are Orlando–Daytona Beach–Melbourne (1.51 million), Sacramento–Stockton–Modesto (1.37 million), and Charlotte–Concord–Gastonia (1.18 million).

If the AL expands at a site in an area not hosting one of its own or a current NL team, a few of these places are viable markets. In addition, they are potential attractive sites for any existing AL clubs with inferior ballparks and who compete for local fans with other teams in the National Basketball Association (NBA), National Football League (NFL), and/or National Hockey League (NHL). Among the group, there has been speculation in the media about MLB locating a new or existing AL (or NL) club in Portland but also in smaller US metropolitan areas that contain the cities of Columbus, Ohio; Indianapolis, Indiana; Las Vegas, Nevada; Nashville, Tennessee; and San Antonio, Texas. Despite failing to support a team during the mid-1990s to early 2000s, another potential site is Montreal, Canada or nearby within the city's metropolis.

Performances

For each regular season, MLB teams have a 25-man or active roster and also a 40-man roster. The former includes the starting eight position players plus pitchers and reserve players. Players on the active roster are also on the 40-man roster. These are generally the only ones dressed in a uniform and who may take the field in a game at any time.[9]

A 25-man roster typically consists of, but not always five starting pitchers, seven relief pitchers, two catchers, six infielders, and five outfielders. In the AL, a full-time DH is usually classified as either an infielder or outfielder because DHs, for the most part, play first base, left field, or right field because of their skills and also inexperience at other positions.

The 40-man or expanded roster is composed of all players in a MLB club's organization who signed a major-league contract. These players are available to be called up to the 25-man roster at any time during a regular season. Also, on the expanded roster are any of them on the 15-day disabled list and also in the minor leagues who signed a major-league contract but are on an "optional assignment" to the minors.

If a team clinches a playoff berth after the regular season, a 25-man post-season roster takes effect. Players who are part of a team's final roster at the end of the regular season are eligible to participate in the postseason besides those traded from a different team, spent time in the minor leagues, or signed a contract later in the season with the team. Rosters for a postseason series are set when the series begins and no changes allowed except when a player is moved to the disabled list or involved in an inactive transaction.

During the AL's 116-year history, the number of teams ranged from eight to 15 per season. Because of differences in the talent of their managers and players, some of them established all-time records as of 2016. For example, the 1954 Cleveland Indians have the highest all-time winning percentage (0.721) but nevertheless lost to the NL's New York Giants in the World Series while the 2001 Seattle Mariners won the most games (116) but lost in the ALCS to the Yankees. Alternatively, the 1916 Philadelphia Athletics have the league's worst all-time losing percentage (0.235) and most losses (117) in a season while finishing more than 54 games behind the champion Boston Red Sox.

For AL teams as of MLB's 2016 season, their all-time performances appear in Table A1.2. Besides winning percentages — which were researched but not listed in the table — the other data in columns denotes the distribution of their seasons and specifically how successful they have competed since becoming members of the league. Following are a summary of their performances in order to compare them from first to 15th based on various results.

Division titles

From 1969 to 2016, the 114-year-old Yankees ranked first among the group by winning 18 (15%) of the league's total division titles — excludes 1994 strike season — followed by the 49-year-old Oakland Athletics with 16 (13%) and 56-year-old Minnesota Twins 10 (8%). In contrast to them, the 4-year-old AL Astros, 19-year-old Rays, and 40-year-old Mariners have won the fewest titles since entering the league.

Besides the 1976–1978 and 1980–1981 MLB seasons, Yankees clubs were successful in winning the ED consecutively during 1998–2006 and 2011–2012. For these periods, their top players included infielders Greg Nettles, Willie Randolph, Derek Jeter, Alex Rodrigues and Robinson Cano, and pitchers Ron Guidry, Andy Pettitte, and Mike Mussina. Managers' Billy Martin, Joe Torre, and Joe Girardi led one or more of these teams to win a majority of their games in regular seasons and also several others in postseasons.

After the Yankees, Athletics and Twins, respectively, teams ranked second by division were the ED Orioles and WD Angels each with nine titles (both 7%) and then the CD Cleveland Indians and Kansas City Royals each with eight (both 6%). Other than the Astros, Rays and Mariners, the ED Toronto Blue Jays, CD Chicago White Sox, and WD Texas Rangers also have ranked among the least competitive divisionally since 1969.

Regarding the distribution of titles, ED clubs won the most at 43 (37%), CD teams second at 38 (33%), and those in the WD third at 35 (30%). Based on teams' standard deviation or spread within divisions, the WD has the largest variation in titles followed by the ED and then CD. Across all AL clubs, the deviation in titles was less than in the WD and ED but greater than the CD's.

Because of such things as decisions made by their owners, general managers and managers, talent of their players on rosters each regular-season, and other factors affecting them as organizations, CD teams were the most equal of the groups or had the greatest parity in winning titles since 1969. In other words, the White Sox and its four intra-divisional rivals have shared titles more equitably than did those in other divisions. Given team performances in recent seasons, the Yankees have not won their division since 2012 and only two of them from 2010 to 2016. The Blue Jays, meanwhile, have improved recently in competitiveness to challenge the Yankees and Red Sox in regular-season games and qualifying for the playoffs while the Rays struggle each year to challenge any of them.

Pennants

Since 1901, the teams in Table A1.2 competed for 101 AL pennants as of 2016. Among the group, the Yankees won forty (39%) of them followed by the 116-year-old Red Sox's 13 (12%) and 116-year-old Tigers' 11 (10%). Alternatively, the Astros and Mariners each with zero pennants and the Rays and Angels with a total of two had the least number of pennants of the 15 teams during the league's entire period.

More specifically, Yankees' teams were successful in numerous MLB seasons by winning six pennants in the 1920s, five each in the 1930s, 1940s and 1960s, eight in the 1950s, three each in the 1970s and 1990s, one in the 1980s, and four in the 2000s. These teams included many great and popular players such as Babe Ruth, Lou Gehrig, Whitey Ford, Yogi Berra, Mickey Mantle, Roger Maris, and Mariano Rivera. As leaders of their teams, managers' Miller Huggins, Casey Stengel, Joe McCarthy, and Joe Torre are in the sport's Hall of Fame.

Following the ED's Yankees and then Red Sox, other clubs with at least five pennants were the ED's Orioles, CD's White Sox, Indians and Tigers, and WD's Athletics. Among all AL teams, the least productive in winning pennants besides the Mariners and Astros with zero of them have been the Rays and Angels each with one. While the Mariners teams played for decades and competed using talented players through 2016, the latter four clubs thus far have been unable to generate a series of successful regular-seasons and consistently advance in the playoffs enough to win at least one pennant (Astros, Mariners) or two (Rays, Angels).

With respect to the distribution of pennants among AL divisions through MLB's 2016 season, the ED leads with a total of 62 (61%), CD second with 30 (30%), and WD third with 9 (9%). These different results occurred primarily because of the historical dominance of the Yankees and Red Sox, a few successful postseasons of the Orioles, White Sox, Indians and Tigers, and inferior performances particularly of the Rays, Astros, Angels, and Mariners.

Within the three divisions — when measured by their standard deviations — the WD had the smallest variation in pennants won or more equality among its teams than those in the ED and CD. Across all teams in the league, the deviation in pennants (nine) was less than in the ED (16) but greater than in the CD (three) and WD (two). Combined, the Yankees and Red Sox won 53 (52%) of them but only 26 (22%) of division titles. This, in part, reflects the different time periods of competition for pennants (115 post-seasons) and divisions (48 regular seasons). In short, there are significant differences among and between teams in each division based on such things as their number of seasons in the league and other factors.

World Series

For this significant sports event as of 2016, the teams in Table A1.2 played a total of 48 of them as of MLB's 2016 season. Those in the ED have won 40 (69%), CD 13 (22%), and WD 5 (9%). Among the group, the Yankees ranked first with 27, Red Sox second with eight, and Tigers and Athletics tied for third each with four. Alternatively, the Rays in 19 years, Astros four, Mariners forty, and Rangers 45 have failed to win a World Series. Put simply, the latter clubs periodically dealt with management and coaching problems, lacked enough talented players on their rosters in most seasons, and had too much competition from others in their division.

To win a World Series, the AL Yankees and other teams succeeded partly because of their Most Valuable Players (MVPs) in this postseason event. The Yankees heroes, for example, included seven pitchers, eight infielders, and one each outfielder and DH. With eight victories, the Red Sox's MVPs were chronologically outfielder Manny Ramirez in 2004, third baseman Mike Lowell in 2007, and DH David Ortiz in 2013. Besides the Tigers' two MVPs — pitcher Mickey Lolich in 1968 and shortstop Alan Trammel in 1984 — Athletics' players winning the award were catcher Gene Tenace in 1972, outfielder Reggie Jackson in 1973, relief pitcher Rollie Fingers in 1974, and starting pitcher Dave Stewart in 1989. As a group, they had exceptional performances at their positions and also some of them as batters.

As measured and explained for the league's pennants and division titles, there are deviations in teams' World Series victories regarding all divisions and also within and between divisions. According to my calculations, the overall variation in winning World Series (6.73) was less than for pennants (9.96) but greater when compared to division titles (4.69). Combined, the Yankees and Red Sox won a relatively larger proportion of total World Series than they did pennants. For division titles, the top-ranked Yankees and second-place Athletics won only about one-third of them. This distribution, in short, is portrayed in Table A1.2.

Within the three groups, the ED's standard deviation in World Series was 11.02, CD's 0.89, and WD's 1.73 as of MLB's 2016 season. In other words, CD teams had the smallest difference in number of World Series victories for several reasons including their competitiveness, rivalries, and the talent and performances of players on their rosters from year-to-year. Meanwhile, the ED's Orioles, Rays, and Blue Jays had fewer opportunities thus far and been less successful in World Series than the dominate Yankees and Red Sox. In the WD, the Athletics have been the only team to win at least two World Series as the Astros, Angels, Mariners, and Rangers struggle to even qualify as wild cards and really compete in ALDS and also ALCS.

Total performances

An MLB team's total performance (TP) includes its number of division titles plus pennants and World Series. Based on the data in Table A1.2 as of 2016, the Yankees had the highest number of TPs with 85, Red Sox second with 29, and Athletics third with 26. The three worst have been the Astros with zero and then the Rays and Mariners each with three. Given this information, these have been the most and least productive teams in MLB relative to their TPs.

There were differences in TPs across all divisions and within and between them. After adding the TPs of fifteen AL teams in Table A1.2, the sum was 275. This included the ED's 145 (52%), CD's 81 (30%), and WD's 49 (18%). In part, this distribution ranks them from first to third in their overall competitiveness and also postseason results.

In deviations of TPs by the three groups, the ED had the largest number followed by those for the WD and then CD. As before for titles, pennants and World Series, the Yankees and Red Sox dominated their division in performances and to lesser extent, so did the Athletics and Angels. The five teams within the CD, however, had the lowest deviation in TPs because of their relatively equal competitiveness during regular-seasons and also comparable ability and opportunity to win in postseasons. Therefore, there has been less parity among teams in the ED and WD but most in the CD.

Although not listed in Table A1.2, another characteristic of teams is their average winning percentages during regular seasons. For those in the AL as of 2016, the Yankees ranked first at 0.569, Athletics second at 0.518, and Red Sox third at 0.517. The bottom three, however, has been the Mariners' 0.470, Rays' 0.462, and Astros' 0.449. In fact, these averages reflect each team's results in TPs.

Regarding divisions, the ED had the highest winning average per team at 0.511, CD second at 0.500, and WD third at 0.486. Because the Yankees, Red Sox, and Orioles are each above 0.512, the White Sox, Indians, and Tigers each greater than 0.503, and the Astros, Mariners, and Rangers each below 0.500, there have been relatively large and real differences in the managerial talent and rosters of these teams for years and sometimes decades. Eventually, the Astros will improve their performances and increase parity across its division.

To avoid duplication or double counting in determining each AL team's TPs, their number of playoffs does not appear in Table A1.2. However, with respect to that data, there were 193 playoffs for those in the table. The Yankees ranked first with 52 (26%), Red Sox second with 21 (10%), and Athletics third with 18 (9%). Alternatively, Rays and Mariners teams each qualified for four playoffs but the Astros only one of them. In short, the Yankees, Red Sox, and Athletics have been competitive enough in regular seasons to perform in more postseasons than did the other twelve clubs.

For distributions by division as of MLB's 2016 season, ED clubs appeared in 95 playoffs, CD's in 57, and WD's in 41. Regarding their deviations within and among divisions, the ED teams had the largest (19.59) and CD smallest (2.88) variations in number of playoffs while the league's equaled 12.08. These differences indicate more parity in number of playoffs among CD teams than those in the ED and WD and also among all divisions combined.

During November 2016, *Baseball Almanac* determined and reported the most dominant MLB teams of all-time. To get this result, the magazine used winning percentage, percentage of runs scored in any given game, playoff record, and pitcher's earned-run average. Based on these metrics, the top five AL teams — in chronological order — was as follows[10]:

• The 1927 Yankees' regular-season win–loss was 110-44. Babe Ruth smashed a record 60 home runs (HRs) while Lou Gehrig hit 0.373 with 47 HRs and 52 doubles. Pitcher Waite Hoyt won 22 games with a 2.63 ERA and closer Wilcy Moore chalked up 19 wins out of the bullpen with an earned-run-average (ERA) of 2.28. The club's run differential — number of runs they outscored opponents — was a staggering 376. In the World Series, Ruth hit 0.400 with seven runs batted in (RBIs) as the Yankees swept the NL's Pittsburgh Pirates in four games.

• Whether the 1910 Philadelphia Athletics were better than the 1929 squad is debatable, the latter took the AL title from Ruth and Gehrig's Yankees. The Athletics' Jimmie Foxx hit 0.354 with 33 HRs and a gaudy 0.463 On-Base-Percentage (OBP) while Al Simmons batted 0.356 with 157 RBIs and totaled 373 bases. With a 104-46 record in the regular season, they finished ahead of the second-place Yankees by 18 games. Besides pitchers' Lefty Grove and George Earnshaw combining for 32 complete games, Philadelphia won the World Series by defeating the NL Chicago Cubs in five games.

• Based, in part on their 411-run differential, the 1939 Yankees rank third best of all-time. Joe DiMaggio hit 0.381 with thirty HRs in a Yankee Stadium where fly balls to left field usually died — 490 feet to left-center and 415 to left. The club had an OBP of 0.448 and somehow struck out only 20 times in 524 plate appearances. During the World Series, Charlie Keller hit 0.438 with three HRs as the Yankees outscored the Reds 20-8 in a four-game sweep. Including the playoffs, the Yankees had an 110-45 record.

• The 1961 Yankees won 109 games and lost 53. Mickey Mantle had a monster season while Roger Maris slugged a MLB record 61 HRs in addition to 142 RBIs. On the mound, pitcher Whitey Ford went 25-4 in the regular season and 14 scoreless innings in two World Series wins to nab MVP honors. The Yankees beat the NL Reds in five games, but the outcome was never really in question.

• Manager Joe Torre had access to the most talented pool of players in the modern era during the Yankees' 114-48 regular-season in 1998. The only vague threat that year came in the playoffs when the Cleveland Indians won game two of the ALCS at old Yankee Stadium, then roughed up starting pitcher Andy Pettitte to take game three in Cleveland. The World Series was more like a vacation for New York, which took home the trophy in a four-game sweep of the San Diego Padres.

For various reasons such as a lack of talented players, manager problems and/or both of them, some AL teams had terrible performances in their regular seasons. Several of these clubs were evaluated based on their ability to win games. According to one study, the following is a list of the five worst clubs in AL history as of MLB's 2016 season.[11]

• As a charter member of the fledgling AL, the Washington Senators had a losing record for the first decade of their existence. The 1904 campaign was an all-time low. The team finished 52-100, last in hits and runs, and its batters struck out more times than any on other teams. In addition, the Senators led the league in errors committed by their players. Embarrassingly, the club's owners tried changing the team's name to Nationals, but that effort also failed.

• One year after falling from first in 1914 to eighth in 1915, the 1916 Philadelphia Athletics had 20 consecutive losses and also set a new league record with 117. That number existed until the 2003 Detroit Tigers lost 119. Among their more dubious achievements in 1916, the Athletics combined with (coincidentally) the Tigers for a record thirty walks in a game on May 9 and a league-high 715 for the season. Ironically, Philadelphia's Wally Schang became the first MLB player to hit HRs from both sides of the plate in the same game.

• Between 1902 and 1914, the Philadelphia Athletics became an early dynasty, winning six pennants and three World Series. Following a 1914 World Series sweep by the NL's Boston Braves, however, and defections to the rival Federal League, Athletics manager Connie Mack released nearly every player of value in favor of younger, less expensive ones. As a result, the team finished last from 1915 to 1921. In the league's 1919 season — shortened to 140 games due to World War I — the Athletics had only a 0.257 winning percentage.

• The 1939 St. Louis Browns featured some of the worst pitching ever seen on a big league diamond, with a team ERA of 6.01. In fact, the staff gave up 700-plus walks or 100 more than the next-worst team. Other than first baseman George McQuinn, who hit 0.318 with 20 HRs, St. Louis was at the bottom of the league in batting average and strikeouts, and near-bottom everywhere else. Starting in mid-August, the club won only nine games the rest of the season, finishing a franchise-worst 43-111 and more than 64 games behind the powerful Yankees.

• The Detroit Tigers were in the midst of a 13-season funk in 2003. Many assumed that the team had bottomed out with a 55-106 record in 2002. Instead, the Tigers set a new AL record for losses with 119. They became the only team in history to have the league's top three losing pitchers on the same staff. On a happier note, the Tigers did manage to rebuild and reach the World Series by 2006, but nevertheless, lost to an underdog St. Louis Cardinals team.

LEAGUE ECONOMICS

As administrative and managerial organizations that include a group of franchises, American professional sports leagues do such things as establish, implement and enforce policies, regulations, and rules; schedule games annually for preseasons, regular seasons, and postseasons; negotiate contracts with cable companies, networks and other types of national and international media; and make decisions and find ways that financially benefit their members' operations. As of MLB's 2016 season, the AL included 15 teams whose economic objective is — and always was and will be — to compete and generate enough revenue from sources in order to maximize profit.

In this section, there are data and other information about the commercial and financial aspects of franchises in the AL and their significance from an economic perspective. Besides attendances at home and away games and anything else that affects teams' income, market value, and wealth is included in the analysis, quantified, and discussed. In other words, the league is an organization consisting of for-profit enterprises that operate to compete each season typically within a division — or conference in other sports — and seek to improve their performances in current and future games.

Franchise Financials

Forbes magazine's sports editors published financial data of MLB franchises as of their 2015 season. As denoted in Columns 2-6 of Table A1.3, these amounts include respectively their estimated market value — which is based on the current stadium deal without deduction for debt — and also total revenue, gate receipts, operating income — earnings before interest, taxes, depreciation, and amortization or simply EBITDA — and debt-to-value (D/V) percentages. For each of three divisions, the information reveals the financial status and wealth of AL teams individually and relative to each other as a group. The following section reviews and highlights the data.[12]

In Column 2 of the table, the 15 clubs' estimated market value averaged $1.24 billion and totaled $18.61 billion. Among divisions, the ED's estimates ranked first on average at $1.65 billion, WD's second at $1.11 billion, and CD's third at $955 million. Within each group, the highest amounts, respectively, belonged to the Yankees and Red Sox, Angels and Rangers, and Tigers and White Sox. These teams — which exist in mostly large and prominent sports markets that contain millions of baseball fans — play their home games in big ballparks with plenty of amenities to generate revenue for them as franchises.

To compare differences between each other, the standard deviation or variation in market values was highest for ED teams ($1.16 billion) and lowest for those in the CD ($142 million) and then WD ($235 million). This means parity or smaller deviation in franchise values existed to a greater extent between the White Sox and their competitors in the CD than among clubs in the other divisions. Although these are financial estimates, the amounts may influence such things as their relative wealth, economic power in the league, and future price if and when sold to potential investors.

Calculated for amounts in Column 3 of Table A1.3, the AL teams' total revenue was $4.16 billion or $277.6 million each in MLB's 2015 season. On average by division, the ED clubs' was $317 million, WD's $267 million, and CD's $248 million. While the Yankees ranked first, Red Sox second, and Angels third among the group of 15, the Rays, Indians, and Athletics each received less revenue than $225 million. These differences, in part, occurred for them because of amounts obtained from such sources as concession sales, gate receipts, fans' expenditures for memorabilia and tickets, and income from television contracts.

Based on each division's standard deviation, ED teams had the largest variation in revenue at $135 million followed by those in the WD at $37 million and CD at $22 million. Because of differences in their market populations, win–loss records and other data, some teams earned much more or less in revenue and thus deviated from their division's average amount by being highest and lowest particularly the ED's Yankees and Rays, CD's Royals and Indians, and WD's Angels and Athletics. These six teams, in turn, were among the most and least fortunate financially based on the distribution of their amounts across the league.

Each AL teams' 2015 gate receipts, in millions, appear in Column 4 of the table. From most to least, ED teams averaged $115 million, CD's $65 million, and WD's $67 million. Similar to market value and revenue, the Yankees ranked first in the league at $259 million and then the Red Sox second at $176 million and Royals (not Angels) third at $99 million. In contrast to them, the Rays, White Sox, Indians, and Athletics each had less than $50 million in gate receipts. These amounts were primarily based on such variables as their home-game attendances, premium and non-premium ticket prices, and win–loss records in the regular-season.

Compared to the league's deviation in gate receipts of $60 million, differences in them were largest for ED clubs at $98 million and smallest for those in the WD at $18 million. Despite being a competitive team in its division and winning a title, the Blue Jays surprisingly earned less than average in gate receipts at $59 million while the less successful Twins and Astros each with $73 million exceeded their division's amount. Although a small market club, the Royals were entertaining and popular at their home games and thus sold plenty of tickets especially to baseball fans in the Kansas City area.

Among the data in Table A1.3, operating income or EBITDA represents these teams' gross earnings but not their net profit. Listed in Column 5, the league's total was $334.2 million in 2015. Compared to an average of $22.2 million for the groups combined, WD franchises led with $30.6 million in EBITDA followed by the CD's $21.3 million and ED's $14.8 million. From mostly an operations perspective, the Astros' had the largest amount at $66.6 million and then the Red Sox and Angels each with more than $41 million.

For various reasons, the WD's Rangers were the only AL franchise with negative operating income in 2015. Such things as simply errors or mistakes in budgeting amounts, failing to prepare for and control major and minor liabilities in the short-run, a relatively large $181 million in players' expenses, and unexpected expenditures to operate contributed in some way to the club's deficit at −$4.7 million.

Regarding deviations in operating income, the league's average was $18.8 million. For each division, WD teams had the largest variation at $26 million, ED's second at $16 million, and CD's third at $10 million. Within each group, respectively, the greatest differences in EBITDA existed between the Red Sox and Blue Jays, Royals and Tigers, and Astros and Rangers. Because their operations each generated a relatively small difference in earnings during the regular season, such ED teams as the Orioles, Rays, and Blue Jays almost broke even financially at less than $9 million in 2015.

After payments for interest, taxes, depreciation and amortization, several AL clubs likely had a net loss. Alternatively, the Astros, Red Sox, Angels, Royals, and Athletics appeared to have enough operating income to be profitable franchises. This was remarkable especially for the small-market Royals whose players' expenses equaled $141 million but not for the Athletics with the lowest amount payments in the league at $98 million. Nevertheless, these five clubs' general manager and budgeting director should be rewarded for their plans and results to operate efficiently.

The sixth column of Table A1.3 lists the D/V percentages of each AL franchise in 2015. On average, the league's was 9.6% or approximately $119 million per team. Among each group, the ED's averaged 7.8%, CD's 12%, and WD's 9.2%. While five clubs had zero debt, the D/V ratios of some others exceeded 12% including the Orioles, Rays, Tigers, Twins, Astros, and Rangers.

As described for other variables in the table, the standard deviations of D/V were unequal among divisions and franchises within divisions. ED teams, for example, had the greatest variation at 10.7% and then the WD at 10.4% and lastly the CD at 6.4%. In order to reduce their ratios for financial reasons and operate more efficiently, such teams as the Orioles and Rays, Tigers and Twins, and Astros and Rangers needed higher market values (Column 2) and/or less amounts of debt on their balance sheets.

Although reported in *Forbes* for being an important, necessary, and periodic payment from an operations perspective, Table A1.3 does not include the players' expenses of these teams in 2015. For the league, they totaled $2.18 billion or $145 million per team. On average, the ED's was $165 million, WD's $137 million, and CD's $134 million. While the Yankees, Red Sox, and Rangers ranked highest, the Rays, Indians, and Athletics each paid less than $104 million in players' expenses. Given these amounts, the Yankees, Rays, and Athletics failed to win enough games in the regular season to compete in the playoffs but not the Red Sox, Rangers, and Indians.

Players' expenses were different but also significantly deviated between the three AL divisions. From most to least in variation among the groups as measured by their standard deviations, these included the ED's $59 million and then WD's $35 million and CD's $24 million. Such amounts denote that the greatest disparity in payments occurred because of the Yankees' $241 million and Red Sox's $208 million versus the Rays' much smaller $92 million in the ED whereas the range in players' expenses in the CD and WD equaled, respectively, only $66 million between the Tigers and Indians and $83 million between the Rangers and Athletics. Thus, AL teams with the greatest revenues and/or largest estimated market values tended to compensate their players more than rivals within their division and across the league.

Ballparks

As of MLB's 2016 season, the fifteen AL teams played their home games in ballparks that differed in age, cost, economic value, and also in such other ways as location, capacity, and ownership. Based on various criteria including their amenities, concessions and sightlines, they were ranked by baseball experts from best to worst overall, most to least accessible, and also highest to lowest as facilities to entertain spectators. Given those criteria, this section provides some data on the league's ballparks and discusses specific character-istics and other information about them.[13]

Among teams' ballparks within each division as of MLB's 2016 season, they ranged in age from Yankee Stadium — which was extensively renovated in 2007 — to the Red Sox's 106-year-old Fenway Park in the ED; from the Twins' 7-year-old Target Field to the Royals' 45-year-old Kauffman Stadium in the CD; and from the Astros' 18-year-old Minute Maid Park to the Angels' 52-year-old Angel Stadium in the WD. Of the 15 venues, five of them are privately owned and another ten publicly, while the Astros organi-zation and Harris County, Texas jointly own Minute Maid Park.

Their construction costs ranked from being relatively cheap to very expensive. From the least to most costly in the ED and then CD and WD, respectively, investors and/or franchise owners and the public jointly spent less than $1 million to erect Fenway Park but more than $1 billion to upgrade Yankee Stadium; from $137 million to build the White Sox's 27-year-old Guaranteed Rate Field (former US Cellular Field) to $435 mil-lion for the Twins' Target Field; and from $117 million to complete Angel Stadium to $517 million for the Mariners' 19-year-old Safeco Field. Regarding the most likely replacement or renovation of a current ballpark in the league, it will be expensive for the team and/or taxpayers to rebuild or significantly refurbish the Athletics' 49-year-old O.co Coliseum in Northern California.

Recently *Forbes* sports editors assigned economic values to AL ballparks. From lowest to highest within divisions, respectively, amounts in the ED were $98 million for the Rays' Tropicana Field in Tampa Bay to $593 million for Yankee Stadium in New York; in the CD, from $107 million for the Indians' Progressive Field in Cleveland to $247 million for Comerica Park in Detroit; and in the WD, from $122 million for the O.co Coliseum in Oakland to $279 million for Globe Life Park in Arlington, Texas. Based on their estimated values, ED teams' ballparks averaged $282 million, CD' $164 million, and WD' $197 million. Because of increasing real estate prices in urban areas and popularity of the sport in America, these facilities will likely appreciate in value especially for those within midsized to large metropolitan areas.

In various studies, AL ballparks have been ranked by baseball experts and sports journalists in the media with respect to their location and different attributes and problems. Although results vary according to each study, a few venues rank among the best while others place in the worst of the group. For example, the most attractive, entertaining and well-structured of them for fans, in no specific order, include the Orioles' Camden Yards and Mariners' Safeco Field. An editor at website' csnatlantic.com evaluated each of them as follows:

"Camden Yards is the original retro ballpark and one of the very best. While many others built in the '90s and '00s tried to duplicate it, none truly could for one good reason: the warehouse. It already existed, so the ballpark was built around it. You can't fabricate something like that. It has to be organic. [Although] starting to age just a bit, it remains a gem, often imitated, never duplicated."

Regarding Safeco Field, the editor wrote these comments:

"It's the best of the domes, in large part because it's not actually a dome. The retractable roof closes when it rains, but it doesn't completely enclose the ballpark. That makes it feel more like you're outdoors. The left-field bullpens and overhanging bleachers are among the best features of the Mariners' home of the last 15 years."[14]

In the study, the two lowest-ranked AL teams' facilities were the Rays' Tropicana Field and Athletics' O.co Coliseum. Among ballparks in the league, they placed fourteenth and fifteenth, respectively, for the following reasons:

"Built eight years before the region even had its own major-league team, the Trop [Tropicana Field] has provided one of the worst environments in baseball history for [more] than 16 years. It's the only permanent dome still being used in the majors. The lack of crowds leaves everything echoing throughout the park. And then there are the catwalks that hover over the field of play, with special ground rules written in case a batted ball strikes one of the four different rings."

With respect to an evaluation of the O.co Coliseum, the author stated:

"The shame is, this once was nice stadium. Back before the [NFL Oakland Raiders owner] built the monstrosity that has overtaken the center-field bleachers as an upper deck for his Raiders, the Coliseum offered up gorgeous views of the mountains in the distance. These days, there are no mountains to be seen, only a decrepit stadium that feels even older than it is. Have we mentioned the recurring raw sewage problem?"[15]

Fan cost index

For several years, a Chicago-based company named Team Marketing Report (TMR) has prepared and published a Fan Cost Index (FCI) for the home games of teams in professional sports leagues. To attend a game for a typical family with two kids, an FCI includes the cost of four average-priced tickets, two cheapest-priced draft beers, four each lowest-priced soft drinks and hot dogs, parking for one vehicle, and two each game programs and least-expensive, adult-sized adjustable caps. Costs are determined by telephone calls with team representatives, venues, and concessionaires and from questions asked during interviews.[16]

In MLB's 2016 season, the average FCI for a family to attend a regular-season game of an AL team was $224. While Red Sox games each cost $360, the Rays had the league's lowest FCI at $154. Among divisions, the average for ED teams equaled $253, CD's $207, and WD's $212. The order from ranking each of them first to third occurred, in part, because FCIs of the Red Sox, Yankees, and Blue Jays each exceeded $230 while those of the White Sox, Indians, Tigers, Royals and Twins, and also the Angels, Athletics, Mariners, and Rangers were each below that amount.

For specific items in TMR's 2016 FCI, the range from most to least expensive or first to fifteenth across the AL were listed as follows: average ticket, Red Sox $54 to Rays $21; average premium ticket, Yankees $305 to Orioles $50; beer, Red Sox $7.75 to Indians $4; soft drink, Rangers $5.25 to

Angels $2.75; hot dog, Rangers $6 to Orioles $1.50; parking, Red Sox and Yankees each $35 to Twins $6 (Rays' not listed); and for a cap, Red Sox and Yankees each $25 to Rays $10. Following economics principles, these prices were set by teams and/or vendors to sell enough units to maximize revenue from their sales at games in the ballparks.

From MLB's 2011 to 2016 season, there have been some significant increases but also relatively small and even decreases in FCIs of teams in the AL. For examples of these changes, the Angels' rose from $129 to $210 or 62% but the Tigers' from only $207 to $214 or 3%, while the While Sox's declined from $258 to $229 or 13%. Because of inflation, number of fans and their spending at games in ballparks, and local economic conditions and other factors, the majority of teams and/or vendors raised their prices each year rather than keeping them constant or reducing amounts.

In evaluating FCIs between MLB's 2015 and 2016 seasons, the Orioles' increased the most, in other words, from $163 to $183 or 12%. Alternatively, fans' costs fell for home games of the Twins, Mariners, Royals, and Rays but remained the same for those of the Yankees at $337 and Tigers at $214. Thus, there were different payments for tickets and other things by families to attend AL teams' home games at their ballparks especially from 2011 to 2016.

ORGANIZATION HIGHLIGHTS

Besides regular-season games and postseason series, the AL and its franchises are involved in — and affected by — community events and business and government affairs, news, and projects. Because these things and other topics influence the league in different but perhaps important ways in the short and/or long run, following are a few of them from online media sources and also the academic and popular literature.[17]

First, the median household income of the five most populous metropolitan areas containing at least one AL team in 2015 was $88,518 in San Francisco–Oakland–Hayward (Athletics); $78,800 in Boston–Cambridge–Newton (Red Sox); $75,331 in Seattle–Tacoma–Bellevue (Mariners); $72,520 in Baltimore–Columbia–Towson (Orioles); and $71,008 in Minneapolis–St. Paul–Bloomington (Twins). Based on these amounts, any of the teams' games in regular-seasons are more affordable for families living within the areas.

Second, in *A Calculus of Color: The Integration of Baseball's AL* — published by McFarland Inc. in 2015 — Robert Kuhn McGregor focuses on the historical integration of the AL, which is often overlooked in the literature on MLB's integration. In the book, the author first provides overviews of the racial histories of both the AL and Negro Leagues. This background information then encouraged him to emphasize the daunting task that faced the owner and president of the Cleveland Indians Bill Veeck and one the club's outstanding players, Larry Doby, whom Veeck recruited from the Negro Leagues in 1947. McGregor offers additional context for Doby's entrance into the AL by detailing the support for integration that arose in black newspapers and the fierce resistance to that effort.

Third, among the central arguments of the bestselling book and movie *Moneyball* was the allegation that the labor market for baseball players was inefficient in 2002. In their article "Quantifying Efficiencies in the Baseball Players Market," the authors determined that the market had in fact already corrected by 2006, and moreover, they argued that the perceived market response to *Moneyball* in 2004 was properly viewed as part of a more gradual but long-term trend. In addition, they used official payroll data from MLB to refute a previous observation that the relationship between team payroll and performance has tightened since the publication of *Moneyball.*

Fourth, the three top and bottom AL teams in total attendance during their 2016 regular-season were, respectively, the Blue Jays (3.39 million), Yankees (3.06 million), and Angels (3.01 million) as opposed to the Rays (1.28 million), Athletics (1.52 million), and Indians (1.58 million). While the former group of clubs played their home games in ballparks within relatively large and wealthy markets, the latter three struggled to attract fans although Cleveland won a pennant and then competed but lost in a seven-game World Series to the NL's Chicago Cubs.

Fifth, through records from the ballpark's owner — Illinois Sports Facilities Authority — the company Guaranteed Rate will pay a lower annual fee than US Cellular did to put its name on the Chicago White Sox's home-site venue. Under the 13-year agreement that renamed the South Side ballpark Guaranteed Rate Field beginning on 1 November 2016, the White Sox will get $20.4 million over the next 10 years for naming rights, or about $2 million per year. That compares to $3.4 million that US Cellular paid the team on average annually since it purchased naming rights to the ballpark originally in 2003 for a 20-year term. Also, Guaranteed Rate's amount is substantially less than the average fee for naming rights regarding other MLB venues. Including US Cellular Field, the 20 MLB parks with naming rights partners pull in an average of $4.4 million per year from contracts according to data published by Chicago-based sponsorship trend research group IEG.

Sixth, besides a municipality's willingness to approve public financing for a new baseball stadium and also such factors as market size, business dynamics and the baseball culture of a particular place, a few potential and perhaps attractive markets for an AL expansion team are Montreal and Vancouver, Canada; Austin, Texas; Mexico City, Mexico or another site somewhere in Latin America; Charlotte, North Carolina; and Nashville, Tennessee. Being the largest metropolitan area in the US or Canada without a MLB franchise, Montreal has a well-documented passion for professional sports despite the history of the former Expos. The city drew an average of more than 48,000 fans per game to Toronto Blue Jays' exhibitions in 2014 and 2015. The Warren Cromartie-led Montreal Baseball Project and Mayor Denis Coderre have continued their passionate advocacy. Furthermore, prospective team owners commissioned a feasibility study for a major-league franchise in Montreal with encouraging results. The city's Olympic Stadium could host a big-league team for two or three seasons while a new ballpark is being built.

Seventh, in April 2016, the Minnesota Twins became the eleventh team in AL history that lost at least its first seven games in a regular season. Others include the 0-8, 1914 Cleveland Indians ; 0-13, 1920 Detroit Tigers; 0-8, 1945 Boston Red Sox; 0-8, 1952 Detroit Tigers; 0-10, 1968 Chicago White Sox; 0-21, 1988 Baltimore Orioles; 0-7, 1992 Kansas City Royals; 0-11, 2002 Detroit Tigers; 0-9, 2003 Detroit Tigers; and 0-7, 2008 Detroit Tigers. Because of their dismal start, these clubs did not finish their season with a winning record.

Eighth, from 1997 to 2013, AL teams won 2,122 interleague games or 52% of them. Because of the DH rule, AL clubs, on average have deeper lineups capable of scoring more runs than those in the NL. This has been true in the interleague era as AL clubs averaged 4.83 runs per game during the 17-year period compared to 4.54 in the NL. Moreover, the NL's typically superior pitching has been inferior in interleague play, while the AL's typically inferior pitching has been more productive. Historically, there was a particularly large difference from 2010 to 2016 when AL pitcher's ERA was 3.84 while the NL's averaged 4.23.

Ninth, half-way through the 2016 MLB season, games on the regional sports networks that hosted them knocked it out of the park in the ratings department for the sports primetime window according to ratings from Nielsen. Since the season started, seven AL teams rated number one in primetime programming in their home markets. Led by the 2015 World Series champion Royals — 13.26 rating with an average of 119,000 households per game — others were the Orioles and then Tigers, Red Sox, Mariners, Indians, and Rangers. Also, the Twins rated number two across both broadcast and cable competition in primetime despite their lackluster performance in the league's standing.

Tenth, since they became principal owners, the Red Sox's John Henry, White Sox's Jerry Reinsdorf, Tigers' Mike Illitch, and Angels' Arturo Moreno each have won more total championships — division titles, pennants, and World Series — than 11 other owners of AL teams. In comparison to them, the least successful with zero championships has been the Astros' Jim Crane. With respect to performances of the group, Henry acquired his team in 2002, Reinsdorf in 1981, Illitch in 1992, Moreno in 2003, and Crane in 2011.

NOTES

1. For the history of professional baseball organizations, especially the AL and its teams, see Jozsa FP Jr. (2016). *American League Franchises: Team Performances Inspire Business Success.* New York, NY: Springer; Quirk J and RD Fort (1992). *Pay Dirt: The Business of Professional Team Sports.* Princeton, NJ: Princeton University Press; *Official Major League Baseball Fact Book 2005 Edition.* St. Louis, MO: Sporting News (2005). Some baseball websites to research for historical data include http://www.mlb.com, http://www.sportsencylopedia.com, and http://www.baseball-almanac.com.
2. See "Baseball-Reference All-Star Game Index," http://www.baseball-reference.com [cited 1 November 2016]; "MLB All-Star Game History," http://www.espn.com [cited 1 November 2016]; "Images: MLB All-Star Game Moments," *Daily Herald* (2015); 1.
3. Jozsa FP Jr. (2009). *Major League Baseball Expansions and Relocations: A History, 1876–2008.* Jefferson, NC: McFarland; Morosi, JP "Which Locations Make the

Most Sense for MLB Expansion?" http://www.foxsports.com [cited 18 November 2016]; Jozsa FP Jr. and JJ Guthrie Jr. (1999). *Relocating Teams and Expanding Leagues in Professional Sports: How the Major Leagues Respond to Market Conditions.* Westport, CT: Quorum Books.

4. The reasons for these franchises' failures are covered in "Defunct AL Teams," http://www.sportsencyclopedia.com [cited 6 November 2016] and "Defunct Baseball Teams," http://www.sportsencyclopedia.com [cited 24 November 2016].

5. "Commissioners of Major League Baseball, and American League Presidents and National League Presidents," http://www.baseball-almanac.com [cited 24 November 2016].

6. A reference for this information is Liebman R. "Schedule Changes Since 1876," http://www.research.sabr.org [cited 7 November 2016].

7. For business aspects of baseball including the AL, see Jozsa FP Jr. (2008). *Baseball in Crisis: Spiraling Costs, Bad Behavior, Uncertain Future.* Jefferson, NC: McFarland and also the author's book, *Baseball, Inc.: The National Pastime as Big Business.* Jefferson, NC: McFarland (2006).

8. Idem, *Major League Baseball Expansions and Relocations: A History, 1876–2008* and *Relocating Teams and Expanding Leagues in Professional Sports: How the Major Leagues Respond to Market Conditions.*

9. An excellent source for this baseball rule is "Baseball Roster History," http://www.baseball-almanac.com [cited 8 November 2016].

10. The online reading to review for this information is Schaal E. "8 Greatest MLB Teams of All Time," http://www.cheatsheet.com [cited 10 November 2016]; Selbe N. "The 10 Greatest MLB Teams Seasons in History," http://www.mlb-teamspointerafter.com [cited 27 November 2016]; "Determining the Best Major League Baseball Team Ever From 1902–2005," http://www.baseball-almanac.com [cited 27 November 2016].

11. See Schaal E. "5 Worst Teams of the Modern Era," http://www.cheatsheet.com [cited 10 November 2016] and "The Ten Worst Major League Baseball Seasons Ever," http://www.writing.jmpressely.net [cited 24 November 2016].

12. Badenhausen, K, Ozanian M and C Settimi. "The Business of Baseball," http://www.forbes.com [cited 1 October 2016] and Edwards C. "Estimated TV Revenues for All 30 MLB Teams," http://www.fangraphs.com [cited 2 December 2016].

13. Jozsa FP Jr. (2016). *Major League Baseball Organizations: Team Performances and Financial Consequences.* Lanham, MD: Lexington Books.

14. These remarks were from a study by Zuckerman M. (2016). "Ranking All 30 MLB Ballparks," http://www.csnmidatlantic.com [cited 17 November 2016]. Another one relating to ballparks is Brown E. "When the New Ballpark is Already Too Old, *Wall Street Journal*, A3.

15. *Idem*, "Ranking All 30 MLB Ballparks."
16. For the facilities of all professional sports teams and families' costs to attend their regular-season games, see editions of "*Fan Cost Index*," http://www.teammarketingreport.com [cited 16 November 2016] and also the issue of "*Team Marketing Report — MLB 2016*," http://www.teammarketing.com [cited 25 January 2016].
17. Organization highlights are discussed in "Median Household Income in the Past 12 Months by 25 Most Populous Metropolitan Areas," http://wwwcensus.gov [cited 18 November 2016]; Smith CM (2015). "A Calculus of Color: The Integration of Baseball's American League," *Choice*, 53, 283; Baumer B and A Zimbalist (2014). "Quantifying Efficiencies in the Baseball Players Market," *Eastern Economic Journal*, 40, 488–498; "MLB Attendance Report — 2016," http://www.espn.com [cited 12 November 2016]; Spedden Z. "Financial Details Emerge on Guaranteed Rate Field," http://www.ballparkdigest.com [cited 18 November 2016]; Morosi JP. "Which Locations Make the Most Sense for MLB Expansion?" http://www.foxsports.com [cited 18 November 2016]; "Other 0–7 starts in American League History," http://www.startribune.com [cited 18 November 2016]; Rymer Z. "Which is Baseball's Superior Overall League, the AL or the NL?" http://www.bleacherreport.com [cited 18 November 2016]; Brown M. "With 2016 Season Half Over, TV Ratings for MLB Shows RSNs Rulings in Prime Time," http://www.forbes.com [cited 21 November 2016]; "List of Major League Baseball Principal Owners," http://www.baseball-reference.com [cited 23 November 2016]; and "MLB Links," http://www.sportsencyclopedia.com [cited 23 November 2016].

Chapter 2

NATIONAL LEAGUE

HISTORY

After rumors that some teams were illegally paying their players, the amateur National Association of Base Ball Players (NABBP) established a professional category in 1869. Two years later, several clubs separated themselves from the NABBP and found the wild and woolly National Association of Professional Base Ball Players (NAPBBP), or simply National Association (NA).[1]

Although some databases, encyclopedias, and baseball experts and organizations consider their ballplayers as major leaguers, the NA's status as an actual major league remains in dispute. Besides dominance by the four-time champion Boston Red Stockings for most of the league's existence — 1871–1875 — other factors limited its lifespan including such things as instability of franchises located in cities too small to financially support professional baseball, absence of a central authority, and influence of crooks and gamblers. In addition, the league was dangerously weak, in part, because there was no strong leadership, unsupervised scheduling of games and unstable membership, alcohol abuse, and an extremely low entry fee giving clubs no incentive to abide by league rules when not convenient for them.

Before early 1876, Chicago businessman and officer of the Chicago White Stockings, William Hulbert, approached several NA members with his plans for a new baseball league that included a strong central authority and exclusive territories for teams in only the larger cities. Hulbert had a problem, however, since some of his star players were threatened with expulsion from the NAPBBP because he signed them to his club using questionable methods. Thus, he had a great vested interest in creating his own league.

After recruiting one NA club privately, the owners of four more of them met in Louisville, Kentucky, during January 1876. With Hulbert representing the group in New York City one month later, the National League of Professional Baseball Clubs, or simply National League (NL) was established with eight charter members.

Besides Hulbert's Chicago White Stockings — renamed Chicago Cubs in 1903 — the other NL teams then were the Philadelphia Athletics from the NA — expelled after the 1876 season; Boston Red Stockings — now Atlanta Braves; Hartford Dark Blues from the NA — which folded after the 1877 season; New York Mutuals from the NA — expelled after the 1876 season; St. Louis Brown Stockings from the NA — folded following the 1877 season after committing to the Louisville Stars for 1878; Cincinnati Red Stockings — a new franchise expelled after the 1880 season; and the Louisville Grays — a new franchise that folded after the 1877 season when four of its players were banned for gambling.[2]

As a result of Hulbert's efforts, the NL's formation meant the end of the NA as the latter's remaining clubs shut down or reverted to amateur or minor status. In fact, the only strong club from 1875 that was excluded in 1876 was a second one in Philadelphia, often nicknamed White Stockings or Phillies.

Between 1880 and 1892, three different professional baseball leagues organized and challenged the NL. These included the American Association (AA), Union Association (UA), and Players League (PL). Because each of them had serious problems in the sport both competitively and economically, the leagues eventually folded their operations.

More specifically, the AA's teams played in non-NL cities such as Indianapolis, Indiana; Rochester, New York; and Toledo, Ohio. Besides scheduling Sunday games, the clubs offered alcoholic beverages where permitted and sold cheaper tickets everywhere — 25 cents versus the NL's 50 cents. Following seven of their regular-seasons, the NL and AA competed in a postseason series, which each lasted from three to 15 games. The NL won four times (1884, 1887, 1888, and 1889), AA once (1886), and twice these leagues' had tied scores (1885 and 1890).

Although they agreed to abide by a uniform rules book in 1887, the NL raided the AA for its teams' best players. After withdrawing from the

National Agreement in February 1891, 10 months later the AA ceased to operate when its clubs in Baltimore, Louisville, St. Louis, and Washington joined the NL.

Established in 1884, the UA consisted of 12 teams. During the season, those in Altoona and Philadelphia, Pennsylvania, disbanded, the club in Chicago transferred to Pittsburgh, and later teams in Wilmington and Pittsburgh were replaced by Milwaukee and Omaha — which after eight days, moved to St. Paul. When only five teams attended UA meetings in December, the league folded in January 1885.

Organized by the Brotherhood of Professional Base Ball Players in 1890 — the sport's first players union — the PL failed to persuade the NL to modify its labor practices including a salary cap and reserve clause that bound players to their teams indefinitely. As a result, several NL players defected to those in the eight-team PL. Nevertheless, because of attendance and financial problems, the PL collapsed after one season and, except for the league's Buffalo franchise, some of their players shifted to NL teams in the same cities such as Boston, Brooklyn, Chicago, Cleveland, Philadelphia, Pittsburgh, and New York.

At the end of the 19th century, the NL was in trouble with its fans. Misconduct among players existed, and fistfights between them frequently occurred at teams' games. Besides fighting with each other about different things, they battled with umpires and used foul language and obscenities. For example, a game between the Baltimore Orioles and Boston Beaneaters in 1894 ended up having tragic consequences when players brawled and several people in the grandstands started a fire. The blaze spread throughout downtown Boston and destroyed or damaged buildings.

In addition, NL franchise owners argued with each other while players despised their $2,400 salary cap. Other clubs, meanwhile, had problems with city governments that forbade recreational activities on Sundays. A prominent outfielder in the 1880s, Billy Sunday became so disgusted with the behavior of his teammates that he quit playing in 1891 to become one of America's most famous evangelical Christian preachers. Baseball fans responded negatively to the league's turmoil as attendances at games continued to plummet by 1900.

After eight years as a 12-team league, the NL reduced in size to eight for its 1900 season by eliminating clubs in Baltimore, Cleveland, Louisville, and Washington. An opportunity to compete for market share, three of these cities received franchises in the new American League (AL) when it opened for business in 1900. But, the NL declared war when it rejected the AL as an equal and pronounced it an 'outlaw league' and outside the National Agreement.

As a result, the AL declined to renew its National Agreement membership when it expired and in January 1901, officially declared itself a second 'major league' in competition with the NL. One year later, the upstart AL had placed new teams in such NL metropolitan areas as Boston, Chicago, New York, Philadelphia, and St. Louis. Only the Cincinnati Reds and Pittsburgh Pirates had no AL team in their markets.

Although the NL initially refused to recognize the AL, reality set in as talent and money were split between the two leagues. After two years of bitter contention, they signed a new version of the National Agreement in 1903. Besides formal acceptance of each other as equal partners in Major League Baseball (MLB), this meant mutual respect of the reserve clause in players' contracts and an agreement to play a postseason championship — and officially named it World Series.

From 1900 to 1961, the NL consisted of eight teams. In 1962 — facing competition from the proposed Continental League (CL) and confronted by the AL's unilateral expansion in 1961 — the NL expanded by adding the New York Mets and the Houston Colt .45s. Three years later, the Colts .45s were renamed Houston Astros and in 1969 the NL added the San Diego Padres and Montreal Expos to become a 12-team league for the first time since 1899.[3]

As a result of expansion, the NL, which for 93 years existed as a single group, was reorganized into two divisions each with six teams. Named the East Division (ED) and West Division (WD) — although geographically it was more like North and South — the division champions met in the NL Championship Series (NLCS) for the right to advance and play in the World Series.

In 1993, the NL league expanded to fourteen teams by adding the Colorado Rockies and the Florida Marlins — who became the Miami Marlins shortly after the 2011 MLB season. Then in 1998, the Arizona Diamondbacks became the league's 15th franchise while the AL's Milwaukee Brewers moved to the NL's Central Division (CD). Thus, there were 16 NL teams for the next 15 seasons.

One year after the Rockies and Marlins joined the NL, it reorganized geographically into the ED, CD, and WD. During the 1994–1997 seasons, the WD had one less team and from 1998 to 2012, the CD had one more of them. Also, a third postseason round was added in 1994 whereby the three division champions plus a wild card team advanced to the preliminary NL Division Series (NLDS). However, due to a general players' strike that year, the postseason was cancelled by MLB franchise owners.

From administrative, organizational, and scheduling viewpoints, it seemed practical to eventually have an even number of teams in both leagues. Even so, in 1998, the AL Milwaukee Brewers were moved from the CD to the NL's CD while the former league's Detroit Tigers transferred from the ED to its CD, which allowed the Tampa Bay Devil Rays to join the New York Yankees, Boston Red Sox, Toronto Blue Jays, and Baltimore Orioles in the ED. Following the move of the Houston Astros from the NL's CD to AL's WD in 2013, both leagues each consisted of 15 teams.

Beginning in MLB's 2012 season, a second wild card was adopted and incorporated into each league. As a result, the NL's two wild card teams faced each other in a one-game playoff with the winner advancing to meet the number one seed in the NLDS. As of October 2016, the league's ED had produced seven of 27 wild card teams led by the New York Mets' three and Atlanta Braves and Florida/Miami Marlins' two each; the WD qualified eight with three each from the Colorado Rockies and San Francisco Giants and two from the Los Angeles Dodgers; and the CD placed 12 with one each from the Cincinnati Reds and Milwaukee Brewers, two each from the Chicago Cubs and Houston Astros, and three each from the Pittsburgh Pirates and St. Louis Cardinals. These results reflect, in part, differences in competitiveness and also the parity between teams within and across divisions of the league.[4]

In contrast to seven expansion teams, six NL clubs moved to sites in other cities. Four of them, for example, were the Boston Braves to Milwaukee in 1953, Brooklyn Dodgers to Los Angeles and New York Giants to San Francisco, each in 1958, and Montreal Expos to Washington in 2005. Several things caused these and other relocations to occur such as lack of local support and declining attendances at the teams' home games in regular seasons; an inferior ballpark prior to relocating and the construction of a modern one at a new site; differences in population, growth in population, and household's disposable and per capita income between the current site and a potentially more prosperous metropolitan area or market; significant changes in the ownership and/or financial status of an existing franchise; deteriorating local or regional economic conditions; and other demographic, financial, social, and sport-specific factors.

As of the NL's 2016 season, a historical overview of the clubs enfranchised in each division was as follows: ED — Atlanta Braves enfranchised in 1871 as the Boston Red Stockings in the NA, who then joined the NL as charter member in 1876, adopted the nickname Braves in 1912 and moved to Milwaukee in 1953 and then to Atlanta in 1966; Miami Marlins in 1993 as the Florida Marlins, who changed their name to Miami Marlins in 2012; New York Mets in 1962; Philadelphia Phillies in 1883 as the Quakers and adopted Phillies as a nickname officially in 1884; Washington Nationals in 1969 as the Montreal Expos, who moved to Washington, D.C. in 2005.

In the league's CD — Chicago Cubs enfranchised in 1870 as an independent professional team and chartered into the NA in 1871, suspended its operations in 1872–1873 following the Great Chicago Fire, joined the NL as charter member in 1876 and was originally nicknamed White Stockings and later Colts, Orphans, and finally Cubs in 1903; Cincinnati Reds in 1882 in the AA, then joined the NL in 1890; Milwaukee Brewers in 1969 as the Seattle Pilots in the AL, moved to Milwaukee in 1970 and transferred to the NL in 1998; Pittsburgh Pirates in 1882 in the AA but joined the NL in 1887; St. Louis Cardinals in 1882 in the AA and ten years later shifted to the NL.

Regarding the league's WD — Arizona Diamondbacks enfranchised in 1998; Colorado Rockies in 1993; Los Angeles Dodgers in 1883 as a minor league team, entered into the AA as the Brooklyn Atlantics in 1884 and acquired the nickname Dodgers, joined the NL in 1890 and moved to Los Angeles in 1958; San Diego Padres in 1969; New York Gothams in 1883, re-nicknamed Giants in 1885, and moved to San Francisco in 1958.[5]

Based on historical records and other information from 1901 to 2016, five former NL franchises ceased to exist and became extinct operationally because of such things as inferior performances in regular seasons, low attendances and lack of support from fans at their home games, financial problems, and other issues. These were the Boston Braves (1876–1952), Brooklyn Dodgers (1890–1957), Milwaukee Braves (1954–1965), Montreal

Expos (1969–2004), and New York Giants (1883–1957). In comparison, there were seven defunct AL teams beginning with the Baltimore Orioles (1901–1902) to the Washington Senators (1961–1971).[6]

From administrative and leadership perspectives, sixteen NL presidents had important roles during the league's development. Besides William Hulbert (1877–1882), others who served five or more years were Nicholas Young (1885–1902), Harry Pulliam (1903–1909), John Tener (1913–1918), John Heydler (1918–1934), Ford Frick (1934–1951), Warren Giles (1951–1969), Chub Feeney (1970–1986), A. Bartlett Giamatti (1986–1989), Bill White (1989–1994), and Leonard Coleman Jr. (1994–1999). In addition to Morgan Bulkeley (1876), former presidents' Hulbert, Frick, and Giles are in the Baseball Hall of Fame. Following MLB's 1999 season, the role of president was eliminated when the NL (and AL) ceased to exist as business entities.[7]

From 1876 to 1903, NL teams officially scheduled from 70 to 140 games each season. Then during 1904–1917, their number of games expanded to 154 as they played each other at least 18 times. But in 1918, the schedule was curtailed during early September on orders from the War Department and therefore each team played approximately 123–129 games. However, when the war ended, the clubs hustled to get some of their players out of a military uniform and into a baseball uniform for a 140-game schedule in 1919. One year later, a 154-game schedule was again implemented and continued without a hitch through World War II. Because of AL expansion, the two leagues played different schedules with a different number of teams in 1961. However, one year later the NL also expanded, which brought about a 10-team, 162-game schedule. Interestingly, when games were cancelled as a result of a players strike on the first 10 days of the 1972 season, NL teams played only 153–156 of them.[8]

In sum, these were highlights but also important and interesting events in the emergence, development, and structure of the NL from 1876 to 2016. Each of them had a major or minor impact on the league and contributed in some way to the popularity, prosperity, and success of MLB and its teams. Although younger than the AL by 26 years and despite economic, financial, and social problems affecting many American small, midsized, large, and very large metropolitan areas, the NL continued to evolve and improve historically and exists now as an organization consisting of 15 geographically-dispersed but competitive and mostly profitable franchises.

TEAMS

Markets

In 1876, NL teams and their home-site population rank (in parentheses) among US cities were roughly New York (1), Philadelphia (2), St. Louis (4), Chicago (5), Boston (7), Cincinnati (8), Louisville (14), and Hartford (34). When MLB formed in 1901, the league's teams existed in metropolitan areas including New York/Brooklyn (1), Chicago (2), Philadelphia (3), Boston (4), Pittsburgh (5), St. Louis (6), and Cincinnati (9). Besides Chicago, Philadelphia, and Boston, AL clubs also played at home in Baltimore (7), Cleveland (11), Detroit (13), Washington (14), and Milwaukee (18). Thus, NL teams' markets on average included more households and potential baseball fans than those in the AL.[9]

From 1902 to 2016, the NL changed in different ways. For various demographic, economic and sport-specific reasons, some new teams joined it and were located in such very large to midsized metropolitan areas as New York and Houston in 1962, Montreal and San Diego in 1969, Denver and Miami in 1993, and Phoenix in 1998. Among the group, five of these expansion clubs continue to perform at their original home sites including the New York Mets, San Diego Padres, Colorado Rockies, Miami (previously-nick-named Florida) Marlins, and Arizona Diamondbacks.

Because of their obsolete ballparks, financial problems, inferior performances, and other reasons, five NL teams moved their operation from one place to another after 1901. Their specific pre-move and post-move sites were, respectively, Boston→Milwaukee (1953); Brooklyn (New York metropolitan area)→Los Angeles (1958); New York→San Francisco (1958); Milwaukee→Atlanta (1966); and Montreal (Canada)→Washington (2005).

To identify and examine some current, interesting, and relevant data about existing NL teams in order to examine the sizes and other elements of their markets, there is information about them in Table A2.1. With respect to the table, variables researched were each team's Metropolitan Statistical Area Population (MSAPOP), number of Designated Market Area Television Homes (DMATVH), and average attendances (AVGATT) at home games in MLB's 2016 season. These criteria are measured, listed, and ranked to reveal the attributes of such competitors and rivals as the ED's Mets and Nationals, CD's Pirates and Cardinals, and WD's Dodgers and Giants.[10]

Based on data in column 2 of the table, the average MSAPOP of NL teams in 2015 was estimated at 6.1 million and marginally lower than the AL's 6.2 million. Because of the very large-market Mets in New York, ED teams had the highest average population at 8.8 million followed by those in the WD at 5.7 million and CD at 3.6 million. Within each group, respectively, the Marlins/Phillies/Nationals, Diamondbacks/Giants, and Reds/Pirates/Cardinals played their home games in similarly-sized areas. However, despite small differences in market populations, their financial results were not similar because of such things as ticket prices at home games, the sport's popularity locally and regionally, and teams' win–loss records during recent seasons.

According to variations in market size within their divisions, the populations of ED teams had the highest standard deviation at 6.3 million. Therefore, they performed within the most unequal markets relative to their divisional rivals primarily due to New York being the biggest and most dense area relative to the smaller areas' of Atlanta and Miami. In contrast to that group, the lowest dispersion in market populations exists among clubs in the CD at 3.6 million people since Cincinnati, Pittsburgh, and St. Louis are roughly similar in size but not compared to Chicago and Milwaukee.

Among only those in the WD, 8.6 million more people live in the Los Angeles–Long Beach–Anaheim statistical area than San Francisco–Oakland–Heyward, while the metropolitan area populations of Phoenix–Mesa–Scottsdale, Denver–Aurora–Lakewood, and San Diego–Carlsbad are within 1.8 million of each other. These gaps in population between divisional teams' areas explain, in part, such things as differences in their attendances at home games, revenues and market values, and even the salaries and contracts of their managers and players. As in the AL, ED clubs had the largest deviation in population followed by those in the WD and then CD.

According to the data in Column 3 of Table A2.1, the league's average among teams is 2.5 million television homes in 2016–2017. While the designated market areas of teams within the ED and WD each averaged about three million television homes, those in the CD have a lower total, especially in Cincinnati and then Milwaukee, Pittsburgh, and St. Louis. Apparently, households in the four latter markets had relatively fewer opportunities to view home games of respectively the Reds, Brewers, Pirates, and Cardinals during their regular seasons and if applicable, in postseasons. Alternatively, households in New York, Los Angeles, and Chicago had the most televisions for games being broadcast, respectively, of the Mets, Dodgers, and Cubs. Compared to AL divisions, the NL's average DMATVH populations were ranked in the same order.

In number of television homes, the largest variation in standard deviations existed in areas of ED teams when compared to those in the CD and WD. The differences between the number of them in New York and Miami are much greater, for example, than Chicago and Cincinnati and also Los Angeles and San Diego. Because the league's standard deviation was relatively low at 1.8 million, television homes across the majority of metropolitan areas are well-dispersed except in the ED. If the New York, Chicago, and Los Angeles areas were excluded in the table, the three divisions would deviate less individually and thus share television homes more proportionately. In contrast to Table A1.1, NL divisions had different results than the AL's in their average deviations.

The data in Column 4 of Table A2.1 denote NL teams' average attendance at home games during MLB's regular season in 2016. Overall, it was 31.4 million per game. Because of their relatively large metropolitan area population and number of television homes, the Mets ranked fifth in AVGATT although considerably less in attendance than the popular and successful Dodgers (first), Cardinals (second), Giants (third), and Cubs (fourth).

The WD teams had the highest average attendance at 34.7 million per game since the Dodgers, and the Giants each played well enough to compete for a title throughout most of the league's regular season. Interestingly, the Cubs won the CD by almost 20 games but nevertheless placed second in its division — fourth in the league and fifth in MLB — in their attendances at Wrigley Field.

Within the ED, the Marlins had the smallest audiences at its home games but nevertheless outperformed the mediocre Braves and Phillies in the division standings. Thus, market size and number of television homes were not the only factors in comparing regular-season ticket sales for each of these teams. Except for the CD, the leagues' ranked differently in the ED and WD because the Dodgers' and Giants' AVGATT each exceeded the Yankees' 37.81 million and Angels' 37.23 million.

Compared to the league's standard deviation of 7.7 million, the variation in average attendances of CD and WD clubs significantly exceeded those in the ED. In fact, the statistic averaged 8.6 million and 8.2 million, respectively, for the two former divisions but only 5.5 million for the latter group of teams. While the Nationals and Marlins had a relatively large difference in attendances at their home games in 2016, the numbers were even greater between the CD's Cardinals and Reds and also the WD's Diamondbacks and Dodgers. Even though they had the largest metropolitan area population or MSAPOP on average, ED teams had the smallest deviation in home-game attendances especially between the Braves, Marlins, and Phillies.

Given the data and its distribution in Table 2.1, the Mets, Cubs, Dodgers, and Giants each play their home games in relatively large markets; the Braves, Marlins, Phillies, Nationals, Cardinals, Diamondbacks, and Rockies in midsized markets; and the Reds, Brewers, Pirates, and Padres in small markets. As computed differently for AL teams in Chapter 2, there were four or approximately 27% of the 15 clubs located in large and also small markets, and the other seven or 46% in midsized markets. According to data in the tables, the teams' markets within and across divisions of both leagues are each unique demographically, they nevertheless represent their economies and the sport's fan base.

For more about two variables in Table A2.1 and their potential to represent baseball markets, the most populated places without a MLB team are such metropolitan statistical areas (MSAs) as Riverside–San Bernardino–Ontario (4.48 million), Charlotte–Concord–Gastonia (2.42 million), and Portland–Vancouver–Hillsboro (2.38 million). With respect to DMAs in the top 25, three without a club are Orlando–Daytona Beach–Melbourne (1.51 million), Sacramento–Stockton–Modesto (1.37 million), and Charlotte–Concord–Gastonia (1.18 million).[11]

If the NL expands at a site in an area not hosting one of its own or a current AL team, a few of these places are viable markets. In addition, they are potential sites for any existing NL clubs with inferior ballparks and that compete for local fans with other teams in the National Basketball Association (NBA), National Football League (NFL), and/or National Hockey League (NHL). Among the group, there has been speculation in the media about MLB locating a new or existing NL (or AL) club in Portland but also in smaller US metropolitan areas that contain such cities as Columbus, Ohio; Indianapolis, Indiana; Las Vegas, Nevada; Nashville, Tennessee; and San Antonio, Texas. Despite failing to support a team during the mid-1990s to early 2000s, another potential site is Montreal, Canada, or somewhere near in the province.[12]

Performances

Each regular season, MLB teams have a 25-man or active roster but also a 40-man roster. The former includes the starting eight position players plus pitchers and reserve players. Players on the active roster are also on the 40-man roster. These are generally the only ones dressed in a uniform and who may take the field in a game at any time.[13]

A 25-man roster typically consists of — but not always — five starting pitchers, seven relief pitchers, two catchers, six infielders, and five outfielders. Unlike the AL, NL teams do not have a designated hitter that, for the most part, plays first base, left field, or right field because of his skills and also inexperience at other positions.

The 40-man or expanded roster is composed of all players in a MLB club's organization who signed a major-league contract. These players are available to be called up to the 25-man roster at any time during a regular season. Also, on the expanded roster are any of them on the 15-day disabled list and those in the minor leagues who signed to a major-league contract but are on an "optional assignment" to the minors.

If a team clinches a playoff berth after the regular season, a 25-man post-season roster takes effect. Players who are part of a team's final roster at the end of the regular season are eligible to participate in the postseason besides those traded from a different team, spent time in the minor leagues, or signed a contract later in the season with the team. Rosters for a postseason series are set when the series begins and no changes are allowed except when a player is moved to the disabled list or involved in an inactive transaction.

During the NL's 141-year history (1876–2016), the number of teams ranged from eight to fifteen per season. Because of differences in the talent of their managers and players, some of them established all-time records as of 2016. For example, the 1906 Chicago Cubs have the highest all-time winning percentage (0.763) and won the most games (116) but nevertheless lost to the Chicago White Sox in the World Series. Alternatively, the 1876 Cincinnati Red Stockings won the fewest number of games (9) while the 1899 Cleveland Spiders have the league's lowest all-time losing percentage

(0.130) and most losses (134) in a season while finishing more than 84 games behind the champion Brooklyn Superbas — renamed Dodgers in 1911.

As of MLB's 2016 season, NL teams' all-time performances appear in Table A2.2. Besides their winning percentages, which were calculated but are not listed in the table, the other data in columns denote the distribution of seasons and overall how well they competed since becoming members of the league. Following is a summary of their performances in order to compare them from first to fifteenth based on various results.[14]

Division titles

According to information in column 5 of the table, the 15 NL teams won 111 division titles — CD clubs with 39, ED 38, and WD 34. Overall, the 51-year-old Atlanta Braves ranked first with 17 (15%) of the total, 59-year-old Dodgers second with 15 (13%), and 125-year-old Cardinals with 13 (11%). Alternatively, the least successful teams have been the Marlins and Rockies each with zero titles and Brewers with only one. While the former group played competitively against others in their division and across the league, the latter three teams had too many inferior players at their positions and were primarily outplayed during regular seasons, respectively, by the ED's Braves and Phillies, WD's Dodgers and Giants, and CD's Cardinals and Reds.

With the most division titles of the group, the Braves and then Dodgers and Cardinals had outstanding managers and talented players. Some of them were manager Bobby Cox and Hall of Fame pitchers' Greg Maddux, Tom Glavine, and John Smoltz for Atlanta from 1991 to 2005; managers' Walter Alston, Tommy Lasorda, Joe Torre, and Don Mattingly, and pitcher Clayton Kershaw, and hitter Pedro Guerrero for Los Angeles in several years since 1969; and manager Tony La Russa and batters' Albert Pujols and Jim Edmonds for St. Louis in the 2000s. Collectively, these men had great careers and won many awards for their success in various regular seasons and postseasons.

After the Braves, Dodgers, and Cardinals, teams ranked second respectively by division were the ED's Philadelphia Phillies with 12 titles (10%) and then the CD's Cincinnati Reds with 11 (9%) and WD's San Francisco Giants with nine (8%). Other than the Marlins, Rockies, and Brewers, the

ED Nationals, CD Cubs, and WD Diamondbacks and Padres also have ranked among the least competitive divisionally since 1969.

Regarding the distribution of titles in each group, the standard deviation of ED clubs was the highest, WD's second, and CD's third. Based on this statistic — which measures the spread or dispersion within divisions — there has more variation in titles won between the Braves and their divisional rivals than among teams in each of the two other groups. Across all NL clubs, however, the deviation in titles was less than in the ED and WD but more when compared to teams within the CD.

Because of such things as decisions approved by their owners, general, and field managers, talent of their players on rosters during each regular season, and other factors affecting them as MLB organizations, CD teams were the most equal of the group or had the greatest parity in winning titles since 1969. In other words, the Cubs and its four intra-divisional rivals have shared titles more equitably than did those in other divisions. Given their performances in recent seasons, the Braves have won only one ED title since 2006 while the Phillies and Nationals, besides the Marlins, struggle each year to challenge any of them.

Pennants

Column 4 of Table A2.2 lists the number of pennants of each NL team by division as of MLB's 2016 season. The CD clubs won 58 (65%) of them and the ED and WD each 19. With the most victories of this title, the Cardinals ranked first (25%), Cubs second (19%), and Dodgers and Reds tied for third (each 10%). Among the least successful in winning pennants thus far have been the Nationals and Brewers with zero of them.

With respect to the all-time leader in postseasons of the league, the Cardinals won 23 pennants, in part, because of such managers as Charlie Comiskey, Billy Southworth, Red Schoendienst, Whitey Herzog, and Tony La Russa, pitchers' Bob Caruthers, Dizzy Dean, and Bob Gibson, sluggers' Frankie Frisch, Stan Musial, and Ken Boyer, and infielders' Ozzie Smith and Orlando Cepeda. Besides them, the organization's owners and executive staffs have made excellent decisions and also they provided leadership and guidance to keep the club competitive during the majority of its regular seasons.

Within the three divisions — when measured by their standard deviations — the ED had the smallest variation in pennants won or most equality among its teams than those in the CD and WD. Across all teams in the league, the deviation in pennants among teams was less than in the CD but greater than in the ED and WD. Combined, the Cardinals and Cubs won 40 (45%) of them but only 19 (17%) division titles. This, in part, reflects the different time periods of competition for pennants (112 post-seasons) and divisions (48 regular-seasons). In short, there are significant differences among and between teams in winning pennants within and among each division based on such things as their number of seasons in the league and other sports-specific factors.

World Series

For this significant sports event as of 2016, the teams in Table A2.2 succeeded in a total of 40 of them as of MLB's 2016 season. Those in the ED won seven (17%), CD 24 (60%), and WD nine (23%). Among the group, the Cardinals ranked first with 11, Reds and Pirates and Dodgers each with five, and Cubs and Giants each with three. Alternatively, the Nationals in 12 years, Brewers in 19, Rockies in 24, and Padres in 48 have failed to win a World Series. Simply put, the latter clubs periodically dealt with management and coaching problems, lacked enough talented players on their rosters in most seasons, and had too much competition from others in their division.

To win a World Series, the Cardinals and other teams succeeded partly because of their Most Valuable Players (MVPs) in this post-season event. For the three most successful of the group, these included, for example, St. Louis' David Freese and David Eckstein, Cincinnati's Pete Rose and Johnny Bench, Pirates' Willie Stargell and Roberto Clemente, and Dodgers' Sandy Koufax and Ron Cey. In 2016, the Cubs' outfielder Ben Zobrist had a 0.357 batting average, 10 hits including a go-ahead runs batted in (RBI) double in the tenth inning of Game 7, and five runs scored in the World Series. As a group, these MVPs had exceptional performances at their positions and also some of them primarily as batters.

As measured by the standard deviation and explained for the league's pennants and division titles, there have been differences in teams' World

Series victories regarding all divisions and also within and between divisions. According to my calculations, the overall variation in winning World Series (2.94) was less than for pennants (6.50) and division titles (5.36). Combined, the Cardinals, Reds, Pirates, and Dodgers won a relatively larger proportion of total World Series than they did pennants. For division titles, the top-ranked Braves, second-place Dodgers, and third-place Cardinals won 45 or about 40% of them. This distribution, in short, is presented in Table A2.2.

Within the three groups, the ED's standard deviation in winning World Series was 0.89, CD's 4.02, and WD's 2.16 as of MLB's 2016 season. In other words, ED teams had the smallest difference or variation in number of World Series victories for several reasons including their competitiveness, various rivalries, managers' experiences, and the talent and performances of players on their rosters from year-to-year. Meanwhile, the CD's Brewers had the fewest opportunities thus far and have been less successful in World Series than the other four teams in the division. In the WD, the Dodgers and Giants have been the only teams to win at least three World Series as the Diamondbacks, Rockies, and Padres struggle in regular seasons to even qualify as wild cards and really compete in NLDS and also NLCS.

Total performances

A MLB team's total performance (TP) includes its number of division titles plus pennants and World Series. Based on the data in Table A3.2 as of 2016, the Cardinals had the best TP with 47, Dodgers second with 29, and Cubs third with 26. The three worst among the group of 15 have been the Brewers and Rockies each with one and then the Nationals with three. Given this information, these have been the most and least productive teams in the NL according to their TPs.

There were differences in TPs across the three NL divisions and within and between them. After adding the TPs of 15 teams in Table A2.2, the sum was 247. Relative to each other's proportion, this included the CD's 121 (49%), ED's 64 (26%), and WD's 62 (25%). In part, this distribution ranks these divisions from first to third in competitiveness during their regular-seasons and also in post-season results.

With respect to the variation of TPs among the three groups of teams, the CD had the largest standard deviation and then those in the WD and

ED. As before for titles, pennants, and World Series, the Cardinals followed by the Cubs and Reds dominated their division in performances and to lesser extent, so did the WD's Dodgers and Giants. The five teams within the ED, however, had the lowest deviation in TPs because of their relatively equal competitiveness during regular seasons and also comparable ability to win games in postseasons. Therefore, there has been less parity among teams in the CD and WD but more in the ED despite low TPs of the Marlins and Nationals.

Although not listed in Table A2.2, another characteristic of teams is their average winning percentages during MLB's regular seasons. For those in the NL as of 2016, the Dodgers ranked first at 0.537, Giants second at 0.520, Braves third at 0.514, and Cubs fourth at 0.513. The bottom four, in contrast, have been the Marlins and Brewers each at 0.469, Rockies at 0.466, and Padres at 0.463. These averages reflect, in part, each team's record in TPs.[15]

Regarding divisions, the CD had the highest winning average per team at 0.500, WD second at 0.494, and ED third at 0.485. Because the Cubs, Reds, Pirates, and Cardinals are each above 0.502, the Dodgers and Giants each greater than 0.519, and the Marlins, Mets, Phillies, and Nationals each below 0.500, there have been relatively large and real differences in the managerial talent and rosters of these teams for decades. Eventually, the Nationals and perhaps Brewers and Padres will improve their performances and increase parity across the NL's three divisions.

To avoid double counting in determining each NL team's total performances or TPs, their number of playoffs does not appear in Table A2.2. However, with respect to that data, there were an aggregate 171 playoffs for clubs in the table as of 2016. The Cardinals ranked first with 28, Dodgers second with 21, and Braves third with 19. Alternatively, Nationals and Rockies teams each qualified for three playoffs, but the Marlins and Brewers combined for only four of them. In short, the Cardinals, Dodgers, and Braves have been competitive enough in regular seasons to perform in more postseasons than the other clubs.

For the distribution of playoffs by division as of MLB's 2016 season, ED clubs appeared in 46, CD's in 80, and WD's in 45. Regarding deviations within and among divisions, CD teams had the largest (9) and ED smallest (7) variation in number of playoffs while the league's averaged eight. These differences indicate more parity or a wider distribution in number of playoffs among CD teams than those in the ED and WD and also among all divisions combined.

During November 2016, *Baseball Almanac* researched and reported the most dominant MLB teams of all-time. To determine this result, the magazine used winning percentage, percentage of runs scored in any given game, playoff record, and pitcher's earned-run average (ERA). Based on these metrics and baseball information from various sources, the top NL teams of all-time — in chronological order — include the following franchises.[16]

- Being the highest-ranked team to not win a World Series, the 1906 Cubs' 116 wins is still tied for the most ever, and their 0.763 winning percentage is easily highest of all time. Third baseman Harry Steinfeldt led the team in batting average (0.327), hits (176), and RBIs (83), Frank Chance in runs (103) and stolen bases (57), and pitcher Mordecai "Three Fingers" Brown in earned run average (1.04). In the World Series, the Cubs played the Chicago White Sox, who were dubbed "Hitless Wonders" after finishing last in the AL with a 0.230 team batting average. Nevertheless, the White Sox pitching prevailed by holding the Cubs to just eighteen runs in six games.

- While there are several statistics that make the 1907 Cubs special, the most significant one is the team's mind-boggling 1.73 ERA. Even in the dead ball era, this pitching staff defined stingy. The club outscored its opponents by nearly 200 runs on its way to a 107-45 record. Besides the Cubs' Brown, who won 20 games, pitcher Orval Overall finished 23-7 and Jack Pfiester led the league with a 1.15 ERA. In the World Series, the pitching staff allowed a total of six runs in five games. How did they manage a four-games-to-none sweep when playing five games in the Series? Game 1 was called off after 12 innings with the teams deadlocked in a 3-3 tie.

- The Pittsburgh Pirates' 0.724 winning percentage in 1909 is the fourth-highest ever and their highest since 1903 (0.650). The team was led by Hall of Fame shortstop Honus Wagner, who had the best batting average (0.339) and most total bases (242) and runs batted in (100) in the league during the regular season. At 35 years old, Wagner finally won his only World Series when the Pirates edged the Detroit Tigers 4-3 in seven games. During the Series, Honus hit 0.333 with seven RBIs and six stolen bases. In addition, his teammate Babe Adams pitched several innings and won three games.

• After 105 victories in the league's regular season, the St. Louis Cardinals faced their crosstown rival — the AL champion St. Louis Browns (now Baltimore Orioles) — in the 1944 World Series. The Cardinals won it in six games because, in part, infielder Stan Musial starred on the biggest stage by hitting 0.304, establishing an on-base percentage of 0.360, and slugging 0.522. On the cusp of superstardom, Musial sat out the 1945 season to serve in the US Navy. He returned in 1946 and led the team to another World Series championship, winning the NL MVP award in the process.

• Though one could argue the "Big Red Machine" of 1975 was one of the best ever, that Cincinnati Reds club needed seven games to defeat the Boston Red Sox and win the World Series. That was not the case for the 1976 Reds who swept the Philadelphia Phillies in the NLCS and then manhandled the New York Yankees in a four-game sweep of the World Series. The Reds' Johnny Bench hit 0.533 in the World Series with two home runs and six RBIs to take home MVP honors while his teammates' George Foster and Dave Concepcion added to the onslaught. In the regular season, players' Joe Morgan, Pete Rose, and Ken Griffey led the offensive juggernaut to 102 wins. Scrappy and scruffy in the way only a 1970s ball club could be, the Reds of 1976 were fun to watch and one of the greatest in the sport's history.

For various reasons such as a lack of talented players, manager problems, and/or both of them, some NL teams had terrible performances in their regular seasons. Several of these clubs were evaluated based on their ability to score runs and win games. In chronological order, the following is a list of the worst clubs in the league's history as of MLB's 2016 season.[17]

• Between 1882 and 1890, the Pittsburgh Allghenys compiled a 441–617 record and ended above 0.500 only twice. In 1890, the team's stars joined many NL players in defecting to the upstart Player's League. The Allghenys' resulting season was historically bad, finishing 23-113 (0.169) and more than 66 games behind the Brooklyn Bridegrooms. Pittsburgh was last or next to last in the league in nearly every major category including at the plate, on the mound, and in the field. The Alleghenys had the last laugh the next season, though, when the Player's League folded. Indeed, the franchise's owners rehired many of their former players and became more successful after being renamed Pittsburgh Pirates.

• Sometime during 1899, the NL's Cleveland Spiders' owners purchased the St. Louis Browns franchise. Although continuing to control the Spiders, they leveraged their newfound conflict-of-interest by trading Cleveland's best players — to themselves (Browns) — thereby decimating the roster and fielding a team that arguably became the worst in baseball history. Indeed, the Spiders won consecutive games only once during the season. Home games were so poorly attended that other teams refused to travel to Cleveland to play them. As a result, the team played only 42 home games and 112 on the road, losing 101 of them. The pitching staff gave up 1,254 runs or 8.1 per game and batters hit only 12 home runs as the Spiders set numerous other undesirable records. In the end, the NL disbanded the Spiders and three other teams as the league contracted from 12 teams to eight.

• In 1912, the Boston Braves claimed their first World Series and won again it in 1914.Then came the dark ages for the franchise until hitting its nadir in the 1935 season. That team went 38-115 (0.248) and finished more than 61 games behind the champion Chicago Cubs. Player Wally Berger's excellent Wins Above Replacement (WAR) — including his NL-leading 34 home runs and 130 RBIs — was wasted along with the presence of former New York Yankees' superstar Babe Ruth in his final year in baseball. It took until the late 1940s, when pitchers' Warren Spahn and Johnny Sain arrived, for the franchise to return to respectability.

• When the New York Mets entered the NL as an expansion team in 1962, they had an awful inaugural season. With legendary Casey Stengel at the helm, they posted a 40-120 record (0.250) and outscored by 331 runs. Slugger Frank Thomas's 34 home runs represented one of the team's few bright spots. If you believe it possible, the Mets actually underachieved. Baseball Reference's Pythagorean won–loss formula had them going 50-110 based on their horrendous run differential. New York fans probably preferred the memory of the former Giants and Dodgers as opposed to the reality of the first Mets team.

• After winning the World Series in 1997, the Marlins descended quickly in their performance. Owner Wayne Huizenga — angry that South Florida taxpayers refused to build his team a new ballpark — systematically dismantled the reigning champs. Gone were core contributors like Kevin Brown, Bobby Bonilla, Moises Alou, Charles Johnson and Gary Sheffield, and replacing them was a pile of young prospects, most of whom turned out to be of little consequence. As a result, the club finished 54-108 in MLB's 1998 regular season. In fact, the Marlins were a combined 0-30 against the Brewers, Giants, Reds, and Yankees.

LEAGUE ECONOMICS

As administrative and managerial parent organizations that include a group of franchises, American professional sports leagues do such things as establish, implement, and enforce policies, regulations, and rules; schedule games and dates annually for preseasons, regular seasons, and postseasons; negotiate contracts with cable companies, networks, and other types of national and international media; and make decisions and find ways that financially benefit their members' operations. As of MLB's 2016 season, the NL included 15 teams whose economic objective was — and always will be — to compete and generate enough revenue from sources in order to maximize their profit.

In this section, there are data and other information about the commercial and financial aspects of franchises in the NL and their significance from an economic perspective. Besides attendances at home and away games, anything else that affects teams' income, market value, and wealth is included in the analysis, quantified, and discussed. In other words, the NL is an organization consisting of for-profit enterprises that operate to compete each season typically within a division and/or the league and seek to improve their performances in current and future games.

Franchise Financials

Forbes magazine's sports editors published financial data of MLB franchises as of their 2015 season. As denoted in Columns 2–6 of Table A2.3, these amounts include respectively their estimated market value — which is based on the current stadium deal without deduction for debt — and also total revenue, gate receipts, operating income — earnings before interest, taxes, depreciation, and amortization (EBITDA) — and debt-to-value (D/V) percentages. For each of three divisions, the information reveals the financial status and wealth of NL teams individually and relative to each other as a group. The following identifies and highlights the data.[18]

As derived from Column 2 of Table A2.3, the NL teams' average but estimated market value equaled $1.33 billion. While the Dodgers ranked first, Giants second, and Cubs third, the Marlins, Rockies, and Brewers had the three lowest amounts. By division from most to least in value, WD teams averaged $1.48 billion, CD's $1.31 billon, and ED's $1.21 billion. There were significant differences between these groups of teams because of such things as their hometown ballpark, geographic location, historical success in the division and league, and size of the metropolitan area's fan base.

To compare their standard deviation or variation in market values, the highest was WD teams ($817 million) and lowest among those in the ED ($349 million) and then CD ($579 million). This means parity or smaller deviation in franchise values existed in 2015 to a greater extent between the Braves and other ED teams than among clubs in the other divisions. Although these were based on estimates, the amounts influence such things as the clubs' relative wealth, economic power in the league, and future price if offered for sale to potential investors.

Each team's revenue in 2015 is listed in Column 3 of Table A2.3. The top three — Dodgers, Giants, and Cubs — ranked the same as did their market values while those with the least revenue were the Marlins, Diamondbacks, and Rockies. Among divisions, WD clubs averaged the most at $308 million followed by the CD's $271 million and ED's $266 million. The differences in amounts occurred for several reasons including their home attendances, range in ticket prices, winning percentage in games, location, and number of baseball fans in the area.

Because of various demographic and sport-specific factors, there were disparities in teams' revenue. While the league's standard deviation equaled $68 million, WD teams had the highest variation in revenue at $106 million and then the CD's at $47 million and ED's at $43 million. The Dodgers' and Giants' amounts combined exceeded $800 million while the Braves and its divisional rivals had relatively small differences in revenue except for the Marlins and Mets. Besides win–loss records in the regular season, this reflects number of jobs among the population of their markets, size of fan bases, popularity, and the income and wealth of local households.

Each NL teams' 2015 gate receipts — in millions of dollars — appear in Column 4 of Table A2.3. While the league's average was $84 million, the Giants had the most ($172 million) and then the Cubs ($144 million) and Dodgers

($130 million). In contrast to these amounts, the Marlins, Diamondbacks, and Padres had the smallest gate receipts in MLB's 2015 season.

Regarding distributions by division, the typical CD team averaged $91 million in revenue, WD clubs $89 million, and ED franchises $71 million. Besides the Cubs and Cardinals, the Reds, Brewers, and Pirates also play in more lucrative and prominent baseball markets from a revenue perspective than one or two in the ED and also WD. As a result, there are differences between them in generating gate receipts from ticket sales at their home games.

The dispersion or disparity in gate receipts was greatest among WD clubs ($58 million) compared to CD teams ($41 million) and those in the ED ($29 million). Because of the gap in amounts between, for example, the Dodgers and Diamondbacks, the division's standard deviation exceeds that of the Cubs and Pirates and also Mets and Marlins. Simply put, Los Angeles and San Francisco are large and more prosperous baseball markets than the majority of others in the league.

Column 5 of Table A2.3 contains the operating income or EBITDA of NL teams in 2015. For the group, it averaged $22.7 million. From most to least by division, CD clubs averaged $36.3 million, ED's $20.8 million, and WD's $11 million. Because of excessive payments for players' salaries and other types of expenses, the Dodgers and Phillies each had a negative EBITDA while the Giants, Cardinals, and Cubs earned the most income by operating efficiently. For various reasons, the Rockies and Reds had marginal results in amounts but less than the small-to-midsized market Marlins in the ED, and small market Brewers and Pirates in the CD and Diamondbacks and Padres in the WD.

Column 6 of Table A2.3 includes the D/V percentages of each NL franchise in 2015. On average, the league's was 13.4% or, in amount, approximately $178 million per team based on their estimated market values. Among each group, the ED's averaged 16.4%, WD's 12%, and CD's 11.8%. Although the Braves had zero debt and six others less than 11%, the D/V ratios exceeded 15% each for the Marlins, Mets, Nationals, Cubs, Cardinals, and Dodgers and Padres.

As described for other variables in the table, the standard deviations of D/V were unequal among NL divisions and franchises within divisions. ED teams, for example, had the greatest variation at 12.8% and then those in the WD at 7.3% and CD at 5.4%. In order to reduce their ratios for financial reasons and operate more effectively, several teams needed to generate higher market values and/or record less amount of debt in accounts on their balance sheet.

Although reported in *Forbes* for being an important, necessary, and periodic payment from an operations perspective, Table A2.3 does not include the players' expenses of these teams in 2015. For the league, they totaled $2.2 billion or $146.6 million per team. On average, the WD's was $179 million, ED's $133 million, and CD's $132 million. While the Dodgers, Giants, and Nationals ranked highest, the Marlins, Diamondbacks, and Pirates each paid less than $112 million in players' expenses. Given these amounts, the first group of clubs had an above-average roster of players and won enough games in the regular season to qualify for the playoffs but the latter three failed to participate in the postseason, in part, because of their relatively small investment in players' salaries.

Players' expenses were different and also significantly deviated between the three NL divisions. From most to least in variation among the groups — as measured by their standard deviations — these included the WD's $99 million and then ED's $38 million and CD's $18 million. Such amounts denote that the greatest disparity in payments occurred because of the Dodgers' $346 million versus the Diamondbacks' $103 million in the WD whereas the range in players' expenses within the ED and CD equaled, respectively, only $98 million between the Nationals and Marlins and also $43 million between the Cubs and Pirates. Thus, NL teams with the greatest revenues and/or largest market values tended to compensate their players more than rivals within their division and across the league.

Ballparks

As of MLB's 2016 season, the 15 NL teams played their home games in ballparks that differed in age, cost and market value, and also in such other ways as location, capacity, and ownership. Based on various criteria including their amenities, concessions and sightlines, they have been ranked from best to worst overall, most to least accessible, and highest to lowest as facilities to entertain spectators at games. Given that overview, this section provides some data and information on the league's ballparks and discusses specific characteristics about them.[19]

Among teams' ballparks within each division as of MLB's 2016 season, they ranged in age as follows: from the Braves' 20-year-old Turner Field to Miami's 6-year-old Marlins Park in the ED; from the Reds' 14-year-old Great American Ball Park to the Cubs' 101-year-old Wrigley Field in the CD; and from the Padres' 13-year-old Petco Park to Los Angeles' 55-year-old Dodger Stadium in the WD. Of the 15 venues, four of them are privately owned and another 10 publicly, while the Padres organization and City of San Diego jointly own Petco Park.

Their construction costs ranked from being relatively cheap to very expensive. From the least to most costly in the ED and then CD and WD, respectively, it was $235 million to erect Turner Field in Atlanta for the Braves compared to $688 million for 9-year-old Citi Field in New York for the Mets; from less than $1 million for investors to build Wrigley Park in Chicago for the Cubs to $365 million for 11-year-old Busch Stadium III for the Cardinals in St. Louis; and from $23 million for Dodger Stadium in Los Angeles to $357 million for 17-year-old AT&T Park for the Giants in San Francisco. Regarding the most likely replacement or renovation of a current ballpark in the league, the Braves will open the $678 million, 41,000-seat SunTrust Park in Cobb County, Georgia, in April 2017 to play a game against the Padres.

Recently *Forbes* sports editors assigned economic values to NL ballparks. From lowest to highest within divisions, respectively, amounts in the ED ranged from $89 million for Marlins Park in Miami to $282 million for Nationals Park in Washington; in the CD, from $153 million for the Pirates' PNC Park in Pittsburgh to $355 million for Wrigley Field in Chicago; and in the WD, from $135 million for Chase Field in Phoenix to $494 million for AT&T Park in San Francisco. Based on their estimated values, ED teams' ballparks averaged $211 million, CD' $245 million, and WD' $281 million. Because of increasing real estate prices in urban areas and popularity of the sport in America, these facilities will likely appreciate in value especially for those within midsized to large metropolitan areas.

In various studies, NL ballparks have been ranked by baseball experts and sports journalists in the media with respect to their location and different attributes and problems. Although results vary according to each study's criteria and requirements, a few venues rank among the best while some others placed in the worst group. For example, the most attractive, entertaining, and well-structured ballparks for fans, in no specific order, include the Pirates' PNC Park and Giants' AT&T Park.

An editor at csnatlantic.com, for example, evaluated each of them as follows:

> "To me [editor], this is the perfect ballpark [PNC Park]. It has everything: An unmatched vista of downtown Pittsburgh beyond the Allegheny River; the Roberto Clemente Bridge ushering fans back and forth; an intimate seating bowl with two decks (the first ballpark with fewer than three decks since Milwaukee's County Stadium in the 1950s); and just enough quirks to make games there distinct without threatening the quality of play. And after two decades of awful baseball, it's been great to see Pirates games become a real event inside the best ballpark in America."

Regarding his description and ranking of AT&T Park, the editor had these comments:

> "There's certainly a valid argument for the Giants' home park to rank No. 1 on the list, and I wouldn't question anyone who picked it. The view of San Francisco Bay is breathtaking. The see-through brick wall in right field is a great touch for pedestrians walking outside the park to be able to see in. The best view of the place, though, actually is from the last seat in the last row of the upper deck down the first base-line. From there, you see not only the field and the bay, but the Bay Bridge and downtown San Francisco behind the third-base line. It's just phenomenal."[20]

According to a similar report, two of the lowest-ranked NL facilities — besides the Braves' Turner Field — were Miami's Marlins Park and the Mets' Citi Field. Among other ballparks in the league, Marlins Park ranked twenty-third and Citi Field twenty-fifth, respectively, for the following reasons:

> "Give [Marlins owner] Jeff Loria this much: He built a ballpark that is uniquely Miami. It may not be your cup of tea, with the Clevelander Bar behind the left-field bullpen, the bright colors and the million-dollar thingamabob sculpture behind the center-field fence. But it doesn't look like any other ballpark in the world, and there's something to be said for that. On the other hand, this feels less like a ballpark than an amusement park. Plus there's the whole swindling [of] local taxpayers to get the place built thing, which never looks good."

With respect to an evaluation of Citi Field, the author stated:

"The problems with Citi Field are many. It's too big. It's too dark. It's too confusing (you can't walk all the way around the main concourse; you have to take stairs or escalators up and then back down). And the original out-field dimensions were so bad, the Mets wound up moving the fences in after only a couple of seasons of play. It's a completely contrived ballpark out in the middle of Flushing Meadows, where the crowds are drowned out by the planes taking off from nearby LaGuardia Airport every couple of minutes. [This is] very much a missed opportunity for the Mets."[21]

Fan cost index

For several years, a Chicago-based company named Team Marketing Report (TMR) has prepared and published a Fan Cost Index (FCI) for the home games of teams in professional sports. To attend a game for a typical family with two kids, an FCI includes the cost of four average-priced tickets, two cheapest-priced draft beers, four each lowest-priced soft drinks and hot dogs, parking for one vehicle, and two each game programs and least-expensive, adult-sized adjustable caps. Costs are determined by telephone calls with team representatives, venues, and concessionaires and from questions asked during interviews.[22]

In the 2016 NL season, the average FCI for a family to attend a regular season game was $213. While Phillies games each cost $258, the Diamondbacks had the league's lowest FCI at $132. Among the three divisions, the average for ED teams equaled $219, CD's $221, and WD's $199. The order from ranking them most to least occurred, in part, because FCIs of the Phillies, Cubs, Cardinals, and Giants each exceeded $242 while those of such teams as the Braves, Marlins, Mets and Nationals, and also Diamondbacks, Rockies, Dodgers, and Padres were each below that amount.

For specific items in TMR's 2016 FCI, the approximate range in amounts from most to least expensive or first to 15th across the NL were listed as follows: average ticket, Cubs $51 to Diamondbacks $18; average premium ticket, Marlins $174 to Brewers $46; beer, Phillies $7.75 to Rockies $3; soft drink, Dodgers $6 to Reds $1; hot dog, Mets $6.25 to Reds $1; parking, Cubs and Giants each $25 to Padres $8; and for a cap, Pirates and Rockies each $22 to Diamondbacks $9.99. Based on economics principles, these prices were set by teams and/or vendors to sell enough units to maximize revenue from their sales at home games in the ballparks.

From MLB's 2011 to 2016 season, there were some significant increases but also relatively small and even decreases in FCIs of teams within the NL. For examples of these changes, the Nationals' FCI rose from $196 to $234 or 19% but the Dodgers' from only $226 to $234 or 4%, while the Mets' declined from $241 to $223 or approximately 5%. Because of inflation, number of — and amount spent by — families at games in ballparks, local economic conditions, and other factors, the majority of teams and/or vendors raised their prices each year rather than keeping them constant or lowering amounts.

In evaluating FCIs between MLB's 2015 and 2016 seasons, the Padres' increased the most, in other words, from $153 to $182 or by 19%. Alternatively, fans' costs fell for home games of the Marlins and Rockies but remained the same for those of the Reds at $166. Thus, there were different payments for tickets and other things by families to attend NL teams' home games at their ballparks especially from 2011 to 2016.

ORGANIZATION HIGHLIGHTS

Besides regular-season and post-season games, the NL and its franchises are involved in — and affected by — community events and also business-related and government affairs, news, and projects. Because these things and other topics influence the league in different but perhaps important and historic ways, the following are a few of them from the academic and popular literature.[23]

First, the median household income of the five most populous metropolitan areas containing at least one NL team in 2015 was $93,294 in Washington–Arlington–Alexandria (Nationals); $88,518 in San Francisco–Oakland–Hayward (Giants); $70,283 in Denver–Aurora–Lakewood (Rockies); $68,743 in New York–Newark–New Jersey (Mets); and $67,320 in San Diego–Carlsbad (Padres). Based on these amounts, local teams' games in regular seasons were more affordable for families living within the areas.

Second, the three top and bottom NL teams in total attendance during their 2016 regular season were, respectively, the Dodgers (3.70 million),

Cardinals (3.44 million), and Giants (3.36 million) as opposed to the Marlins (1.71 million), Reds (1.89 million), and Phillies (1.91 million). While the former group of clubs played their home games in ballparks within relatively large and wealthy markets and at least competed for a division title, the latter three struggled to attract fans and finished with a losing record.

Third, besides a municipality's willingness to approve public financing for a new baseball stadium and also such factors as market size, business dynamics, and the baseball culture of a particular place, a few attractive markets for an NL expansion team are Montreal and Vancouver, Canada; Austin, Texas; Mexico City, Mexico or another site in Latin America; Charlotte, North Carolina; and Nashville, Tennessee. Being the largest metropolitan area in North America without a MLB franchise, Montreal has a well-documented passion for professional sports, and perhaps again for baseball. The city, for example, drew an average of more than 48,000 fans per game to Toronto Blue Jays' exhibitions in 2014 and 2015. The Warren Cromartie-led Montreal Baseball Project and Mayor Denis Coderre have continued their passionate advocacy. Furthermore, prospective team owners commissioned a feasibility study for a major league franchise in Montreal with encouraging results. The city's Olympic Stadium could host a big-league team for two or three seasons while a new ballpark is being built somewhere in the area.

Fourth, from 1997 to 2013, AL teams won 2,122 interleague games or 52% of them. Because of the DH rule, AL clubs have deeper lineups capable of scoring more runs. This has been true in the interleague era as AL clubs averaged 4.83 runs per game during the 17-year period compared to 4.54 for those in the NL. Moreover, the NL's typically superior pitching has been inferior in interleague play, while the AL's typically inferior pitching has been more productive. There has been a particularly big divide since the start of 2010 to 2016, as AL pitcher's ERA was about 3.84 while the NL's averaged 4.23.

Fifth, since they became principal owners, the Cardinals' William DeWitt Jr., Phillies' David Montgomery, and Giants' Charles Johnson have each won more total championships — division titles, pennants, and World Series combined — than 12 other owners of NL teams. The least successful with zero championships has been the Pirates' Robert Nutting and Padres' Ron Fowler. For the group, Dewitt acquired his team in 1995, Montgomery in 1981, Johnson in 1992, Nutting in 2007, and Fowler in 2012. Until

2016, the Cubs' Tom Ricketts also had no championships since becoming an owner in 2009.

Sixth, during early 2016, MLB commissioner Rob Manfred revealed that the NL could adopt the DH rule as soon as 2017. Speaking at quarterly owners meetings, Manfred told reporters that the sport's newer owners "have demonstrated willingness" to consider such a radical change. Despite a slight uptick in 2015, offensive production across the league is still at its lowest point since the 1970s. Pitchers, in fact, had a collective on-base-plus-slugging percentage of 0.329 in 2015, the third-lowest mark since 1974. The only years in which pitchers have done worse over that span were 2012 (0.327) and 2014 (0.306). Although NL purists will bemoan the demise of "true baseball," the extra bat will help in the long run since AL teams have a 14-11 record in the last 25 World Series.

Seventh, in a 2014 study that listed each MLB team's popularity on the google.com website, the relative size of its television market — markets with two teams are divided evenly between them and then the (ratio) between the two — the Cardinals ranked second (2.29), Cubs fourth (1.90) and Giants fifth (1.87), and the Nationals 25th (.53), Marlins 27th (0.47), and Diamondbacks 29th (0.39). Thus, such NL teams as the Cardinals, Cubs, Giants, Pirates (1.57), and Reds (1.53) tend to over-perform relative to their market size. Among all clubs in the study, the Red Sox were first (2.95) and Yankees third (1.95), but the Angels 30th (0.35).

Eighth, based on their local cable deals, the three NL clubs with the most and least television revenue in 2016 were respectively the Dodgers at $204 million, Cubs $65 million, and Phillies $60 million, but then alternatively the Brewers at only $24 million and Marlins and Rockies each at $20 million. The Dodgers, for example, have a 25-year deal valued at $8.35 billion that started in 2014 and ends in 2038 with 100% ownership, while the Rockies signed a 10-year contract worth $200 million from 2011 to 2020 with no ownership. Following the Dodgers in annual amounts were the AL's Angels at $118 million, Yankees at $98 million, and Red Sox at $80 million, with the Royals and Rays each earning less than $23 million.

Ninth, in 2016, Turner Broadcasting Systems' AL wild card game did poorly in ratings while Entertainment Sports Programming Network's NL wild card did great. The latter league's top media markets for games were Los Angeles ranked second, Chicago third, San Francisco fifth, and Washington D.C.

seventh. These teams drive ratings up because of casual viewers outside of their endemic market. Most fans know the Dodgers, Cubs, Giants, and Nationals and also their reputation and star players. In fact, the NL all-star team could have been filled with just players from the four squads.

Tenth, two corporate strategic and management observations about why the Cubs' ownership succeeded in 2016 after others failed for so long are vision and strategic patience. Regarding vision, the team's owners spent millions on the organization's infrastructure and smartly bolstered its business-side and baseball operations. About strategic patience, Cubs management remained steadfastly committed to its overall strategy and did not backslide, or meander, from its ultimate plan. The group knew real progress was being made in the minor leagues and soon would, and actually did, have an impact at the major league level.

NOTES

1. For the history of professional baseball organizations, especially the National League and its teams, see Jozsa FP Jr. (2016), *National League Franchises: Team Performances Inspire Business Success.* New York, NY: Springer; Quirk J and Fort RD, (1992). *Pay Dirt: The Business of Professional Team Sports.* Princeton, NJ: Princeton University Press; and the *Official Major League Baseball Fact Book 2005 Edition.* St. Louis, MO: Sporting News (2005). Some baseball websites to research for historical data include http://www.mlb.com, http://www.sportsen cylopedia.com, and http://www.baseball-almanac.com.

2. Read "Defunct NL Franchises," http://www.sportsencyclopedia.com [cited 6 November 2016] and "Defunct Baseball Teams," http://www.sportsencyclope-dia.com [cited 24 November 2016].

3. Jozsa FP Jr., (2009). *Major League Baseball Expansions and Relocations: A History, 1876–2008.* Jefferson, NC: McFarland and Jozsa FP Jr. and Guthrie JJ Jr. (1999). *Relocating Teams and Expanding Leagues in Professional Sports: How the Major Leagues Respond to Market Conditions.* Westport, CT: Quorum Books.

4. Regarding wild card teams and their success, one source is Mather V, "A Brief History of the Single-Elimination Wild-Card Game," http://www.nytimes.com [cited 6 November 2016].

5. *Idem, Major League Baseball Expansions and Relocations: A History, 1876–2008* and *Relocating Teams and Expanding Leagues in Professional Sports: How the Major Leagues Respond to Market Conditions.*

6. *Idem,* "Defunct NL Franchises" and "Defunct Baseball Teams."

7. "National League Presidents," http://www.sportsencyclopedia.com [cited 24 November 2016] and "Commissioners of Major League Baseball, and American League Presidents and National League Presidents," http://www.baseball-almanac. com [cited 24 November 2016].

8. There are readings on this topic such as Liebman R, "Schedule Changes Since 1876," http://www.research.sabr.org [cited 7 November 2016].

9. See "Median Household Income in the Past 12 Months by 25 Most Populous Metropolitan Areas," http://wwwcensus.gov [cited 18 November 2016].

10. The results for AL teams appear in this book's Table A1.1 of Chapter 1, which denote how they ranked in MSAPOP, DMATVH, and AVGATT. Among them, the most prominent demographically were the New York Yankees, Los Angeles Angels, Chicago White Sox, and Texas Rangers.

11. "Population Estimates 2015," http://www.census.gov [cited 12 November 2016] and "Metropolitan Statistical Areas of the United States of America," https//en.wikipedia.org [cited 12 November 2016].

12. An article for this topic is Morosi JP, "Which Locations Make the Most Sense for MLB Expansion?" http://www.foxsports.com [cited 18 November 2016].

13. An excellent source for this baseball rule is "Baseball Roster History," http://www.baseball-almanac.com [cited 8 November 2016].

14. See Table A2.2 in the appendix for the all-time performances of AL teams. The New York Yankees and then Boston Red Sox led in each championship category while the league's Houston Astros, Tampa Bay Rays, and Seattle Mariners had the worst results.

15. For the average winning percentages and number of playoffs of NL teams, the data is available in sections of websites' http://www.baseball-reference.com, http://www.mlb.com, and http://www.baseball-almanac.com.

16. Three online sources for this topic are Eric Schaal, "8 Greatest MLB Teams of All Time," http://www.cheatsheet.com [cited 10 November 2016]; Selbe N, "The 10 Greatest MLB Teams Seasons in History," http://www.mlb-teamspoin tafter.com [cited 27 November 2016]; "Determining the Best Major League Baseball Team Ever From 1902–2005," http://www.baseball-almanac.com [cited 27 November 2016].

17. See Schaal E, "5 Worst Teams of the Modern Era," http://www.cheatsheet.com [cited 10 November 2016] and "The Ten Worst Major League Baseball Seasons Ever," http://www.writing.jmpressely.net [cited 24 November 2016].

18. Ozanian M, Badenhausen K, and Settimi C, "The Business of Baseball," http://www.forbes.com [cited 27 June 2016]. Comparable data and financial results for AL teams are in this book's Table A1.3 of the Appendix.

19. Jozsa FP Jr. (2016). *Major League Baseball Organizations: Team Performances and Financial Consequences.* Lanham, MD: Lexington Books.

20. These remarks were from a study by Zuckerman M, "Ranking All 30 MLB Ballparks," http://www.csnmidatlantic.com [cited 17 November 2016].

21. *Idem*, "Ranking All 30 MLB Ballparks."

22. For the facilities of all professional sports teams and costs for families to attend regular season games, see various editions of the "Fan Cost Index," http://www.teammarketingreport.com [cited 16 November 2016] and also the publication "Team Marketing Report — MLB 2016," http://www.teammarketing.com [cited 25 January 2017].

23. "Median Household Income in the Past 12 Months by 25 Most Populous Metropolitan Areas," http://wwwcensus.gov [cited 18 November 2016]; "MLB Attendance Report — 2016," http://www.espn.com [cited 12 November 2016]; "Which Locations Make the Most Sense for MLB Expansion?" http://www.foxsports.com [cited 18 November 2016]; "Which is Baseball's Superior Overall League, the AL or the NL?" http://www.bleacherreport.com [cited 18 November 2016]; "List of Major League Baseball Principal Owners," http://www.baseball-reference.com [cited 23 November 2016]; Diamond J, "Why a National League Designated Hitter is Inevitable," http://www.wsj.com [cited 2 December 2016]; Silver N, "Which MLB Teams Overperform in Popularity?" http://www.fivethirtyeight.com [cited 2 December 2016]; Edwards C, "Estimated TV Revenues for All 30 MLB Teams," http://www.fangraphs.com [cited 2 December 2016]; Colangelo M, "Alternating American League, National League Coverage Favors Fox Over Turner This Year," http://www.thefieldsofgreen.com [cited 2 December 2016]; Reed R, "Fly the 'W' for Cubs Business Strategy," http://www.chicagotribune.com [cited 3 December 2016].

Part II
National Basketball Association

Chapter 3

EASTERN CONFERENCE

HISTORY

Because of financial and economic problems, low attendances at their home games and other reasons, four teams moved from the National Basketball League (NBL) to the rival Basketball Association of America (BAA) in 1948. One year later, the BAA absorbed several other NBL clubs. Consisting of only three teams — Calumet Buccaneers in Hammond, Indiana, and the All-Stars in Oshkosh, Wisconsin, and Rens in Dayton, Ohio — the NBL folded its operations.[1]

In its 1948–1949 or final season, the BAA's Eastern Division (ED) included the Baltimore Bullets, Boston Celtics, New York Knicks, Philadelphia Warriors, Providence Steam Rollers, and Washington Capitols. Alternatively, the Western Division (WD) teams were the Chicago Stags, Fort Wayne Pistons, Indianapolis Jets, Minneapolis Lakers, Rochester Royals, and St. Louis Bombers. In the league's postseason, the Lakers defeated the Capitols in six games to win the championship.

Based, in part, on the NBL's failure and other factors, the BAA changed its name to National Basketball Association (NBA) and opened to play the league's 1949–1950, or simply 1949, season with five teams in the Central Division (CD) and six each in the ED and WD. Besides the Bullets, Capitols, Celtics, Knicks, and Warriors, the Syracuse Nationals also played in the ED.

In 1950, six NBA teams were unable to continue operating for various economic and sports-specific reasons. Thus, they dropped out of the league.

As a result, the NBA restructured itself by eliminating the CD and admitting six clubs in the ED and five in the WD. With respect to the ED, these were the Bullets, Capitols Celtics, Nationals, Knicks, and Warriors, while the WD was composed of the Lakers, Pistons, Royals, and also the Indianapolis Olympians and Tri-Cities Blackhawks.

From their 1950–1951 to 1969–1970 season, the ED and WD each changed in size when some teams joined the league due to expansion while others relocated from a site in one metropolitan area to another. Respectively, new clubs and their (initial year) were the Chicago Packers (1961); Chicago Bulls (1966); San Diego Rockets and Seattle Supersonics (1967); and the Milwaukee Bucks and Phoenix Suns (1968). Subsequently, the league's expansion teams included the Buffalo Braves, Cleveland Cavaliers, and Portland Trail Blazers (1970); New Orleans Jazz (1974); Dallas Mavericks (1980); Charlotte Hornets and Miami Heat (1988); Orlando Magic and Minnesota Timberwolves (1989); Toronto Raptors and Vancouver Grizzlies (1995); and Charlotte Bobcats (2004).[2]

Because of a small number of spectators at their home games, financial difficulties, and such problems as substandard arenas and the transfer of ownership to a different individual or group of investors, 21 NBA clubs moved their headquarters to exist at home in another city or municipality. By decade, there were four relocations in the 1950s, five in the 1960s, seven in the 1970s, two in the 1980s, and three from 2001 to 2008. While several of these teams were renamed after relocating, 11 of the group played in the league's 2015–2016 season.

After its 1969–1970 season, the NBA reorganized by renaming the ED and WD respectively to Eastern Conference (EC) and Western Conference (WC). While the EC consisted of four teams each in the Atlantic Division (AD) and CD, the WC's had four in the Midwest Division (MWD) and five in the Pacific Division (PD). Then in 2004, the EC added a Southeast Division (SED) and the WC replaced the MWD with the Northwest Division (NWD) and Southwest Division (SWD). To remain consistent within the league and establish rivalries between teams in each division, there are five clubs each in American geographic regions except for the Raptors in Toronto, Canada.

Based on information and data from the literature, this chapter focuses on and discusses EC teams' markets, historical performances, financial accounts, home arenas, organizational highlights, and/or other conference topics as of 2016. From the research, Tables A3.1–A3.3 in the appendix contain specific demographic, economic, and sports-related results about them and their success as business enterprises and NBA franchises.

TEAMS

Markets

In 1970, the eight EC clubs existed in relatively large, midsized, and small cities. Geographically, they ranged east to west or in other ways from New York to Buffalo in the AD and Baltimore to Cincinnati in the CD. Their metropolitan areas' populations were also different and within the two divisions ranked from most to least in (millions) as follows: in the AD were teams based in New York (11.5), Philadelphia (4.8), Boston (2.7), and Buffalo (1.3) and in the CD, one each in Baltimore (2.1), Cleveland (2.0), Atlanta (1.4), and Cincinnati (1.3). Although there were no EC clubs in areas east and north of Boston, west of Cincinnati, and south of Atlanta, three in the WC had home sites in the Midwest including Chicago (6.9), Detroit (4.2), and Milwaukee (1.4).[3]

During the NBA's 1971–1972 to 2015–2016 season, new EC teams began to play at home in such locations — with Metropolitan Statistical Area (MSA) populations in (millions) — as Charlotte (1.1), Miami (3.1), and Orlando (1.0) besides Toronto (4.2). In addition, existing clubs in the conference relocated to such areas as Washington, D.C. (2.8), Newark (.6), New Orleans (1.3), and Brooklyn (18.8). Most occurred, in part, because of attendance problems at home games, changes in ownership, and their hometown's dilapidated arena, and also because the post-move MSAs contained households with increasing disposable and/or per capita incomes.

Within the EC, several teams either relocated or decided to move from one division to another or into a division of the WC. Them and their (years) in the AD — Buffalo Braves (1970–1978) relocated to San Diego; Washington Bullets/Wizards (1978–2004) transferred to the SED; Charlotte Hornets (1988–1989) shifted to the MWD; and the Miami Heat (1989–2004) and Orlando Magic (1991–2004) each moved to the SED.

Regarding the conference's CD and its changes in structure — Atlanta Hawks (1970–2004) moved to the SED; Baltimore/Capital/Washington

Bullets (1970–1978) transferred to the AD and then SED; Cincinnati Royals (1970–1972) relocated to Kansas City; Houston Rockets (1972–1980) moved to the MWD and then to the WC's SWD; New Orleans Jazz (1974–1979) relocated to Utah; San Antonio Spurs (1976–1980) shifted to the MWD and then to the WC's SWD; Orlando Magic (1989–1990) moved to the MWD and then the SED; Charlotte Hornets (1990–2002) relocated to New Orleans; and the Toronto Raptors (1995–2004) moved to the AD and New Orleans Hornets/Pelicans (2002–2004) to the WC's SWD.

Prior to 1970, fifteen BAA/NBA teams folded their operation because of such things as low attendances at their home games, failure to win games, ownership issues, bad short-term financial problems, and/or restructuring of the league. The group and their (final seasons) included such clubs as the ED's Baltimore Bullets (1954–1955), Providence Steam Rollers (1948–1949), Toronto Huskies (1946–1947), and Washington Capitols (1950–1951).[4]

In eight seasons, the Bullets had a 158-292 record, appeared in three playoffs, and won one championship. The team folded on 27 November, 1954 with a 3-11 record, making it the last NBA franchise to do so as of 2016. Of all defunct NBA franchises, the Bullets were members of the association for the longest time and the only failed one to win a championship.

One of the original eleven BAA franchises, the Steam Rollers, posted an all-time record of 46-122 (0.274) and holds the dubious NBA record for the fewest games won in a season with six. Also, during the 1947–1948 season, the team's coach Nat Hickey activated himself as a player for one game two days before his 46th birthday, setting a still-standing record as the oldest player in NBA history.

A member of the BAA in the 1946–1947 season, the Toronto Huskies won 36% of their games and did not qualify for the postseason. Given the worst possible home dates, the team's hardships started almost immediately when co-owner Ben Newman's father became ill soon after the first game, forcing him to leave the Huskies and take over the family scrap and steel metal business in St. Catharine's, Ontario. Furthermore, lack of cooperation from the local media and lack of talent on the court kept crowds low at games, despite the team using such gimmicks as free stockings to all women in attendance.

From 1946 to 1951, the Capitols won approximately 57% of their games and also two divisional championships in four playoffs. The team is noteworthy for two long win streaks during their short history. In 1946, they won 17 consecutive games — a single season streak that remained the NBA's longest until 1969. Also, the club's 15-0 start of the 1948–1949 season was the best in NBA history until the Golden State Warriors broke it in 2015–2016 by starting 24-0, although the Houston Rockets previously tied the Capitols' record in 1993–1994.

To provide and examine some current and relevant data and interesting facts about existing EC teams in order to examine the sizes and other elements of their markets, there is information about them in Table A3.1. Within the table, variables researched were each team's Metropolitan Statistical Area Population (MSAPOP), number of Designated Market Area Television Homes (DMATVH), and average attendances (AVGATT) at home games in the NBA's 2015–2016 season. These criteria are measured, listed, and ranked in order to reveal the fan bases and markets of such competitors and rivals as the AD's Boston Celtics and New York Knicks, CD's Chicago Bulls and Cleveland Cavaliers, and SED's Orlando Magic and Miami Heat.

Based on data listed in Column 2 of Table A3.1 as of the league's 2015 season, the typical EC team had a MSAPOP of 5.27 million. More specifically, AD teams' areas were ranked first in population at 7.42 million, followed by those in the SED at 4.52 million, and then the CD at 3.89 million. While the Nets, Knicks, and Bulls had the largest group of people within their markets, the three smallest were in areas of the Cavaliers, Pacers, and Bucks. These differences, in turn, affected each club's potential and actual ticket sales, revenue, and market value especially those identical or similar in size such as the ED's Nets and Knicks and also 76ers and Raptors, CD's Pacers and Bucks, and SED's Heat and Wizards in addition to the Hornets and Magic.

Besides averages for the league and by division, the variation or dispersion in MSAPOPs was determined using the standard deviation. While it averaged 2.92 million across the 15 teams in 2015, the AD's ranked highest at 3.49 million, CD's second at 3.33 million, and WD's third at 1.94 million. In other words, the least equal in market population were areas of the Nets, Knicks, and their divisional rivals, but most alike are those of WD teams particularly the Hornets and Magic and also the Heat and Wizards. Because of such widespread variation in MSAPOPs, teams' locations influenced in various ways their attendances at home games and other sport-specific and financial variables of these franchises as reflected in other tables of this chapter.

In Table A3.1, Column 3 is the number of television homes in each team's designated market area (DMATV) in years' 2016–2017. While it averaged 2.24 million across the conference, the AD teams' on average equaled 3.12 million television homes and those in the SED 1.85 million and CD 1.75 million. Similar to the distribution of the MSAPOPs, the largest number of homes with televisions was in the New York and then Chicago areas while the fewest existed in Charlotte, Indianapolis, and Milwaukee. This variable, in turn, affects each club's home attendances and its gate receipts, operating income, and revenue.

As explained before for the MSAPOP, the standard deviation of television homes in teams' areas denotes differences across the conference and also between and within divisions. While the variation was 0.94 or 940,000 television homes among the entire group in the EC, CD clubs had the largest at 1.02 or marginally above one million, SED's at 0.56 or 560,000, and the AD's at 0.54 or 540,000. Within divisions, for example, the difference between the number of television homes in Chicago and Milwaukee was much greater than New York and Boston, and also Washington and Charlotte. Thus, the Atlanta Hawks and its divisional rivals are the most equal in this characteristic of their market, but less so for teams in the SED and AD. This data, however, does not mean more or fewer fans actually watch their games on television at home.

Column 4 of Table A3.1 lists the average attendance of each EC team while playing games on its home court in the 2015 season. For this statistic, the Bulls ranked first at the United Center in Chicago, Cavaliers second at Quicken Loans Arena in Cleveland, and Raptors third at the Air Canada Center in Toronto. In contrast to them, teams' with the smallest attendances at their home were the Bucks at the Bradley Center in Milwaukee, Nets at the Barclays Center in Brooklyn, and 76ers at the Wells Fargo Center in Philadelphia.

While the conference's attendance was 17,870 per game, CD teams averaged 18,170, SED's 17,850, and AD's 17,580. Ranked first and second within their division, respectively, games of the Bulls and Cavaliers were more popular, for example, than those of the Raptors and Knicks, and also the Heat and Wizards. However, the AD's Nets and 76ers had the lowest-ranked combined attendances and not the CD's Bucks and Pistons or SED's Hawks and Hornets. Undoubtedly such things as these teams' win–loss records, ticket prices, advertising promotions and marketing campaigns, and number of superstar players affected weekday and weekend attendances at their home games.

Regarding the deviation in teams' average attendances in the league's 2015 season, it was 2,110 per game for the conference, but from most to least by division it was as follows: 2,850 in the CD, 2,430 in the AD, and 1,110 in the SED. This suggests that CD clubs had the largest variation in number of fans at their games, in part, because of sellouts at the Bulls' United Center and Cavaliers' Quicken Loans Arena and not at the other three teams' venues. For various reasons including their competitiveness and ability to entertain fans, the smallest difference in attendances occurred in the SED at the Hawks' Philips Arena, Hornets' Time Warner Arena (renamed Spectrum Arena), Heat's American Airlines Arena, Magic's TD Waterhouse Center, and Wizards' Verizon Center.

Given the data and its distribution in Table A3.1, the Nets, Knicks, Raptors, Bulls, and Wizards each played their home games in relatively large markets; the Celtics, 76ers, Cavaliers, Pistons, Hawks, Heat, and Magic in mid-sized markets; and the Pacers, Bucks, and Hornets in small markets. Thus, approximately 33% of NBA teams existed in MSAs with plenty of fans and television homes during 2015, while 47% had home sites in less populated areas and another 20% performed within inferior markets. According to data in the table — except for the Nets and Knicks in New York–Newark–New Jersey — the teams' markets within and across divisions are each different demographically and roughly represent their economies and the sport's fan base.

For more about variables in Table A3.1 and their power to represent future basketball markets, the most populated places without an NBA team are such MSAs as Riverside–San Bernardino–Ontario (4.4 million), Seattle–Tacoma–Bellevue (3.7 million), San Diego–Carlsbad (3.2 million), Tampa–St. Petersburg–Clearwater (2.9 million), St. Louis (2.8 million), and Baltimore–Columbia–Towson (2.7 million). With respect to DMAs in the top 25, a few without a club — besides Seattle–Tacoma and St. Louis — are Orlando–Daytona Beach–Melbourne (1.5 million), Sacramento–Stockton–Modesto (1.3 million), and Pittsburgh and Raleigh-Durham (1.1 million).[5]

If the league expands at a site in an area not hosting a current NBA team, a few of these places are viable markets. In addition, they are potential sites for any existing NBA clubs with inferior arenas and who compete for local fans with other teams in Major League Baseball (MLB) and any in the National Football League (NFL) and/or National Hockey League (NHL). Among the group, there has been speculation in the media about locating a new or existing club in Las Vegas, Nevada, and also in smaller US metropolitan areas that contain the cities of Columbus, Ohio; Kansas City, Missouri; Nashville, Tennessee; and Cincinnati, Ohio.

Despite being homes of former ABA teams that folded during the late 1960s/early 1970s or were not admitted into the NBA in 1976, the former group includes such cities as Baltimore, Maryland, and New Orleans, Louisiana, while in the latter are Lexington, Kentucky, and St. Louis, Missouri. In short, a number of places are adequate sites to host an NBA expansion team or one that struggles to get local fans to attend its home games and earn enough money to operate efficiently within a division of the EC.

Performances

According to rules established in the league's most recent collective bargaining agreement (CBA) with the player's union, an NBA team may have a maximum of 15 players on its active roster and at least eight of them must suit up for every game. Any remaining players are placed in the inactive list and cannot play in games.[6]

Teams may have a maximum of two players on the inactive list. This can drop to zero for up to two weeks at a time, and also, temporary inactive positions may be added with league approval in hardship cases. The inactive list can change up to one hour before the opening tipoff by informing the official scorer of the game. A player can be inactive for as little as one game.

Players sent to the NBA Development League will continue to count on a team's inactive list. While individual teams must carry a minimum of 13 — 12 active plus one inactive — players, the NBA guarantees a league-wide average of at least 14 players per team. The league is surcharged if they do not meet the average.

Prior to the 2005 CBA, injured players could be placed on an injured list but were forced to sit out a minimum of five games. The NBA's latest CBA includes an "amnesty clause" or one-time opportunity for teams to remove their worst contracts from the books. Players can be traded between teams in exchange for other players, draft picks, and/or a limited amount of cash. Coaches may only be traded for draft picks or cash. Trades are not allowed to be contingent on the completion of other trades.

During the ED/EC's 71-year history, the number of teams ranged from four in the 1947–1948 season to 15 in 2015–2016. Because of differences in the talent of their coaches and players, some of them established all-time records as of 2016. For example, the Celtics have the highest winning percentage (0.588) and won the most titles plus championships (56) while the Bulls' Michael Jordan, 76ers'/Bucks' Wilt Chamberlain, and Heat'/Cavaliers' LeBron James are among the top 10 all-time leaders in points scored, and the Celtics' Bill Russell, Robert Parrish, and Larry Bird in number of rebounds. A few coaches with outstanding careers, in part, with ED/EC teams were the Celtics' Red Auerbach, Bucks'/Bulls' Larry Costello, and 76ers' Billy Cunningham.

For 15 EC teams as of the NBA's 2015–2016 season, their all-time performances appear in Table A3.2. Besides their total performances, which were calculated but are not given in the table, the columns report the distribution of seasons and overall how well they have competed and succeeded since becoming members of the league. At their current sites, the following is a summary of their performances in order to compare them from first to 15th based on various results. The teams' years range from the Boston Celtics and New York Knicks in the BAA's 1946–1947 season to the Brooklyn Nets in 2012–2013.

Winning percentage

For this number of teams, the conference's win–loss in column 3 averaged 48.7% or 0.487. By division, the AD ranked first at 0.496, CD second at 0.495, and SED third at 0.469. Within each group, respectively, the highest and lowest winning percentages were the Celtics and Raptors, Bulls and Cavaliers, and Heat and Bobcats/Hornets. Despite being the 2016 NBA champion, Cavaliers had ranked 11th in the league and worse than such inferior teams as the Nets, Pistons, and Magic.

In 2007–2008, the Celtics won more than 80% of their regular-season games and at least 70% consecutively in NBA seasons' 1958–1964, 1979–1981, and 1983–1984. Alternatively, the club finished under 20% in 1996–1997 and less than 30% in 2006–2007 and below 40% in 1949–1950, 1978–1979 to 1979–1980, 1993–1994, and 1998–1999. During the latter periods, the Celtics were not competitive because of coaching problems, a below-average roster of players, and simply too much competition from such divisional rivals as the Knicks and 76ers.

Based on its long-run average winning percentage in the conference, the Celtics were able to consistently recruit, hire, and retain such outstanding head coaches as Red Auerbach and former great player Tom Heinsohn, and also Bill Fitch, K.C. Jones, Jim Rogers, Chris Ford, Jim O'Brien, and Doc Rivers. Auerbach, Heinsohn, and Rick Pitino are in the Naismith Basketball Hall of Fame. After coaching Butler University in two National Collegiate Athletic Association (NCAA) Division I Tournament final fours, Brad Stevens joined the Celtics in 2013 and his teams finished second twice in the AD but lost in the conference's first round of the playoffs.

In the EC, the standard deviation or variation in win–loss was 4.5% or 0.045. For each group of teams, the AD's equaled 0.056, SED's 0.053, and CD's 0.022. Because of such things as competition and rivalries among teams and differences in coaches and talents of their players, the largest deviation occurred in the AD and smallest in the CD. In other words, there was a wider gap in average win–loss percentages between the Celtics and others in its division as compared to those particularly in the CD, including the Cavaliers, Pistons, and Pacers.

Playoffs

Within each conference, the eight teams with the most wins qualify for the playoffs with seeding based on their record. Each conference's bracket is fixed with no reseeding. All rounds are best-of-seven series, and the team with four wins advances to the next round. All rounds, including the NBA Finals, are in a home-away format of 2–2–1–1–1. Home court advantage in any round does not necessarily belong to the higher-seeded team, but instead to the one with the better regular season record. If two teams with the same record meet in a round, standard tiebreaker rules are applied to the games. The rule for determining home court advantage in the NBA Finals is their winning percentage and then head-to-head record followed by record versus opposite conference.[7]

During September 2015, the NBA announced changes to how playoff teams get seeded. Previously, the division champions were guaranteed no worse than the fourth seed, while the team with the second-best record in the conference was guaranteed no worse than the second seed even if it not a division champion. However, beginning with the 2016 playoffs, the eight playoff qualifiers in each conference were seeded solely based on their regular-season record. If two teams finished with identical records, the team that won the regular-season series earned the higher seed. If the regular-season series is tied, and one of the teams is a division champion, it received the higher seed.

From a historical perspective, the number of playoffs for each EC team appears in Column 4 of Table A3.2. In total, there were 365 of them. By division, AD teams were in 139 or 38% of the playoffs, CD clubs in 138 or approximately 38%, and SED teams in 88 or 24%. Within each group, respectively, the most and least playoffs occurred for the Celtics and Nets, Bulls and Cavaliers, and Hawks and Bobcats/Hornets.

While Boston was in back-to-back playoffs during NBA seasons' 1950–1968, 1971–1976, 1979–1992, 2001–2004, 2007–2012, and 2014–2015, the Nets qualified in 2012–2014; Bulls in 1966–1967, 1969–1974, 1984–1997, 2004–2006, and 2008–2014; Cavaliers in 1975–1977, 1987–1989, 1991–1995, 2005–2008, and 2014–2015; and Hawks in 1968–1972, 1977–1979, 1981–1983, 1986–1988, 1992–1998, and 2007–2015. Interestingly, the Bobcats/Hornets lost in the first round of conference playoffs during the league's 2010, 2013, and 2015 seasons.

While the ED's Knicks, CD's Pistons, and SED's Wizards ranked second in number of playoffs as of 2016, such competitors as the 76ers (tied for fourth), Bucks (7th), and Heat (11th) also had some success by playing well enough to qualify for postseasons. Similarly, each club won a majority of its games in several regular seasons because of smart coaches and the talents and skills of players including superstars and reserves.

Their total seasons and average winning percentages aside, how much did the three groups of clubs differ with respect to the distribution of playoffs in the conference from 1947 to 2016? Based on the standard deviation, the CD's equaled six playoffs, SED's ten, and AD's 21. Thus, more equality or less variation existed in allocating playoffs among such teams as the Pistons and Bucks than the 76ers and Raptors or Hawks and Magic. In fact, for 365 EC playoffs, the Celtics were in 14% of them and Knicks 11%, while the

Nets and Bobcats/Hornets each appeared in less than 1%. In short, the Celtics, Knicks, Bulls, 76ers, Pistons, and Hawks have been productive enough in regular seasons to be in the most playoffs within the conference.

Division titles

Column 5 of Table A3.2 lists 117 division titles for the fifteen EC teams as of 2016. Among the three groups, AD clubs won 50 or approximately 43% of them and those in the CD 42 or 36% and the SED 25 or 21%. The most and least successful, respectively, have been the Celtics, Bucks, and Heat, but at the bottom of the conference, the Nets and Bobcats/Hornets and then Wizards.

Following the Celtics, the Bucks won their division five times in the 1970s, seven times in the 1980s, and in 2001. Led by head coaches Larry Costello, Don Nelson, and George Karl, such players as Kareem Abdul-Jabbar, Marques Johnson, Sidney Moncrief, and Ray Allen had great performances in scoring points and leading their teams to victories in regular seasons. While Coach Nelson and center Abdul-Jabbar are in the sport's Hall of Fame, such players as Oscar Robertson, Junior Bridgeman, and Bob Dandridge had their uniform numbers retired by the club.[8]

With three division titles in the 1990s and also nine from 2000 to 2016, the Heat has been very competitive within the SED. Besides 1997 Coach of the Year Pat Riley, its other effective head coaches were Stan Van Gundy and Eric Spoelstra. Such former Miami players as Alonzo Mourning, Tim Hardaway, Dwyane Wade, and LeBron James became superstars by scoring points, getting rebounds, and/or being organized on defense with their teammates. While Mourning earned Defensive Player of the Year awards in 1999–2000, James won two NBA Most Valuable Player (MVP) trophies.[9]

Other than the Celtics, Bucks, and Heat, other teams with above-average division titles include the Bulls, Pistons, Knicks, and 76ers. In contrast to these clubs, the AD's Nets and Raptors, CD's Cavaliers and Pacers, and SED's Hawks, Bobcats/Hornets, Magic, and Wizards each have below-average results. With their current roster including superstar James, the Cavaliers have considerably improved and will likely win more games and compete in additional postseasons.

Between the three groups of teams, those in the AD have the highest deviation or dispersion in division titles followed by those in SED and then CD.

Because of the dominant Celtics and also number of mediocre clubs in the latter two divisions, they are not equal performance-wise in winning titles during their seasons in the conference. Thus, less parity exists within the AD as with total years in the league, winning percentages, and playoffs.

In the future, the Nets might be more competitive within their division along with the CD's Cavaliers and SED's Wizards. Each club has experienced but talented players who will lead their team to victories. Currently, the Celtics, Bucks, and Hawks are not a dynasty and therefore vulnerable to challenges from others across the conference. This, in turn, means more balance and competitiveness among the groups and increased attendances at their home games.

Conference titles

After the regular season, eight teams from each of the league's two conferences qualify for the playoffs. At the end of the playoffs, the top two teams play each other in the conference finals to determine the conference champion from each side, which proceed to play each other in the NBA Finals. At the conclusion of the conference finals, winning players are presented with a silver trophy, caps, and tee shirts, and then advance to the NBA Finals.

In Table A3.2, Column 6 lists the conference titles for each club as of 2016. The total number is 45 with AD teams winning 18 or 40% of them, CD 17 or 38%, and SED 10 or 22%. Those with most and fewest of these titles are, respectively, the Celtics with nine, Bulls six, and the 76ers, Pistons, and Heat each with five. Alternatively, the Nets, Raptors, Hawks, and Bobcats/Hornets have never won an EC title, and the 40-year-old Pacers only one.

Because of great teams, the Bulls won their division and conference six times from 1991 to 1998 and also finished second and third each once in the CD. Coached by Phil Jackson, the club featured such great players as shooting guard Michael Jordan and also forwards' Scottie Pippen and Dennis Rodman. During the period, Jackson was Coach of the Year in 1996 and Jordan a four-time NBA MVP. In addition, Pippen and Rodman made several conference all-star teams and won awards for being outstanding on defense.

Besides the Celtics and Bulls, the 76ers, Pistons, and Heat each ranked third in EC titles. The 76ers competed for three championships during the early 1980s as did the Pistons in the late 1980s/early 1990s. The Heat, meanwhile, were conference titlists five times between 2005 and 2015. Among their greatest players in some of these years included, respectively, Philadelphia's Wilt Chamberlain and Charles Barkley, Detroit's Isiah Thomas and Joe Dumars, and Miami's Dwayne Wade and LeBron James.

For various reasons, the 70-year-old Knicks, 40-year-old Pacers, and 43-year-old Wizards have not been successful in winning the EC, respectively, more than four times, once, and three times. Besides frequent and distracting coaching problems, these clubs failed to be consistent from season-to-season and also traded some of their outstanding talent after a few years. As a result, they struggle against rivals in other divisions especially in postseasons. Unless the three develop a winning tradition and more consistency, the outlook is bleak for them to win another conference title within a few years.

Similar to division titles, the deviation in 45 conference titles measures the disparity in wins between each five-team group as of 2016. According to calculations using an Excel program, the variations between divisions are almost the same across the conference. In fact, they were two titles each for the CD and SED, and three for the ED. This indicates small differences among teams within divisions although the gap between the Celtics and Nets/Raptors is nine titles and five each for the Bulls and Pacers and also for the Heat compared to the Hawks and Bobcats/Hornets. In part, this distribution reflects which clubs dominant their rivals within the EC.

NBA championship

This is the league's most popular and successful series and conclusion of the sport's post-season. All finals have been played in a best-of-seven format and contested between winners of the EC and WC — former ED and WD, respectively, before 1970 — except in 1950 when the ED champion faced the winner of games between the WD and CD champions. Prior to 1949, the playoffs were a three-stage tournament where the two semifinal winners played each other in the finals. For its award, the winning team receives the Larry O'Brien Championship Trophy.

The home-and-away format in the NBA Finals is 2-2-1-1-1 and the team with the better regular season record plays on its home court in Games 1, 2, 5, and 7. During 1949, 1953–1955, and 1985–2013, it was a 2-3-2 format in which the team with the better regular season record played on its home court in Games 1, 2, 6, and 7; in a 1-1-1-1-1-1-1 format during 1956 and 1971; and in a 1-2-2-1-1 format during 1975 and 1978.

In Table 3.2, Column 7 gives the number of league championships of each team in the conference as of 2016. Ranked from first to third by group, those in the AD had won 21 or 58% of NBA championships and in the CD 11 or 31% and SED four or 11%. During various seasons, the most and least successful clubs have been, respectively, the Celtics, Bulls, Pistons and Heat, and with zero championship the Nets, Raptors, Pacers, Hawks, Bobcats/ Hornets, and Magic.

Besides better coaches and more talent and leaders, the former four teams were consistent and played together throughout each regular season and post-season despite injuries and other problems. The other six, however, failed to score enough points in games, get a sufficient number of rebounds, and/or defend their opponents' top players. Thus, they lacked the teamwork to be NBA champions in any post-season.

Regarding the 15 teams' performances statistically, the differences in deviations divisionally ranged from seven championships in the AD to one in the SED versus four on average for the conference. While the Celtics dominated the former division, there was more equality among clubs in the SED despite the Heat and also less inequality within the CD even though the Bulls and Pistons combined won nine or 25% of the league's total championships. To compare teams' performances across the NBA, the data for WC teams appears in the next chapter.

Total performances

This result — or the total performance (TP) for each team — includes their division and conference titles plus NBA championships as listed in Columns 5–7 of Table A3.2. Among 198 TPs, AD clubs won 89 or 45% of them followed by the CD's 70 or 35% and SED's 39 or 20%.

While the Celtics ranked first with 56 in TPs, Bulls second with 21, and Heat third with 20, the Nets and Bobcats/Hornets each had zero. Other teams in the conference with at least 10 (in parentheses) are the Knicks (14), 76ers (15), Bucks (16), and Pistons (17). Considering only their average winning percentage and number of playoffs combined, top-ranked are the Celtics followed by the Bulls, Knicks, 76ers, Bucks and Hawks, and then Heat and Pacers. In contrast to them, the Bobcats/

Hornets, Raptors, Hawks, and Pacers, Magic, and Wizards had the fewest TPs in the EC as of 2016.

After sports experts researched and published the history of all teams, some of these articles reported the most dominant and/or successful NBA teams of all-time. To get results, different criteria were used including the Elovation App (Elo) rating, which focuses on wins and losses and considers the margin of victory, whether road games, and strength of the team's opponent. Based partly on this metric and basketball information from various sources, among the best since the 1970–1971 season — in chronological order — are the following clubs from the EC.[10]

• K.C. Jones coached the 1985–1986 Boston Celtics team to a 67-15 regular-season finish, a 15-3 record in the playoffs, and an eventual championship over the Houston Rockets. Led by Larry Bird — who averaged 25.8 points and 9.8 rebounds per game — and Kevin McHale — 21.3 points and 8.1 rebounds per game — this group had the third-best offensive rating in the league at 111.8 and the best defensive rating at 102.6. The peak Elo rating for this team was 1816. However, the club finished with a rating of 1801 and, throughout the season, ended up with an average mark of 1735. And yet, by managing a composite Elo rating of 1784, these Celtics are — according to some experts — about the fourth-best NBA team of all time following the 1995–1996 and 1996–1997 Chicago Bulls' clubs and the 2014–2015 or 2015–2016 Golden State Warriors.

• The 1991–1992 Bulls defeated the Portland Trail Blazers in six games in the 1992 NBA Finals. This win marked the second NBA championship in the organization's history. The group had a peak Elo rating of 1782 and an average mark of 1759, and they ended the season with a rating of 1762. This team averaged 109.9 points per game, which was fifth in the league, and led the NBA with an offensive rating of 115.5. It was also talented on the defensive end of the floor, finishing the season with a defensive rating of 104.5 (fourth in the league) and only allowing opponents to score 99.5 points per contest (third in the league). With an eventual composite Elo of 1768, the 1991–1992 Bulls played their way to a top five position on the list of the best teams in ED/EC history.

• Most people agree that the 1995–1996 Chicago Bulls have been the best team in NBA history. This group achieved a then-record 72 regular-season wins and, of course, tied its season up with a pretty bow by defeating the Seattle SuperSonics in the finals in six games. The Bulls averaged 105.2 points per game, which was first in the league; allowed 92.9 points per contest or third in the league; had the league's top offensive rating at 115.2; and was also the most defensively-efficient bunch in the NBA with a 101.8 rating. According to its Elo results, this group dominated in that metric as well.[11]

• At 69-13 (0.841 winning percentage) in its regular-season, the 1996–1997 Bulls were an impressive squad, especially on the offensive end of the floor. This group led the NBA in points per game (103.1) and offensive efficiency (114.4). With a postseason mark of 15-4, it is no surprise that Chicago ended up with a composite Elo rating of 1802. At its best, this club reached a peak mark of 1811. However, throughout the season, the Bulls had an average rating of 1792 and ended the year with a tally of 1802. Still, this group was a force to be reckoned with, and the Utah Jazz had no answer for them — losing in the NBA Finals in six games.

• After finishing the regular season with a 62-20 record and going 15-6 in the post-season, the 1997–1998 Bulls took home the NBA title, while also completing the second three-peat in franchise history. This group, led by Michael Jordan — who averaged 28.7 points in the regular season — was third in the NBA in opponents' points per game (89.6), third in defensive rating (99.8), and ninth in offensive rating (107.7). Although this team scored a composite Elo of 1764, at one point during the year it achieved a peak Elo rating of 1788. In the end, this team will always be remembered for Jordan's game winner against the Utah Jazz in the NBA Finals.

For various reasons such as a lack of talented players, coaching problems and/or both of them, some NBA teams had terrible performances in their regular seasons. Several of these clubs were evaluated based on their ability to score points and win games. In chronological order, the following is a list of a few of the worst EC clubs as of the league's 2016 season.[12]

• Sometimes, there are multiple squads during the same season that are relatively close in their levels of putridity, but that was not so for Cleveland in the league's 1970–1971 season. Of the 17 teams in the NBA, the Cavaliers finished last in offensive rating, scoring 1.4 fewer points per 100 possessions than the second-worst Buffalo Braves. And on defense, Cleveland allowed 102.4 points per 100 possessions, or 2.3 more than the Seattle SuperSonics and everyone else in the league. In fact, 2.3 points was nearly as big as the gap between the Sonics at sixteenth and the Philadelphia 76ers at tenth. Then again, they never strung together three victories and only won back-to-back games twice.

• The 1972–1973 76ers were a run-and-gun team that used 115.2 possessions per 48 minutes. While the Rockets played with the same pace during their 1972–1973 season, every other squad in the 17-team NBA played more slowly. Thing is, that did not work out too well for the Sixers. In fact, it gave their opponents more chances to take advantage of a porous defense, one that had plenty of trouble keeping the other team from drilling one shot after another, and not like they were making the most of their extra offensive possessions. The team was devoid of much scoring talent, as three of its top five scorers — Tom Van Arsdale, Bill Bridges and Kevin Loughery — were unable to even hit 40% from the field. The other two starters, Fred Carter and John Block, shot 42.1% and 44.1%, respectively. As a whole, Philadelphia shot just 42%, which was the worst mark in the league. The Cavaliers were the next worst, but they still made 43.5% of their shots. Everyone else was at 44.4% or higher.

• The 1988–1989 Miami Heat dropped its first game as an NBA franchise to the Clippers, losing by 20 points. And things did not get much better for quite some time. Though the Heat took the Warriors to overtime during their stretch of winless basketball, they lost their first 17 games, which was an ignominious NBA record at the time. The losing skid has since been topped by the 2009–2010 New Jersey Nets, but the Heat will always be in the record books for their seriously lackluster start to NBA life.

• The 1998–1999 Bulls had the third-worst offense in NBA history, better than only the 2002–2003 Nuggets and 1987–1988 Clippers. No team in the league struggled more with its shot during the 1998–1999 season, and the Bulls made things worse on themselves by turning the ball over often, failing to crash the offensive boards, and rarely getting to shoot free throws. Players' Toni Kukoc and Dickey Simpkins came close, but not a single member of the roster managed to earn three win shares during the lockout-shortened campaign.

• As if a 16-game losing streak was not awful enough, the 2011–2012 Bobcats managed to drop each of its last 23 contests, giving them the worst winning percentage of any team in NBA history. Frankly, it is hard to imagine them getting off the schedule even if the regular season had been extended, as only eight of their 23 losses came by single digits. "It has been tough, but we are just trying to move forward," Augustin told the press near the end of the season. "Many people are laughing at us and making the losing streak a joke, but we take it very seriously. We are just trying to stay positive and play hard until the end." Even if they played hard, the Bobcats still go down as one of the worst teams in NBA history.

LEAGUE ECONOMICS

As administrative and managerial parent organizations that include a group of franchises, American professional sports leagues do such things as establish, implement and enforce policies, regulations, and rules; schedule games annually for pre-seasons, regular seasons, and post-seasons; negotiate contracts with cable companies, networks, and other types of national and international media; and make decisions and find ways that financially benefit their members' operations. As of the NBA's 2015–2016 season, the EC included fifteen teams whose economic objective was — and always will be — to compete and generate enough revenue from sources in order to maximize their profit.[13]

In this section, there are data and other information about the commercial and financial aspects of franchises in the EC and their significance from an economic perspective. Besides attendances at home and away games, anything else that affected these teams' income, market value, and wealth is included in the analysis, quantified, and discussed. In other words, the league is an organization consisting of for-profit enterprises that operate to compete each season typically within a division of a conference and seek to improve their performances in current and future games.

Franchise Financials

Forbes magazine's sports editors' published financial data of NBA franchises as of their 2015–2016 season. As denoted in Columns 2–7 of Table A3.3, these amounts include, respectively, their estimated market value — which is based on the current stadium deal without deduction for debt — and also total revenue, gate receipts, operating income — earnings before interest, taxes, depreciation, and amortization (EBITDA) — debt-to-value (D/V) percentages, and players' expenses. For each of three divisions, the information reveals the financial status and wealth of EC teams individually and relative to each other as a group. The following section identifies and highlights the data.[14]

In Table A3.3, Column 2 is the estimated market value of each NBA team, by division, as of 2015. Ranked from most to least, AD clubs averaged $1.5 billion, CD's $1.1 billion, and SED's $947 million. While the Knicks were first at $3 billion, Bulls second at $2.3 billion, and Celtics third at $2.1 billion, least in value included the Bucks at $675 million, 76ers at $700 million, and Hornets at $750 million. In comparison to the typical club's average of $1.2 billon, only four or approximately 26% of the group exceeded that amount.

Several factors caused differences in NBA teams' market values. In no specific order, these were their history, tradition, and success in the league, whether located in big, midsized, or small markets, size of each's fan base, number of titles and championships, and such financial data as their revenue, operating income, and gate receipts. Based on these and other reasons, they ranged in value by more than $2.3 billion in 2015.

To compare their standard deviation or variation in market values, the highest was AD teams ($955 million) and lowest among those in the SED ($212 million) and then CD ($658 million). This means parity or smaller deviation in these NBA franchise's values existed in 2015 to a greater extent between the Hawks and other SED teams than among clubs in the other divisions. Although these were only estimates, the amounts influence such things as the clubs' relative wealth, economic power in the league, and future price when offered for sale to potential investors. Interestingly, only the Bucks' market value fell below the conference's average deviation of $686 million.

Each team's revenue — net of stadium revenues used for debt payments — is displayed in Column 3 Table A3.3. While the Knicks had the highest at $307 million followed by the Bulls' $228 million and Nets' $220 million, the three lowest-ranked in revenue were the Pacers' $138 million at 13th, Bucks' $126 million at 14th, and 76ers' $124 million at 15th. The differences in amounts occurred for several reasons including their home attendances, range in ticket prices, winning percentage in games, and number of basketball fans in the area.

Because of various demographic and sport-specific factors, there were disparities in teams' revenue. While the league's standard deviation equaled $48 million, AD teams had the highest variation in revenue at $69 million and then the CD's at $41 million and SED's at $16 million. The latter division's revenues had the smallest difference in amounts because similar data existed for the Hawks, Hornets, Magic, and Wizards, but not the Heat. Besides win–loss records in the regular season, the deviations reflect the population of their markets, popularity at home, and per capita income and the type of jobs and also wealth of local households.

Column 4 of Table A3.3 contains the operating income or EBITDA of EC teams in 2015. For the group, it averaged $26 million. From most to least by division, AD clubs averaged $39 million, CD's $27 million, and SED's $13 million. Because of excessive payments for players' salaries and other types of fixed and variable expenses, the Nets had a negative EBITDA while the Knicks, Bulls, and Celtics earned the most income by operating efficiently. For various reasons, the Hawks, Hornets, and Wizards were also marginally profitable but significantly less so, for example, than the large-market Raptors in the AD, and midsized Cavaliers in the CD, and Magic in the SED.

Each EC teams' 2015 gate receipts — in millions of dollars — appear in Column 5 of Table A3.3. While the conference's average was $46 million, the Knicks had the most ($128 million) and then the Bulls ($72 million), and then Heat ($67 million). In contrast to these amounts, the Pistons ($22 million), 76ers ($21 million), and Pacers ($20 million) had the smallest gate receipts in the NBA's 2015 season.

The dispersion or disparity in gate receipts was greatest among AD clubs ($39 million) compared to CD teams ($23 million) and those in the SED ($17 million). Because of the gap in amounts between, for example, the Knicks and 76ers, the division's standard deviation exceeds that of the CD's Bulls and Pacers, and SED's Heat and Hornets. Simply put, New York and Boston are large and more prosperous basketball markets than the majority of others.

In Table A3.3, Column 6 includes the D/V percentages of each EC franchise in 2015. On average, the conference's was 15% or in amount, approximately $183 million per team based on their estimated market values. Among each group, the AD's averaged 11%, CD's 17%, and SED's also 17%. Although the Knicks had zero debt and four others less than 15%, the D/V ratios exceeded 20% each for the 76ers, Pistons, Bucks, and Hawks.

As described for other variables in the table, the standard deviations of D/V were unequal among divisions and franchises within divisions. CD teams, for example, had the greatest variation at 9% and then those in the SED at 8% and AD at 7%. In order to reduce their ratios for financial reasons and operate more effectively, several teams needed to reform in order to generate higher market values and/or record less amount of debt in accounts on their balance sheet.

As reported in *Forbes* for being an important, necessary, and periodic payment from an operations perspective, in Table 3.3. Column 7 gives the players' expenses — including benefits and bonuses — of these teams in 2015. For the conference, they totaled approximately $1.1 billion or about $79 million per team. On average, the AD's was $80 million and the CD's and SED's each $78 million. While the Nets, Heat, and Wizards ranked highest, the 76ers, Hawks, and Magic each paid less than $70 million in players' expenses. Given these amounts, the first group of clubs had an above-average roster of players and, other than the Nets and Wizards, won enough games in the regular season to qualify for the playoffs while the latter three failed to participate, in part, because of their relatively small investment in players' salaries.

Players' expenses were different and also significantly deviated between the EC's three divisions. From most to least in variation among the groups — as measured by their standard deviations — these included the AD's $15 million, and then SED's $11 million and CD's $8 million. Such amounts denote that the greatest disparity in payments occurred because of the Nets' $99 million versus the 76ers' $60 million in the AD, whereas the range in players' expenses within the SED and CD equaled, respectively, only $23 million between the Heat/Wizards and Hawks and also $16 million between the Bulls/Cavaliers and Pistons/Bucks. Thus, EC teams with the greatest revenues and/or largest market values tended to compensate their players more than rivals within their division.

Arenas

As of the NBA's 2015–2016 season, the 15 EC teams played their home games in venues that differed in age, cost and market value, and also in such other ways as location, capacity, and ownership. Based on various criteria including their amenities, concessions, and sightlines, they have been ranked from best to worst overall, most to least accessible, and top to bottom as facilities to host and entertain spectators at games. Given those criteria, this section provides some data and other information regarding the facilities of EC clubs and discusses specific characteristics about them.[15]

Among teams' home courts within each division as of the NBA's 2015 season, they ranged in age as follows: within the conference's AD, from the Nets' 5-year-old Barclays Center in Brooklyn to the Celtics' 22-year-old TD Garden in Boston; within the CD, from the Pacers' 18-year-old Bankers Life Fieldhouse in Indianapolis to the Bucks' 29-year-old Harris Bradley Center in Milwaukee and Pistons' 29-year-old Palace of Auburn Hills in Detroit; and within the SED, from the Magic's 7-year-old Amway Center in Orlando to the Wizards' 20-year-old Verizon Center in Washington. Of teams' 15 venues in the EC, eight or 53% of them are privately owned and seven or 47% publicly. Interestingly, none are jointly owned by the team and a municipality and/or state government.

Their construction costs ranked from being relatively cheap to very expensive as of 2015. From the least to most costly in the AD and then CD and WD, respectively, it took approximately $160 million to erect TD Garden in Boston for the Celtics compared to $1 billion to completely renovate Madison Square Garden in New York for the Knicks; from $70 million to build the Palace of Auburn Hills in Detroit for the Pistons to $183 million for Bankers Life Fieldhouse in Indianapolis for the Pacers; and from $213 million each for American Airlines Arena in Miami for the Heat and Philips Arena in Atlanta for the Hawks to $380 million for the Amway Center in Orlando for the Magic.

Regarding the most likely replacements or renovation of current venues in the EC, the Bucks' BMO Harris Bradley Center is — according to some fans — falling apart and has smelly seats and zero charm. The team's new owners have less than two years to secure funding for a new stadium or the NBA expects to buy the team back via force sale and move it to Seattle, Washington. According to a contract when the team was sold, it specifies the requirements regarding financing a new venue in Milwaukee.[16]

Recently *Forbes* sports editors assigned economic values to venues of teams in the EC. From lowest to highest within divisions, respectively, amounts in the AD were $80 million for the Wells Fargo Center in Philadelphia to $907 million for Madison Square Garden in New York; in the CD, from $76 million for the BMO Harris Bradley Center in Milwaukee to $629 million for the

United Center in Chicago; and in the SED, from $132 million for the Spectrum Center — former Time Warner Cable Arena — in Charlotte to $308 million for the American Airlines Arena in Miami. Based on their estimated values, AD teams' venues averaged $430 million, CD' $250 million, and SED' $195 million. Because of increasing real estate prices in urban areas and popularity of the sport in America, these facilities will likely appreciate in value, especially for those within midsized to large metropolitan areas.

In various studies, NBA arenas have been ranked by basketball experts and sports journalists in the media with respect to their location and different attributes and problems. Although results vary according to each study's parameters, a few venues rank among the best while some others placed in the worst group. For example, the most attractive, entertaining, and well-structured facilities within the EC based on their name, aesthetics, and experience for fans are the Knicks' Madison Square Garden and Bulls' United Center.[17]

In a recent article published online, the two best buildings were rated as follows:

> "The oldest [and recently renovated] arena in the NBA remains iconic in every aspect, especially with a name that imparts a certain regal magnificence. Madison Square Garden is a classic stadium, filled with enough rich history and entertainment that it's a better reason to go than the Knicks themselves. With the court's theater lighting, the design on the court gets full exposure, which is why it's perfect that the Knicks chose to emphasize the blue and not overdo the designs. Like the Staples Center [in Los Angeles], there is an element of high drama with that theater lighting. The wide range of food choices, the professional and efficient staff and the non-stop entertainment (even in between the quarters) reflects the city in which it is located."

For why the United Center ranked second in the EC, the editor provided these comments:

> "The name 'United Center' has a galvanizing effect, creating a groundswell of unified support from the fans. The court is great, with the killer Bulls logo at the center and FOUR logos complement the best use of black and red in the NBA. The six championship banners are all prominent, and the shared color scheme with the [Chicago] Blackhawks allows the symbolism for both teams to never clash. The court design is intimidating, and it

makes up for the fact that the rest of the arena is an eyesore with limited views of the action on the floor."

Within the same study, two of the lowest-ranked EC facilities — besides the Bucks' BMO Harris Bradley Center — were the 76ers' Wells Fargo Center and Cavaliers' Quicken Loans Arena. Among others in the conference, the former ranked 15th (27th in the NBA) and the latter 14th (24th in the league).

The study's author evaluated each of them, respectively, as follows:

"The Wells Fargo Center is truly a reflection of the city it inhabits: unwelcoming and self-conscious about its inferiority. As far as sponsorships go, this is a little above average and the name has some music to it. Compared to the Bradley Center, Wells Fargo is intimate rather than cramped, and that allows the energy of the game to be translated more easily. Red, white & blue is overdone, but for this team it is appropriate, and the court design emphasizes the blue and brings out tasteful, balanced shades. Going to a Sixers game is the least angry Philly sports experience, which still means you are probably going to get things thrown at you anyway."

For the Cavaliers' home venue, he remarked:

"It [Quicken Loans Arena] reminds fans of daytime television commercials and midday depression. The court design is among the worst in the NBA, as the Cavs choose to emphasize the wine red and navy blue over the mustard-y gold, a sin similar to the Pelicans over-reliance on their navy blue. On TV, the stadium looks atrocious. In person, it's much better, with good viewing and solid sound. The actual ticket-buying experience is a hassle, where you are essentially forced to buy Cavs tickets off of 'Flash Seats,' a site that gives off the classy vibe of a low-grade flea market. One major positive is the location, which is directly in downtown Cleveland rather than somewhere randomly off of the Cuyahoga River."

Fan Cost Index

For several years, a Chicago-based company named Team Marketing Report (TMR) has prepared and published a Fan Cost Index (FCI) for the home games of teams in professional sports. To attend a game for a typical family with two kids, an FCI includes the cost of four average-priced tickets, two cheapest-priced draft beers, four each lowest-priced soft drinks and hot dogs, parking for one vehicle, and two each game programs and least-expensive, adult-sized adjustable caps. Costs are determined by telephone calls with team representatives, venues, and concessionaires and from questions asked during interviews.[18]

In the 2015–2016 NBA season, the average FCI for a family to attend a regular season game of an EC team was $344. While Knicks games each cost $676, the Hornets had the conference's lowest FCI at $212. Among divisions, the average for AD teams equaled $419, CD's $309, and SED's $303. The order from ranking them first to third occurred, in part, because FCIs of the Celtics, Nets, and Knicks each exceeded $400 while those of such teams as the Cavaliers, Pistons, Pacers, Hawks, Hornets, and Magic were each below $300.

For specific items in TMR's 2015–2016 FCI, the approximate range in amounts from most to least expensive or first to 15th across the EC were listed as follows: average ticket, Knicks $129 to Hornets $30; cheapest tickets, Knicks $54 to Pistons $7.98; beer, Knicks $10.50 to Cavaliers $4; soft drink, Bulls $5.75 to Cavaliers $3; hot dog, Heat $7 to Cavaliers $3; parking, Celtics $45 to Hornets $5; and for a cap, Nets $28 to Pacers $17.76. Based on economics principles, these prices were set by teams and/or vendors to sell enough units to maximize revenue from their sales at home games in the arenas.

From the NBA's 2011 to 2015 season, there were some significant increases but also relatively small and even decreases in FCIs of teams in the EC. For examples of these changes, the Wizards' FCI rose from $212 to $322 or approximately 52% but the Raptors' from only $319 to $323 or about 1%, while the Pistons' declined from $257 to $215 or 16%. Because of inflation, number of — and amount spent by — families at games in arenas, local economic conditions and other factors, the majority of teams and/or vendors raised their prices each year rather than kept them constant or lowered amounts.

In evaluating FCIs of teams between the EC's 2014–2015 and 2015–2016 seasons, the Wizards' increased the most, in other words, from $258 to $322 or approximately 24%. Alternatively, fans' costs fell for home games of the Celtics, 76ers, Pistons, and Heat, but remained the same for those of the Nets, Knicks, Bulls, Bucks, Hornets, and Magic. Thus, there were different payments for tickets and other things by families to attend EC teams' home games at their arenas, especially from 2011 to 2016.

ORGANIZATION HIGHLIGHTS

Besides regular-season and post-season games, the NL and its franchises are involved in — and affected by — community events and also business-related and government affairs, news, and projects. Because these things and other topics influence the league in different but perhaps important and historic ways, following are a few of them from the academic and popular literature.[19]

First, ED/EC teams won 37% or 56% of all-star games during NBA seasons' 1951–1998 and 2000–2015 (the 1999 all-star game was canceled due to a league lockout). Such outstanding and popular players as the Celtics' Bob Cousy, Royals' Oscar Robertson, Pistons' Isiah Thomas, Bulls' Michael Jordan, 76ers' Allen Iverson, and Cavaliers' LeBron James were each MVPs in at least two of these games.

Second, since the NBA divided teams into two conferences with divisions as of its 1970–1971 season, the EC has won 21 championships and the WC 26. Of those in the EC, the Celtics and Bulls each won six championships, Pistons three, Knicks two, and one each for the Bucks, Cavaliers, 76ers, and Bullets (renamed Washington Wizards). The most successful WC clubs have been the Lakers with 11 championships, Spurs five, Heat three, Rockets and Warriors each with two, and one each for the Mavericks, Trail Blazers, and Supersonics (renamed Oklahoma City Thunder).

Third, the top and bottom three EC clubs in home attendances per game (in thousands) during the NBA's 2015–2016 season were, respectively, the Bulls (21.8), Cavaliers (20.5), and Raptors (19.8), while the lowest included the 76ers (14.8), Nets (15.1), and Bucks (15.2). At away games, the Cavaliers ranked first in followed by the Bulls and Knicks with the Raptors, Magic, and Celtics finishing at the end of the conference. Across all teams in the league, the Bulls and Cavaliers placed first and second, respectively, in attendances at their home games. Alternatively, the WC's Mavericks, Warriors, and Trail Blazers had the most fans at games in their arenas, while fewest attended those of the Nuggets, Timberwolves, and 76ers.

Fourth, as of early 2016, a study ranked the worst principal owners of EC franchises. These were the Knicks' James Dolan, who ran the team into the ground after getting his job the old-fashioned way, from his father; 76ers' Josh Harris, who bought the club for a song ($260 million), then hired general manager Sam Hinkie to destroy it, dumping players Jrue Holiday, Thaddeus Young, and Andre Igoudala to finish low in the standings but draft high; Nets' Mikhail Prokhorov, the Russian billionaire who despite lavish spending, set a new standard for absentee ownership; Bucks' Wes Eden and Marc Lasry, classic modern owners and New York hedge fund biggies confident they could operate a team after a lifetime of ardent fanhood; Cavaliers' Dan Gilbert, who puffed up his diminutive self to torch LeBron James' so-called cowardly desertion in 2010, then was bailed out after years of failure when LeBron forgave all in his desire to come home in 2014; and the Hornets' Michael Jordan, who hired Steve Clifford turning the Hornets into a respectable team, but Jordan's tribute to the Lakers' Kobe Bryant was typical, sending in a video from wherever he vacationed.

Fifth, two of the best owners of EC teams are the Heat's Micky Arison and Celtics' Wyc Grousbeck. Regarding Arison, he knows how to put a winning team together, and that extends far beyond just assembling winning pieces to put on the court on a given night. The man has learned how to let Pat Riley do his thing, which has been a major reason why the Heat became dominant over the years. Indeed, Arison has been a part of a winning culture. Meanwhile, Grousbeck pieced together a front office headed by Danny Ainge and also negotiated deals that sped up the rebuilding process after throwing together others that brought a title to Boston. Although you may credit Ainge with moves the Celtics make, Grousbeck deserves credit for putting the right pieces in place so the team did not become a train wreck like their cross-country rivals.

Sixth, the richest owner of an EC franchise is the Nets' Mikhail Prokhorov at approximately $9 billion. A self-made billionaire, he owns the private investment holding company Onexim Group. Created in 2007, some of its assets are metal companies, financial services, media outlets, real estate development, utilities, and high technology. Prokhorov also aspires to become a Russian political leader through his party named Civic Platform. Despite owning the Nets since 2010, he has no interest in relocating to the US. The next wealthiest of a conference team is the Heat's Micky Arison. At

$7 billion, he is the chairman of Carnival Corporation, which is the world's largest cruise operator. His father Ted Arison co-founded Carnival Corporation with business partner Meshulam Riklis in 1972. Micky was one of the leaders in acquiring P&O Princess Cruises, a deal worth approximately $8.2 billion. As a result, the two companies merged forming Carnival Corporation.

Seventh, the five biggest media markets without an NBA team in 2016 are Tampa/St. Petersburg/Sarasota, Seattle, St. Louis, Pittsburgh, and Raleigh/Durham/Chapel Hill. About each of them in order: one, while low attendance for MLB's Tampa Bay Rays likely keeps the NBA away from the Gulf Coast, basketball games would have higher attendances because teams play in the winter and not summer; two, an investment team offered to forgo public financing to build a new sports arena in Seattle's SoDo neighborhood and also would cover the current funding gap to build an overpass over Lander Street; three, the Spirits of St. Louis played in this city for nearly a decade in the American Basketball Association (1968–1976) and if you have seen the ESPN 30 For 30 episode "Free Spirits", you would understand what an amazing team this really was, and how it supplied a ton of talent to the NBA, not just on the court; four, considering there are only 12 metropolitan areas with teams in all four major sports, the Steel City in northwest Pennsylvania would actually be the smallest of them if it became number thirteen. Once with four teams, it was one of the first to lose their fourth team as American factory work began to dry up; five, Raleigh/Durham/ Chapel Hill is a transient area in eastern North Carolina with a ton of money-people based in the medical industry and the home to three premier college basketball teams all within about a 30-mile radius.

Eighth, an ESPN forecast panel rated each NBA team's front-office management on its guidance and leadership in terms of how it affects overall on-court success, both in the short and long term. In the EC, the top three in 2015 were the Heat, Celtics, and Hawks, while the Hornets, Nets, and Knicks finished at the bottom of the group. With respect to coaches, the panel ranked the Hawks' Mike Budenholzer first, Bulls' Tom Thibodeau second, and the Heat's Erik Spoelsta third. At the bottom of the group were the Wizards' Randy Wittman, Magic's James Borrego (interim), and the Knicks' Derek Fisher.

Ninth, the NBA became the first professional sports league to pass one billion social media likes and followers across all league, team, and player accounts as of mid-2016. The league broke its all-time attendance record with nearly 22 million fans streaming into stadiums throughout the 2015–2016 regular season; television viewership increased by 19%; the number of NBA League Pass subscriptions was 10% higher than in 2014–2015; and the league's website saw visits rise by 27%. These deals have reportedly greatly increased in value due to the league's revolutionary social media strategy, which caused its reach and popularity to boom.

Tenth, the National Basketball Players Association (NBPA) announced in the summer of 2016 that its player representatives voted unanimously to fund health insurance for all retired NBA players with at least three years of service in the league. The first of its kind among North American professional sports, it exemplifies the NBPA's focus on the health and welfare of its current, retired, and future members. "The game has never before been more popular, and all the players in our league today recognize that we're only in this position because of the hard work and dedication of the men who came before us," said Chris Paul, NBPA President and nine-time All-Star. "It's important that we take care of our entire extended NBA family, and I'm proud of my fellow players for taking this unprecedented step to ensure the health and well-being of our predecessors."

NOTES

1. For the history of the NBA and its teams, see Jozsa FP Jr. (2015). *National Basketball Association Strategies: Business Expansions, Relocations, and Mergers*. New York, NY: Springer; Kirchberg C, (2007). *Hoop Love: A History of the National Basketball Association*. Jefferson, NC: McFarland; Surdam DG, (2012). *The Rise of the National Basketball Association*. Urbana, IL: University of Illinois Press; and the *Official National Basketball Association Guide 2015–16*. New York, NY: NBA Properties (2015).

2. Besides the *National Basketball Association Strategies: Business Expansions, Relocations, and Mergers*, the league's new franchises were also discussed in Jozsa FP Jr. and Guthrie JJ, (1999). *Relocating Teams and Expanding Leagues in Professional Sports: How the Major Leagues Respond to Market Conditions*. Westport, CT: Quorum Books.

3. See "Top U.S. Metropolitan Areas by Population, 1790–2010," http://www.peakbagger.com [cited 5 December 2016] and "Rankings of U.S. Standard Metropolitan Statistical Areas," *World Almanac & Book of Facts* (1972), 154–155.

4. "NBA and ABA Team Index," http://www.basketball-reference.com [cited 1 December 2016].

5. Along with historical population data from the U.S. census, another source is "The 382 Metropolitan Statistical Areas of the United States of America," http://www.en.wikipedia.org [cited 12 October 2016].

6. References include "CBA 101," http://www.nba.com [cited 8 December 2016] and "NBA Collective Bargaining Agreement," http://www.npba.com [cited 8 December 2016].

7. Charlie Zegers, "About the NBA Playoffs," http://www.basketball.about.com [cited 13 December 2016].

8. For outstanding former and/or current coaches, executives, owners and players, there is "The Naismith Memorial Basketball Hall of Fame," http://www.hoophall.com [cited 1 December 2016].

9. "NBA History — MVP," http://www.espn.com [cited 2 December 2016] and "NBA Most Valuable Player Recipients," http://www.basketball.realgm.com [cited 2 December 2016].

10. There are several articles on this topic including Alsher J, "The Ten Best NBA Teams of All-Time," http://www.cheatsheet.com [cited 2 December 2016].

11. Nate Silver and Reuben Fischer-Baum, "How We Calculate NBA Elo Ratings," http://www.fivethirtyeight.com [cited 5 December 2016].

12. The articles for this topic are Fromal A, "Each NBA Franchise's Worst Team Ever," http://www.bleacerreport.com [cited 10 December 2016] and also "10 Worst Records in NBA History," http://www.cheatsheet.com [cited 12 December 2016].

13. The author assumed profit maximization in Jozsa FP Jr. (1977). "An Economic Analysis of Franchise Relocation and League Expansions in Professional Team Sports, 1950–1976," Ph.D. diss., Georgia State University.

14. Badenhausen K, Ozanian M, and Settimi C, "The Business of Basketball," http://www.forbes.com [cited 27 June 2016].

15. See "Present National Basketball Association Arenas," http://www.basketball.ballparks.com [cited 11 December 2016] and "NBA Arenas," http://www.hoopsonline.com [cited 11 December 2016].

16. Reference Hill J, "NBA: 5 Arenas That Need to be Torn Down Right Now," http://www.fansided.com [cited 12 December 2016].

17. Dahlgren L, "Power Rankings: NBA Arenas," http://www.fansided.com [cited 11 December 2016].

18. For this data online, see the "Fan Cost Index," http://www.teammarketingreport.com [cited 16 November 2016] and more specifically, "Team Marketing Report — NBA 2015–16," http://www.teammarketing.com [cited 12 December 2016].

19. "NBA All-Star Game Results," http://www.nba.com [cited 12 December 2016]; "NBA Championships: Winners by Conference," http://www.landofbasketball. com [cited 12 December 2016]; "NBA Attendance Report — 2016," http:// www.espn.com [cited 5 December 2016]; Heisler M, "Heisler: From Bad to Worse to Vivek: Top Ten Worst Owners in NBA," http://www.dailynews.com [cited 12 December 2016]; Hill J, "NBA Owners Power Ranking: Who is the Best Owner in Basketball?" http://www.fansided.com [cited 12 December 2016]; Khan A, "Top Ten Richest NBA Owners," http://www.thesportster.com [cited 12 December 2016]; Gonos D, "Top Ten Media Markets Without an NBA Team," http://www.sportsgrid.com [cited 12 December 2016]; "NBA Front-Office Rankings: 2015," http://www.espn.com [cited 13 December 2016]; Anzilotti E, "How the NBA's Progressivism is Helping it Thrive," http:// www.theatlantic.com [cited 13 December 2016]; "Players Union to Fund Health Insurance for NBA Retirees," http://www.nba.com [cited 13 December 2016].

Chapter 4

WESTERN CONFERENCE

HISTORY

Before they merged in 1949 and became known as the National Basketball Association (NBA) — or simply Association — the Basketball Association of America (BAA) and National Basketball League (NBL) each consisted of an Eastern Division (ED) and Western Division (WD). Prior to their 1948–1949 seasons, the NBL's Fort Wayne Pistons, Indianapolis Jets, Minneapolis Lakers, and Rochester Royals transferred to the BAA's WD to join the Chicago Stags and St. Louis Bombers. This, in turn, left the Denver Nuggets, Oshkosh All-Stars, Sheboygan Redskins, Tri-Cities Blackhawks, and Waterloo Hawks in the NBL's WD.[1]

Following the BAA–NBL merger, the NBA formed three divisions. Besides five teams in the Central Division (CD) and six in the ED, the Association's WD included the Anderson Packers, Denver Nuggets, Indianapolis Olympians, Sheboygan Red Skins, Tri-Cities Blackhawks, and Waterloo Hawks. After defeating the WD Packers in the semifinals, the CD Lakers beat the ED Syracuse Nationals in the finals and won an NBA championship.

Between the NBA's 1950–1951 and 1969–1970 seasons, some teams moved their operations from one metropolitan area to another while others became new members of the league. These actions changed several things within the organization such as decisions involving business, economic and financial activities, marketing the sport to fans and on the radio stations and television networks, creating rivalries among clubs within divisions, scheduling games in regular seasons and post-seasons, and enforcing policies, regulations, and rules.

With respect to the chronological relocation of NBA teams from and/or to the WD before 1970, these were the Tri-Cities Blackhawks→Milwaukee in 1951; Milwaukee Hawks→St. Louis in 1955; Fort Wayne Pistons→Detroit and Rochester Royals→Cincinnati both in 1957; Minneapolis Lakers→Los Angeles in 1960; Philadelphia Warriors→San Francisco in 1962; Chicago Zephyrs→Baltimore in 1963; and St. Louis Hawks→Atlanta in 1968. For movements within the ED, the only one was Syracuse Nationals→Philadelphia in 1963. Thus, the former eight changes occurred, in part, for teams to relocate from mostly small and small-to-midsized areas to play within larger markets containing arenas with more amenities and revenue potential.

Expansion was also an important way for the Association to grow demographically and financially before 1970. Sequentially, the new teams in the WD were the Chicago Packers in 1961; Chicago Bulls in 1966; San Diego Rockets and Seattle Supersonics both in 1967; and Phoenix Suns in 1968. In the ED, the Milwaukee Bucks joined the league in 1968. Regarding relocations in the WD, the Chicago, San Diego, Seattle, and Phoenix metropolitan areas had enough people, households with jobs and incomes, and also sports fans to support a basketball team at least for a few years or perhaps decades.

Because of a declining local economy, lack of attendance at their home games, poor performances in regular seasons and other troubles, some WD teams had to terminate operations and withdraw from the BAA. Prior to 1950, these were the Cleveland Rebels, Detroit Falcons and Pittsburgh Ironmen each in 1947, and Indianapolis Jets in 1949. The following are some facts about each of them.[2]

While playing at the Cleveland Arena, the Rebels defeated the Toronto Huskies in their first game. The club, however, had its ups and downs as Roy Clifford took over for Dutch Dehnert as head coach for its final 23 games. After finishing with a 30-30 record and qualifying for the first BAA playoffs, the Rebels lost to the New York Knicks in a best-of-three series. Unable to make a profit and attract enough fans to its home games, the Rebels folded after one season. It took another 23 years before the NBA returned to Cleveland with the expansion Cavaliers in 1970.

Five of six National Hockey League (NHL) arenas were the home of 11 charter members of the BAA. The basketball Falcons, for example, shared Olympia Stadium with the NHL Detroit Red Wings, who also were previously named Falcons. Coached by legendary Glenn Curtis, the Falcons did not have much success starting 12-22 before Philip Sachs replaced Curtis. The Falcons did not fare much better under Sachs, winning just eight more games as they posted a 20-40 record and finished fourth in the league's WD. After its season, the Falcons and three other BAA teams disbanded because of financial problems and other reasons. A decade later, Detroit got another shot at professional basketball when the NBA Pistons moved from Fort Wayne to the Motor City.

Playing at the old Duquesne Gardens, the Ironmen were a charter franchise in the BAA in 1946–1947 and coached by Paul "Polly" Birch, a native of western Pennsylvania. After a 56-51 loss to the St. Louis Bombers in their first game, the Ironmen made their home debut two nights later against the Washington Capitols and lost 71-56. Wins were scarce for the Ironmen, who were the new league's weakest team in 1946–1947 posting a 15-45 record and finishing in last place in the WD. As a result, they did not play another season and folded their operations. Pittsburgh ventured into professional basketball again two decades later with a team nicknamed Pipers in the American Basketball Association (ABA).

In 1948, the Indianapolis Kautskys were among four teams that left the NBL and joined the BAA. Since the BAA did not allow corporate names for its teams, the Kautskys became the Indianapolis Jets. The Jets won their BAA debut beating the St. Louis Bombers 84-80 at Butler Fieldhouse. However, the Jets lost their next eight games as Coach Bruce Hale was fired after a 4-13 start. The team did not fare much better under the reigns of Burl Firddle as they finished last in the WD with an 18-42 record. After only one season in the league, the Jets shut down their operations before the BAA–NBL merger. The Indianapolis Olympians — who expected to replace the Kautskys in the NBL — would instead join the NBA in 1949 to replace the Jets but nevertheless, they disbanded four years later.[3]

After the merger in 1949, defunct WD teams included the Anderson Packers, Denver Nuggets, Indianapolis Olympians, and Sheboygan Red Skins. In addition to them, such BAA/NBA clubs in the CD or ED failed including the Toronto Huskies in 1947, Providence Steam Rollers in 1949,

Chicago Stags and St. Louis Bombers both in 1950, and Baltimore Bullets in 1955. Located in larger markets with better arenas and enough resources to survive and prosper, more teams in the league's ED were able to continue after the early-to-mid 1950s like the Boston Celtics, New York Knicks, Philadelphia Warriors, and Syracuse Nationals.

For interesting highlights about each defunct club in the WD, the Packers swept the Oshkosh All-Stars in three straight games to claim the NBL championship in 1949. Upon joining the NBA, the club rotated through three coaches and played competitive basketball most of the season, to finish second in the division with a 37-27 record. In the playoffs, they won a three-game series against the Tri-Cities Blackhawks and Indianapolis Olympians. But in the semifinals, the Packers were overmatched by the Lakers who won both games on the way to a championship. Despite their success, the Packers withdrew from the NBA in 1950. They played another year in the National Professional Basketball League (NPBL) along with other NBL teams unhappy with the merger. The NPBL, meanwhile, lasted only one season and never hosted a championship.

Despite their struggles in the NBL, the Denver Nuggets joined the NBA in 1949. The westernmost team in the league, the Nuggets lost their first 15 games and suffered an 11-game losing streak. After the club finished with an 11-51 record in the WD, it folded following the season leaving Colorado without any major league sports teams until the birth of the American Football League's Denver Broncos in 1960.

During their 1949–1951 NBA seasons, the Olympians won one division title and also qualified for three consecutive playoffs. Still reeling from the loss of players' Alex Groza and Ralph Beard because they admitted to point shaving while at the University of Kentucky and thus banned for life by NBA Commissioner Maurice Podolof, the Olympians lost their first five games in the 1952–1953 season. Despite being a bad team, they slipped into the playoffs by finishing fourth in the WD with a 28-43 record. However, once again they were overmatched by the eventual champion Lakers. That would also be the Olympians final game after which they folded following the season.

After 11 seasons and winning a championship in the NBL, the Red Skins joined the NBA despite playing in the smallest arena and market and also being the oldest but most experienced team. They were inconsistent, however, and lost nine straight games. Although the Red Skins played well at home, the team had injuries and struggled in away games to finish the NBA's 1949–1950 season in fourth place at 22-40. In the playoffs, the team battled hard but lost a three-game series to the Olympians. A month after the play-offs ended, Sheboygan withdrew from the NBA. Then they played in the NPBL, which folded before completing its first season.

After its 1969–1970 season, the NBA reorganized by renaming the ED and WD respectively Eastern Conference (EC) and Western Conference (WC). While the EC consisted of four teams each in the Atlantic Division (AD) and CD, the WC's had four in the Midwest Division (MWD) and five in the Pacific Division (PD). In 2004, the EC added a Southeast Division (SED) and the WC replaced the MWD with the Northwest Division (NWD) and Southwest Division (SWD). To remain consistent across the league and create rivalries between teams in each division, there are five clubs each in US regions except for the Raptors in Toronto, Canada.

Based on information and data from the literature, this chapter focuses on and discusses fifteen WC teams' markets, historical performances, finan-cial accounts, home arenas, organizational highlights, and/or conference topics as of 2016. As a result of the research, Tables A4.1–A4.3 contain spe-cific demographic, economic, and sports-related results about them and their experiences and success as business enterprises and NBA franchises.

TEAMS

Markets

In 1970, the NBA's eight WC clubs originally existed in relatively large, midsized, and small markets. Geographically, they ranged north to southwest or in other words from Milwaukee to Phoenix in the MWD and Portland to San Diego in the PD. Their metropolitan areas' populations were also differ-ent and within the two divisions ranked from most to least in (millions) as follows: in the MWD were teams based in Chicago (6.9), Detroit (4.1), Milwaukee (1.4), and Phoenix (1.0), and in the PD, one each in Los Angeles (7.0), San Francisco (3.1), Seattle (1.4), San Diego (1.3), and Portland (1.1). Although there were no EC clubs in areas east and north of Boston, west of Cincinnati, and south of Atlanta, three in the WC had home sites in the Midwest.[4]

During the NBA's 1971–1972 to 2015–2016 seasons, new WC teams began to play at home in such locations — with Metropolitan Statistical Area (MSA) populations in (millions) — as Dallas (2.9), Minneapolis (2.4), and Vancouver (1.8). In addition, existing clubs in the conference relocated to such areas as Los Angeles (7.4), Oakland (3.1), San Diego (1.8), Sacramento (1.4), New Orleans (1.3), Kansas City (1.2), Oklahoma City (1.2), Memphis (1.1), and Salt Lake City (1.0). Most occurred, in part, because of changes in ownership and/or construction of new arenas at the post-move sites, and also because these MSAs contained more people including households with increasing discretionary, disposable, and/or per capita incomes.

Within the WC, several teams either relocated or simply moved from one division to another or into a division of the other conference. For example, them and their (years) in the MWD — Detroit Pistons (1970–1977) shifted to the EC's CD; Milwaukee Bucks (1970–1979) to the EC's CD; Chicago Bulls (1970–1979) to the EC's CD; Indiana Pacers (1977–1978) to the EC's CD; and Phoenix Suns (1970–1971) to the WC's PD.

To provide and examine some current and interesting data and also relevant facts about existing WC teams in order to examine the sizes and other elements of their markets, there is information about them in Table A4.1. Within the table, variables researched were each team's Metropolitan Statistical Area Population (MSAPOP), number of Designated Market Area Television Homes (DMATVH), and average attendances (AVGATT) at home games in the NBA's 2016 season. These criteria are quantified, listed, and ranked in order to reveal the attributes and characteristics of such competitors and rivals as the NWD's Denver Nuggets and Utah Jazz, PD's Golden State Warriors and Los Angeles Clippers, and SWD's Houston Rockets and San Antonio Spurs.

Based on data listed in Column 2 of Table A4.1, as of the league's 2015 season, the typical WC team had a MSAPOP of 3.65 million. More specifically, PD teams' areas were ranked first on average in population at 4.96 million followed by those in the SWD at 3.74 million and then the NWD at 2.24 million. While the Mavericks, Clippers, and Lakers had the largest group of people within their markets, the three smallest were in areas of the Grizzlies, Pelicans, and Jazz. These differences, in turn, affect and influence each club's potential and actual ticket sales, revenue from games and other sources, and market value especially those identical or similar in size within divisions such as the NWD's Nuggets and Trail Blazers, PD's Warriors and Suns, and SWD's Mavericks and Rockets.

Besides averages for the league and by division, the variation or dispersion in MSAPOPs was determined mathematically using the standard deviation. While it averaged 2.22 million across the 15 teams in 2015, the SWD's ranked highest at 2.89 million, SWD's second at 1.82 million, and PD's third at 0.99 million. In other words, the least equal in market population were areas of the Grizzlies, Pelicans, and their divisional rivals, but most alike are those of NWD teams particularly the Nuggets and Trail Blazers and also the Thunder and Jazz. Because of such widespread variation in MSAPOPs by division, teams' home-site populations impacted in various ways their attendances at home games, media coverage, travel costs, and other variables of these franchises. In fact, some of these effects appear in other tables of the chapter.

In Table A4.1, Column 3 is the number of television homes in each team's designated market area (DMATV) in years' 2016–2017. While it averaged 1.64 million for the conference, the PD teams' on average equaled 2.24 million television homes and those in the SWD 1.47 million and NWD 1.22 million. Similar to the distribution of MSAPOPs, the largest number of homes with televisions was in the Los Angeles and then Dallas and San Francisco–Oakland–Hayward areas, while the fewest existed in Oklahoma City, New Orleans, and Memphis.

As explained before for the MSAPOP, the standard deviation of television homes in teams' areas denotes differences across the conference and also between and within divisions. While the variation was 0.81 or 810,000 television homes among the entire group in the WC, SWD clubs had the largest at 1.02 or marginally above one million, PD's at 0.59 or 590,000, and NWD's at 0.44 or 440,000. Within divisions, for example, the difference between the number of television homes in Dallas and Memphis was much greater than Los Angeles and Sacramento, and Minneapolis and Oklahoma City. Thus, the Trail Blazers and their divisional rivals are the most equal in this characteristic of their market but less so for teams in the PD and SWD. This, however, does not mean more or fewer fans actually watch their NBA games on television at home or in other places.

In Table A4.1, Column 4 lists the average attendance of each WC team while playing games on its home court in the 2015 season. For this statistic, the Mavericks ranked first at the American Airlines Center in Dallas, Warriors second at the Oracle Arena in Oakland, and the Trail Blazers third at the Rose Garden in Portland. In contrast to them, teams' with the smallest attendances at their home-site were the Grizzlies at the FedEx Forum in Memphis, Timberwolves at the Target Center in Minneapolis, and Nuggets at the Pepsi Center in Denver.

While the conference's attendance was 17,810 per game, PD teams averaged 18,420, SWD's roughly 18,000, and NWD's approximately 17,000. Ranked first and second within their division, respectively, games of the Trail Blazers and Jazz were more popular, for example, than those of the Nuggets, Timberwolves, and Thunder. In addition, the NWD's Nuggets and Timberwolves had the lowest-ranked combined attendances and not the PD's Suns and Kings or SWD's Grizzlies and Pelicans. In fact, such things as these teams' win–loss records, ticket prices, advertising campaigns and marketing promotions, and number of superstar players affected in some way weekday and weekend attendances at their home games.

Regarding the deviation in teams' average attendances in the league's 2015 season, it was 1,830 per game for the conference but from most to least by division as follows: 2,680 in the NWD, 1,610 in the PD, and 1,410 in the SWD. This suggests that NWD clubs had greater variation in number of fans at their games, in part, because of sellouts at the Trail Blazers' Rose Garden and Jazz's Delta Center and not at the other three teams' venues. For various reasons including their competitiveness and ability to entertain fans, the smallest difference in attendances occurred at the Suns' Talking Stick Resort Arena, Kings' Sleep Train Arena (now Golden 1 Center) and Rockets' Toyota Center, and also the Grizzlies' FedEx Forum and Pelicans' New Orleans Arena.

Given the data and its distribution in Table A4.1, the Clippers, Lakers, Warriors, Rockets, and Mavericks each played their home games in relatively large markets; the Nuggets, Timberwolves, Thunder, Trail Blazers, Jazz, Suns, Kings, and Spurs in midsized markets; and the Grizzlies and Pelicans in small markets. Thus, approximately 33% of NBA teams existed in MSAs with plenty of fans and television homes during 2015 while 53% had home sites in less populated areas and another 14% performed within inferior markets. According to data in the table — except for the Clippers and Lakers in Los Angeles–Long Beach–Anaheim — the teams' markets within and across divisions are each different demographically and roughly represent their economies and the sport's fan base.

For more about variables in Table A4.1 and their potential to be future basketball markets, the most populated places without an NBA team are such MSAs as Riverside–San Bernardino–Ontario (4.4 million), Seattle–Tacoma–Bellevue (3.7 million), San Diego–Carlsbad (3.2 million), Tampa–St. Petersburg–Clearwater (2.9 million), St. Louis (2.8 million), and Baltimore–Columbia–Towson (2.7 million). With respect to DMAs in the top 25, a few without a club — besides Seattle–Tacoma and St. Louis — are Orlando–Daytona Beach–Melbourne (1.5 million), Sacramento–Stockton–Modesto (1.3 million), and Pittsburgh/Raleigh–Durham (1.1 million).

If the league expands at a site in an area not hosting a current team, a few of these places are viable markets. In addition, they are potential sites for any existing NBA clubs with inferior arenas and who compete for local fans with other teams in Major League Baseball (MLB) and any in the National Football League (NFL) and/or NHL. Among the group, there has been speculation in the media about locating a new or existing club in Las Vegas, Nevada and also in smaller US metropolitan areas that contain such cities as Columbus, Ohio; Kansas City, Missouri; Nashville, Tennessee; and Cincinnati, Ohio.

Despite being homes of former ABA teams that folded during the late 1960s/early 1970s or were not admitted into the NBA in 1976, the former group includes such cities as Baltimore, Maryland, and New Orleans, Louisiana, while in the latter are Lexington, Kentucky, and St. Louis, Missouri. In short, a number of places could be adequate sites to host an NBA expansion team or one that struggles to get local fans to attend its home games and earn enough money to operate efficiently within a division of the WC.

Performances

According to rules established in the league's most recent collective bargaining agreement (CBA) with the player's union, an NBA team may have a maximum of 15 players on its active roster and at least eight of them must suit up for every game. Any remaining players are placed in the inactive list and cannot participate in games.[5]

Teams may have a maximum of two players on the inactive list. This can drop to zero for up to two weeks at a time, and also, temporary inactive positions may be added with league approval in hardship cases. The inactive list can change up to one hour before the opening tipoff by informing the official scorer of the game. A player can be inactive for as little as one game.

Players sent to the NBA Development League will continue to count on a team's inactive list. While individual clubs must carry a minimum of 13 — 12 active plus one inactive — players, the NBA guarantees a league-wide average of at least fourteen players per team. The league is surcharged if they do not meet the average.

Prior to the 2005 CBA, injured players could be placed on an injured list but were forced to sit out a minimum of five games. The NBA's latest CBA includes an "amnesty clause" or one-time opportunity for teams to remove their worst contracts from the books. Players can be traded between teams in exchange for other players, draft picks, and/or a limited amount of cash. Coaches may only be traded for draft picks or cash. Trades are not allowed to be contingent on the completion of other trades.

During the WD/WC's 70-year history, the number of teams extended from four in the 1947–1948 season to 15 in 2015–2016. Because of differences in the talent of their coaches and players, some of them established all-time records as of 2016. For example, the Spurs had the highest winning percentage (0.621) and Lakers the most titles plus championships (57) while the Lakers' Kareem Abdul-Jabbar and Kobe Bryant, Jazz's Karl Malone, and Rockets' Elvin Hayes is among the top 10 all-time leaders in points scored; Spurs' Tim Duncan, Timberwolves' Kevin Garnett, and Lakers' Wilt Chamberlain in number of rebounds; and the Jazz's John Stockton, Suns/Lakers' Steve Nash, and Lakers' Magic Johnson in assists. A few coaches with outstanding careers, in part, with WD/WC teams were the Lakers' Phil Jackson, Bucks'/Golden State's Don Nelson, and Jazz's Jerry Sloan, and currently, the Spurs' Gregg Popovich.[6]

For 15 WC teams as of the NBA's 2015–2016 season, their all-time performances appear in Table A4.2. Besides their total performances, which were calculated but are not given in the table, the columns report the distribution of seasons and overall how well they competed and succeeded since becoming members of the league. At their current sites, the following is a summary of their performances in order to compare them from first to 15th based on various results. The teams' history ranges from the 56-year-old Lakers and 48-year-old Suns to the 8-year-old Thunder and 14-year-old Pelicans.

Winning percentage

For this number of teams, the conference's win–loss in column three averaged 50.9% or 0.509. By division, the SWD ranked first at 0.523, NWD second at 0.516, and SED third at 0.489. Within each group, respectively, the highest and lowest winning percentages were the Spurs and Hornets/Pelicans, Thunder and Timberwolves, and Lakers and Clippers. Despite being the 2014–2015 NBA champion and runner-up in 2015–2016, the Warriors' winning percentage ranked only 11th in the conference but much higher than that of such inferior teams as the Timberwolves, Kings, and Clippers.

In 2015–2016, the Spurs won more than 80% of their regular-season games and at least 70% consecutively in NBA seasons' 1994–1995, 2000–2002, and 2010–2013 but also individually in 1998–1999, 2004–2005, and 2006–2007. Alternatively, the club finished below 30% in 1988–1989 and 1996–1997, between 30% and 40% in 1986–1987 and 1987–1988, and from 40% to 50% in several other years. During the latter periods, the Spurs were not competitive because of coaching problems, an inferior roster of players, and simply too much competition from such divisional rivals as the Mavericks and Rockets.

Based on their average winning percentage historically within the conference, the Spurs were able to recruit, hire, and retain such outstanding head coaches as Doug Moe, Stan Albeck, Cotton Fitzsimmons, Bob Hill, and Gregg Popovich, and even such former great players as centers Artis Gilmore and David Robinson, forwards Sean Elliot and George Gervin, and guards Johnny Moore, Avery Johnson, and James Silas. Besides Popovich, retired forward Tim Duncan and current guards Tony Parker and Manu Ginobilli led San Antonio to five championships since the late 1990s/early 2000s. Most importantly, former coaches Larry Brown and Jerry Tarkanian are in the Naismith Basketball Hall of Fame along with seven Spurs' players.[7]

Except for eight seasons, the Timberwolves failed to win a majority of their games. They struggled, for example, during consecutive years while coached by Bill Musselman, Jimmy Rodgers, Bill Blair, Dwane Casey, Randy Wittman, Kent Rambis, and Rick Adelman. Led by Coach Frank Saunders, however, Minnesota qualified for the playoffs during seasons' 1996–2003 but lost in the conference's first round seven times and once in the finals. Although not yet inducted into the Basketball Hall of Fame, forward Kevin Garnett has been the club's best player. Until the Timberwolves hire more productive coaches and sign better players who perform as a group above expectations, they will not win an NBA championship.

In the WC, the standard deviation or variation in win–loss was 7.4% or 0.074. For each group of teams in the conference, the NWD's equaled 0.084, PD's 0.088, and SWD's 0.059. Because of such things as competition among teams and differences in coaches and talents of their players, the largest deviation occurred in the PD and smallest in the SWD. In other words, there was a wider gap or variation in average win–loss percentages between the Lakers and others in their division as compared to those particularly in the SWD including the Mavericks and Rockets, Grizzlies, and Hornets/Pelicans, but not the Spurs. Moreover, the PD's Warriors, Clippers, and Kings have each won less than 50% of their games all-time but not the Lakers and Suns.

Playoffs

Within each conference, the eight teams with the most wins qualify for the playoffs with seeding based on their record. Each conference's bracket is fixed with no reseeding. All rounds are best-of-seven series, and the team with four wins advances to the next round. All rounds, including the NBA Finals, are in a home-away format of 2-2-1-1-1. Home court advantage in any round does not necessarily belong to the higher-seeded team, but instead to the one with the better regular season record. If two teams with the same record meet in a round, standard tiebreaker rules are used. The rule for determining home court advantage in the NBA Finals is winning percentage and then head to head record followed by record versus opposite conference.[8]

During September 2015, the NBA announced changes to how playoff teams get seeded. Previously, the division champions were guaranteed no worse than the fourth seed, while the team with the second-best record in the conference was guaranteed no worse than the second seed even if it not a division champion. However, beginning with the 2016 playoffs, the eight playoff qualifiers in each conference were seeded solely based on regular-season record. If two teams finished with identical records, the team that won the regular-season series earned the higher seed. If the regular-season series was tied, and one of the teams is a division champion, it gets the higher seed.

From a historical perspective, the number of playoffs for each WC team appears in Column 4 of Table A4.2. In total, there were 308 of them. By division, NWD teams were in 95 or 31% of the playoffs, PD clubs in 112 or approximately 36%, and SWD teams in 101 or 33%. Within each group, respectively, the most and least playoffs occurred for the Trail Blazers and Thunder, Lakers and Clippers, and Spurs and Hornets/Pelicans.

While Portland was in back-to-back playoffs during years' 1977–1981, 1983–2003, 2009–2011, and 2014–2016, Oklahoma City qualified in 2010–2014; Los Angeles Lakers in 1961–1974, 1977–1993, 1995–2004, and 2006–2013; Clippers in 1992–1993 and 2012–2016; San Antonio in 1977–1983, 1990–1996, and 1998–2016; and New Orleans in 2003–2004 and 2008–2009.

Regarding the newest member of the conference, the Thunder appeared in six playoffs in eight seasons and lost once each in the conference's first round and semifinals and three times in the finals, and once in the NBA finals. Led by coaches' Scott Brooks and Billy Donovan, the club's best players in those years included superstars Kevin Durant and Russell Westbrook. Following Durant's departure to the Warriors after the club's 2015–2016 season, the Thunder's winning percentage and opportunities to be in playoffs will likely decline if Westbrook and his teammates fail to score enough points, get plenty of rebounds, and/or generate many assists.

While the NWD's Jazz, PD's Suns, and SWD's Rockets each ranked second in number of playoffs within their divisions, overall such competitors as the Nuggets (seventh), Warriors (ninth), and Mavericks (eighth) also had some success playing well enough to get into post-seasons. Similarly, each club won a majority of its games in several regular seasons because of smart coaches and the talents and skills of their players including superstars and reserves.

Their total seasons and average winning percentages aside, how much did the three groups of clubs differ with respect to the distribution of playoffs within the conference from 1947 to 2016? Based on their standard deviations, the NWD's equaled eleven playoffs, PD's 16, and SWD's 12. Thus, more equality existed in allocating playoffs among such teams as the Clippers and Kings than the Nuggets and Trail Blazers or Rockets and Spurs. Furthermore, of total conference playoffs, the Lakers were in approximately 16% of them and Spurs 12%, while the Timberwolves, Thunder, Clippers, Grizzlies, and Hornets/Pelicans each appeared in less than 3%. Besides the Laker and Spurs, others like the Trail Blazers, Suns, and Rockets have also been very productive in regular seasons to qualify for the playoffs.

Division titles

Column 5 of Table A4.2 lists 98 division titles for the 15 WC teams as of 2016. Among the three groups, NWD clubs won 26 or approximately 27% of them and those in the PD 42 or 43% and SWD 30 or 30%. The most and least successful, respectively, have been the Lakers and then Spurs and Jazz, and at the bottom by division, the Timberwolves, Clippers/Kings, and Grizzlies.

Ahead of the Spurs in total, the Lakers won their division five times each in the 1960s and 1970s, nine times in the 1980s, once in the 1990s, and eight times in the 2000s. Led by head coaches Fred Schaus, Bill Sharman, Paul Westhead, Pat Riley, Mike Dunleavy, Don Harris, and Phil Jackson, such players as Jerry West, Kareem Abdul-Jabbar, Magic Johnson, Gail Goodrich, James Worthy, and Kobe Bryant had great performances in scoring points and leading their teams to victories in regular seasons. While coaches' Sharman, Riley, and Jackson are in the sport's Hall of Fame, such players as Elgin Baylor, Jamaal Wilkes, and Shaquille O'Neal had their uniform numbers retired by the club.

With two division titles in the 1980s and three each during the 1990s and 2000s, the Jazz has been competitive within the NWD. Besides 1984 Coach of the Year Frank Layden, its other effective head coach was Jerry Sloan. Such former Utah players as Adrian Dantley, Karl Malone, John Stockton, Pete Maravich, Jeff Hornacek, and Darrell Griffith became stars by scoring points, getting rebounds, making assists, and playing with their teammates on defense. While center Mark Eaton earned Defensive Player of the Year awards in 1985 and 1989, Malone won two NBA Most Valuable Player (MVP) trophies.[9]

Other than the Lakers, Spurs, and Jazz, other team's with above-average division titles include the Nuggets and Suns. In contrast to these clubs, the NWD's Timberwolves, Thunder, and Trail Blazers, PD's Warriors, Clippers, and Kings, and SWD's Mavericks, Rockets, Grizzlies, and Hornets/Pelicans each have below-average results. With their current roster, the Warriors and Rockets have greatly improved and will likely win more games and compete in additional post-seasons.

Between the three groups of teams, those in the PD have the highest deviation or dispersion in division titles followed by those in SWD and then NWD. Because of the dominant Lakers and also number of mediocre clubs in the latter two divisions, they are not equal proportionately in winning titles during their seasons in the conference. Thus, less parity exists within the PD for this performance as it did with such variables as winning percentages and playoffs.

In the future, the Nuggets might be more competitive within their division along with the PD's Clippers and SWD's Mavericks. Each club has experienced but talented players who will lead their team to victories. Currently, such division titlists as the Jazz, Lakers, and Spurs are not a dynasty and therefore vulnerable to challenges from others within the conference. This, in turn, means more balance in performances, competitiveness among the groups, and increased attendances at their home games.

Conference titles

After the league's regular season, eight teams from each of the league's two conferences qualify for the playoffs. At the end of the playoffs, the top two teams play each other in the conference finals to determine the conference champion from each side, which then proceed to play each other in the NBA Finals. At the conclusion of the conference finals, winning players are presented with a silver trophy and also caps and tee shirts, and advance to the NBA Finals.

In Table A4.2, Column 6 is the conference titles for each club as of 2016. The total is 41 with PD teams winning 23 or 56% of them and those in the SWD 12 or 29% and NWD six or 15%. Teams with most of these titles are, respectively, the Lakers with eighteen, Spurs six, and Rockets four. Alternatively, the Nuggets, Timberwolves, Clippers, Kings, Grizzlies, and Hornets/Pelicans have not won their conference.

Because of great teams, the Lakers won their conference twice in the 1970s, eight times in the 1980s, once in the 1990s, and seven times from 2000 to 2015. Coached by Phil Jackson and others, the club featured several outstanding players and many good to very good at the center, forward, and guard positions. Besides members of the sport's Hall of Fame, some of them became conference and NBA all-stars and also won awards for being leaders offensively and also on defense.

Besides the Lakers, Spurs, and Rockets, the Trail Blazers and Warriors tied for fourth in WC titles. The Trail Blazers were successful in 1977, 1990, and 1992, and the Warriors in 1975, 2015, and 2016. The Jazz,

Suns, and Mavericks each won two conference titles and the Thunder one. Among the three latter teams' greatest players in some of these years included, respectively, the Jazz's John Stockton and Karl Malone, Suns' Paul Westphal and Charles Barkley, and Mavericks' Jason Terry and Dirk Nowitzki.

For various reasons within each division, the 40-year-old Nuggets, 27-year-old Timberwolves, 32-year-old Clippers, 31-year-old Kings, 15-year-old Grizzlies, and 14-year-old Hornets/Pelicans have not been successful in winning the WC even once. Besides frequent coaching problems, these clubs failed to be consistent from season-to-season and also traded some of their outstanding talent after a few years. As a result, they struggled against rivals in other divisions especially in postseasons. Unless the six develop a winning tradition and more consistency, the outlook is bleak for them to win their first conference title within a few years.

Similar to division titles, the deviation in 41 conference titles measures the disparity between each five-team group as of 2016. According to calculations using an Excel program, the variations between divisions are different across the conference. In fact, these were seven titles in the PD, two in the SED, and one in the NWD. There is a relatively large difference among teams within the PD primarily because of the Lakers and Clippers/Kings results or 18 titles although the gap between the Blazers and Nuggets/Timberwolves is three and the Spurs and both Grizzlies and Hornets/Pelicans six. In short, this distribution reflects which clubs have been most and least competitive against their rivals during and after regular seasons within and among divisions of the WC.

NBA championships

This is the NBA's final series and conclusion of the sport's postseason. All series have been played in a best-of-seven format and contested between winners of the EC and WC — former ED and WD respectively before 1970 — except in 1950 when the ED champion faced the winner between the WD and CD champions. Prior to 1949, the playoffs were a three-stage tournament in which the two semifinal winners played each other in the finals. Since 1977, the Larry O'Brien Championship Trophy has been awarded to the NBA finals winning team.

In Table A4.2, Column 7 is the number of championships won by each team in the conference as of 2016. Ranked from first to third by group, those in the PD have won 13 or 59% of NBA championships and in the SWD eight or 36% and NWD one or 5%. During various postseasons since 1971, the most and least successful clubs in the conference have been respectively the Lakers, Spurs, and then Warriors and Rockets, and with zero championships such teams as the NWD's Nuggets and Timberwolves, PD's Clippers and Kings, and SWD's Grizzlies and Hornets/Pelicans.

Besides having better coaches as leaders and more talent on their rosters, the former four teams were consistent and played together throughout each regular season and in the playoffs despite injuries and other problems. The other six, however, failed to score enough points in games, get many rebounds, and/or defend their opponents' top players. Thus, they lacked teamwork and the ability to be NBA champions in any season.

Regarding the 15 teams' performances, the differences in deviations divisionally ranged from four championships in the PD to less than one in the NWD versus three for the conference. While the Lakers dominated their division, there was more equality among clubs in the SWD despite the Spurs and also less inequality within the NWD in which the Trail Blazers won only one or approximately 4% of the league's total championships. To compare performances across the NBA, see those of EC divisions and their teams in Chapter 3.

Total performances

This result — or the total performance (TP) for each team — includes their division and conference titles plus NBA championships as listed in columns 5–7 of Table A4.2. Among 161 TPs, PD clubs won 78 or 48% of them followed by the SWD's 50 or 31% and NWD's 33 or 21%.

While the Lakers ranked first with 57 in TPs, Spurs were second with 32 and Rockets third with 11, the Grizzlies had zero, and the Timberwolves and Hornets/Pelicans each had one. Other teams with at least nine include the Trail Blazers, Jazz, and Warriors. Considering only their average winning percentage and number of playoffs combined as of measure of their performances, those with the most impressive statistics have been the Spurs followed closely by the Lakers and then the Trail Blazers, Suns, Jazz,

Rockets, Mavericks, Thunder, Nuggets, and Warriors. In contrast to them, the Timberwolves, Hornets/Pelicans, and Clippers had the worst-ranked numbers of the group as of 2016.

After sports experts researched and published the history of all teams, some articles reported the most dominant and/or successful NBA teams since the early 1970s. To get results, different criteria were used including the Elovation App (Elo) rating, which focuses on wins and losses and also the margin of victory, whether home or road games, and strength of teams' opponent. Based on this metric and basketball information from various sources, among the best of the modern era — in chronological order — are the following clubs from the league's WC.[10]

- After changing its logo to more closely reflect the state of Utah by featuring purple mountains and sky blue in the script, the 1996–1997 Jazz posted a 31-4 record after the all-star break and finished first in their conference with a franchise-best record of 64-18. In the playoffs, the team swept the Clippers in three straight games and then in the semifinals, continued to roll easily ousting the Lakers four games to one. In the conference finals, Utah defeated the Rockets in six games when playmaker John Stockton nailed a three-point buzzer beater that launched them to the NBA Finals for the first time in franchise history. However, the Jazz lost 4-2 to the Bulls. A blend of Utah's peak, average, and end Elo rating was 1735 or 17th highest of all-time.[11]

- The 2008–2009 Lakers were a dynamic bunch. They finished the regular season with a 65-17 record, went 16-7 in the post-season, and defeated the Magic in the NBA Finals in five games. At their best, this team would have a 1790 Elo rating, which also represented the team's season-ending rating. However, throughout the season, the club had an average Elo score of 1726. It was third in the NBA in offensive efficiency (112.8 rating) and sixth in defensive efficiency (104.7 rating). After the Lakers suffered a disappointing loss in the finals the season before, this team became the group that finally helped Kobe Bryant return to the top of the NBA.

- Led by guard Stephen Curry, the 2013–2014 Warriors are an interesting case. Heading into Game 4 of the 2015 conference finals, the Warriors had a composite Elo rating of 1773, based on a peak score of 1791, an average of 1737, and an end rating of 1791. At the time, these numbers put Golden State in the fourth position of all-time. However, by destroying the Rockets in Game 3 of the WC finals, the Warriors reached a new peak Elo rating of 1813. With this score, the team's season-ending mark increased as its average Elo jumped to 1738. After demolishing the Cavaliers, Golden State finished up with an Elo of 1796, making them one of the best teams in NBA history.

• The offseason addition of LaMarcus Aldridge helped the 2015–2016 Spurs reach a peak Elo rating of 1800 and finish the year with a final regular-season mark of 67-15. Although they did not win an NBA championship, these Spurs, statistical speaking, were one of the best teams ever. Under Coach Gregg Popovich, the Spurs limited the opposition to just 92.9 points per game, finished with the best defensive rating in the NBA, and had a season-ending Elo rating of 1759 to go along with an average tally of 1768. Had this group not been eliminated by the Thunder in the conference semi-finals, it would rank in the top five of all-time.

• Even as the 2015–2016 Warriors achieved history by compiling a now-record 73 regular-season victories, they blew a 3-1 lead to Cleveland in the NBA Finals, failing to capture a second straight title and shot at immortality. This stumble, in turn, affected their place in history. Based on numbers, the Warriors' finished the year with a composite Elo rating of 1798, placing them at third on the all-time list. Despite setting the bar for regular-season excellence, the club's season-ending Elo rating of 1756 dragged everything down, preventing them from even earning a spot in the top two of all-time.

For various reasons such as lacking talented players, coaching problems, and/or both of them, some NBA teams had terrible performances in their regular seasons. Several of these clubs were evaluated based on their ability to score points and win games. In chronological order, the following is a list of a few of the worst clubs in the conference's history as of its 2016 season.[12]

• Of four offensive and defensive factors, not even a single category saw the 1982–1983 Rockets ranked in the top half of the group. The closest they came was in turnover percentage, where only a dozen squads fared better than them. Behind that were opponent's turnover percentage at 15th, free throws allowed per field-goal attempt at 17th, and both effective field-goal percentage allowed and defensive rebounding percentage at 18th. The Rockets offense was also atrocious during the season. Six players managed to score in double figures during the average outing, but the team's leading point-producer put up only 14.8 per game.

• The 1992–1993 Mavericks actually had two separate two-game winning streaks, but they also went double-digit contests without winning even once three times during the campaign. There was a 12-game skid in late November and early December, a 15-game losing streak that surrounded New Year's Eve, and a 19-game stretch of winless outings that lasted until mid-March. Among the NBA's 27 teams, Dallas finished at the bottom of the pile in both offensive and defensive ratings. The offense was so bad that despite using the league's sixth-fastest pace, the Mavericks still scored more points per game than only the Timberwolves, who were third-slowest in the Association.

• The Vancouver Grizzlies are the only franchise in the NBA with two of the worst 10 teams in the sport's history. Even with the terrible performance of the 1995–1996 Grizzlies, the 1996–1997 squad was somehow even worse. Bryant Reeves, who was drafted one year prior with the intent of making him into the face of the franchise, needed help in the frontcourt supplied by Shareef Abdur-Rahim. The two aforementioned young guns and another were the only three players on the Vancouver roster who earned more than two-win shares. Meanwhile, six other players each managed to finish below zero.

• With Bill Hanzlik at the helm, the 1997–1998 Nuggets only won 11 games throughout the year, struggling as a handful of relatively non-descript players attempted to lead the squad. Making just over $4 million, the team's highest-paid player had injuries limiting him to only 31 games throughout the season. Though Denver managed to string together 23 losses in a row at one point and had a separate 16-game stretch of winless basketball, the team emerged victorious from back-to-back contests only once all season.

• Legal troubles and on-court issues plagued the 2005–2006 Trail Blazers squad. Of eight factors — four on offense and the same on defense — the team mustered up a single-digit finish in only one. They were great at preventing opponents from getting to the free-throw line, but that was about it. They never forced turnovers, struggled to keep their opponents from making their looks from the field, could not grab defensive rebounds, and so forth. Basically, they were really bad at almost everything, which explains their status as one of the worst teams in NBA history.

LEAGUE ECONOMICS

In this section, there are data and other information about the commercial and financial aspects of franchises in the WC and their significance from an economic perspective. Besides attendances at their home and away games, anything else that affects these teams' income, market value, and wealth is included in the analysis, quantified, and discussed. In other words, the NBA is an organization consisting of for-profit enterprises that operate to compete each season typically within a division of a conference and seek to improve their performances in current and future games.

Franchise Financials

Forbes magazine's sports editors' published financial data of NBA franchises as of their 2015–2016 season. As denoted in Columns 2–7 of Table A4.3, these amounts include, respectively, their estimated market value — which is based on the current stadium deal without deduction for debt — and also total revenue, gate receipts, operating income — earnings before interest, taxes, depreciation, and amortization (EBITDA) — debt-to-value (D/V) percentages, and players' expenses. For each of three divisions, the information reveals the financial status and power of WC teams individually and relative to each other as a group. The following section identifies and highlights the data.[13]

In Table A4.3, Column 2 is the estimated market value of each NBA team, by division, as of 2015. Ranked from most to least, PD clubs averaged $1.7 billion, SWD's $1.1 billion, and NWD's $875 million. While the Lakers were first at $2.7 billion, Clippers second at $2 billion and Warriors third at $1.9 billion, least in value included the Grizzlies at $780 million, Timberwolves at $720 million, and Pelicans at $650 million. In comparison to the typical club's $1.2 billon, only five or 33% of the group exceeded that amount.

Several factors caused differences in teams' market values. In no specific order, these were their history, tradition, and success in the league; location within a big, midsized, or small market; size of each's fan base; number of titles and championships; and such financial data as their revenue, operating income, and gate receipts. Based on these and other reasons, they ranged in value by more than $2 billion.

To compare their standard deviation or variation in market values, the highest was PD teams ($745 million) and lowest among those in the NWD ($100 million) and then SWD ($373 million). This means parity or smaller deviation in these NBA franchise's values existed in 2015 to a greater extent between the Nuggets and other NWD teams than among clubs in the other divisions. Although these were only estimates, the amounts influence such things as the clubs' relative wealth, economic power in the league, and future price if offered for sale to potential investors. Interestingly, there were no clubs whose market value fell below the conference's average deviation of $577 million.

Each team's revenue — net of stadium revenues used for debt payments — is displayed in Column 3 of Table A4.3. While the Lakers had the highest at $304 million followed by the Rockets' $237 million and Warriors' $201 million, the three lowest-ranked were the Pelicans' $142 million at 13th, Kings' $141 million at 14th, and Nuggets' $140 million at 15th. The differences in amounts occurred for several reasons including their home attendances, range in ticket prices, winning percentage in games, and number of basketball fans in the area.

Because of various demographic and sport-specific factors, there were disparities in teams' revenue. While the league's standard deviation equaled $44 million, PD teams had the highest variation in revenue at $64 million and then the SWD's at $37 million and NWD's at $7 million. The latter division had the smallest difference in revenue because the same amounts existed for the Timberwolves and Jazz and also Thunder and Trail Blazers. Besides win–loss records in the regular season, the deviations reflect the population and growth in population of their markets, popularity at home, and per capita income and type of jobs of local households.

In Table A4.3, Column 4 contains the operating income or EBITDA of WC teams in 2015. For the group, it averaged $32 million. From most to least by division, PD clubs averaged $47 million, SWD's $31 million, and NWD's $18 million. Because of excessive payments for players' salaries and other types of expenses, the Trail Blazers and Kings had the smallest EBITDA's while the Lakers and Rockets earned the most income by operating efficiently. For various reasons, the Timberwolves, Clippers, and Grizzlies were also marginally efficient along with some others located in small, mid-sized, and large markets.

Each EC team's 2015 gate receipts — in millions of dollars — appears in Column 5 of Table A4.3. While the conference's average was $47 million, the Lakers had the most ($98 million) and then the Warriors ($77 million) and Rockets ($75 million). In contrast to these amounts, the Grizzlies ($27 million), Nuggets ($26 million), and Timberwolves ($19 million) had the smallest gate receipts in the NBA's 2015 season.

The dispersion or disparity in gate receipts was greatest among PD clubs ($28 million) compared to SWD teams ($20 million) and those in the NWD ($11 million). Because of the gap in amounts between, for example, the Lakers and Kings, the division's standard deviation exceeds that of the SWD's Rockets and Grizzlies, and NWD's Thunder and Timberwolves. Simply put, the Los Angeles and San Francisco–Oakland–San Jose areas are large and more prosperous basketball markets than the majority of others in the conference.

The sixth column of Table A4.3 includes the D/V percentages of each WC franchise in 2015. On average, the conference's was 11% or in amount, approximately $134 million per team based on estimated market values. Among each group, the NWD's averaged 9%, PD's 11%, and SWD's 12%. Although the Nuggets and Clippers had zero debt and five others less than 10%, the D/V ratios exceeded 20% each for the Kings and Grizzlies.

As described for other variables in the table, the standard deviations of D/V were unequal among divisions and franchises within divisions. PD teams, for example, had the greatest variation at 10%, and then those in the SWD at 7%, and NWD at 5%. In order to reduce their ratios for financial reasons and operate more effectively, several teams needed to reform in order to generate higher market values and/or record less amount of debt in accounts on their balance sheet.

As reported in *Forbes* for being an important, necessary, and periodic payment from an operations perspective, Column 7 in Table A4.3 shows the players' expenses — including benefits and bonuses — of these teams in 2015. For the league, they totaled approximately $1.2 billion or $80 million per team. On average, the SWD's was $82 million, PD's $81 million, and NWD's $77 million. While the Trail Blazers, Clippers, and Mavericks ranked highest in the conference, the Nuggets and Jazz each paid less than $70 million in players' expenses. Given these amounts, the first group of clubs had an above-average roster of players and won enough games in the league's

2015–2016 regular season to qualify for the playoffs but the latter two failed to participate, in part, because of their relatively small investment in players' salaries.

Players' expenses were different and also deviated between the three WC divisions. From most to least in variation among the groups — as measured by their standard deviations — these included the NWD's $12 million and then PD's $6 million and SWD's $5 million. Such amounts denote that the greatest disparity in payments occurred because of the Trail Blazers' $94 million versus the Nuggets' $64 million in the NWD whereas the range in players' expenses in the PD and SWD equaled, respectively, only $16 million between the Clippers and the Lakers and Suns and also $14 million between the Mavericks and Spurs. Thus, WC teams with the greatest revenues and/or largest market values did not necessarily compensate their players more than rivals within their division.

Arenas

As of the NBA's 2015–2016 season, WC teams — except for the Clippers and Lakers — played their home games in venues that differed in age, cost and market value, and also in such other ways as location, capacity, and ownership. Based on various criteria including their amenities, concessions, and sightlines, they have been ranked from best to worst overall, most to least accessible, and highest to lowest as facilities to entertain and support spectators at games. Given that overview, this section provides some data and other information regarding the facilities of WC clubs and discusses specific characteristics about them.[14]

Among teams' home courts within each division as of the NBA's 2015 season, they ranged in age as follows: within the conference's NWD, from the Thunders' 15-year-old Chesapeake Energy Arena in Oklahoma City to the Timberwolves' 27-year-old Target Center in Minneapolis; within the PD, from the Clippers' and Lakers' 18-year-old Staples Center in Los Angeles to the Warriors' 51-year-old Oracle Arena in Oakland; and within the SWD, from the Grizzlies' 13-year-old FedExForum in Memphis to the Pelicans' 18-year-old Smoothie King Center in New Orleans. Of teams' 14 venues in the WC, six or 43% of them are privately owned and eight or 57% publicly. Interestingly, none in the group are jointly owned by the team and a municipality and/or state agency.

Their construction costs ranked from being relatively cheap to very expensive. From the least to most costly in the NWD and then PD and SWD, respectively, it was approximately $89 million to erect the Chesapeake Energy Arena in Memphis for the Thunder compared to $262 million for the Trail Blazers' Moda Center in Portland; from $40 million to build the Sleep Train Arena in Sacramento for the Kings to $400 million for the Staples Center in Los Angeles for the Clippers and Lakers; and from $114 million for the Smoothie King Center in New Orleans for the Pelicans to $420 million for the American Airlines Center in Dallas for the Mavericks.

Regarding the most likely replacements or renovation of current venues in the WC, the Chase Center is a planned 18,000-seat multipurpose arena to be built in San Francisco and finished sometime in 2019. It will be privately financed, primarily used for basketball games, and become the new home of the Warriors. However, the plan for the Chase Center to open in the city's Mission Bay area has been delayed multiple times due to complaints about the location. Opposed by the Mission Bay Alliance, the building would increase traffic, create a shortage of parking, and limit space for expansion of the University of California–San Francisco campus.

Recently *Forbes* sports editors assigned economic values to venues of teams in the WC. From lowest to highest within divisions, respectively, amounts in the NWD were from $118 million for the Target Center in Minneapolis to $207 million for the Moda Center in Portland; in the PD, from $156 million for Sleep Train Arena in Sacramento to $537 million for the Staples Center in Los Angeles — when occupied by the Lakers but not the Clippers; and in the SWD, from $117 million for the Smoothie King Center in New Orleans to $408 million for the Toyota Center in Houston. Based on their estimated values, PD teams' venues averaged $347 million, SWD' $263 million, and NWD' $168 million. Because of increasing real estate prices in urban areas and popularity of the sport in America, these facilities will likely appreciate in value especially for those within midsized to large metropolitan areas.

In various studies, NBA arenas have been ranked by various basketball experts and sports journalists in the media with respect to their location and different amenities and problems. Although results vary according to each study's parameters, a few venues rank among the best while some others placed in the worst group. For example, the most attractive, entertaining, and well-structured facilities within the WC based on their name, aesthetics, and experience for fans, are the Moda Center and Staples Center.[15]

In a recent study, the two best buildings of the group were rated as follows:

"The Portland Trail Blazers will always play in the Rose Garden [renamed Moda Center], a picturesque name that relates to the city of Portland, a.k.a. 'Rose City.' This is perhaps the worst rebranding in NBA arena history. Portland's only major sports team is their basketball team, and as a result the Trail Blazers inspire an electrifying atmosphere. Certainly the prices for food and drink are obscene, but the building is well located across the river from the Pearl District and near good food. The Rose Garden [Moda Center] is an energizing and vibrant NBA arena."

For why the Staples Center ranked second in the WC, the editor provided these comments:

"These [aesthetics] are great for Lakers fans, who have one of the best looking courts in the NBA — gotta love the stars at center court representing the championships and a series of classic banners hanging from the ceiling. For Clippers fans, this is contrasted with a disgusting, over-black court and those same Lakers banners. The theater lighting gives the game a sense of high drama. The Staples Center is one of the busiest arenas in sports, housing the Lakers, Clippers and the NHL's Los Angeles Kings. It makes sense that they know what they're doing, as the seats are always comfortable, the food is decently priced and at least one of the teams is generally relevant."

Within the same study, two of the lowest-ranked facilities were the Kings' Sleep Train Arena and Pelicans' Smoothie King Center. Among others in the conference, the former ranked 15th (29th in the NBA) and the latter 14th (26th).

The study's author criticized each of them, respectively, as follows:

"This is a wonderful arena [Sleep Train Arena] if you hope to be bombarded with advertisement. Next time you look up to the center of the ceiling to see the video scoreboard, remember through all of those advertisements that, to the Kings, you are more than a fan. You are a consumer.

The purple-infused court design itself is average and not too distracting. Getting there is difficult, as the arena is in the middle of nowhere away from any real civilization. Being there is difficult, as the seats are uncomfortable and the place smells like old food. The arena is notoriously cramped and uncomfortable, and so there is really no motivation to watch a sporting event here."

For the Smoothie King Center, he remarked:

"Whoooo boy. In stark contrast to Sleep Train [Arena], I could see the executives at Smoothie King [Center] setting their sights on stadium naming rights. I could even see them pitching the 'Smoothie King FroYo Free Throw Fieldhouse.' This stadium name is the strongest argument against free market capitalism since Karl Marx. For a city known for its bright, flamboyant personality, it's strange that the Pelicans chose to emphasize the most boring color in professional sports, the overused navy blue. The court tends to be heavy on the navy, unfortunately. Otherwise, the visual experience of the game is functional without being notable."

Fan cost index

In the 2015–2016 NBA season, the average Fan Cost Index (FCI) for a family to attend a regular season game of a WC team was $332. While the Lakers' games each cost $545, the Pelicans had the conference's lowest FCI at $221. Among divisions, the average for PD teams equaled $416, NWD's $297, and SWD's $285. The order from ranking them first to third occurred, in part, because FCIs of the Warriors, Clippers, and Lakers each exceeded $436 while those of such teams as the Timberwolves, Thunder, Jazz, Mavericks, Grizzlies, and Pelicans were each below $300.[16]

For specific items in TMR's 2015–2016 FCI, the approximate range in amounts from most to least expensive or first to fifteenth across the WC were listed as follows: average ticket, Lakers $103.27 to Pelicans $30; cheapest tickets available, Lakers $36 to Grizzlies $7; beer, Suns $10.25 to Mavericks and Thunder each $5; soft drink, Suns $6.25 to Spurs $2.50; hot dog, Trail Blazers/Clippers/Rockets/Warriors each $6 to Suns/Mavericks/Thunder/Jazz each $3.50; parking, Warriors $30 to Spurs $5; program, seven teams each $5 to eight not reported; and for a cap, Spurs $30 to Mavericks $12.99.

Based on economics principles, these prices were set by teams and/or vendors to sell enough units to maximize revenue from their sales at home games in the arenas.

From the NBA's 2011–2012 to 2015–2016 season, there were some significant increases but also relatively small, and even, decreases in FCIs of teams in the WC. For examples of these changes, the Warriors' FCI rose from $252 to $471 or approximately 87% but the Spurs' from only $319 to $325 or about 1–2%, while the Mavericks' declined from $311 to $281 or 9–10%. Because of inflation, number of — and amount spent by — families at games in arenas, local economic conditions and other factors, the majority of teams and/or vendors raised their prices each year rather than keeping them constant or reducing amounts.

In evaluating FCIs between the WC's 2014–2015 and 2015–2016 seasons, the Warriors' increased the most, in other words, from $336 to $471 or approximately 40%. Alternatively, fans' costs fell for home games of the Nuggets, Mavericks, and Spurs but remained the same for those of the Timberwolves, Jazz, Suns, Grizzlies, and Pelicans. Thus, there were different payments for tickets and other things by families to attend WC teams' home games at their arenas especially from late 2011 and 2014 to early 2016.

ORGANIZATION HIGHLIGHTS

Besides regular-season and post-season games, the NBA and its franchises are involved in — and affected by — community events and also business-related and government affairs, news, and projects. Because these things and other topics influence the league in different but perhaps important and historic ways, following are a few of them from the academic and popular literature.

First, WD/WC teams won 29 or 44% of all-star games against ED/EC clubs during NBA seasons' 1951–1998 and 2000–2015 (the 1999 game was cancelled due to a league lockout). Such outstanding and popular players as the Hawks' Bob Petit, Lakers' Magic Johnson, Shaquille O'Neal, and Kobe Bryant, Jazz's Karl Malone, and Thunders' Russell Westbrook were each MVPs in at least two of these games.[17]

Second, since the NBA divided teams into two conferences as of the 1970–1971 season, the WC has won 26 championships and the EC 21.

The most successful WC clubs have been the Lakers with 11 championships, Spurs five, Heat three, Rockets and Warriors each with two, and one each for the Mavericks, Trail Blazers, and Supersonics (renamed Oklahoma City Thunder). In the EC, the Celtics and Bulls each won six championships, Piston three, Knicks two, and one each for the Bucks, Cavaliers, 76ers, and Bullets (renamed Washington Wizards).

Third, the top and bottom three WC clubs in home attendances per game (in thousands) during the NBA's 2015–2016 season were, respectively, the Mavericks (20.1), Warriors (19.5) and Trail Blazers (19.3), while the lowest included the Nuggets (14.0), Timberwolves (14.1), and Grizzlies (16.6). At away games, the Lakers ranked first followed by the Warriors and Thunder with the Suns, Kings, and Jazz at the end of the conference. Across all teams in the league, the EC's Bulls and Cavaliers placed first and second, respectively, in attendances at both their home and road games while the WC's Grizzlies ranked 24th, Timberwolves 29th, and Nuggets 30th.

Fourth, as of early 2016, a study ranked the worst principal owners of WC franchises. These were the Kings' Vivek Ranadive, who despite having never touched a basketball until he coached his daughter's team in the 1950s, is on his third coach — and counting — in two-plus seasons; Suns' Robert Sarver, who despite his vow to keep everyone upon arrival in their heyday in 2004 — everyone from paterfamilias Jerry Colangelo down — found themselves on the way out. He blew up the young team that won 48 games three seasons ago, putting Isaiah Thomas alongside Eric Bledsoe and Goran Dragic, but upsetting everyone so badly that they traded Thomas and Dragic; Nuggets' Stan Kroenke, who despite marrying into the Walmart fortune, is so thrifty that general manager Masai Ujiri bailed in 2013 after being named executive of the year; and the Grizzlies' Robert Pera, who arrived with his analytics aces in 2013 and determined to turn the grind-it-out team, coming off a 50-6 win season, into an up-tempo team. Head coach Lionel Hollins lasted one season and Dave Joerger had to slow them back down to post 50, 55, and 42-win seasons.

Fifth, two of the best owners of EC teams are the Spurs' Peter Holt and Mavericks' Mark Cuban. Holt helped usher in a boom in international players thanks to branding out for players like Manu Ginobili and Tony Parker and getting Becky Hammon into a position where she could become the first female head coach in NBA history. While the Spurs are a dynasty and an institution in the NBA, Holt is perhaps the best owner in not just basketball but top five in all of professional sports. Regarding Dallas's owner, you can fault Cuban for being over-the-top in passion for this team, which is a unique brand of passion exclusive to him. Although not cuddly, he takes credit for good decisions and owns the bad ones.

Sixth, the richest owner of a WC franchise is the Clippers' Richard Ballmer. Worth at least $22 billion, Ballmer worked at Microsoft for more than 20 years and headed several Microsoft divisions including operations, operating systems development, and sales and support. After leaving Microsoft, the value of his shares significantly increased and, thus, he became the company's largest single shareholder in April 2014. Four months later, Ballmer was the highest bidder among several investors and paid $2 billion for the team.

Seventh, an Entertainment Sports Programming Network (ESPN) forecast panel rated each NBA team's front-office management on their guidance and leadership in terms of how it affects overall on-the-court success, both in the short and long term. In the WC, the top three offices in 2015 were those of the Spurs, Warriors, and Mavericks, while the Timberwolves, Nuggets, and Lakers ranked last in the conference. With respect to ranking coaches, the Spurs' Popovich was first followed by the Warriors' Kerr and Mavericks' Carlisle, but the bottom five included the Timberwolves' Saunders, Nuggets' Hunt (replaced by Michael Malone), and Lakers' Scott.

Eighth, which WC teams have the highest and lowest salaries in the NBA's 2016–2017 season? Ranked from first to third as of late 2016 are the Trail Blazers at approximately $120 million, then the Clippers at $114 million, and Spurs at $111 million. With the smallest salaries, however, are the Timberwolves at $83 million, Jazz at $80 million, and Nuggets at $75 million. Overall, the EC Cavaliers had the highest amount in salaries and Nets lowest.

Ninth, the WC again was better than the EC during the regular season — for the 16th time in 17 seasons — but the separation was much closer this time. In head-to-head competition, the WC was fourteen games over 0.500 against the EC in 2015–2016, compared to a 76-game separation in 2014–2015 and 118-game advantage in 2013–2014. The WC, likewise, has dominated championships, though not by as wide a margin. Beginning with 2000, WC teams won 11 or 68% of them and those in EC five or 32%.

Tenth, according to financial information in Tables A4.3 and A5.3 of this book, the two conferences had different results except for their teams' total estimated market values each at $1.2 billion. Based on amounts in 2015, the WC led the EC in average revenue, operating income, gate receipts, and player expenses, but not D/V percent. Their average standard deviations also were not the same with WC teams, as a group, having more variation in operating income but less in estimated market value, revenue, gate receipts, D/V percent, and player expenses. Among divisions in each conference, the WC's PD with the Lakers and Warriors, and EC's AD with the Knicks and Celtics, were the most important within the NBA from a financial perspective.

NOTES

1. For the history of the NBA and its teams, see Jozsa FP Jr., (2015). *National Basketball Association Strategies: Business Expansions, Relocations, and Mergers.* New York, NY: Springer; Kirchberg C, (2007). *Hoop Love: A History of the National Basketball Association.* Jefferson, NC: McFarland; Surdam DG, (2012). *The Rise of the National Basketball Association.* Urbana, IL: University of Illinois Press; and the *Official National Basketball Association Guide 2015–16.* New York, NY: NBA Properties 2015.

2. Please read "Historical Moments," http://www.sportsencyclopedia.com [cited 25 June 2016]. For defunct BAA/NBA teams, review "NBA and ABA Team Index," http://www.basketball-reference.com [cited 1 December 2016].

3. See "This Day in History: The NBA is Born," http://www.history.com [cited 14 December 2016] and Quirk J and Fort RD, (1992). *Pay Dirt: The Business of Professional Team Sports.* Princeton, NJ: Princeton University Press.

4. Besides the sources in Table A4.1 of the appendix, two others are the "Top U.S. Metropolitan Areas by Population, 1790–2010," http://www.peakbagger.com [cited 5 December 2016] and "Rankings of U.S. Standard Metropolitan Statistical Areas," *World Almanac & Book of Facts* (1972), 154–155.

5. See "CBA 101," http://www.nba.com [cited 8 December 2016]. For the new proposed deal, read David Aldridge, "NBA, NBAP Reach Tentative Seven-Year CBA Agreement," http://www.nba.com [cited 15 December 2016].

6. The historical performances of NBA teams and their coaches and players are available on such websites as http://www.nba.com, http://www.sportsencyclopedia.com, and http://www.basketball-reference.com.

7. For its members and their achievements, research "The Naismith Memorial Basketball Hall of Fame," http://www.hoophall.com [cited 1 December 2016].

8. The reference is Charlie Zegers, "About the NBA Playoffs," http://www.basketball.about.com [cited 13 December 2016].

9. There are several references for this information including "NBA History — MVP," http://www.espn.com [cited 2 December 2016].

10. Among readings about this topic, see for example Jason Alsher, "The Ten Best NBA Teams of All-Time," http://www.cheatsheet.com [cited 2 December 2016].

11. An explanation is in Silver N and Fischer-Baum R, "How We Calculate NBA Elo Ratings," http://www.fivethirtyeight.com [cited 5 December 2016].

12. Two references are Fromal A, "Each NBA Franchise's Worst Team Ever," http://www.bleacerreport.com [cited 10 December 2016] and "10 Worst Records in NBA History," http://www.cheatsheet.com [cited 12 December 2016].

13. For financial information about these professional sports franchises, see Badenhausen K, M, Ozanian and C Settimi, "The Business of Basketball," http://www.forbes.com [cited 27 June 2016].

14. "NBA Arenas," http://www.hoopsonline.com [cited 11 December 2016] and on pages 235–236 of Jozsa FP Jr. (2011). *The National Basketball Association: Business, Organization and Strategy*. Hackensack, NJ: World Scientific.

15. L. Dahlgren, "Power Rankings: NBA Arenas," fansided.com [cited 11 December 2016] and "Present National Basketball Association Arenas," http://www.basketball.ballparks.com [cited 11 December 2016].

16. Besides the league and its teams, the best source for this financial data is "Fan Cost Index," http://www.teammarketingreport.com [cited 16 November 2016] and more specifically, "Team Marketing Report — NBA 2015–16," http://www.teammarketing.com [cited 12 December 2016].

17. "NBA All-Star Game Results," http://www.nba.com [cited 12 December 2016]; "NBA Championships: Winners by Conference," http://www.landofbasketball.com [cited 12 December 2016]; "NBA Attendance Report — 2016," http://www.proxy.espn.com [cited 5 December 2016]; Heisler M, "Heisler: From Bad to Worse to Vivek: Top Ten Worst Owners in NBA," http://www.dailynews.com [cited 12 December 2016]; Hill J, "NBA Owners Power Ranking: Who is the Best Owner in Basketball?" http://www.fansided.com [cited 12 December 2016]; Khan A, "Top Ten Richest NBA Owners," http://www.thesportster.com [cited 12 December 2016]; "NBA Salaries," http://www.hoopshype.com [cited 20 December 2016]; "NBA Front-Office Rankings: 2015," http://www.espn.com [cited 13 December 2016]; Exner R, "NBA's Western Conference Tops East for Sixteenth Time in Seventeen Seasons, But Separation Much Tighter in 2015–16," http://www.cleveland.com [cited 20 December 2016].

Part III
National Football League

Chapter 5

AMERICAN FOOTBALL CONFERENCE

HISTORY

Established in Canton, Ohio, the American Professional Football Association (APFA) consisted of 14 teams in 1920 — with Akron Pros winning the championship — and included 21 in 1921 led by the Chicago Staleys. One year later, the APFA changed its name to National Football League (NFL), and fielded eighteen teams. In wins–losses–ties, the Canton Bulldogs finished 10-0-2 and emerged as the league's first true powerhouse.[1]

From its 1933 to 1949 season, the NFL had an Eastern Division (ED) and Western Division (WD). In 1950, these became respectively the American Conference (AC) and National Conference (NC) for three years and then Eastern Conference (EC) and Western Conference (WC) for the next 17 years. Meanwhile, to expand the sport geographically and competitively in the United States (US), the American Football League (AFL) was created in 1960 and financed by a number of investors who had been denied NFL expansion franchises or currently owned minor shares of them. Structurally, the AFL included an EC and WC for one season and then an ED and WD through 1969.[2]

Although the AFL had lopsided competition but different rivalries between its teams within a few years and low-to-moderate attendances at their home and road games, the league was buttressed by a generous television contract with the American Broadcasting Corporation (ABC) followed by a contract with the National Broadcasting Corporation (NBC) for games starting with the 1965 season while the Columbia Broadcasting System (CBS) acquired rights to NFL regular season games in 1966–1967 with an option for 1968.

Continuing to attract talented football players from colleges and the NFL by the mid-1960s, as well as successful franchise shifts of the Chargers from Los Angeles to San Diego in 1961 and the Texans from Dallas to Kansas City and renamed Chiefs in 1963, the AFL established a dedicated following. Also, the transformation of the struggling Titans into the New York Jets in 1963 under new ownership further solidified the league's reputation among many fans and the major media.

Regarding performances, the most successful AFL teams were the Dallas Texans/Kansas City Chiefs with three titles, two each for the Buffalo Bills and Houston Oilers, and one each for the New York Titans/Jets, Los Angeles/ San Diego Chargers, and Oakland Raiders. Alternatively, the Boston Patriots, Miami Dolphins, Cincinnati Bengals, and Denver Broncos had several losing records during their seasons in the league.

Because fierce competition caused player salaries to skyrocket in both leagues — especially after a series of raids by each other — they agreed to a merger after a series of meetings between them in 1966. According to conditions in the agreement, they would combine to form an expanded league with 26 teams with no franchises being transferred outside their metropolitan areas; hold a common draft; play a world championship game named the Super Bowl between league champions beginning in 1966; and replace their existing conferences/divisions alignment in 1970 with the American Football Conference (AFC) and National Football Conference (NFC). While the AFC was originally composed of nine pre-merger AFL teams plus three from the NFL, the NFC's 13 came from the NFL's former Capitol, Central, Century, and Coastal Divisions.

Being the focus of this chapter, the AFC had five teams in the ED and four each in the Central Division (CD) and WD in its 1970–1971 or simply 1970 season. However, because of expansion and other factors, the conference changed in 2002 and reassigned their groups of teams to be members of the ED, North Division (ND), South Division (SD), or WD. Moreover, from 1970 to 2002, the number of clubs increased from 13 to 16, with four in each division.

Between 1970 and 2016, some AFC teams changed plans and moved from one city to another within a metropolitan area or to a completely different area. Chronologically, these were the Oakland Raiders→Los Angeles in 1982; Baltimore Colts→Indianapolis in 1984; Los Angeles Raiders→Oakland in 1995; Cleveland Browns→Baltimore in 1996; Houston Oilers→Memphis in 1997; and Tennessee Oilers→Nashville in 1998. While some teams relocated to more-populated and wealthier areas, others moved to play in a new or renovated publicly financed stadium and perform before a larger number of fans at the new site.[3]

Besides movements, such new teams joined the AFC as the Jacksonville Jaguars in 1995, Cleveland Browns in 1999, and Houston Texans in 2002. As denoted later in this chapter, they have not performed up to expectations within the conference and/or their division for several reasons including ownership issues and various problems with coaches and/or players during seasons and postseasons.

By decade, a few important facts about and within the AFC were memorable: in the 1970s, Boston Patriots was renamed New England Patriots; Seattle Seahawks moved from the NFC to AFC WD and Tampa Bay Buccaneers from the AFC WD to the NFC; Kansas City Chiefs' owner Lamar Hunt was elected president of the conference; NBC televised conference games for four years; and in the 1970s, the AFC's Pittsburgh Steelers became the first team to win four Super Bowls; a jury ruled against the NFL thereby allowing the Raiders to move from Oakland to Los Angeles; and the league, representing its conferences, signed new, multiyear broadcasting contracts with major television and radio networks.

In the 1990s, the Denver Broncos won the conference's only two Super Bowls; according to an agreement, the city of Cleveland retained the Browns' heritage and records including the club's name, logo, colors, history, trophies, and memorabilia; and NFL team owners' Robert Irsay (Colts) and Leon Hess (Jets) died in addition to Paul Brown, who founded the Bengals and Browns franchises. During the 2000s, teams approved additional league-wide revenue sharing; the Patriots became the second in NFL history to win three Super Bowls in four seasons and five in 17; and AFC teams remembered the courage and resilience that followed the events of September 2001 with special tributes in each stadium and on television during their games on 11 September, 2011.[4]

TEAMS

Markets

From 1920 to 2016, many NFL franchises became "defunct", including some within the APFA, pre-ED, and also ED, EC, and AFC. Of the total, 45 failed in the 1920s, four in the 1930s, and two in the 1940–1950s. In addition, 12 teams applied for membership in the league but were refused entry. Some existed only as proposals, but others had full organizations. Among the group were the Massillon Tigers, Union Quakers of Philadelphia, and Youngstown Patricians in the 1920s, Los Angeles Bulldogs in the 1930s, Pennsylvania Keystoners in the 1940s, Buffalo Bills in the 1950s, Orlando Suns and Memphis Grizzlies in the 1970s, New Jersey Generals in the 1980s, and the Baltimore Bombers, Memphis Hound Dogs, and St. Louis Stallions in the 1990s.

As a result of the merger following their 1969 season, 10 teams shifted from their current league to the other one. Specifically, the AFL's Jets, Patriots, Bills, and Dolphins transferred to the NFL's AFC ED and Oilers to its CD, while the AFL's Raiders, Chiefs, Chargers, and Broncos moved to the NFL's AFC WD and also Bengals to its CD.

In 1970, the 13 AFC clubs originally existed in relatively large, midsized, and small cities. Geographically, they ranged north to southwest or in other ways from Boston to Miami in the ED, Pittsburgh to Houston in the CD, and Kansas City to San Diego in the WD. Their metropolitan areas' populations were also different and within the three divisions ranked from most to least in (millions) as follows: in the ED was teams based in New York (11.5), Boston (2.7), Baltimore (2.1), Buffalo (1.3), and Miami (1.2); in the CD, they included Pittsburgh (2.4), Cleveland (2.0), Houston (1.9), and Cincinnati (1.4); and in the WD, one each in Oakland (3.1), San Diego (1.3), Denver (1.2), and Kansas City (1.2). Although there were no AFC clubs in areas north of Boston or Buffalo and south of Houston or Miami, at least six in the NFC had home sites in the Midwest.[5]

During the NFL's 1971–1972 to 2015–2016 season, new AFC teams began to play at home in such locations — with Metropolitan Statistical Area (MSA) populations in (millions) — as Houston (4.7), Cleveland (2.9), and Jacksonville (1.0). In addition, existing clubs in the conference relocated to such areas as Baltimore (7.6), Los Angeles (7.4), Oakland (7.0), Nashville

(1.2), Indianapolis (1.1), and Memphis (1.1). Most occurred, in part, because of changes in ownership and construction of new stadiums at the post-move sites, and also because these MSAs contained more people including households with increasing disposable and/or per capita incomes.

To provide and examine some current, interesting, and relevant data and facts about existing AFC teams in order to examine the locations, sizes and other elements of their markets, there is information about them in Table A5.1. Within the table, variables researched were each team's Metropolitan Statistical Area Population (MSAPOP), number of Designated Market Area Television Homes (DMATVH), and average attendances (AVGATT) at home games as of 2016 in the NFL. These criteria are measured, listed, and ranked in order to reveal the attributes, characteristics, and problems of such competitors and rivals as the ED's New England Patriots and New York Jets, ND's Cincinnati Bengals and Cleveland Browns, SD's Houston Texans and Indianapolis Colts, and WD's Denver Broncos and Oakland Raiders.

Based on data listed in Column 2 of Table A5.1 as of the league's 2015 season, the typical AFC team had a MSAPOP of 3.3 million. More specifically, ED teams' areas were ranked first at 5.5 million followed by those in the SD at 2.9 million, WD at 2.6 million, and ND at 2.3 million. While the Jets, Texans, and Dolphins had the largest group of people within their markets, the three smallest areas hosted the Titans, Jaguars, and Bills. These differences, in turn, affected and will influence each club's potential and actual ticket sales, revenue from games and other sources, and their market value especially those identical or similar in size within divisions such as the Dolphins and Patriots, Bengals and Steelers, Colts and Titans, and Broncos and Chargers.

Besides averages for the league and by division, the variation or dispersion in MSAPOPs was determined mathematically using standard deviation. While it averaged 2.3 million people across the AFC's 16 teams in 2016, the ED's ranked highest at 3.6 million, SD's second at 2.4 million, WD's third at 0.5 million, and ND's fourth at 0.3 million. In other words, the least equal in market population were areas of the Bills, Dolphins, and their divisional rivals, but most alike are those of ND teams particularly the Bengals and Browns and also Ravens and Steelers. Because of such widespread variation in MSAPOPs, teams' locations impacted them in various ways such as their attendances at home and away games, media coverage, travel costs, and other variables of these franchises.[6]

In Table A5.1, Column 3 gives the number of estimated television homes in each team's designated market area (DMATVH) in years' 2016–2017. While it averaged 1.4 million across the conference, the ED teams' on average equaled 2.1 million television homes and those in the SD 1.3 million, WD 1.2, and ND 1.1 million. Similar to but not exactly ranked like the distribution of the MSAPOPs, the largest number of homes was in the New York and then Houston and Boston–Manchester market areas, while the fewest existed in Cincinnati, Jacksonville, and Buffalo.

As explained before for the MSAPOP, the standard deviation of television homes in teams' areas denotes differences across the conference and also between and within divisions. While the variation was 0.8 or 800,000 television homes among the entire group in the AFC, ED clubs on average had the largest at 1.29 million, SD's at 0.78 or 780,000, WD at 0.31 to 310,000, and the ND's at 0.25 or 250,000. Within divisions, for example, the difference between the number of television homes in New York and Buffalo was much greater, for example, than in Houston and Jacksonville, Denver, and Kansas City, and Cleveland and Cincinnati. Thus, the Baltimore Ravens and their divisional rivals are the most equal in this characteristic of their market, but it is less so for teams within the ED, SD, and WD. This, however, does not mean more or fewer fans actually viewed their games on television at home or other places.

In Table A5.1, Column 4 lists the average attendance of each AFC team while playing games on its home field in the 2015 season. For this statistic, the Jets ranked first at 82,500-seat MetLife Stadium in East Rutherford, New Jersey, Broncos second at 76,100-seat Sports Authority Field at Mile High in Denver, and Chiefs third at 76,400-seat Arrowhead Stadium in Kansas City. In contrast to them, teams' with the smallest attendances at their home were the Bengals at 65,500-seat Paul Brown Stadium in Cincinnati, Chargers at 71,500-seat Qualcomm Stadium in San Diego, and Raiders at 53,200-seat O.com Coliseum in Oakland.

While the conference's attendance was 66,550 per game, ED teams averaged 69,740 fans, ND's almost 65,100, SD's about 65,990, and WD's roughly 65,420. Ranked first and second within their division, respectively, games of the ED's Jets and Bills were more popular, for example, than those of the Dolphins and Patriots. In addition, the WD's Raiders and Chargers had the lowest-ranked combined attendances and not the ND's Bengals and Browns or SD's Jaguars and Titans. In fact, such things as these teams' win–loss records, average ticket prices, advertising promotions and marketing campaigns, and number of superstar quarterbacks and other players affected in some way their Sunday afternoon crowds and other nighttime attendances at home games.

Regarding the deviation in teams' average attendances in the league's 2015 season, it was 6,560 spectators per game for the conference but from most to least by division as follows: 11,240 in the WD; 5,740 in the ED; 4,400 in the ND; and approximately 4,200 in the SD. This suggests that WD clubs had greater variation in number of fans at their games, in part, because of sellouts at the Broncos' Sports Authority Field at Mile High and Chiefs' Arrowhead Stadium but not at the two other teams' venues.

For various reasons including a strategy to be competitive while entertaining fans given the capacity of their stadiums, very small differences in attendances between them occurred, for example, at the Browns' FirstEnergy Stadium, Steelers' Heinz Field, and Titans' Nissan Stadium, and also at the Patriots' Gillette Stadium and Colts' Lucas Oil Stadium. Although the Patriots, Colts and Steelers each won at least five more regular-season games than the Browns and Titans as of 2016, they each sold about the same number of seats to fans at their home games.

Given the data and its distribution in Table A5.1, the ED's Dolphins, Patriots, and Jets, SD's Texans, and WD's Broncos each played their home games in relatively large markets; the ND's Ravens, Bengals, Browns, and Steelers, SD's Colts and Titans, and the WD's Chiefs, Raiders, and Chargers in midsized markets; and the ED's Bills and SD's Jaguars in small markets. Thus, approximately 32% of AFC teams existed in MSAs with plenty of fans and television homes during 2016, while 56% had home sites in less populated areas with fewer television homes, and another 12% performed within inferior markets. According to data in the table — except for the Jets in the New York–Newark–New Jersey area and the Raiders in San Francisco–Oakland–Hayward metropolis, the other teams' markets within and across divisions are each different demographically and roughly represent their economies and the sport's fan base.

For more about variables in Table A5.1 and their potential to be future football markets after the league's 2016–2017 season, the most populated places without an NFL team are such MSAs as Riverside–San Bernardino–Ontario

(4.4 million), St. Louis (2.8 million), Portland–Vancouver–Hillsboro (2.3 million), Orlando–Kissimmee–Sanford (2.3 million), San Antonio–New Braunfels (2.3 million), Sacramento–Roseville–Arden–Arcade (2.2 million), and Las Vegas–Henderson–Paradise (2.1 million). With respect to DMAs in the top 40, those without a club — besides San Antonio and Las Vegas — are Raleigh–Durham–Fayetteville, Hartford–New Haven, Columbus, Salt Lake City, Milwaukee, Greenville–Spartanburg–Ashville, West Palm Beach–Ft. Pierce, and Austin.[7]

If the league expands at a site in an area not hosting a current NBA team, a few of these places are viable markets. In addition, they are potential sites for any existing NFL clubs with inferior stadiums and who compete for local fans with other teams in Major League Baseball (MLB) and any in the National Basketball Association (NBA) and/or National Hockey League (NHL). Among the group, there has been speculation in the media about locating a new or existing club in especially Las Vegas, Nevada, and also in smaller US metropolitan areas such as Columbus, Ohio, and San Antonio, Texas.

Despite being homes of former NFL teams that folded in years from 1920 to 2000 or were not admitted into the NFL, this group includes such cities as Akron, Dayton, and Toledo, Ohio; Duluth, Minnesota; Louisville, Kentucky; Rochester, New York; Milwaukee, Wisconsin; and St. Louis, Missouri. In short, a number of places are adequate sites to host an NFL expansion team or one that struggles to get local fans to attend its home games and/or earn enough money to operate effectively within a division of the AFC.

Before discussing teams' performances in the next section of this chapter, the NFL Players Association (NFLPA) signed a Collective Bargaining Agreement (CBA) with the NFL in 2011. It covered several specific things such as the roster of players and their employment rights. Regarding the size of teams during seasons, the active list limit increased from 45 players per club to 46. The limit cannot be reduced by clubs for the duration of the CBA, although they may carry less than 46 players on their active list during the regular season but no less than 43. Players on the active and inactive lists receive the same benefits and protections and in any league year, these lists do not exceed 53.[8]

A team's practice squad consists of the following players — provided they have not served more than two previous seasons on a practice squad: first, players who do not have an accrued season of NFL experience and any free agent players who were on the active list for fewer than nine regular-season games during their only accrued season(s). An otherwise eligible player may be on a practice squad for a third season only if the club by which he is employed that season has at least 53 players on its active/inactive list during the entire period of his employment.

Second, a player shall be deemed to have served on a practice squad in a season if he has passed the club's physical and been a member of the club's practice squad for at least three regular-season or post-season games during his first two practice squad seasons, and for at least one regular season or post-season game during his third practice squad season. According to a section of the CBA, a bye week counts as a game provided the player is not terminated until after the regular season or post-season weekend in question.

Performances

During the league's 97-year history, the number of pre-AFC/AFC teams ranged from five in various seasons to 16 from 1999 to 2016. Because of differences in performances, some of their players were among all-time leaders in the sport. These include, for example, such quarterbacks as Peyton Manning, Tom Brady, and Dan Marino in passes completed; runners' LaDainian Tomlinson, Edgerrin James, and Marcus Allen in rushing yards; receivers' Marvin Harrison, Tim Brown, and Reggie Wayne in receptions; and Morten Andersen, Gary Anderson, and Jeff Feagles in number of games. A few head coaches with outstanding careers as leaders of conference teams were, in part, the Dolphins/Colts' Don Shula, Bengals/Browns' Paul Brown, and currently the Patriots' Bill Belichick.[9]

For 16 AFC teams as of the NFL's 2015–2016 season, their all-time performances appear in Table A5.2. Besides their total performances — which were calculated but are not given in the table — the columns denote the distribution of seasons and overall how well these clubs competed and whether they succeeded since becoming members of the league. Based on various results and other information, the following is an overview of their performances in order to compare and rank them from first to 16th.

Besides differences in the quality of coaches and players, their total seasons in the league — as listed in Column 2 of Table A5.2 — partly influenced them. From most to least, ED clubs averaged 46 seasons, WD's 42, ND's 41, and SD's 21. As a group, their histories ranged from the 14-year-old Texans to the 83-year-old Steelers.

Winning Percentage

While the conference average in wins was approximately 290 (Column 3 of Table A5.2), ED teams' equaled 364, WD's 337, ND's 295, and SD's only 166. As of the league's 2015–2016 season, the Steelers won 590 games and led the group of 16 followed by the Broncos and Dolphins. However, with the least number of wins were the Browns and then Texans and Titans.

Given each club's number of seasons and wins, another important factor in ranking AFC teams is their win–loss record or simply winning percentage. According to data in Column 4 of Table A5.2, the most successful in the conference have been the Broncos, Dolphins, and Patriots, while the lowest winning percentages belong to the Browns and then Texans and Jets. By groups, ED teams have an average of 0.512, WD's 0.507, SD's 0.479, and ND's 0.461.

Since 1970, the Broncos have won more than 58% of their regular-season games because of such coaches as Red Miller, Dan Reeves, Mike Shanahan and John Fox, and also quarterbacks' Craig Morton, John Elway, Jake Plummer and Peyton Manning. Besides them, running back Terrell Davis, tight end Shannon Sharpe, offensive tackle Gary Zimmerman, and cornerback Willie Brown had successful careers with the club. In fact, these players contributed greatly to Denver teams being well above 0.500, play many winning seasons, and qualify for 22 playoff in 46 years.

Because of various problems including competition from the Ravens, Bengals, and Steelers, the Browns have mostly finished fourth in their division since 1999. The club's best teams finished in second-place divisionally in 2002 and 2007, and appeared in one playoff game but lost it. In other seasons, the Browns lost the majority of their regular-season games despite hiring new coaches and making changes to improve the active roster of players.

Other than the Browns, the worst clubs in each division have been the Jets, Texans, and Chargers. The Jets appeared four times in back-to-back playoffs and played in two conference finals but failed to win them.

In addition, the Texans lost games three times in the divisional playoffs and once in the conference finals, while the 46-year-old Chargers competed for titles especially in the early 1980s and from 2006 to 2009. In sum, these teams have been inconsistent and not able to advance very far in postseasons because of not enough depth at key positions, coaching issues, and simply bad draft choices.

Statistically, the standard deviation is used to measure the variation or inequality in winning percentages between and within divisions of the AFC. The widest variation occurred among teams in the ND (0.09 or 9%) and then the ED (6%), WD (5%), and SD (4%). Although these were relatively small differences in deviations between divisions, the average winning percentages of the highest and lowest indicated, for example, that the ND's Browns compared to the Ravens' exceeded those of the ED's Dolphins and Jets, WD's Broncos and Chargers, and SD's Colts and Texans. Consequently, in evaluating and ranking winning percentages, ND teams have been the most unequal competitively among themselves in the conference.

Playoffs

Other than team relocations and franchise expansions, some specific but interesting things about the 46-year-old AFC have affected the sport and league in different ways. For example, each team plays the others in its respective division twice — home and away — during the regular season, in addition to 10 other games assigned to their schedule by the NFL. Two of these games are assigned on the basis of a particular team's final divisional standing from the previous season. The remaining eight games are split between the rosters of two other NFL divisions. This assignment shifts each year and follows a standard cycle.

At the end of each season, the top six teams in the conference continue to compete in the playoffs. These teams consist of the four division winners and the top two wild card teams. The AFC playoffs culminate in the AFC championship game with the winner receiving the Lamar Hunt Trophy. Then, the AFC and NFC champions play each other in the Super Bowl.

Based on their records in NFL regular seasons through 2016, the Steelers qualified for 29 playoffs and the Dolphins, Patriots, and Broncos each 22. In contrast to them, the Browns have been in one, Texans three, and Jaguars and Titans each six. Of 222 total playoffs, the ED ranks first with 69 or 31% of them, WD second with 67 or 30%, ND third with 54 or 25%, and SD fourth with 32 or 14%.

Regarding differences between the most and least successful within each division of the AFC, the Dolphins and Patriots have been in 10 more playoffs than the Jets, Steelers 28 more than the Browns, Colts fourteen more than the Texans, and Broncos nine more than the Chargers. From a historical perspective, these results indicate greater difficulty in getting into the playoffs among least competitive teams in the ND and SD in comparison to those in the ED and WD.

Division titles

According to Column 5 of Table A5.2, the 16 AFC clubs accumulated 132 division titles during their years in the league. From most to least, those in the WD won forty or 30% of the total, ED 39 or 29%, ND 34 or 26%, and SD 19 or 15%. More specifically, the Steelers ranked first in number of them as of 2016, Patriots second, and Broncos third, while the Texans and Titans tied for 12th and Jets and Jaguars for 14th, as the Browns finished 16th.

With respect to the distribution of their division titles, the Steelers won seven in the 1970s, two in the 1980s, five in the 1990s, and another seven between 2000 and 2015. While owned by businessman Dan Rooney, such outstanding head coaches as Chuck Noll and Bill Cowher challenged their players to win enough regular-season games to lead their division. Some of these players included Hall of Fame quarterback Terry Bradshaw, running backs Jerome Bettis and Franco Harris, receivers John Stallworth and Lynn Swann, and on defense, linebackers Jack Ham and Jack Lambert, cornerbacks Mel Blount and Ron Woodson, and defensive tackle Mean Joe Greene. Besides 1992 Coach of the Year Cowher, they won awards for being the best at their positions.

In division titles, the Steelers best season was in 2004. They finished 15-1, but were defeated 30-13 by the Baltimore Ravens after Pittsburgh's starting quarterback Tommy Maddox suffered an elbow injury. That, in turn, forced rookie Ben Roethlisberger into action who led the club to 14 consecutive wins and the ND title. Later, they lost to the Patriots 41-27 in the AFC championship game.

As a group, the Jets, Texans, Jaguars, and Titans have won ten total division titles and the Browns zero of them in a total of 116 regular seasons. Sequentially, the Jets were titlists in 1998 and 2000; Texans in 2011, 2012, and 2015; Jaguars in 1998 and 1999; and Titans in 2000, 2002, and 2008. With a 9-7 record and finishing second in the ND in 2002, the Browns qualified for the playoffs for the first time since returning to the NFL in 1999. On the road against the Steelers, Cleveland had a 33-21 lead with 5 minutes left in the game but its defense suffered a letdown allowing Pittsburgh to score 15 points to take a 36-33 lead in the final minute. However, time ran out and ended the Browns' season.

Eventually Patriots quarterback Tom Brady and Steelers Ben Roethlisberger will retire from the sport. This, in turn, will provide an opportunity for other ED and ND teams, respectively, to better compete and win a division title in the conference. The Colts' Andrew Luck and Titans' Marcus Mariota, for example, are young but very talented quarterbacks with the potential to lead their teams to victories along with such veterans as the Ravens' Joe Flacco and Chiefs' Alex Smith.

Conference titles

The 16 AFC teams in Table A5.2 won a total of 44 conference titles during their multiple seasons in the league. Of the four groups, ED clubs won 17 or 39% of them and those in the ND and WD each 12 for a total of 54%, and in the SD only three or 7%. The most and least successful have been, respectively the Patriots, Steelers, and Broncos each with eight titles but then the Jets, Browns, Texans, Jaguars, and Chiefs with zero.

The Patriots won the conference once each in the 1980s and 1990s but six times between 2000 and 2015; the Steelers four times in the 1970s, once in the 1980s, and in three seasons during the 2000s; and the Broncos once in the 1970s, three times in the 1980s, and twice each in the 1990s and 2000s. Ranked behind these teams are the Dolphins with five titles, Bills four, Raiders three, and with two each the Ravens, Bengals, and Colts.

Although they failed to win a conference championship through 2016, the Chiefs won six division titles and in 1993, advanced to the AFC championship game with a 28-20 decision. However, their magic run ended in Buffalo as the Bills won their fourth straight Lamar Hunt Trophy to advance to the Super Bowl. Kansas City head coaches Marv Levy and Hank Stram are in professional football's Hall of Fame along with such players as quarterbacks Len Dawson and Warren Moon, linebackers Bobby Bell, Willie Lanier and Derrick Thomas, and placekicker Jan Stenerud.

Some teams have recently improved and may eventually win either their first, second, third, or fourth conference title. These include the ND's Ravens and Bengals, SD's Texans and Colts, and WD's Chiefs and Raiders. But such inferior clubs as the ED's Bills and Jets, for example, struggle to be conference titlists because the Dolphins and Patriots are consistent and have too much talent, especially at key positions on both offense and defense, and also have excellent coaching staffs.

Super bowls

According to Column 8 in Table A5.2, the 16 AFC teams won a total of 21 Super Bowls through 2016. Among divisions, ND clubs won eight or 38% of the championships and those in the ED and WD each six for a total of 58%, and the SD one or 4%. While the most successful have been the Steelers, Patriots, and Broncos, nine conference teams have failed to win any Super Bowls.

With respect to their championships, players who won Super Bowl Most Valuable Player (MVP) awards include the Steelers' Franco Harris, Lynn Swann, Terry Bradshaw (twice), Hines Ward, and Santonio Holmes; Patriots' Tom Brady (three times) and Deion Branch; and Broncos' Terrell Davis, John Elway, and Von Miller. Some of these players were also NFL MVPs and/or defensive and offensive player of the year in the AFC.

Besides them, other clubs in the conference played in but lost one or more Super Bowls. The Broncos were defeated in five championship games, Bills four, Dolphins three, Bengals two, and the Colts, Titans, Raiders, and Chargers one each. Most interesting, Buffalo won the AFC in four consecutive seasons (1990–1993) but failed to win a championship despite head coach Marv Levy and Hall of Fame quarterback Jim Kelly, running back Thurman Thomas, wide receiver Andre Reed, and defensive end Bruce Smith.

After becoming the first team ever to play in three consecutive Super Bowls, the Bills were heavy underdogs facing the NFC Cowboys in a rematch at the Georgia Dome in Atlanta. Throughout the first half, the Bills played solid football taking a 13-6 lead into halftime. However, just 55 seconds into the third quarter, Thomas was stripped of the football by James Washington who returned it 47 yards for a game-tying touchdown. As a result of Buffalo's mistake, Dallas scored 17 more points and won the game 30-13.

In the 2015–2016 season, the Broncos had the top ranked defense in the NFL and faced the Carolina Panthers, who had the league's best offense. In most Super Bowl match ups with the top defense and top offense facing each other, the defense won. During the game, Denver's defense frequently harassed Panthers' quarterback Cam Newton while the Broncos' Peyton Manning led the offense. Winning its third Super Bowl, Denver's Von Miller had five tackles, two and half sacks, two forced fumbles, and was named the game's MVP as Manning rode off into the sunset with a championship just like Broncos' quarterback John Elway did 17 years earlier.

Regarding those who have never won a Super Bowl through 2016, the most likely team to become champion within a few seasons, in my judgement, is the Texans. With three-time defensive player of the year J.J. Watt, and recruiting an efficient but stable rookie or veteran quarterback to lead its offense, Houston will be more competitive and a threat to win the SD and then the AFC and eventually a Super Bowl.

Total performances

This result — or the total performance (TP) for each team — includes their division and conference titles plus championships as listed in Columns 5–8 of Table A5.2. Among 196 TPs, ED clubs won 62 or 32% of them followed by the WD's 57 or 29%, ND's 54 or 28%, and SD's 23 or 11%.

While the Steelers ranked first with 35 TPs, Patriots second with 29 and Broncos third with 26 as of 2016, the Browns had zero and the Jets and Jaguars each had two. Other teams with at least 14 TPs are the Dolphins, Colts, and Raiders. Considering only their average winning percentage and number of playoffs combined as a measure of their performances, those with the most impressive results have been the Steelers followed closely by the Patriots and then the Broncos, Dolphins, Colts, Ravens, Chiefs, Raiders, Bengals, and Titans. In contrast to them, the Browns, Texans, and Jaguars had the worst-ranked results of the group through the league's 2015–2016 season.

After sports experts researched data and published the history of all teams, some of these articles reported the most dominant and/or successful AFC teams since 1970. To rank them, different criteria were used including the Elovation App (Elo) rating, which focuses on wins and losses and margin of victory and also whether home or road games and strength of teams' opponent. Based on this metric and football information from various sources, among the best — in chronological order — are the following clubs from the AFC.[10]

• At 14-0 in the regular season and Super Bowl VIII champions, the 1972 Dolphins are a no-brainer. Not only is this the best Dolphins team, a strong case can be made that it has been the greatest NFL team ever. The club was filled with such Hall of Famers as players' Larry Csonka, Nick Buoniconti, Bob Griese and Paul Warfield, and also coach Don Shula. However, the biggest feather in their cap is that they remain the only group in NFL history to go through the regular season and playoffs undefeated. Many have tried and several came close, but no team has matched this feat for more than four decades and counting. While the team's Elo blend equaled 1754, its peak and end were each 1776 with a mean of 1711.

• The Steelers have several candidates for being great teams, but the 1975 season shines bright among the franchise's six Super Bowl winners. This team was loaded with Hall of Famers and impressively won consecutive division titles and championships, thus framing a 1970s dynasty the game had not seen before. The Steelers could beat you with quarterback Terry Bradshaw's arm passing or running back Franco Harris' yards from scrimmage. Eight of 14 regular-season opponents scored 10 points or fewer on what became the Steel Curtain defense. In three playoff games, opposing offenses averaged 12.3 points against the Steelers. While wide receiver Lynn Swann had his breakout in the Super Bowl, Harris played his best all year. Everything fell into place in this season. The team's Elo blend equaled 1760, peak and end each 1777, and mean 1724.

• Hall of Fame quarterback John Elway was able to ride off into the sunset after winning his second straight championship with the 1998 Denver Broncos. The team finished its regular season with a 14-2 record in the WD, defeated the Dolphins in the divisional playoffs and then the Jets for the AFC title, and finally the Falcons in Super Bowl XXXIII. However, while this group only managed to hit a peak Elo rating of 1784 and finish the year with a mark of 1781, because these Broncos were able to acquire an average mark of 1747, their Elo blend score wound up being just higher — 1771 — than that of the 1989 San Francisco 49ers. Based on website http://www.five thirtyeight.com's calculations, this Broncos team is the fourth best in the league's history.

• Since coach Bill Belichick and quarterback Tom Brady came together to form one of the greatest head coach–quarterback combinations the NFL has ever seen, the New England Patriots have had some pretty special teams. However, if we look at it from a strictly Elo perspective, the 2004 team finds itself in some pretty historic company. After finishing 14-2 in its division and toppling the Steelers to win the AFC championship and then the NFC-champion Carolina Panthers in Super Bowl XXXIX, these Patriots finished with a season-ending (and peak) Elo of 1817, as well as a mean score of 1743. Once averaged out, New England's Elo blend of 1792 is enough to make this team among the best since 1920.

• Considering the 2007 Patriots came up short in the Super Bowl, it would be easy to find their place at the top of history's best in the AFC to be controversial. However, do not forget that prior to losing their final game of the season, this team finished the regular season 16-0, scored 38.6 points per game, and came within one "Helmet Catch" of running the table. The Patriots ended the year with an Elo rating of 1824 — and an average mark of 1797 — but at the height of their domination, their peak Elo was a whopping 1849. Therefore, if one were to go off Elo ratings alone, New England's blended rating of 1824 would make it among the best teams in the history of the NFL.

For various reasons such as lacking talented players, coaching problems and/or both of them, some AFC teams had terrible performances in their regular seasons. Several of these clubs were evaluated based on their ability to score points and win games. In chronological order, the following is a list of a few of the worst clubs in the conference's history as of its 2016 season.[11]

• Just before the start of the 1971 NFL season, Bills head Coach John Rauch called it quits and resigned, which forced Buffalo to hand the reins of the team over to their pro personnel director Harvey Johnson. Of course, things turned out about as well as expected when making a big change like that immediately before the club's first game. The Bills offense and its defense both ranked last in the league during the season. Despite having future NFL great O.J. Simpson on the team, who rushed for just 750 yards that season, the Bills did not accomplish much on either side of the ball and finished 1-13 in the conference. The result was so disastrous, forcing the Bills to change their offensive philosophy and run the ball more — a lot more — the following season.

• During the 1973 NFL season, the Houston Oilers' offense stunk. They could not run the ball — finishing last in the conference in rushing with 1,388 yards — failed to get many first downs — managing only 193 — and they could not protect their quarterback Dan Pastorini, who routinely played with broken ribs in the early 1970s and became the first quarterback to wear a flak jacket. Furthermore, the team was not much better on defense, giving up 447 points that season. Those things combined created a recipe for failure, which was exactly what the 1973 season was for the Oilers.

• The Tampa Bay Buccaneers debut season (1976–1977) was football's equivalent of the 1962 MLB's New York Mets but without the wit of manager Casey Stengel to make things a bit more entertaining. At 0-14 in the regular season, the team was shut out five times and averaged fewer than nine points per game. Its' defense was almost as futile with a margin of defeat of 20 points per game. Tampa Bay's quarterback, Steve Spurrier, threw only seven touchdown passes all season. His longest completion was 38 yards. Despite switching to the NFC's CD, the Bucs carried their losing momentum into the 1977–1978 season, losing another twelve, to begin their franchise history of 26 consecutive games in losses. "The coach (John McKay) stopped talking to us after the third game," defensive lineman Pat Toomay told the *Columbus Dispatch* in 2001. "During the week, he wanted nothing to do with us. I can't blame him, really. We had so many guys get injured that nobody knew who was hurt and who wasn't. By the end of the season we were getting guys out of the Canadian league and off the streets."

• The Patriots were bad both on and off of the football field. During the 1990 season, they finished 1-15-0 by scoring just 181 points while giving up 446. This was the worst point differential in the NFL during the 1990s. If that was not bad enough, the club also managed to spoil the only win they had during the season. After beating the Indianapolis Colts 16-14 in week two of the season, New England's tight end Zeke Mowatt, running back Robert Perryman, and wide receiver Michael Timpson were accused of sexually harassing Lisa Olson of the *Boston Globe* in the Patriots' locker room. Basically, the season could not have gone any worse for the Patriots.

• Despite the fact that the Indianapolis Colts had six-time Pro Bowl running back Eric Dickerson in their backfield in 1991, they were unable to manufacture any offense. They scored just 143 points, the lowest total of any NFL team in a 16-game season until that year. Things actually got so bad that Dickerson more or less told fans to stop coming to games. "I wouldn't come out and watch a [Colts] game," he said. "No way I'd pay to see someone play the way we are." Fortunately, Indianapolis squeaked out a one-point win against the New York Jets in week 11. Otherwise, they very well could have finished 0-16 and gone down as the worst NFL team ever.

• The San Diego Chargers were awful — in fact, real bad — when it came to gaining rushing yards but nevertheless, they were forced to rush a lot since Ryan Leaf was their quarterback at the time. They ended the 2000 NFL season with just 1,062 yards on the ground, making them the least successful rushing team of all time. They actually lost a handful of games by three points or less including three games by a point and two others by two points but, unfortunately, a loss is a loss regardless of how many points you score. And the Chargers ended the season with 15 losses. The only good thing about their results was allowing them to draft college running back LaDainian Tomlinson the following spring.

LEAGUE ECONOMICS

In this section, there are data and other information about the commercial and financial aspects of franchises in the AFC and their significance from an economic perspective. Besides attendances at home and away games, anything else that affects teams' income, market value, and wealth is included in the analysis, quantified, and discussed. In other words, the NFL is an organization consisting of for-profit enterprises that operate to compete each season typically within a division of a conference and seek to improve their performances in current and future games.

Franchise Financials

Forbes magazine's sports editors' published financial data of AFC franchises as of their 2015–2016 season. As denoted in Columns 2–7 of Table A5.3, these amounts include, respectively, their estimated market value — which is based on the current stadium deal without deduction for debt — and also total revenue, operating income — earnings before interest, taxes, depreciation, and amortization (EBITDA) — gate receipts, debt-to-value (D/V) percentages, and players' expenses. For each of four divisions, the information reveals the cash flows, financial status, and wealth of these teams both individually and relative to each other as a group. The following section identifies and highlights the data.[12]

In Column 2 of Table A5.3 is the estimated market value of each AFC team, by division, as of its 2015 season. Ranked from most to least, ED clubs averaged $2.50 billion, SD's $2.18 billion, WD's $2.11 billion, and ND's $2.01 billion. While the Patriots were first at $3.40 billion, Jets second at $2.75 billion, and Texans third at $2.60 billion, least in value included the Browns at $1.85 billion, Bengals at $1.67 billion, and Bills at $1.50 billion. In comparison to the typical club's market value of $2.20 billon, only seven or approximately 43% of the group actually exceeded that amount.

Several factors caused differences in teams' market values. In no specific order, these were their history, tradition, and success in the league, being located at a site within a big, midsized, or small market, size of each's fan base, number of titles and championships, and such financial data as their revenue, operating income, and gate receipts. Based on these and other reasons, they ranged in value by almost $2 billion.

To compare their standard deviation or variation in market values, the highest within groups was ED teams ($793 million) and lowest among those in the WD ($216 million), SD ($295 million), and then ND ($305 million). This means inequality or greater deviation in these AFC franchise's values existed in 2015–2016 to a greater extent between the Patriots and other ED teams than among clubs in the other divisions. Although these were just estimates, the amounts influence such things as the clubs' relative wealth, economic power in the league, and future price if offered for sale to potential investors. Interestingly, there were no teams whose market value fell below the conference's average deviation of $455 million.

Each team's revenue — net of stadium revenues used for debt payments — is displayed in Column 3 of Table A5.3. While the Patriots had the highest at $523 million followed by the Jets' $423 million and Texans' $416 million, the three lowest-ranked in the group were the Bengals' $329 million at fourteenth, Bills' $326 million at fifteenth, and Raiders' $301 million at sixteenth. The differences in amounts occurred for several reasons including their home attendances, range in non-premium and premium ticket prices, winning percentage in games, and number of basketball fans in the area.

Because of various demographic and sport-specific factors, there were disparities in teams' revenue. While the conference's standard deviation equaled $52 million, ED teams had the highest variation in revenue at $86 million and then the SD's at $37 million, WD's at $35 million and lastly the ND's at $23 million. The latter division's franchises had the smallest difference in revenue because similar amounts existed for the Colts, Jaguars, and Titans but not for the Texans. Besides win–loss records in the regular season, the deviations in revenue reflect the population and growth in population of their markets, popularity at home, and per capita income and wealth and also the number and type of jobs of local households.

In Table A5.3, Column 4 contains the operating income or EBITDA of AFC teams as of their 2015 season. For the group, it averaged $80 million. From most to least in amounts by division, ED clubs averaged $99 million, SD's $90 million, ND's $71 million, and WD's $62 million. Because of excessive payments for players' salaries and other types of expenses, the Browns, Raiders, and Bills had the three smallest EBITDA's while the Patriots, Texans, and Ravens earned the most income by operating efficiently. For various reasons, the Bengals, Chargers, and Dolphins were also marginally but not overwhelmingly efficient along with some others within different areas of NFL markets.

While $43 million was the average deviation in operating income of these AFC teams, the ED's equaled $81 million, SD's $27 million, ND's $22 million, and WD's $14 million. The gap or variation between the most and least EBITDA within divisions occurred, respectively, for the Patriots and Bills, Texans and Colts, Ravens and Browns, and Broncos and Raiders. Simply put, their earnings varied because each of them operated differently while applying historical and also new business practices, strategies, and tactics of the sports industry.

Each AFC teams' 2015 gate receipts — in millions of dollars — appear in Column 5 of Table A5.3. While the conference's average was $59 million, the Patriots had the most ($99 million) and then the Jets ($77 million) and Broncos ($71 million). In contrast to these amounts, the Raiders ($40 million),

Bengals and Titans (each $48 million), and Bills ($50 million) had the smallest gate receipts in the NFL that year.

The dispersion or disparity in gate receipts was greatest among ED clubs ($21 million) compared to WD teams ($12 million) and also to those in the ND ($8 million) and SD ($6 million). Because of the large gap in amounts between, for example, the ED's Patriots and Bills, that division's standard deviation exceeds that of the WD's Broncos and Raiders, ND's Ravens and Bengals, and SD's Texans and Titans. Simply put, the Boston–Cambridge– Newton, Denver–Aurora–Lakewood, Houston–The Woodlands–Sugar Land, and Baltimore–Columbia–Towson areas are midsized-to-large and also more prosperous football markets than the majority of others.

The sixth column of Table A5.3 includes the D/V percentages of each AFC franchise in 2015. On average, the conference's was 9% or, in amount, approximately $198 million per team based on estimated market values in column 1. Among each group, the ED's averaged 15%, ND's 9 percent, SD's 5%, and WD's 7%. Although six clubs had debt percentages less than 7%, the D/V ratios exceeded 10% each for the Bills, Dolphins, Jets, Ravens, Browns, and Raiders.

As discussed for other variables in the table, the standard deviations of D/V were unequal among divisions and franchises within divisions. ED teams, for example, had the greatest variation at 7% and then those in the WD at 4% and ND and SD each at 2%. In order to reduce their ratios for financial reasons and operate more effectively, several teams needed to reform themselves as businesses in order to generate higher market values and/or record less amount of debt in accounts on their balance sheet.

As reported in *Forbes* for being an important, necessary, and periodic payment from an operations perspective, Column 7 in Table A5.3 gives the players' expenses — including benefits and bonuses — of these 16 teams in 2015. For the conference, they totaled approximately $2.9 billion or about $182 million per team. On average, the ED's was $192 million, WD's $184 million, ND's $182 million, and SD's $170 million. While the Bills, Chargers, and Steelers ranked highest, the Ravens, Jaguars, Titans, and Raiders each paid less than $170 million in players' expenses. Given these amounts, neither group of clubs had an outstanding roster of players and, other than the Steelers, won enough games in the regular season to qualify for the playoffs. Indeed, six of them failed to be competitive and participate in the conference's postseason partly because of their relatively small investment in players' salaries.

Players' expenses were different and also significantly deviated between the three AFC divisions. From most to least in variation among the groups — as measured by their standard deviations — these included the SD's $13 million and then WD's $12 million, ND's 11 million, and ED's $10 million. Such amounts denote that the greatest disparity in payments occurred because of the Texans' $182 million versus the Jaguars' $152 million in the SD whereas the range in players' expenses within the WD, ND, and ED equaled, respectively, only $30 million between the Chargers and Raiders, $26 million between the Steelers and Ravens, and $24 million between the Bills and Patriots. Thus, not all AFC teams with the highest revenues and/or largest market values always compensated their players more than rivals within their division.

STADIUMS

As of the NFL's 2015–2016 season, the sixteen AFC teams played their home games in venues that differed in age, cost and market value, and also in such other ways as location, capacity, and ownership. Based on various criteria including their amenities, concessions, and sightlines, they have been ranked from best to worst overall, most to least accessible, and highest to lowest as facilities to entertain spectators at games. Given those viewpoints, this section provides some data and other information regarding the facilities of the conference's clubs and discusses specific characteristics about them.[13]

Among teams' home sites within each division as of the AFC, they ranged in age as follows: within the conference's ED, from the Jets' 6-year-old MetLife Stadium in New York to the Bills' 43-year-old Ralph Wilson Stadium in Buffalo; within the ND, from the Steelers' 15-year-old Heinz Field in Pittsburgh to the Ravens' 18-year-old M&T Bank Stadium in Baltimore; within the SD, from the Colts' 8-year-old Lucas Oil Stadium in Indianapolis to the Jaguars' 21-year-old EverBank Field in Jacksonville; and within the WD, from the Broncos' 15-year-old Sports Authority Field in Denver to the Raiders' 50-year-old O.com Coliseum in Oakland. Of teams' 16 different venues in the AFC, one or approximately 6% of them is privately owned and five or 31% publicly. Furthermore, the other 10 or

63% are jointly owned by the team and a municipality and/or state organization.

Their construction costs ranked from being relatively cheap to very expensive. From the least to most costly within the conference's ED and then ND, SD and WD, respectively, amounts were $22 million to erect Ralph Wilson Stadium in Buffalo for the Bills compared to $1.6 billion for MetLife Stadium in New York for the Jets (and NFC New York Giants); from $220 million to construct M&T Bank Stadium in Baltimore for the Ravens to $450 million for Paul Brown Stadium in Cincinnati for the Bengals; from $134 million to build EverBank Field in Jacksonville for the Jaguars to $720 million for Lucas Oil Stadium in Indianapolis for the Colts; and $25 million to erect the O.com Coliseum in Oakland for the Raiders to $364 million for Sports Authority Field in Denver for the Broncos.

Regarding the most likely replacements or renovation of current venues in the AFC, the Raiders' O.com Coliseum, Chargers' Qualcomm Stadium, and Bills' Ralph Wilson Stadium — according to fans and several football experts — are old and lack modern amenities of newer venues, have tight or uncomfortable seats and tight space in the concourses, and simply outdated in their architecture and personality to host NFL games.

Recently *Forbes* sports editors assigned economic values to venues of teams in the AFC. From lowest to highest within divisions, respectively, amounts in the ED were $139 million for Ralph Wilson Stadium in Buffalo to $1.43 billion for MetLife Stadium in New York; in the ND, from $142 million for Paul Brown Stadium in Cincinnati to $280 million for M&T Bank Stadium in Baltimore; in the SD, from $193 million for EverBank Field in Jacksonville to $394 million for NFG Stadium in Houston; and in the WD, from $107 million for O.com Coliseum in Oakland to $292 million for Sports Authority Field in Denver. For each division, ED teams' venues averaged $637 million in value, ND's $220 million, SD's $258 million, and WD's $329 million [14]

According to their standard deviations, teams' stadiums in the ED and ND, respectively, had the most and least variability in construction costs and estimated values. Nevertheless, because of increasing real estate prices in urban areas and popularity of the sport in America, most of them will likely appreciate economically, particularly those within the largest markets and wealthiest metropolitan areas.

In various studies, NFL stadiums have been ranked by various football analysts and sports journalists in the media with respect to their location and different attributes and problems. Although results vary given each study's parameters, a few venues rank among the best, while some others are placed in the worst group. For example, the most attractive, entertaining, and well-structured facilities within the AFC based on their name, aesthetics, and experience for fans are Lucas Oil Stadium and M&T Bank Stadium.

As reported in the *Stadium Journey*, the two best buildings were rated highest for these reasons[15]:

"Lucas Oil Stadium [in Indianapolis for the Colts] offers a near perfect game day experience. Here you'll find outstanding fans, a fantastic downtown location, energetic game day experience, reasonable pricing, and some of the friendliest game day staff that you will ever encounter. It all comes together to create one of the best stadium experiences on the planet."

For why the Ravens' stadium ranked second in the conference, the editor provided these comments:

"From the Ravenswalk area outside of the stadium to the purple seats and concourse lighting, the Ravens have set a fine stage for enjoyment of NFL football. Expect the games to be loud inside the walls of the stadium. Every play, whether it is on defense or offense, will have the fans screaming at every detail. Even special teams plays are paid attention in great detail. The fans are knowledgeable about all aspects of the game."

In another study, two of the lowest-ranked AFC facilities were the Raiders' O.com Coliseum and Dolphins' Sun Life Stadium. Among others in the conference, the former ranked fifteenth (thirtieth in the NFL) and the latter fourteenth (twenty-ninth in the league). The study's author evaluated each of them, respectively, as follows:[16]

"The nostalgic part of me loves that there's still an NFL stadium [Qualcomm] that has infield dirt for the first few weeks of the season. The rational part of me says, hey bub, it's 2015. Surely we can figure out a way around literally playing on a sandlot."

Regarding why Sun Life Stadium ranked almost last in the conference and league, comments were as follows:

"The Marlins have a better stadium than you. The Marlins! This stadium was crumbling when I went to the 2002 Orange Bowl (which I was stunned to find out wasn't played at the Orange Bowl). I can't imagine what it's like now. Renovations are underway at least. Going up a jam-packed, four-story escalator to the upper deck was one of the more terrifying sporting experiences of my life and that's coming from someone who once wore at Art Monk jersey to The Vet."

Fan cost index

For several years, a Chicago-based company named Team Marketing Report (TMR) has prepared and published a Fan Cost Index (FCI) for the home games of teams in professional sports. To attend a game for a typical family with two kids, an FCI includes the cost of four average-priced tickets, two cheapest-priced draft beers, four each lowest-priced soft drinks and hot dogs, parking for one vehicle, and two each game programs and least-expensive, adult-sized adjustable caps. Costs are determined by telephone calls with team representatives, venues, and concessionaires and from questions asked during interviews.[17]

In the 2015–2016 NFL season, the average FCI for a family to attend a regular season game of an AFC team was $481. While Patriots' games each cost $652, the Jaguars had the conference's lowest FCI at $367. Among divisions, the average from most to least was ED teams at $552, WD's $474, ND's $469, and SD's $432. The order from ranking them first to fourth occurred, in part, because FCIs of the Dolphins, Patriots, and Jets each exceeded $500 while those of such teams as the Jaguars and Titans were each below $400.

For specific items in TMR's 2015–2016 FCI, the approximate range in amounts from most to least expensive — or first compared to 16th across the AFC — were listed as follows: average ticket, Patriots $130 to Jaguars $61; average premium ticket, Patriots $566 to Raiders $148; beer, Raiders $9.75 to Jets/Texans/Bengals/Browns each $5; soft drink, Ravens $8 to Jets $3; hot dog, Bills $7 to Ravens $3; parking, Patriots/Ravens/Steelers each $40 to

Dolphins/Colts each $20; and for a cap, Dolphins $25.99 to Jaguars $14.99. Based on economics principles, these prices were set by teams and/or vendors to sell enough units to maximize revenue from their sales at home games in the stadiums.

From the NFL's 2011–2012 to 2015–2016 season, there were some significant increases but also relatively small and even decreases in FCIs of teams in the AFC. For examples of these changes in fans' costs, the Bills' FCI rose from $361 to $494 or approximately 36% but the Bengals' from $397 to only $402 or about 1%, while the Jets' declined from $617 to $543 or 12%. Because of inflation, number of — and amount spent — by families at games in arenas, local economic conditions and other factors, the majority of teams and/or vendors raised their prices each year rather than keeping them constant or reducing amounts.

In evaluating year-to-year FCIs between, for example, the AFC's 2014–2015 and 2015–2016 seasons, the Dolphins' increased the most, in other words, from $398 to $520 or approximately 30%. Alternatively, fans' costs fell for home games of the Jets, Browns, Titans, and Chargers, but remained the same for those of the Colts' at $462. Thus, there were different payments for tickets and other things by families to attend conference teams' home games at their stadiums especially from 2011 to 2016.

ORGANIZATION HIGHLIGHTS

Besides regular-season and post-season games, the AFC and its franchises are involved in — and affected by — community events and also business-related and government affairs, news, and projects. Because these things and other activities influence the division, conference, and/or league in different but perhaps important and historic ways, following are a few of them from the academic and popular literature.[18]

First, in games between teams in the conferences since 1970, the AFC's Ravens, Bengals, Broncos, Chiefs, Dolphins, Patriots, Raiders, and Steelers have winning records. In the NFC, winners include the Cowboys, Eagles, Giants, and 49ers but not others such as the Cardinals, Falcons, Lions, Panthers, Packers, and Saints. Among all franchises in the NFL as of its' 2013–2014 season, the difference in total victories is 101 — excluding eleven ties — with AFC clubs ahead in wins of those within the NFC. During specific seasons, the

AFC won more games than the NFC in seven of them in the 1970s, four in the 1980s, five in the 1990s, and eight from 2000 to 2013.

Second, during late 2016, Oakland's mayor Libby Schaaf announced that the city reached a framework agreement with the Ronnie Lott group of investors for a new stadium, with the hopes of keeping the Raiders in northern California. The framework agreement, however, did not include the Raiders, nor has Raiders owner Mark Davis agreed to stay in Oakland. The agreement needs to be approved by the Board of Supervisors and the Oakland City Council before the group could move forward. Nevertheless, Davis and the Raiders have a financing plan in place for a $1.9 billion stadium to be built in Las Vegas after the Nevada state legislature approved a tax plan in October 2016 to raise $750 million toward the project. Nevada Governor Brian Sandoval signed the bill, clearing the way for the stadium, which would also be used by the University of Las Vegas's football team.

Third, San Diego Chargers chairman Dean Spanos and his group involved in the stadium effort were not surprised by the failed vote in November 2016 on the team's proposed $1.8 billion downtown stadium and the convention center citizens' initiative. Despite spending more than $10 million to promote the campaign, the Chargers received just 43% approval from city voters. Measure C, however, required two-thirds of the vote for approval. Instead of pursuing a new stadium deal in San Diego or a massive overhaul of dilapidated Qualcomm Stadium, the Chargers decided to partner with Los Angeles Rams owner Stan Kroenke on the Inglewood stadium project. Besides securing land for a practice facility, the Chargers agreed to host home games at the 30,000-seat StubHub Center in nearby Carson, California, for two seasons until joining the Rams and sharing their new $2.6 billion stadium in 2019.

Fourth, the Buffalo Bills have been playing at Ralph Wilson Stadium (originally Rich Stadium) since 1973. Until recently, the organization was in no rush to build a new stadium. However, NFL Commissioner Roger Goodell's remarks about the team's future moved the Bills into considering the possibility. Speaking on WGR-AM in Buffalo during June 2016, Bills owner Terry Pegula said the NFL made it clear that a new stadium plan probably should be part of the franchise's goals. According to Pegula, "I think they [NFL] think we need a new stadium, that's where they're coming from, so you need to listen to that and you make your own judgment. Our stadium is one of the older venues in the league. We're not going to make any hasty decisions, but we're evaluating."

Fifth, Jacksonville Jaguars owner Shad Khan has no intention of moving his franchise to somewhere in the Midwest. This is not a surprise to anyone in Jacksonville who knows what Khan has done with the franchise since he purchased it in November 2011 for $770 million. He spent $31 million of his own money to finance improvements to EverBank Field — $11 million to renovate the locker room and weight room and $20 million to partially pay for the $63 million video board/pools project. In addition, he supposedly paid one-half of the $90 million project to upgrade club seats and add an indoor practice facility and amphitheater outside the south end of the stadium. In total, that is approximately $76 million to improve a stadium owned by the city.

Sixth, for the NFL's recent season, the three AFC teams with the most and least average attendances at their home games (in thousands) were each, respectively, the Jets (78.1), Broncos (76.7), and Chiefs (73.7), but alternatively the Bengals (60.5), Chargers (57.0), and Raiders (54.5). While the Broncos filled Sports Authority Field with fans as did the Jets at MetLife Stadium and Chiefs at Arrowhead Stadium to about 95% of capacity, the Bengals' Paul Brown Stadium was at 92% of its capacity, Chargers' Qualcomm Stadium 80%, and Raiders' O.com Coliseum 86%.

Seventh, the 2017 NFL Draft depends on teams' records and using their strength of schedule as a tiebreaker in order to determine the draft order. Regarding AFC teams, the Browns draft first, Jaguars fourth and Titans fifth, and lastly the Steelers 28th, Chiefs 30th, and Patriots 30-second. Each of the former group needs positional players including a young quarterback for the Browns, a tackle, guard, and safety for the Jaguars, and a tight end for the Titans.

Eighth, with 719,000 television households, Las Vegas is larger than only four markets with NFL teams: Green Bay, Buffalo, New Orleans, and Jacksonville. However, it does have some advantages over other cities from the NFL's perspective because tourists there might buy tickets to NFL games while in town, and the market has historically strong television ratings for NFL games. Most importantly, Las Vegas has a plan in place for a new stadium which would be financed with $150 million from the Sands Corporation and $750 million from taxpayers. If the Nevada legislature approves an expenditure of $750 million, the NFL seems ready to accept the deal.

Ninth, according to one sports analyst, the AFC has been better than the NFC since 2000 because of the following reasons: its' teams have won more pro bowls and they draft better defensive rookies; the conference has New England Patriots coach Bill Belichick and quarterback Tom Brady; and AFC clubs have the best home field advantages, more NFL MVPs, and won more Super Bowls.

Tenth, FTW magazine ranked the 32 NFL teams by wins over the last decade and while New England, Indianapolis, and Pittsburgh lead the pack with Cleveland, St. Louis, and Oakland at the bottom, what about each of the NFL's eight divisions? Which one dominates and which one is the four-team equivalent of the Raiders? For example, the AFC ND and NFC ED have clearly been the two most consistent divisions, while New England's 122 wins — 37% of its division's total — prop up an otherwise mediocre AFC ED. The recent power of Indianapolis and Houston override problems at Jacksonville and Tennessee. As expected, no division has averaged more than nine wins per season and none has averaged less than seven, a nod to both the guarantee of a 0.500 record in divisional play and overall parity in the league.

NOTES

1. For the history of the APFA (renamed NFL in 1922) and its various seasons and teams and their coaches and players, see Jozsa FP Jr. (2016). *National Football League Franchises: Team Performances, Financial Consequences.* Lanham, MD: Lexington; and also Quirk J and Fort RD, (1992). *Pay Dirt: The Business of Professional Team Sports.* Princeton, NJ: Princeton University Press.

2. These facts are in the *2014 Official NFL Record & Fact Book.* New York, NY: National Football League (2014).

3. Jozsa FP Jr. and Guthrie JJ Jr. (1999). *Relocating Teams and Expanding Leagues in Professional Sports: How the Major Leagues Respond to Market Conditions.* Westport, CT: Quorum Books.

4. Football information and data is available on such websites as http://www.nfl.com, http://www.sports-reference.com, http://www.sportsencyclopedia.com, and http://www.pro-football-reference.com.

5. For demographic data and other details about actual and potential sports markets, see such references as "The 382 Metropolitan Statistical Areas of the United

States of America," http://www.en.wikipedia.org [cited 12 October 2016]; "Population Estimates 2015," http://www.census.gov [cited 12 November 2016]; and "Top U.S. Metropolitan Areas by Population, 1790–2010," http://www.peakbagger.com [cited 5 December 2016].

6. Standard Deviation (SD) is the measure of spread of the numbers in a set of data from its mean value. It is represented using the symbol σ (sigma). The SD can also measure variability or volatility in a given set of data. Find the mean, variance (sigma squared), and SD of given numbers by using the free arithmetic standard deviation calculator online. Or, enter 'n' number of values in a calculator for the SD, mean and variance See "Standard Deviation Calculator," http://www.easycalculation.com [cited 3 January 2017].

7. *Idem*, "The 382 Metropolitan Statistical Areas of the United States of America."

8. For other details about provisions between the league and players union, see the "NFL Collective Bargaining Agreement," http://www.nfllabor.com [cited 24 December 2016].

9. See "Team Encyclopedias and Records," http://www.pro-football-reference.com [cited 1 December 2016].

10. The Elo rating is a metric for evaluating a team's skill level at any given moment. Elo is not the only power rating, but it's a relatively simple algorithm with an elegant, endlessly customizable design that makes the most of the information it receives. See Neil Paine, "The Best NFL Teams of All Time, According to Elo," http://www.fivethirtyeight.com [cited 23 December 2016]; "Picking the Best Team Ever for All 32 NFL Franchises," http://www.espn.com [cited 23 December 2016]; Daniel Zimmer, "All 32 NFL Franchises Statistically Ranked in All-Time Greatness." http://www.nflspinzone.com [cited 14 January 2017].

11. Two references are Angel Diaz, "The 25 Worst NFL Teams of All Time," http://www.complex.com [cited 29 December 2016] and "Worst NFL Teams of All Time," http://www.espn.com [cited 29 December 2016].

12. For financial data about teams, see Mike Ozanian, "2016 NFL Valuations," http://www.forbes.com [cited 1 December 2016].

13. Stadium data and other information about them appear in such sources as "NFL Stadium Comparisons," http://www.stadiumsofprofootball.com [cited 25 December 2016] and "Tour Every NFL Stadium," http://www.espn.com [cited 25 December 2016].

14. See Table A5.3 in the Appendix for the estimated economic value of all AFC teams as of their 2015–2016 season.

15. Readings include Paul Swaney, "2015 NFL Stadium Experience Rankings," http://www.scout.com [cited 31 December 2016] and Dan Muret, "Ranking All NFL Stadiums," http://www.sportingnews.com [cited 10 January 2017].

16. Please read Chase C, "Ranking the Best and Worst NFL Stadium, From No. 1 (Lambeau) to 31 (Soldier)," http://www.ftwusatoday.com [cited 31 December 2016] and "Tour Every NFL Stadium," http://www.espn.com [cited 25 December 2016].

17. "Fan Cost Index," http://www.teammarketingreport.com [cited 16 November 2016] and "Team Marketing Report — NFL 2016," http://www.teammarket ing.com [cited 15 January 2017].

18. The references for this section include: *Idem, 2014 Official NFL Record & Fact Book*, pp. 518–522; Ratto R, "The 'Raiders Stadium Deal' That Isn't a Stadium Deal at All," http://www.csnbayarea.com [cited 1 January 2017]; "Oakland Mayor Announces Framework for Stadium Agreement," http://www.espn.com [cited 2 January 2017]; Williams E, "Failed Stadium Vote Leaves Little Time to Mull Options," http://www.espn.com [cited 2 January 2017]; Dragon T, "Buffalo Bills Evaluating Potential New Stadium Options," http://www.nfl.com [cited 2 January 2017]; DiRocco M, "Shad Khan: Jaguars Moving to St. Louis Isn't a Possibility," http://www.espn.com [cited 2 January 2017]; "NFL Attendance — 2016," http://www.espn.com [cited 2 January 2017]; Lance Zierlein, "2017 NFL Draft Order and Needs for Every Team," http://www.nfl. com [cited 2 January 2017]; Smith MD, "Las Vegas Would be the NFL's Fifth-Smallest Media Market," http://www.profootballtalknbcsports.com [cited 2 January 2017]; Daniel Wolf, "10 Reasons Why the AFC is Better Than the NFC Since 2000," http://www.bleacherreport.com [cited 2 January 2017]; Chase C, "The AFC North Has Been the NFL's Best Division in Past Decade," http://www.ftwusatoday.com [cited 2 January 2017].

Chapter 6

NATIONAL FOOTBALL CONFERENCE

HISTORY

Established in 1920, the American Professional Football Conference — renamed American Professional Football Association (APFA) and after two years the National Football League (NFL) — originally consisted of 14 teams. These were the Akron Pros, Canton Bulldogs, Cleveland Tigers, Columbus Panhandlers, and Dayton Triangles from Ohio; Chicago Tigers, Decatur Staleys, Racine Cardinals (based in Chicago but took the name of a local street), and Rock Island Independents from Illinois; Hammond Pros and Muncie Flyers from Indiana; Buffalo All-Americans and Rochester Jeffersons from New York; and Detroit Heralds from Michigan.[1]

During 1921–1932, a few clubs disbanded or moved while others joined the league such as the Green Bay Packers in 1921, Oorang Indians in 1922, Frankford Yellow Jackets in 1924, New York Giants in 1925, Portsmouth Spartans in 1930, and Boston Braves in 1932. When the Philadelphia Eagles, Pittsburgh Pirates, and Cincinnati Reds became new members in 1933, the NFL divided itself into the Eastern Division (ED) and Western Division (WD) each with five teams.

In 1950, the divisions were replaced respectively by the American Conference (AC) — renamed Eastern Conference (EC) in 1953 — and National Conference (NC) — renamed Western Conference (WC) also in

1953. The latter group consisted of six teams, which ranged east to west from Baltimore to Los Angeles and San Francisco and north to south from Green Bay to Chicago and Detroit. Meanwhile, the EC had clubs based in Chicago, Cleveland, New York, Philadelphia, Pittsburgh, and Washington D.C.

After 14 seasons, the league's structure changed again by adding the Capital Division and Century Division to the EC and Coastal Division and Central Division (CD) to the WC. This arrangement continued until 1970 when the American Football League (AFL) and NFL merged and then reorganized into the American Football Conference (AFC) and National Football Conference (NFC). Besides five in the ED, each conference had four teams in their CD and also WD.[2]

Between 1970 and 2016 inclusive, a few NFC teams moved from one city to another within a metropolitan area or to a completely different area. Chronologically, these were the St. Louis Cardinals→Phoenix in 1988; Los Angeles Rams→St. Louis in 1995; and St. Louis Cardinals→Los Angeles in 2016. Within the AFC, these were the Oakland Raiders→Los Angeles in 1982; Baltimore Colts→Indianapolis in 1984; Los Angeles Raiders→Oakland in 1995; Cleveland Browns→Baltimore in 1996; Houston Oilers→Memphis in 1997; and Tennessee Oilers→Nashville in 1998. While some teams relocated to more populated and/or prosperous areas, others moved in order to play in a new or renovated publicly financed stadium and perform before a larger number of fans at the new site.[3]

Besides movements, such new teams joined the NFC as the Seattle Seahawks in 1976 and Carolina Panthers in 1995, while the AFC added the Tampa Bay Buccaneers in 1976, Jacksonville Jaguars in 1995, Cleveland Browns in 1999, and Houston Texans in 2002. As denoted later in this chapter, some of these expansion clubs have not performed up to expectations within the conference and/or their division for several reasons including ownership issues and various problems with coaches and players during seasons and postseasons.

By decade, a few important facts about and within the NFC were memorable: in the 1970s, for example, the conference signed a four-year television contract with the Columbia Broadcasting System (CBS) to broadcast all its games but divide those of the Super Bowl and Pro Bowl with the AFC; divisional winners with the highest win–loss percentage were made the home team in the divisional playoffs, and the surviving winners with the highest percentage became home teams in championship games; and such leaders died as former head coach Vince Lombardi (Packers), president and general manager Dan Reeves (Rams), and president Lloyd Nordstrum (Seahawks).

In the 1980s, New York Giants executive officer Wellington Mara became president of the NFC; the conference's number-one seed, Washington Redskins, defeated the AFC's number-two seed, Miami Dolphins, in Super Bowl XVII at the Rose Bowl in Pasadena, California; franchise owners voted to continue the instant replay system; and a 24-day players strike reduced the 1987 regular season from 16 to 15 games; in the 1990s, New York businessman Robert Tisch purchased a 50% interest in the Giants franchise; clubs adopted a package of changes including modification in line play, chucking rules, roughing-the-passer rules, and a two-point conversion after touchdowns; and league teams approved an extension of the Collective Bargaining Agreement through 2003 and created a $100 million fund for youth football programs.

And in the 2000s, all clubs approved league-wide revenue sharing and to pool the visiting team's share of gate receipts for all preseason and regular-season games and divide the pool equally starting in 2002; franchise owners unanimously approved $10 million in additional spending for retired players to help pay for their medical assistance; for the first time, an NFC game was broadcast by the National Broadcasting Corporation (NBC) and also streamed live to fans on the Internet via websites' nfl.com and nbcsports.com.

Besides those historical details about the conference, two others are interesting to remember: first, parity has generally been greater at least recently among NFC than AFC teams. Since realignment in 2002, the only time an NFC team made back-to-back Super Bowl appearances and won one game was the Seattle Seahawks in 2014 and 2015. But from 2000 to 2016, the NFC sent eleven different teams to the Super Bowl, whereas the AFC's New England Patriots appeared six and Pittsburgh Steelers three times, and also the Baltimore Ravens, Denver Broncos, and Indianapolis Colts each twice. Second, the original NFC logo, used during seasons' 1970–2009, depicted a blue "N" with three stars across it. That represented three divisions — Eastern, Central, and Western — in the conference from 1970 to 2001. The 2010 NFL season, however, brought an updated NFC logo. Largely similar to the old logo, the new one has a fourth star to represent four divisions — East, North, South, and West — that comprised the NFC beginning in 2002.[4]

TEAMS

Markets

From 1920 to 2016, many NFL franchises terminated or became "defunct" including some within the pre-NFC. Of the total, 45 failed in the 1920s, four in the 1930s, and two in the 1940–1950s. In addition, 12 teams applied for membership in the league but were refused entry. While some of these existed only as proposals to join, others had full organizations. Among the group, for example, were the Brooklyn Lions, Evansville Crimson Giants, and Louisville Colonels in the 1920s, Cleveland Indians and St. Louis Gunners in the 1930s, Pennsylvania Keystoners in the 1940s, Baltimore Colts and Buffalo Bills in the 1950s, Orlando Suns and Memphis Grizzlies in the 1970s, New Jersey Generals in the 1980s, and the Baltimore Bombers, Memphis Hound Dogs, and St. Louis Stallions in the 1990s.[5]

As a result of the merger following their 1969 season, ten teams shifted from the AFL to the NFL's AFC, while five of 10 former NFL EC clubs transferred to the NFC's ED. In the latter group were the Dallas Cowboys, New York Giants, St. Louis Cardinals, Washington Redskins, and Philadelphia Eagles.

In 1970, the 13 NFC clubs each had front offices and existed at home in relatively large, midsized, and small cities. Geographically, they ranged north to south or in other ways from New York to Dallas in the ED, Green Bay to Minneapolis in the CD, and Atlanta to San Francisco in the WD. Their metropolitan areas' populations were also different and within the three divisions ranked from most to least in (millions) as follows: in the ED were teams based in New York (11.5), Philadelphia (4.8), Washington (2.8), St. Louis (2.3), and Dallas (1.5); in the CD, they included Chicago (6.9), Detroit (4.1), Minneapolis (1.8), and Green Bay (.2); and in the WD, one each in Los Angeles (7.1), San Francisco (3.1), Atlanta (1.3), and New Orleans (1.0). Although there were no NFC clubs in areas north of Minneapolis or Green Bay and southeast of Atlanta, at least four in the AFC had home sites in the Midwest plus one each in the southeast and southwest.

During the NFL's 1971–1972 to 2015–2016 season, new NFC teams began to play at home in such locations — with Metropolitan Statistical Area

(MSA) populations in (millions) — as Seattle (1.8) and Charlotte (1.1). In addition, existing clubs in the conference relocated to such areas as Los Angeles (18.6), St. Louis (2.6), and Phoenix (2.2). Most of these occurred, in part, because of changes in ownership and construction of new stadiums, and also because these MSAs contained more people including households with increasing disposable and/or per capita incomes.[6]

To identify and discuss some current, interesting, and relevant data and facts about existing NFC teams in order to examine the sizes and other elements of their markets, there is information about them in Table A6.1. Within the table, variables researched were each team's Metropolitan Statistical Area Population (MSAPOP), number of Designated Market Area Television Homes (DMATVH), and average attendances (AVGATT) at home games. These are measured, listed, and ranked in order to reveal the attributes and problems of such competitors and rivals as the ED's New York Giants and Philadelphia Eagles, ND's Detroit Lions and Green Bay Packers, SD's Atlanta Falcons and Carolina Panthers, and WD's Denver Broncos and Oakland Raiders.

Based on data listed in Column 2 of Table A6.1, the typical NFC team had a MSAPOP of approximately 5.2 million. More specifically, ED teams' areas were ranked first at 7.3 million followed by those in the WD at 5.9 million, ND at 4.4 million, and SD at 3.1 million. While the Rams, Giants — who split New York with the AFC's Jets — and Bears had the largest group of people within their markets, the three smallest were in areas of the 49ers — shared market with the AFC's Raiders — and then the Saints and Packers. These differences, in turn, affect and will influence each club's potential and actual ticket sales, revenue from games and other sources, and their market value, especially those identical or similar in size within divisions such as the Eagles and Redskins, Lions and Vikings, Panthers and Buccaneers, and Cardinals and Seahawks.

Besides averages for the league, conference, and by division, the variation or dispersion in MSAPOPs were determined mathematically using the standard deviation. While it averaged 3.48 million people across the 16 teams, the WD's ranked highest at 4.98 million, ND's second at 3.83 million, ED's third at 1.89 million, and SD's fourth at 1.88 million. In other words, the least equal in market population were areas of the Cardinals and their divisional rivals, but most alike include those of SD teams particularly the Panthers and Buccaneers but not the Falcons or Saints. Because of such widespread variation in MSAPOPs, teams' locations impacted them in various ways such as their attendances at home games, media coverage, travel costs, and other variables of these franchises.[7]

In Table A6.1, Column 3 is the number of television homes in each team's designated market area (DMATV) in years' 2016–2017. While it averaged 2.23 million across the conference, the ED teams' on average equaled 2.94 million television homes and those in the ND 1.87 million, WD 1.54, and ND 1.53 million. Similar to but not exactly like the distribution of the MSAPOPs, the largest number of homes with televisions is in the Los Angeles and then New York and Chicago DMAs while the fewest existed in Charlotte, New Orleans, and Green Bay.

As explained before for the MSAPOP, the standard deviation of television homes in teams' areas denotes differences across the conference and also between and within divisions. While the variation was 1.25 or 1,250,000 television homes among the entire group in the NFC, ND clubs on average had the largest at 1.24 or 1,240,000, SD's at 0.78 or 780,000, ED's at 0.51 to 510,000, and the WD's at 0.36 or 360,000. Within divisions, for example, the difference between the number of television homes in Chicago and Green Bay was much greater, for example, than Atlanta and New Orleans, New York and Washington, and Los Angeles and Seattle. Thus, the Arizona Cardinals and two of their three divisional rivals are the most equal in this characteristic of their market but less so for teams in the ND, SD, and ED. This, however, does not mean more or fewer fans actually watch their NFL games on television while at home or other places.

In Table A6.1, Column 4 lists the average attendance of each NFC team while playing games on its home field as of 2016. For this statistic, the Cowboys ranked first at 80,000-seat AT&T Stadium in Arlington, Texas; Rams second at 93,607-seat Los Angeles Memorial Coliseum in Los Angeles, California; and Giants third at 82,566-seat MetLife Stadium in East Rutherford, New Jersey. In contrast to them, teams' with the smallest attendances at their home were the Lions at 65,000-seat Ford Field in Detroit, Michigan; Buccaneers at 65,890-seat Raymond James Stadium in Tampa, Florida; and Bears at 61,500-seat Soldier Field in Chicago, Illinois.

While the conference's attendance was 71,870 per game, ED teams averaged 79,800 fans, WD's roughly 71,800, SD's 69,370, and ND's about

66,530. Ranked first and second within their division, respectively, games of the ED's Cowboys and Giants were more popular, for example, than those of the Packers and Vikings, Panthers and Saints, and Rams and 49ers. In addition, the ND's Bears and Lions had the lowest-ranked combined attendances and not the SD's Falcons and Buccaneers or WD's Cardinals and Seahawks. In fact, such things as these teams' win–loss records, average ticket prices, advertisements and marketing campaigns, and number of superstar quarterbacks and other players affected in some way their Sunday and other nighttime attendances at home games.

Regarding the deviation in teams' average attendances, it was 8,810 spectators per game for the conference but from most to least by division as follows: 9,470 in the ED; 8,310 in the ND; 7,910 in the WD; and approximately 6,060 in the SD. This suggests that ED clubs had greater variation in number of fans at their games, in part, because of sellouts at the Cowboys' AT&T Stadium in Arlington, near sellouts at the Giants' MetLife Stadium in East Rutherford, and Redskins' FedEx Field in Hyattsville, Maryland, but not at the Eagles' Lincoln Financial Field in Philadelphia.

For various reasons including competitiveness and the ability to entertain fans and also capacity of their stadiums, very small or marginal differences in attendances between them occurred, for example, at the Bears' Soldier Field, Lions' Ford Field, Buccaneers' Raymond James Stadium, and Cardinals' University of Phoenix Stadium. Although the Lions and Buccaneers each won two more regular-season games than the Cardinals and six more than the Bears in 2015–2016, they each sold about the same number of seats to fans at their home games.

Given the data and its distribution in Table A6.1, the ED's Cowboys, Giants and Redskins, ND's Bears, and WD's Rams each played their home games in relatively large markets; the ED's Eagles, ND's Lions and Vikings, SD's Falcons and Buccaneers, and WD's Cardinals and Seahawks in midsized markets; and the ND's Packers, SD's Panthers and Saints, and WD's 49ers in small markets. Thus, approximately 31% of NFC teams existed in MSAs with plenty of fans and television homes during the league's 2016–2017 while 44% had home sites in less populated areas with fewer television homes and another 25% performed within markets with inferior data. According to rankings in the table — except for the Giants in the New York–Newark–New Jersey area and 49ers in the San Francisco–Oakland–Hayward metropolis, the other teams' markets within and across divisions are each different demographically and roughly represent their economies and the sport's fan base.

For more about variables in Table A6.1 and their potential to be future football markets after the league's 2016–2017 season, the most populated places without an NFL team are such MSAs as Riverside–San Bernardino–Ontario (4.48 million), St. Louis (2.81 million), Portland–Vancouver–Hillsboro (2.39 million), Orlando–Kissimmee–Sanford (2.38 million), San Antonio–New Braunfels (2.38 million), Sacramento–Roseville–Arden–Arcade (2.27 million), and Las Vegas–Henderson–Paradise (2.11 million). With respect to DMAs in the top forty, those without a club — besides San Antonio and Las Vegas — are Raleigh–Durham–Fayetteville, Hartford–New Haven, Columbus, Salt Lake City, Milwaukee, Greenville–Spartanburg–Ashville, West Palm Beach–Ft. Pierce, and Austin.[8]

If the league expands at a site in an area not hosting a current NBA team, a few of these places are viable markets. In addition, they are potential sites for any existing NFL clubs with inferior stadiums and who compete for local fans with other teams in Major League Baseball (MLB) and any in the National Basketball Association (NBA) and/or National Hockey League (NHL). Among the group, there has been speculation in the media about locating a new or existing club in especially Las Vegas, Nevada or another one in Chicago, and also in smaller US metropolitan areas such as Columbus, Ohio, and San Antonio, Texas.

Despite being homes of former NFL teams that folded in years from 1920 to 2000 or were not admitted into the NFL, the group includes such cities as Akron, Dayton and Toledo, Ohio; Duluth, Minnesota; Louisville, Kentucky; Rochester, New York; Milwaukee, Wisconsin; and St. Louis, Missouri. In short, a number of places are potentially adequate sites to host an NFL expansion team or one that struggles to get local fans to attend its home games and/or earn enough money to operate effectively within a division of the NFC.

Before discussing teams' performances in the next section of this chapter, the NFL Players Association (NFLPA) signed a Collective Bargaining Agreement (CBA) with the NFL in 2011. It covered several specific things such as the roster of players and their employment rights. Regarding the size of teams during seasons, the active list limit increased from 45 players per club to 46. The limit cannot be reduced by clubs for the duration of the

CBA, although they may carry less than 46 players on their active list during the regular season but no less than 43. Players on the active and inactive lists receive the same benefits and protections, and in any league year, these lists do not exceed 53.[9]

A team's practice squad consists of the following players — provided they have not served more than two previous seasons on a practice squad: First, players who do not have an accrued season of NFL experience and any free agent players who were on the active list for fewer than nine regular-season games during their only accrued season(s). An otherwise eligible player may be on a practice squad for a third season only if the club by which he is employed that season has at least 53 players on its active/inactive list during the entire period of his employment.

Second, a player serves on a practice squad in a season if he has passed the club's physical and has been a member of the club's practice squad for at least three regular-season or post-season games during his first two practice squad seasons, and for at least one regular season or post-season game during his third practice squad season. According to a section of the CBA, a bye week counts as a game provided the player is not terminated until after the regular season or post-season weekend in question.

Performances

During the league's 96-year history, the number of pre-NFC/NFC teams ranged from four in the 1943 season to 16 during 1999–2016. Because of differences in performances and other factors, some of their players were among all-time leaders in the sport. These include, for example, such quarterbacks as Brett Farve, Eli Manning, and Fran Tarkenton in passes completed; runners' Emmitt Smith, Walter Payton, and Barry Sanders in rushing yards; receivers' Cris Carter, Jason Witten, and Anquan Boldin in receptions; and George Blanda, Jason Hanson, and Darrell Green in number of games. A few coaches with outstanding careers, in part, with conference teams were the Bears' George Halas, Cowboys' Tom Landry, and Packers' Curly Lambeau and Vince Lombardi.[10]

For 16 NFC teams as of the NFL's 2015–2016 season, their all-time performances appear in Table A6.2. Besides their total performances, which were calculated but are not given in the table, the columns denote the distribution of seasons and overall how well they competed and succeeded since becoming members of the league. At their current sites, the following is a summary of their performances in order to compare them from first to 16th based on various results. These teams' histories ranged from the 21-year-old Panthers to the 95-year-old Bears and Packers.

Winning percentage

Besides differences in the abilities of coaches and players, their total seasons in the league — as listed in Column 2 of Table A6.2 — partly influenced results. While the conference's average was approximately 444 wins (Column 3), the ND's equaled 601, ED's 563, WD's 346, and SD's only 267. As of 2015–2016, the Bears led the group of sixteen teams followed by the Packers and Giants. With the least number of wins were the Panthers and then Cardinals and Buccaneers.

Given number of seasons and also wins, an important fact in ranking these NFC teams is their all-time winning percentage. According to data in column four of the table, the most successful in the conference have been the Cowboys, Packers, and Bears, while the lowest winning percentages belong to the Buccaneers, Cardinals, and Falcons. Based on groups, ND teams averaged 52% or 0.520 in wins, ED's 0.515, WD's 0.497, and SD's 0.436.

Since 1960, the Cowboys have won more than 56% of their games because of such coaches — besides Tom Landry — as Jimmy Johnson, Bill Parcells and Wade Phillips, and also quarterbacks' Roger Staubach, Troy Aikman, and Don Meredith. Besides them, running backs Tony Dorsett and Emmitt Smith, tight end Jackie Smith, offensive tackles Rayfield Wright and Larry Allen, defensive tackles Bob Lilly, Randy White, and Don Perkins, receivers Bob Hayes, Michael Irvin, and Drew Pearson, and safeties Cliff Harris and Darren Woodson had successful careers with the club. In fact, these players contributed to Dallas teams having many winning seasons and qualifying, in part, for 32 playoffs in 56 years.

Because of various problems including competition from the SD's Falcons, Panthers and Saints, and from the Bears, Packers, and Vikings while in the CD, the Buccaneers have mostly finished fourth or fifth in their division since 1977. Tampa Bay's best teams finished as titlists once each in the 1970s, 1980s, and 1990s, three times in the 2000s, and also when they won the NFC and Super Bowl XXXVII in 2002. In other seasons, they lost the majority of their regular-season games despite making changes to improve the coaching staff and active roster of players.

Other than the SD's Buccaneers with a 0.383 winning percentage, some of the worst clubs in each division have been the ED's Eagles, ND's Lions, and WD's Cardinals. The Eagles appeared in back-to-back playoffs six times and won three NFL championships but zero Super Bowls in 83 seasons. Similarly, the Lions have won only eight division titles although four NFL championships but zero Super Bowls in 82 years, while the 28-year-old Cardinals have been in just five playoffs and won one conference title. In sum, these teams have been inconsistent and not able to advance in postseasons because of not enough depth at key positions on their roster, coaching failures, and simply bad draft choices.

Statistically, the standard deviation is used to measure the variation or inequality in winning percentages between and within divisions of the NFC. The widest variation occurred among teams in the WD (0.06 or 6%) and then the ND (5%), SD (4%), and ED (3%). Although these were relatively small differences in deviations between divisions, the average winning percentages of the highest and lowest in the groups indicated, for example, that the Rams' compared to the Cardinals' exceeded those of the Packers and Lions, Panthers and Buccaneers, and Cowboys and Eagles. Thus, in evaluating and ranking by winning percentages, WD teams have been the most unequal competitively among themselves and also relative to those in other divisions of the conference.

Playoffs

Other than relocations and franchise expansions, some specific but interesting things about the 46-year-old NFC have affected the sport and league in different ways. For example, each team plays others in its respective division twice — home and away — during the regular season, in addition to ten other games assigned to their schedule by the NFL. Two of these games are assigned on the basis of a particular team's final divisional standing from the previous season. The remaining eight games are split between the rosters of two other NFL divisions. This assignment shifts each year and follows a standard cycle.

At the end of each season, the top six teams in the conference continue to compete in the playoffs. These teams consist of four division winners and the top two wild cards. The NFC playoffs culminate in a championship game with the winner receiving the George Halas Trophy, which is named after the founder and longtime owner of the Chicago Bears franchise. Lastly, the NFC and AFC champions play each other in a Super Bowl.

Based on their records in NFL regular seasons through 2016, the Cowboys, Giants, and Packers each qualified for 32 playoffs, Vikings 28, and the Bears and 49ers each 25. In contrast to them, the Cardinals have been in five, Panthers seven, and Saints and Buccaneers each 10. With respect to NFC teams' total number of playoffs by division, the ED ranks first with 111 or 35%, ND second with 102 or 32%, WD third with 67 or 21%, and SD fourth with 40 or 12%.

Regarding differences between the most and least successful clubs within each division of the NFC, the Cowboys and Giants each have been in nine more playoffs than the Redskins, Packers 15 more than the Lions, Falcons six more than the Panthers, and 49ers 20 more than the Cardinals. From a historical perspective, these results indicate greater difficulty in getting into the playoffs among teams in the SD and WD in comparison to those in the ED and ND.

Division Titles

According to Column 5 of Table A6.2, the 16 NFC clubs claimed 208 division titles during their years in the league. From most to least, those in the ED won 71 or 34% of the total, ND 70 or approximately 33%, WD 45 or 22%, and SD 22 or 11%. More specifically, the Giants ranked first in number of them as of 2016, Packers second, and Cowboys third, while the Panthers and Buccaneers tied for 12th and Falcons and Saints for 14th, and the Cardinals finished at 16th.

With respect to the distribution of their division titles, the Packers won three in the 1930s, two in the 1940s, six in the 1960s, one in the 1970s, three in the 1990s, and another eight between 2000 and 2016. While owned first by the Indian Packing Company and then the Green Bay Football Corporation, such outstanding Green Bay head coaches — besides Curly Lambeau and Vince Lombardi — as Bart Starr, Mike Holmgren, and Mike

McCarthy challenged their players to win enough regular-season games to lead their division.

Some of these players included Hall of Fame quarterbacks Bart Starr and Brett Favre, running back Paul Horning and fullback Jim Taylor, receivers Don Hutson and James Lofton, on defense, linebackers Ray Nitschke and Dave Robinson, defensive ends Willie Davis and Reggie White, offensive tackles Cal Hubbard and Forrest Gregg, and safety Willie Wood. Besides 1961 Coach of the Year Vince Lombardi and also Lindy Infante in 1989, Favre and the other Packers won awards for being the best at their positions in regular-seasons and some post-season games.

In division titles, one of the Packers best seasons was 2011–2012. While waiting for the divisional round with a playoff bye, the Packers family was hit by tragedy as Michael Philbin — son of offensive coordinator Joe Philbin — was found dead in a frozen river in Oshkosh, Wisconsin. Despite Green Bay battling back to tie their divisional playoff game, the New York Giants scored 10 unanswered points in the last two minutes of the first half. Although Mason Crosby's third-quarter field goal made it closer, the Giants pulled away in the fourth quarter stunning the Packers at Lambeau Field 37-20.

As a group, the Falcons, Saints, and Cardinals won thirteen division titles in 127 regular seasons through 2016. Respectively, Atlanta and New Orleans are each five-time titlists while Arizona won the WD in the conference's 2008, 2009, and 2015 seasons. In fact, these teams' most impressive seasons include 1998 when the Falcons finished 14-2 and runner-up to the Broncos in Super Bowl XXXIII; 2009 when the Saints were 13-3 in the regular season and defeated the Indianapolis Colts 31-17 in Super Bowl XLIV; and 2015 when the Cardinals had thirteen wins in its regular season and beat the Packers in the divisional playoffs but then lost to the Carolina Panthers 49-15 in the NFC championship game.

Eventually Giants' quarterback Eli Manning and the Packers' Aaron Rodgers will retire from the sport. This, in turn, should provide an opportunity for other teams to better compete and win a division title in the conference. The Seahawks' Russell Wilson and Panthers' Cam Newton, for example, are young but talented quarterbacks with the potential to lead their teams to more victories along with such veterans as the Saints' Drew Brees, Lions' Matt Stafford, and Cardinals' Carson Palmer.

Conference titles

The 16 NFC teams in Table A6.2 won a total of 67 conference titles during their post-seasons in the league. Of the four groups, ED clubs won 27 or 40% of them and those in the ND 20 or 31%, WD 14 or 21%, and SD five or 8%. The most and least successful have been, respectively, the Giants, Packers, and Cowboys and with fewest in number the Falcons, Saints, Buccaneers, and Cardinals each with one.

Before 2017, the Giants won the conference three times each in the 1950s and 1960s, once each in the 1980s and 1990s, and in 2000, 2007, and 2011; the Packers six times in the 1960s, twice in the 1990s, and in 2010; and the Cowboys five times in the 1970s and three in the 1990s. Ranked behind these three teams are the 49ers with six titles, Redskins five, the Bears, Lions, Vikings, and Rams each with four, Eagles and Seahawks each with three, and five others with at least one.

While located in Los Angeles for 49 seasons before 2016, the Rams won their conference in 1950–1951, 1955, and 1979. When coached by Joe Stydahar, Sid Gillman, or Ray Malavasi, one or more of these clubs were led by such quarterbacks as Norm Van Brocklin and Pat Haden, running backs Dan Towler, Ron Waller, and Wendell Tyler, and also receivers Tom Fears, Elroy Hirsch, and Preston Dennard. Although they did not win the NFC, the club was 12-2 in 1973 and also 1975, but was defeated in the divisional playoffs, and then in 1975, lost to the Cowboys in the conference's title game. After moving from St. Louis to Los Angeles, the Rams had difficulty winning four games in the league's 2016–2017 season. Nevertheless, they finished seventh among 31 others in average home attendance.

Some teams have recently improved and may eventually win another NFC title. These include the ED's Cowboys and Redskins, ND's Lions and Packers, SD's Falcons and Panthers, and WD's Cardinals and Seahawks. But such experienced clubs as the ND's Bears and Vikings struggle to be conference titlists because the Lions and Packers are more consistent and have too much talent especially at key positions on both offense and defense, and also excellent coaching staffs.

Super bowls

According to Column 8 in Table A6.2, the 16 NFC teams won a total of 25 Super Bowls as of 2016. Among divisions, ED clubs had victories in 12 or

48% of them and those in the WD six or 24%, ND five or 20%, and SD two or 8%. While the most successful clubs have been the Cowboys and 49ers followed by the Giants and Packers, seven or approximately 28% of the group have failed to win a Super Bowl.

With respect to their championships, some players who won Super Bowl Most Valuable Player (MVP) awards include the Cowboys' Chuck Howley, Larry Brown, and Troy Aikman; 49ers' Jerry Rice, Joe Montana, and Steve Young; Giants' Phil Simms, Ottis Anderson, and Eli Manning; and Packers' Bart Starr, Desmond Howard, and Aaron Rodgers. Some of these players were also NFL MVPs and/or defensive and offensive player of the year in the NFC.

Besides them, other clubs in the conference played in but lost one or more Super Bowls. The Vikings, for example, were defeated in four championship games; Redskins, Panthers, Seahawks, and Eagles each twice; and the Bears, Falcons, Rams, Colts, and Cardinals each once. Most interesting, Minnesota won consecutive division and conference titles (1974–1975) but failed to win a championship despite head coach Bud Grant and such Hall of Fame players as quarterback Fran Tarkenton, defensive tackle Alan Page, defensive end Carl Eller, safety Paul Krause, and center Mick Tinglehoff.

Especially important in prestige for the conference, Green Bay won the league's first Super Bowl on 15 January, 1967. For the first time ever, NFL and AFL winners faced each other in a game for the undisputed world champion of football. It took place with little fanfare at the half-empty Los Angeles Memorial Coliseum as the Packers played the AFL's Kansas City Chiefs. Although the Packers had a 14-10 lead at halftime, the Chiefs proved to be pesky. However, the Packers scored 21 unanswered points in the second half to claim the championship with a 35-10 victory. Within a few years, the game became an American institution.

Following the "Ice Bowl" between the Packers and Cowboys for the NFC championship in 1967, Super Bowl II was a walk in the park. After playing in conditions suited for a polar bear at Lambeau Field in Green Bay, the Packers faced the AFC champion Oakland Raiders in the warm sun at Miami's Orange Bowl. More of a coronation than a championship game, the Packers easily beat the Raiders 33-14. The champions were led by quarterback Bart Starr who again won the game's MVP award. As Green Bay's head coach Vince Lombardi grasped the game's trophy that eventually bore his name, it became evident his era was over.

Regarding those who have never won a Super Bowl through 2016, the most likely NFC team to become champion within a few seasons, in my judgement, is the Panthers. With one of the league's best defenses led by all-pro linebackers Luke Kuechly and veteran Thomas Davis and on offense by 2016 MVP quarterback Cam Newton and also tight end Greg Olsen, Carolina is competitive and a threat to win the SD again in 2018 or 2019, and then the conference, and eventually a Super Bowl. To achieve these results, the club needs someone to replace Davis when he retires and either draft or trade for better players to protect Newton from being sacked and/or injured.

Total performances

This result — or the total performance (TP) for each team — includes their division and conference titles plus championships as listed in Columns 5–8 of Table A6.2. Among 331 TPs, ED clubs won 119 or 36% of them followed by the ND's 117 or 35%, WD's 66 or 20%, and SD's 29 or 9%.

While the Packers ranked first with 45 in TPs, Giants second with 43, and Cowboys third with 35, the Saints had only seven, Falcons six, and Cardinals four. Other teams with at least 20 are the Redskins, Bears, Vikings, and 49ers. Considering only their average winning percentage and number of playoffs combined as of measure of their performances, those with the most impressive results have been the Cowboys followed closely by the Packers and then the Giants, Bears, Vikings, 49ers, Rams, Redskins, and Seahawks. In contrast to them, the Cardinals, Buccaneers, and Falcons had the worst-ranked results of the group as of 2016.

After sports experts researched and published the history of all teams in the league, some of these articles reported the most dominant and/or successful teams of all-time. To get results, different criteria were used including the Elovation App (Elo) rating, which focuses on wins and losses and considers the margin of victory, whether home or road games, and strength of the team's opponent. Based on this metric and football information from various sources, among the best of all-time — in chronological order — are the following clubs from the WC/NFC.[11]

• Almost a dozen Hall of Famers played on Vince Lombardi's 1962 Packers championship team, which went 13-1 and led the NFL in points scored (415) and fewest points allowed (148). Led by Bart Starr, Paul Hornung, Jim

Taylor, Forrest Gregg, Ray Nitschke, Herb Adderley, Willie Davis, Jim Ringo, Willie Wood, and Henry Jordan, the team capped its season with a 16-7 win over the EC's New York Giants to become league champion.

• The 1985 Bears rank as one of the greatest NFL teams of all time. Led by future Hall of Famers Walter Payton, Mike Singletary, Richard Dent, Dan Hampton, and Mike Ditka, plus other enigmatic personalities such as Jim McMahon, Steve "Mongo" McMichael, William "Refrigerator" Perry, Otis Wilson, Buddy Ryan, and Willie Gault, the Bears lit the football world on fire. Behind arguably the best defense in league history by allowing only 198 points, the Bears finished 18-1 and decimated the AFC Patriots 46-10 in Super Bowl XX at the Louisiana Superdome in New Orleans. To this day, the team is treated like royalty in Chicago.

• A strong case could be made for the 1984 San Francisco 49ers team that went 17-1 and blew out the Dolphins 38-16 in Super Bowl XIX. But the 1989 49ers were marginally better. They lost two home games by a combined five points, one to the Rams who they played and defeated 30-3 in the NFC title game. San Francisco's 1989 team dominated the post-season, defeating the 10-6 Vikings, 11-5 Rams, and 13-5 Broncos by a combined 126-26, including a 55-10 demolition of Denver in Super Bowl XXIV. With Hall of Famers Joe Montana, Jerry Rice, Ronnie Lott, and Charles Haley at the height of their powers, one could argue that the 1989 49ers — who won back-to-back championships — are the best team in NFL history.

• The Washington Redskins had three teams under head coach Joe Gibbs that won a Super Bowl and a fourth, the 1983 team, might have earned this distinction had it won a championship. Of the three that did win, the 1991 club jumps out in a big way for its wire-to-wire dominance. That year, the Redskins won their first 11 games in route to a 14-2 regular-season record, with seven of their wins by 20 or more points. Besides leading the NFL in points scored (485) and being second in fewest points allowed (224), they never trailed in the post-season and capped it with a 37-24 win over Buffalo in Super Bowl XXVI.

• With five Super Bowl championships, it is difficult to pick the best Dallas Cowboys team. But the one in 1993 stands above the rest with the other in 1977 coming in a close second. The 1993 Cowboys lost their first two games without running back Emmitt Smith but went 12-2 in the remaining regular season and defeated the Buffalo Bills 30-13 in Super Bowl XXVIII at the Georgia Dome in Atlanta. That Dallas team had four Hall of Famers in Troy Aikman, Emmitt Smith, Michael Irvin, and Charles Haley and a Ring of Honor member in Darren Woodson, plus an offensive line that had three pro bowlers. Alternatively, the 1977 Cowboys had Hall of Famers in Roger Staubach, Tony Dorsett and Randy White, plus Ring of Honor members Drew Pearson and Cliff Harris and franchise staples such as Ed "Too Tall" Jones, Harvey Martin, Jethro Pugh, Charlie Waters, and John Fitzgerald. What separated the two teams? The 1993 Cowboys had an average margin of victory of 15.3 points compared with 12.9 points for the one in 1977.

For various reasons such as lacking talented players, coaching problems, and/or both of them, some NFC teams had terrible performances in their regular seasons. Several of these clubs were evaluated based on their ability to score points, deny first downs, and win games. In chronological order, the following is a list of a few of the worst clubs in the WD/pre-NFC/NFC's history as of the league's 2016 season.[12]

• The 1934 Cincinnati Reds had trouble scoring points on offense. Through eight games in the NFL season, they tallied just one touchdown and a field goal. The club also had a very porous defense, which gave up 6.4 rushing yards per attempt. It made them the worst run defense in the history of the NFL, a distinction they still hold. Things got so bad for the Reds that they actually threw in the white towel and folded as a franchise with a few games left in the season. In other words, this was likely the worst team to ever play in the league.

• The 1952 Dallas Texans had no identity or talent. After an unsuccessful 1951 season at 1-9-2 in New York City while named New York Yankees or simply "Yanks," the team moved to Dallas the next year. While there, they lost the first half of their games by an average of 20 points and could not compete with other NFL teams. In fact, with five games remaining on their schedule, the NFL took control of the 0-11 Texans and moved them out of Dallas. They ended up playing their final home game — which, miraculously, they won because the Chicago Bears sent their second-string players to match up against them — in Akron, Ohio. Indeed, it was a strange season for the Texans.

• During their 1976 and 1977 seasons, the Buccaneers lost 26 consecutive games. They went 0-14 as a member of the AFC's WD in 1976 and then lost their first 12 games in 1977 while in the CD of the NFC. During the latter year, they were pitiful on offense, scoring just six touchdowns the entire season and setting a league record by getting shut out in six of their fourteen games. They finally won a game in Week 13 — a 33-14 victory over the New Orleans Saints that earned them a celebration in Tampa the following day. Although the event featured more than 8,000 fans welcoming them home, that was not enough to save the club from cementing their legacy as one of the worst NFL teams of all-time.

• There have been many NFC teams with really bad offenses. But, the 1992 Seahawks were among the worst in the group. During the NFL season, Seattle scored just 140 points — or less than nine points per game — and only managed to string together 1,778 passing yards. Strangely, the Seahawks did have a great defense — defensive tackle Cortez Kennedy was named the NFL Defensive Player of the Year in 1992 — but their offense could not help Seattle to avoid finishing its regular season with the lowest winning percentage (0.125) in franchise history.

• The Detroit Lions had plenty of chances to win at least one game during the 2008 NFL season. Although they suffered their share of blowouts throughout the year, they also lost four games by a touchdown or less. Rather than finishing 1-15, 2-14, or even 3-13, they ended at 0-16 scoring 268 points but allowing 517. Their season was summed up perfectly by their radio play-by-play announcer Dan Miller after they lost their final game of the season to the Green Bay Packers. He said, "For 16 weeks, starting in Atlanta back in September, they [Lions] took the field thinking this was gonna be their day. Sixteen times they were wrong. They are the worst team in league history."

LEAGUE ECONOMICS

In this section, there are data and other information about the commercial and financial aspects of franchises in the NFC and their significance from an economic perspective. Besides attendances at home and away games, anything else that affects teams' income, market value, and wealth is included in the analysis, quantified, and discussed. In other words, the NFL is an organization consisting of for-profit enterprises that operate to compete each season typically within a division and/or conference and seek to improve their performances in current and future games.

Franchise Financials

Forbes magazine's sports editors' published financial data of NFC franchises as of 2016. As denoted in Columns 2–7 of Table A6.3, these amounts include respectively their estimated market value — which is based on the current stadium deal without deduction for debt — and also total revenue, operating income — earnings before interest, taxes, depreciation, and amortization (EBITDA) — gate receipts, debt-to-value (D/V) percentages, and players' expenses. For each of four divisions, the information reveals the financial status and wealth of these teams both individually and relative to each other as a group. The following section identifies and highlights the data.[13]

In Table A6.3, Column 2 is the estimated market value of each NFC team, by division, as of 2016. Ranked from most to least, ED clubs averaged $3.1 billion, WD's $2.5 billion, ND's $2.2 billion, and SD's $1.9 billion. While the Cowboys were first at $4.2 billion, Giants second at $3.1 billion, and 49ers third at $3 billion, least in value included the Buccaneers at $1.8 billion, Saints at $1.7 billion, and Lions at $1.6 billion. In comparison to the typical club's market value of $2.4 billon, only seven or approximately 43% of the group actually exceeded that amount.

Several factors caused differences in teams' market values. In no specific order, these were their history, tradition, and success in the league, location in a big, midsized, or small market, size and growth of each's fan base, number of titles and championships, and such financial data as their revenue, operating income, and gate receipts. Based on these and other things, they ranged in value by more than $2.5 billion.

To compare their standard deviation or variation in market values, the highest within groups was ED teams ($721 million) and lowest among those in the SD ($189 million), ND ($436 million), and then WD ($484 million). This means inequality or greater deviation in these NFC franchise's values existed in 2016 to a greater extent between the Cowboys and other ED teams than among clubs within other divisions. Although these were just estimates, the amounts influence such things as the clubs' relative wealth, economic power in the league, and future price if offered for sale to potential investors. Interestingly, there no teams whose market value fell below the conference's average deviation of $653 million.

Each team's revenue — net of stadium revenues used for debt payments — is displayed in Column 3 of Table A6.3. While the Cowboys had the highest at $700 million followed by the Redskins' $447 million and 49ers' $446 million, the three lowest-ranked were the Lions' $321 million at 14th, Rams' $317 million at fifteenth and Vikings' $306 million at 16th. The differences in amounts occurred for several reasons including their home attendances, range in non-premium and premium ticket prices, winning percentage in games, and number of football fans in the metropolitan area.

Because of various demographic and sport-specific factors, there were disparities in teams' revenue. While the conference's standard deviation equaled $93 million, ED teams had the highest variation in revenue at $134 million and then the WD's at $55 million and ND's at $43 million and lastly SD's at $12 million. The latter division's teams had the smallest difference in revenue because similar amounts existed for the Falcons and Buccaneers and also the Panthers and Saints. Besides win–loss records in the regular season, the deviations reflect the population and population growth of their markets, popularity at home, and per capita income and the type of jobs and spending trends of local households.

In Table A6.3, Column 4 contains the operating income or EBITDA of NFC teams as of 2016. For the group of 16, it averaged $101 million. From most to least by division, ED clubs averaged $163 million, WD's $95 million, ND's $80 million, and SD's $68 million. Because of excessive payments for players' salaries and other types of expenses, the Lions, Panthers, and Vikings had the three smallest EBITDA's while the Cowboys, 49ers, and Giants earned the most income by operating efficiently. For various reasons, the Redskins, Eagles, and Bears were also very efficient along with some others within different areas of NFL markets.

While $60 million was the average deviation in operating income of these NFC teams, the ED's equaled $91 million, WD's $41 million, ND's $26 million, and SD's $10 million. The gap or variation between the most and least EBITDA within divisions occurred, respectively, for the Cowboys and Eagles, 49ers and Rams/Seahawks, Packers and Vikings, and Saints and Panthers. Simply put, their earnings varied because each of them operated by applying well-known and also new business practices, strategies, and tactics of the sports industry.

Each NFC teams' 2015–2016 gate receipts — in millions of dollars — appear in Column 5 of Table A6.3. While the conference's average was $65 million, the Cowboys had the most ($98 million) and then the Giants ($96 million) and Redskins ($80 million). In contrast to these amounts, the Buccaneers ($49 million), Vikings ($46 million), and Rams ($43 million) had the smallest gate receipts in the NFL that season.

The average dispersion or disparity in gate receipts was greatest among WD clubs ($14 million) compared to ED teams ($13 million) and also to those in the ND ($10 million) and SD ($7 million). Because of the large gap in amounts between, for example, the 49ers and Rams, the division's difference of highest and lowest gate receipts greatly exceeded that of the SD's Panthers and Buccaneers and ND's Bears and Vikings but interestingly, not much more than the ED's Cowboys and Eagles. Simply put, the Dallas–Fort Worth–Arlington, New York–Newark–Jersey City, Washington–Arlington–Alexandria, and San Francisco–Oakland–Hayward areas are large-to-very-large and more prosperous football markets than the majority of others.

In Table A6.3, Column 6 includes the D/V percentages of each NFC franchise in 2016. On average, the conference's was 12% or in amount, approximately $296 million per team based on estimated market values. Among each group, the WD's averaged 15%, SD's 14%, ND's 12%, and ED's 9%. Although nine clubs had debt percentages less than 9%, the D/V ratios exceeded 22% each for the Vikings, Falcons, and Rams.

As described for other variables in the table, the standard deviations of D/V were unequal among divisions and franchises within divisions. SD teams, for example, had the greatest variation at 17% and then those in the WD at 11%, ND at 9%, and ED at 4%. In order to reduce their ratios for financial reasons and operate more effectively, several teams needed to restructure themselves operationally as businesses in order to generate higher market values and/or record less amount of debt in accounts on their balance sheet.

As reported in *Forbes* for being an important, necessary, and periodic payment from an operations perspective, Column 7 in Table 6.3 lists the players' expenses — including benefits and bonuses — of these NFC teams in 2016. For the league, they totaled approximately $2.8 billion or $177 million per team. On average, the ED's was $188 million, SD's $182 million, WD's $170 million, and ND's $167 million.

While the Seahawks, Panthers, and Redskins ranked highest, the Lions, Vikings, Cardinals, Rams, and 49ers each paid less than $170 million in players' expenses. Given these amounts, only two of these eight clubs had an above-average or talented roster of players and won enough games in the regular season to qualify for the playoffs. Indeed, the other six failed to be competitive and participate in the conference's postseason partly because of their relatively small or misallocated investment in players' salaries.

Players' expenses were different and also significantly deviated between the four NFC divisions. From most to least in variation among the groups — as measured by their standard deviations — these included the WD's $18 million and then SD's $12 million, ND's 11 million, and ED's $4 million. Such amounts denote that the greatest disparity in payments occurred because of the Seahawks' $197 million versus the 49ers' $157 million in the WD, whereas the range in players' expenses within the SD, ND, and ED equaled, respectively, only $24 million between the Panthers and Falcons/ Buccaneers, $26 million between the Packers and Lions, and $11 million between the Redskins and Giants. Thus, not all NFC teams with the greatest revenues and/or largest market values always compensated their players more than rivals within their division.

Stadiums

As of the NFL's 2015–2016 season, the sixteen NFC teams played their home games in venues that differed in age, cost and market value, and also in such other ways as location, capacity, and ownership. Based on various criteria including their amenities, concessions and sightlines, they have been ranked from best to worst overall, most to least accessible, and highest to lowest as facilities to entertain spectators at games. Given those comparisons, this section provides some data and other information regarding the facilities of the conference's clubs and discusses specific characteristics about them.[14]

Among NFC teams' home sites within each division as of 2016, they ranged in age as follows: within the conference's ED, from the Giants'

7-year-old MetLife Stadium in East Rutherford, New Jersey, to the Redskins' 20-year-old FedEx Field in Landover, Maryland; within the ND, from the Vikings' 1-year-old US Bank Stadium in Minneapolis to the Packers' 60-year-old Lambeau Field in Green Bay; within the SD, from the Buccaneers' 19-year-old Raymond James Stadium in Tampa to the Saints' 42-year-old Mercedes-Benz Superdome in New Orleans; and within the WD, from the 49ers' 3-year-old Levi's Stadium in San Francisco to the Rams' 94-year-old Los Angeles Memorial Coliseum in Los Angeles. Of teams' 16 venues in the NFC, two or approximately 13% of them are privately owned and five or 31% publicly. Interestingly, the other nine or 56% are jointly owned by the team and a municipality and/or state agency.

Their construction costs ranked from being relatively cheap to very expensive. From the least to most costly within the conference's ED and then ND, SD and WD, respectively, it was $250 million to erect FedEx Field for the Redskins compared to $1.4 billion for MetLife Stadium for the Giants (and also AFC Jets); from less than $1 million to build Lambeau Field for the Packers to $1.1 billion for U.S. Bank Stadium for the Vikings; from $134 million to construct the Mercedes-Benz Superdome for the Saints to $242 million for Bank of America Stadium for the Panthers; and from $360 million for CenturyLink Field for the Seahawks to $1.2 billion for Levi's Stadium for the 49ers.

Regarding the most likely replacement or renovation of current venues in the NFC, a retractable-roof, privately–publicly financed, 65,000-seat, $1 billion Mercedes–Benz Stadium is scheduled to open during the summer of 2017 in Atlanta, Georgia, for the Falcons. Such others as the Rams' Los Angeles Memorial Stadium and the Saints' Mercedes-Benz Superdome — according to many football fans — are old and lack modern amenities of newer venues, have tight or uncomfortable seats and small spaces in the concourses, and are simply outdated in their appearance and design to host big-time football games.

Recently *Forbes* sports editors assigned economic values to venues of teams in the NFC. From lowest to highest within divisions, respectively, amounts in the ED were $371 million for Lincoln Financial Field in Philadelphia to $1.1 billion for AT&T Stadium in Dallas; in the ND, from $122 million for Ford Field in Detroit to $330 million for Soldier Field in Chicago; in the SD, from $197 million for Mercedes-Benz Superdome in

New Orleans to $260 million for Bank of America Stadium in Charlotte; and in the WD, from $208 million for University of Phoenix Stadium in Phoenix to $516 million for Levi's Stadium in San Francisco.[15]

Based on their estimated values, ED teams' venues averaged $632 million, ND' $215 million, SD' $214 million, and WD's $305 million. Furthermore, according to their standard deviations, those in the ED and SD, respectively, had the most and least variability in construction costs and also in estimated values. Nevertheless, because of increasing real estate prices in urban areas and popularity of the sport in America, most of them will likely appreciate economically, particularly those within the largest and most-populated markets and wealthiest metropolitan areas.

In various studies, NFL stadiums have been ranked by various football experts and sports journalists in the media with respect to their location and different amenities and problems. Although results vary according to each study's parameters, a few venues rank among the best while some others placed in the worst group. For example, the most attractive, entertaining, and well-structured facilities within the NFC based on their name, aesthetics, and experience for fans, are Lambeau Field and AT&T Stadium.

As reported in the *Stadium Journey*, the first of two best football buildings was rated highest for these reasons[16]:

"Packers fans are intelligent and well informed. They take the time to know the opponent as well as the home team. At times, it would appear that there are 70,000 NFL head coach candidates in the stands, but for the most part people share rational opinions about the match-up prior to kick-off or how situations are unfolding on the field. When the game starts, people are dialed in. Most are smart about getting up to go to the bathroom in between plays or series. No time is wasted on the wave during a crucial offensive possession, but the place can rock in the right 3rd and long situation."

For why the Cowboys' stadium ranked second in the conference, the editor provided these comments:

"Overall, the stadium, fans, and the amazing architectural structure with its retractable roof and doors provide a good atmosphere to see a game. Although, don't expect to have the roof or the doors opened as it is has been customary to keep them closed due to the Texas weather. The fantastic artwork located throughout the stadium adds an interesting touch and brings another reason any sports fan would enjoy their visit."

In another study, two of the lowest-ranked NFC facilities were the Falcons' Georgia Dome and Redskins' FedEx Field. Among others in the conference, the former ranked 16th (29th in the NFL) and the latter 15th (28th in the league). The study's author evaluated each of them, respectively, as follows[17]:

> "The dirty birds will play out their string at the Georgia Dome before moving to a new stadium next door in 2017. The new venue features a radical retractable roof design influenced by a popular children's toy. The 23-year-old dome [25-year-old as of 2016] has served its purpose, though. It's played host to the NCAA Final Four, Super Bowl and SEC football championship. Many fans take public transportation to Falcons games and those driving must pick their spots to find parking. One lot south of the dome, dubbed 'The Gulch,' is named for the original street level for Atlanta in the 1800s."

For why FedEx Field ranked almost last in the conference and league, comments were as follows:

> "Redskins owner Dan Snyder just can't sit still. He wants to move the team back to Washington and build a new stadium 18 years after the Skins moved to Maryland. FedEx Field has seen its fair share of improvements. Some worked, some didn't. The same can be said for the revolving door tied to FedEx Field's food providers. For this season, the team unveils a new traffic plan to ease help congestion. It's welcome news for Skins fans familiar with 2-hour waits to exit the lots after games."

Fan cost index

For several years, a Chicago-based company named Team Marketing Report (TMR) has prepared and published a Fan Cost Index (FCI) for the home games of teams in professional sports. To attend a game for a typical family with two kids, an FCI includes the cost of four average-priced tickets, two cheapest-priced draft beers, four each lowest-priced soft drinks and hot dogs, parking for one vehicle, and two each game programs and least-expensive, adult-sized adjustable caps. Costs are determined by telephone calls with team representatives, venues, and concessionaires and from questions asked during interviews.[18]

In the 2015–2016 NFL season, the average FCI for a family to attend a regular season game of an NFC team was $522. While Bears' home games each cost $685, the Buccaneers had the conference's lowest FCI at $418. Among divisions, the average from most to least was ED teams at $600, ND's $541, WD's $499, and SD's $449. The order from ranking them first to fourth occurred, in part, because FCIs of the Cowboys, Giants, and Redskins each exceeded $600, while those of such teams as the Falcons, Panthers, and Rams were each below $450.

For specific items in TMR's 2016 FCI, the approximate range in amounts from most to least expensive — or first compared to sixteenth across the NFC — were listed as follows: average ticket, Bears $131 to Rams $72; average premium ticket, Giants $509 to Lions $180; beer, 49ers $10 to Giants/Seahawks/Lions/Panthers each $5; soft drink, Lions/Falcons each $6.50 to Giants/Vikings each $3; hot dog, Lions $6.25 to Vikings/Seahawks each $3; parking, Cowboys $75 to Cardinals $14; and for a cap, Redskins $30 to Packers $14.95. Based on economics principles, these prices were set by teams and/or vendors to sell enough units to maximize revenue from their sales at home games in the stadiums.

From the NFL's 2011–2012 to 2015–2016 season, there were some significant increases but also relatively small and even decreases in FCIs of teams within the NFC. For examples of these changes, the Redskins' FCI rose from $461 to $657 or approximately 43% but the Buccaneers' from only $391 to $418 or about 6%, while the Cowboys' actually declined from $634 to $614 or 3%. Because of inflation, number of — and amount spent by — families at games in stadiums, and local economic conditions and other factors, the majority of teams and/or vendors raised their prices each year rather than keeping them constant or reducing amounts.

In evaluating year-to-year FCIs between, for example, the NFC's 2014–2015 and 2015–2016 seasons, the Bears' increased the most, in other words, from $601 to $685 or approximately 14%. Alternatively, fans' costs fell for home games of the Cowboys, Giants, Eagles, and 49ers but remained approximately the same for those of the Falcons at $437–$438. Thus, there were different payments for tickets and other things by families to attend conference teams' home games at their stadiums especially from 2011 to 2016.

The largest deviation in FCIs in 2016 occurred among ND clubs ($96) than those in the WD ($91), ED ($61), and SD ($46). Of the highest and lowest in each division, the Bears' amount exceeded the Lions by $207 compared to $202 for the 49ers and Rams, $144 for the Redskins and Eagles, and $100 for the Saints and Buccaneers. These gaps in FCI's reflect differences in teams' pricing policies and other factors such as their attendances at home games, win–loss record, stadium capacity, and popularity in the local and regional sports market.

ORGANIZATION HIGHLIGHTS

Besides regular-season and post-season games, the NFC and its franchises are involved in — and affected by — community events and also business-related and government affairs, news, and projects. Because these things and other topics influence the conference and also league in different but perhaps important and historic ways, following are a few of them from the academic and popular literature.[19]

First, based on information in Tables A5.1 and A6.1, the average metropolitan statistical area population (MSAPOP) of NFC teams is a larger number than in the AFC. Among eight divisions, the NFC's ED ranks first, WD second, ND fourth, and SD fifth. In addition, the NFC had the highest standard deviation in MSAPOP. Similar results occurred for other market data — designated market area television homes (DMATVH) and average attendance (AVGATT). Compared demographically, the NFC is the superior conference because of its teams' locations and their history, tradition, and success in the league. The AFC, meanwhile, was organized in 1970 with 10 former clubs of the AFL plus the NFL's Baltimore Colts, Cleveland Browns, and Pittsburgh Steelers.

Second, regarding averages of teams' historical performances in Tables A5.2 and A6.2, the NFC led the AFC in seasons, wins, winning percentage, and number of titles and championships. After combining each of the conference teams' titles and championships and referring to them as "TPs," the NFC had 331 and AFC 196. Among the top five TPs (ranked) were the

Packers with 45 (first), Giants 43 (second), Cowboys and Steelers each 35 (tied for third), and Bears 33 (fifth). For the most part, this result reflects the pre-1970 era when ED and WD/Conference teams won titles and NFL championships from 1933 to 1969. Also, the NFC's clubs were in 98 more playoffs through the league's 2015–2016 season especially those in the conference's ED, ND, and SD but not the WD where four teams in the two groups each qualified for 67 playoffs.

Third, according to Tables A5.3 and A6.3, NFC teams combined had a higher average market value and revenue, operating income, gate receipts, and D/V ratios relative to those in the AFC. For specific amounts in each conference by financial category, these were, respectively, the Cowboys and Patriots each first at $4.2 billion and $3.4 billion in value; Redskins and Jets each second at $447 million and $423 million in revenue; Giants and Ravens each third at $133 million and $103 million in operating income; 49ers and Ravens each fourth at $76 million and $68 million in gate receipts; and Giants/Lions and Ravens each fifth at 16% and 12% in D/V.

Fourth, the AFC teams as a group had higher average players' expenses ($182 million) than those in the NFC ($177 million). While such mediocre teams as the Bills, Chargers, and Jets overpaid their players in the league's 2015–2016 season, the Super Bowl-champion Broncos ranked sixth in their conference at $188 million and the runner-up Panthers second at $195 million within the NFC. However, the variation or deviation in players expenses were about the same in the conferences at $13–$14 million. The smallest and largest amounts across divisions ranged from $4 million to $18 million in the NFC's ED compared to the conference's WD, and $10 million to $13 million in the AFC's ED to SD. As explained in Chapter 6, these amounts indicate, in part, whether differences in players' expenses actually affected their teams' performances in the NFL's regular season and also its' post-season.

Fifth, NFC teams' stadiums were statistically but also marginally different in age, cost, funding, market value, and capacity than those in the AFC as of 2016. The former conference's venues, on average, tended to be younger in age, more expensive in construction costs, and higher in market value. However, their stadiums were funded with about the same proportions from private, public, and private–public sources. Averaged by groups, the oldest stadiums exist within the AFC's WD at 39-years-old and most costly in the

NFC's ND at $540 million and valuable at $637 million in the AFC's ED. With respect to funding those in the NFC, two of them were built with private money — MetLife Stadium and Back of America Stadium, five with funds only from government, and nine privately–publicly. In the AFC, these funding sources were respectively one, five, and 10. Also, from smallest to largest by division, NFL stadiums' capacities ranged from approximately 67 million for teams in the AFC's ND and SD to 77 million for those in the NFC's ED.

Sixth, as denoted in Chapters 5 and 6, NFC teams' average FCI in 2016 was $522 or about 8% more than those in the AFC. From most to least expensive for families to attend games in the league's 2015–2016 season, the NFC's ED clubs ranked first at $600 and AFC's SD teams eighth at $432. While typical fans of the Cowboys, Giants, Redskins, Bears, 49ers, and Patriots each paid at least $614 per game, it cost less than $400 to see home games of the Browns, Jaguars, and Titans. Among divisions, the NFC's ND teams had the largest variation or deviation in FCIs at $96 and the conference's SD smallest at $46. While a Bears' game at Soldier Field was $190 more than one of the Vikings' at US Bank Stadium, it was only $100 more to watch the Saints perform at the Mercedes-Benz Superdome than see the Buccaneers compete at Raymond James Stadium.

Seventh, the Cowboys have America's team power in terms of television ratings. Their victory over the rival Redskins on Thanksgiving Day in late November 2016 was a television ratings bonanza. Fox Sports said the game averaged 35.1 million viewers, more than any regular-season game in the network's history, which dates to 1994. According to NFL spokesman Greg Aiello, it was the most-watched regular-season game for any network since the 1995 Thanksgiving Day game between the Cowboys and Chiefs, which drew 35.7 million viewers. Of the NFL season's five most-watched games, the Cowboys played in four of them, with the Thanksgiving Day game leading the way. Dallas also drew big numbers against the Steelers (28.9 million) earlier in November and against the Packers (28.0 million) in October and Giants (27.5 million) in September's season opener. The only game in the top five that did not include the Cowboys was when the Lions and Vikings drew 27.6 million television viewers.

Eighth, statistically ranked in all-time greatness according to a sports website, the NFC Packers were first and Panthers 30th. Owned by their fans,

Green Bay had numerous periods of success including their dynasty of the 1960s — which some consider the NFL's first real dynasty. Prior to that period, they won a league-high nine world championships and then four Super Bowl trophies. They have the second-most Hall of Fame inductees and made the playoffs 32 times. The club's combination of ancient, modern, and current success put it atop the list. Established in 1995, the Panthers had three separate rosters find relative success with seven playoff appearances and two conference titles. The club, however, has not been consistent with no Hall of Fame inductees as of 2016.

Ninth, the NFC Buccaneers and AFC Dolphins should greatly improve in the league's 2017–2018 season. Tampa Bay quarterback Jameis Winston can work with two top receivers while playing in a division that features two currently terrible defenses. If it keeps Lavonte David and Gerald McCoy, Tampa Bay could be as good as the Panthers three years after drafting Cam Newton. The Dolphins have upgraded their offensive line, and rookie receiver DeVante Parker has drawn rave reviews. With the addition of Jordan Cameron and Kenny Stills, quarterback Tannehill has a better chance to succeed.

Tenth, former APFA Decatur/Chicago Staleys and NFL Chicago Bears coach George Halas is second in all-time wins to Don Shula. Besides being a player and the founder and owner of the Staleys/Bears organization, he coached them for 48 years. Halas was lesser known as an inventor, jurist, radio producer, philanthropist, philatelist, and MLB player. In 1963, he became one of the first 17 inductees into the Pro Football Hall of Fame. Awarded by the NFL, the NFC champion receives the George Halas Trophy while the Pro Football Writers Association gives the George S. Halas Courage Award to the player or coach who performed with abandon despite injury or personal problems.

NOTES

1. For the history of the APFA (renamed NFL in 1922) and its various teams and their coaches and players, see Jozsa FP Jr. (2016). *National Football League Franchises: Team Performances, Financial Consequences*. Lanham, MD: Lexington; and also Quirk J and Fort RD (1992). *Pay Dirt: The Business of Professional Team Sports*. Princeton, NJ: Princeton University Press.

2. These and other facts are in the *2014 Official NFL Record & Fact Book*. New York, NY: National Football League (2014).

3. Jozsa FP Jr. and Guthrie JJ Jr. (1999). *Relocating Teams and Expanding Leagues in Professional Sports: How the Major Leagues Respond to Market Conditions.* Westport, CT: Quorum Books.

4. Football information and data is available on such websites as http://www.nfl.com, http://www.sports-reference.com, http://www.sportsencyclopedia.com, and http://www.pro-football-reference.com.

5. "Defunct Teams Histories," http://www.sportsencyclopedia.com [cited 15 January 2016].

6. For demographic data and other details about actual and potential sports markets, see such references as "The 382 Metropolitan Statistical Areas of the United States of America," http://www.en.wikipedia.org [cited 12 October 2016]; "Population Estimates 2015," http://www.census.gov [cited 12 November 2016]; and "Top U.S. Metropolitan Areas by Population, 1790–2010," http://www.peakbagger.com [cited 5 December 2016].

7. Standard Deviation (SD) measures spread of the numbers in a set of data from its mean value. It is represented using the symbol σ (sigma). This also measures variability or volatility in the given set of data. Find the mean, variance, and SD of the given numbers using this free arithmetic standard deviation calculator online. Enter 'n' number of values in the calculator and find the SD (σ), mean, and variance. See "Standard Deviation Calculator," http://www.easycalculation.com [cited 3 January 2017].

8. *Idem,* "The 382 Metropolitan Statistical Areas of the United States of America."

9. For other details about its provisions, see the "NFL Collective Bargaining Agreement," http://www.nfllabor.com [cited 24 December 2016].

10. Please read "Team Encyclopedias and Records," http://www.pro-football-reference.com [cited 1 December 2016].

11. "Picking the Best Team Ever for All 32 NFL Franchises," http://www.espn.com [cited 23 December 2016] and Neil Paine, "The Best NFL Teams of All Time, According to Elo," http://www.fivethirtyeight.com [cited 23 December 2016]. The Elo rating is a metric for evaluating a team's skill level at any given moment. Elo is not the only power rating, but a relatively simple algorithm with an elegant, endlessly customizable design that makes the most of the information it receives.

12. Two references are Angel Diaz, "The 25 Worst NFL Teams of All Time," http://www.complex.com [cited 29 December 2016] and "Worst NFL Teams of All Time," http://www.espn.com [cited 29 December 2016].

13. For financial data about teams, see Mike Ozanian, "2016 NFL Valuations," http://www.forbes.com [cited 1 December 2016].

14. Stadium data and other information about them appear in such sources as "NFL Stadium Comparisons," http://www.stadiumsofprofootball.com [cited 25 December 2016] and "Tour Every NFL Stadium," http://www.espn.com [cited 25 December 2016].

15. See Table A6.3 in the Appendix for the estimated economic value of all NFC teams as of the league's 2015–16 season.

16. Swaney P, "2015 NFL Stadium Experience Rankings," http://www.scout.com [cited 31 December 2016].

17. Muret RD, "Ranking All NFL Stadiums," http://www.sportingnews.com [cited 10 January 2017].

18. "Fan Cost Index," http://www.teammarketingreport.com [cited 16 November 2016].

19. Besides Tables A6.1–A6.3 in the appendix, the references for this section include: "Dallas Cowboys Dominating NFL TV Ratings," http://www.upi.com [cited 14 January 2017]; Daniel Zimmer, "All 32 NFL Franchises Statistically Ranked in All-Time Greatness," http://www.nflspinzone.com [cited 14 January 2017]; Arthur K, "What the NFL Will Look Like in 2018," http://www.sportsonearth.com [cited 14 January 2017]; Doleiden Z, "George Halas Trophy: 5 Fast Facts You Need to Know," http://www.heavy.com [cited 15 January 2017]; "George Halas Award," http://www.profootballwriters.org [cited 15 January 2017].

Part IV
National Hockey League

Chapter 7

EASTERN CONFERENCE

HISTORY

Before the late 1910s, several ice hockey leagues existed throughout North America. These included, for example, the Amateur Hockey Association of Canada (1886–1898), Eastern Canada Amateur Hockey Association (1905–1909), and the Canadian Hockey Association (1909–1910). After these failed, the National Hockey Association (NHA) (1910–1918) became a prominent organization in the sport despite such rivals as the Ontario Professional Hockey League (1908–1911), Maritime Professional Hockey League (1911–1914), and Pacific Coast Hockey Association (1912–1924) or simply PCHA.[1]

Since forming in 1910, the NHA was involved in conflicts and disputes that, in turn, affected its growth, popularity, and success. Besides competing with other sports for hockey fans within local, regional, and national markets, the league also experienced problems with officials including team owners and their coaches and players. During World War I, the league struggled most years to schedule games in regular seasons and post-seasons, generate enough revenue to continue operations, supervise and regulate teams' behavior, and maintain an honest but competent and efficient administrative staff.

Toronto Blueshirts' owner Edward J. Livingstone was the most controversial, disliked, and mistrusted executive in the NHA. Specifically, some hockey officials accused him of such things as ignoring and even undermining league policies, regulations and rules, bribing and offering illegal contracts to hire other clubs' players, campaigning to remove the Montreal Wanderers from the NHA, and threatening to campaign for and establish another professional but competitive ice hockey organization somewhere in Canada.

These and other problems, in part, caused NHA President Frank Robinson to suspend a Toronto club and then later, he resigned from his position while team owners joined to oust Livingstone from the sport. In fact, they demanded to sell the Blueshirts team sometime during the spring of 1917. Nonetheless, Livingstone negotiated a deal whereby the Toronto Arena Gardens Company would temporarily operate the club as a commercial venture until he eventually regained control of it.

During autumn of 1917, the NHA suspended operations in order to review and perhaps revise its business model but more significantly, to form a new professional hockey league without Livingstone's participation in it. At its annual meeting that year, the NHA announced a breakup because its officials declared that five teams were not a feasible number for the organization to operate efficiently and profitably at their respective home sites. Furthermore, there were simply not enough talented hockey players available to perform in games due to them being inducted into the military and actual combat service during World War I in Europe.

In November 1917, key representatives from the Montreal Canadiens and Montreal Wanderers and also the Ottawa Senators and Quebec Bulldogs met at the Windsor Hotel in Montreal, Canada. While there, they established the National Hockey League (NHL). In addition, the group agreed to adopt the NHA's constitution and its reserve list of players. As a result of organizing the NHL, this meant that control, decision-making, and power in the sport would gradually shift from clubs with self-interested owners such as Livingstone to the new league's hierarchy including such officials as newly-elected president, Frank Calder.

Although the NHL struggled as an organization from 1917 to the early 1920s, it stabilized and actually improved relations with such other hockey leagues as the PCHA and Western Canada Hockey League. Because of some teams' revenue from the Stanley Cup playoffs and competing for a championship plus Calder's excellent leadership skills, the NHL became gradually more popular and marginally profitable in the expanding commercialized hockey industry.

Before the NHL's 1923 season, however, some of its teams had financial troubles while others successfully attracted fans to their games and thrived in their respective markets. Because the Quebec Bulldogs and Montreal Wanderers folded, the league consisted of clubs that played at home in Montreal, Ottawa, and Toronto in the 1917–1918 and 1918–1919 seasons. Then in 1919, the Quebec Athletic Club/Bulldogs reentered the league, but one year later, it moved from Quebec City to Hamilton, Ontario, and renamed itself the Hamilton Tigers. In short, from the 1920–1921 to 1923–1924 seasons, the NHL included one team each in Hamilton, Montreal, Ottawa, and Toronto.

Regarding another historically important event of the period, former NHA executive and maverick team owner Edward Livingstone threatened to organize an international hockey league with money he received from settling a lawsuit filed against the Toronto Arena Gardens. Fearing his efforts to sell the sport as an entertainment commodity and responding to an expanding American economy in years following World War I, NHL franchise owners decided to adopt and implement an innovative strategy. That is, they appointed hockey entrepreneur and pioneer Tom Duggan to study the feasibility of locating new teams in markets throughout the US and some more within Canada.

From 1924 to 2016, the league approved four new teams in the 1920s, six in the 1960s, 10 in the 1970s (including four from the World Hockey Association), seven in the 1990s, and two in the 2000s. Being current members in a division of the NHL's Eastern Conference (EC), they and their expansion (years) sequentially were the Boston Bruins (1924), Detroit Red Wings (1926), New York Rangers (1926), Philadelphia Flyers (1967), Pittsburgh Penguins (1967), Buffalo Sabres (1970), New York Islanders (1972), Washington Capitols (1974), Ottawa Senators (1992), Tampa Bay Lightning (1992), Florida Panthers (1993), and Columbus Blue Jackets (2000). ENDNOTE: Cutler Klein, "From Six Teams to 31: History of NHL Expansion," nhl.com, cited 15 February 2017.

Besides them, other clubs in the conference as of 2016 include the Montreal Canadiens, Toronto Maple Leafs, Carolina Hurricanes, and New Jersey Devils. While the Canadiens and Maple Leafs joined the NHL originally in 1917, the Whalers moved from Hartford, Connecticut, to Raleigh, North Carolina, in 1997 and were nicknamed Hurricanes, and the Rockies from Denver, Colorado, to East Rutherford, New Jersey, in 1982 and were renamed New Jersey Devils. In addition to those facts, Toronto was previously nicknamed Arenas and then Patricks, and Detroit the Cougars and then Falcons. Thus, within the EC, 12 or approximately 74% of the group are expansion teams, two or 12.5% lifetime members, and another two or 12.5% moved from different areas.

Before discussing topics relative to the growth, development, and success of the NHL and its franchises and their stadiums and organizations, the World Hockey Association (WHA) formed in 1972 and had several teams playing their home and away games in non-NHL and large US markets. While the New England Whalers, Quebec Nordiques, and Winnipeg Jets each existed for seven seasons and the Edmonton Oilers and Houston Astros each for six, some others folded or relocated from one area to another after one or more years in the league.

Although competitive in interleague games, the WHA's problems included such things as undercapitalized franchises, low attendances at teams' games, relatively high players' salaries, a number of inferior and disgruntled team owners, poor scheduling of games especially during weekdays, lack of sponsors and a major television contract, and resistance from the NHL. After negotiating — even sometimes in bad faith — the two professional hockey leagues merged their operation before the sport's 1979–1980 season. As a result, the Whalers (renamed Hartford Whalers) and Nordiques joined divisions of the NHL's Prince of Wales Conference as did the Jets and Oilers of the Clarence Campbell Conference. Individually treated as expansion franchises, their entry fee into the NHL was each $6 million.[2]

TEAMS

Markets

From 1917 to 2016, five NHL franchises became "defunct" and folded their operations. Of the total, the Montreal Wanderers disbanded in 1918, Philadelphia Quakers in 1931, St. Louis Eagles in 1935, Montreal Maroons in 1938, and New York Americans in 1942. In addition to them, some clubs moved to different areas. Specifically, these were the Quebec Bulldogs→Hamilton in 1920; Hamilton Tigers→New York in 1925; Pittsburgh Pirates→Philadelphia in 1930; and Ottawa Senators→St. Louis in 1934.[3]

After the league realigned into the Clarence Campbell and Prince of Wales Conferences in 1974 and then 19 years later renamed EC and Western Conference (WC), more teams transferred to other areas. These included the California Golden Seals→Cleveland and Kansas City Scouts→Colorado both in 1976; Atlanta Flames→Calgary in 1980; Colorado Rockies→New Jersey in 1982; Minnesota North Stars→Dallas in 1993; Quebec Nordiques→Colorado in 1995; Winnipeg Jets→Phoenix in 1996; Hartford Whalers→Carolina in 1997; and Atlanta Thrashers→Winnipeg in 2011.

In 1993, the 14 EC clubs existed in relatively large, midsized, and small cities. Geographically, they ranged north to south or in other ways from New York to Miami in the Atlantic Division (AD) and from Quebec City to Hartford in the Northeast Division (NED). Their metropolitan areas' populations were also different and within the two divisions ranked from most to least in (millions) as follows: in the AD were teams based in New York–Jersey City–Newark (19.3), Washington (6.7), Philadelphia (5.8), Miami (3.1), and Tampa Bay (2.1); in the NED, they included Boston (5.4), Montreal (3.1), Pittsburgh (2.3), Buffalo (1.2), Hartford (1.1), Ottawa (0.9), and Quebec (0.5). Although there were no EC clubs in areas west of New York State or in the south, at least three each in the WC had home sites in the US Midwest and on the west coast, one in the southwest, and five in Canada.

During the NHL's 1993–1994 to 2016–2017 season, new EC teams began to play at home in such locations — with Metropolitan Statistical Area (MSA) populations in (millions) — as Atlanta (4.2), Miami (3.1), and Columbus (1.5). In addition, the Whalers moved from Hartford (1.1) to Raleigh-Durham (1.1). These and others occurred, in part, because of such things as changes in franchise owners, construction of new arenas at the post-move sites, and also because the MSAs contained enough people including households with increasing disposable and/or per capita incomes.

To provide and examine some current, interesting, and relevant data and facts about the league's existing EC teams in order to examine the economics, sizes, and other elements of their markets, there is information about them in Table A7.1. Within the table, variables researched were each team's Metropolitan Statistical Area Population (MSAPOP), number of Designated Market Area Television Homes (DMATVH), and average attendances (AVGATT) at home games in the NHL as of 2016. These criteria are measured, listed, and ranked in order to reveal the attributes and characteristics of such competitors and rivals as the AD's Boston Bruins and Detroit Red Wings, and MD's New Jersey Devils and New York Rangers.

Based on data listed in Column 2 of Table A7.1, the typical EC team had a MSAPOP of 4.28 million. More specifically, MD teams' areas on average were ranked first at 4.74 million followed by those in the AD at 3.82 million. While the Devils, Islanders, and Rangers had the largest number of people within their markets, the three smallest were in areas of the Senators, Hurricanes, and Sabres partly because of their economic development, growth, and prosperity. These differences, in turn, affected and will influence each club's potential and actual ticket sales, revenue from games and other sources, and market value, especially those identical or similar in size within divisions such as the AD's Panthers and Maple Leafs and also Red Wings and Canadiens, and the MD's Flyers and Capitals in addition to the Devils, Islanders, and Rangers.[4]

Besides averages for the conference and by division, the variation or dispersion in MSAPOPs was determined mathematically using the standard deviation. While it averaged 2.14 million people across 16 teams in the EC, the MD's deviation ranked highest at 2.40 million followed by the AD's 1.89 million. In other words, the least equal in market population were areas of the Blue Jackets and their divisional rivals but most alike are those of AD teams particularly the Sabres and Senators but not, for example, the Panthers or Lightning. Because of such widespread variation in MSAPOPs, teams' locations impacted them in various ways such as their attendances at home games, media coverage, travel costs, and other variables of these franchises.

In Table A7.1, Column 3 is the expected number of television homes in each team's designated market area (DMATVH) in years' 2016–2017. While it averaged 1.86 million across the conference, the AD teams' on average equaled 1.72 million television homes and those in the MD 1.99 million. Similar to but not exactly like the distribution of the MSAPOPs, the largest number of homes with televisions for these clubs is in the Philadelphia and then Toronto, Washington, and New York–New Jersey DMAs while the fewest existed in Columbus, Buffalo, and Ottawa.

As explained before for the MSAPOP, the standard deviation of television homes in teams' areas denotes differences across the conference and also between and within divisions. While the variation was 0.78 or 780,000 television homes among the entire group in the EC, AD clubs had the largest at

0.80 or 800,000 compared to the MD's 0.77 or 770,000. Within divisions, for example, the difference between the number of television homes in Philadelphia and Columbus was close but not exactly the same, for example, as between Toronto and Ottawa or Boston and Buffalo. Interestingly the MD's Devils, Islanders, Rangers, and Capitals and also the AD's Red Wings and Lightning are each similar with respect to this characteristic of their market. This, however, does not mean more or fewer fans actually viewed their games on television at home or other places.

In Table A7.1, Column 4 lists the average attendance of each EC team while playing games in its home stadium in the league's 2015–2016 season. For this statistic, the Canadiens ranked first at 21,273-seat Centre Bell complex in Montreal, Canada, Red Wings second at 20,066-seat Joe Louis Arena in Detroit, Michigan, and Flyers third at 19,500-seat Wells Fargo Center in Philadelphia. In contrast to them, teams' with the three smallest attendances at their home were the Islanders at 18,103-seat Barclays Center in Brooklyn, New York, Blue Jackets at 18,500-seat Nationwide Arena in Columbus, Ohio, and Hurricanes at 18,600-seat PNC Arena in Raleigh, North Carolina.

While the conference's attendance was 17,510 per game, AD teams averaged 18,790 fans and those in the MD about 16,220. Ranked among the highest and lowest within their division, respectively, home games of the AD's Maple Leafs and Lightning were more popular, for example, than those of the Bruins and Sabres. In addition, the MD's Hurricanes and Islanders had the lowest-ranked combined attendances and not the AD's Panthers and Senators. In fact, such things as these teams' win–loss records, ticket prices, advertising and marketing campaigns, and number of superstar goalies and other players affected in some way their Sunday and other night attendances at home games.

Regarding the deviation in teams' average attendances in the league's 2015–2016 season, it was 2,520 spectators per game for the conference, but from most to least by division it was as follows: 2,650 people in the AD and 1,690 in the MD. This suggests that MD clubs had a greater variation in number of fans at their games, in part, because of sellouts at the Flyers' Wells Fargo Center in Philadelphia and near sellouts at the Penguins' PPG Paints Arena in Pittsburgh, Capitals' Verizon Center in Washington and Rangers' Madison Square Garden in New York, but not at the Blue Jackets' Nationwide Arena in Columbus or the Devils' Prudential Center in Newark.

For various reasons including competitiveness and ability to entertain fans and the capacity of their stadiums, very small differences in attendances between them occurred, for example, at the Penguins' PPG Paints Arena and Capitals' Verizon Center, and Bruins' TD Garden and Sabres' KeyBank Center. Although the Penguins and Capitals won more regular-season games and scored more points than the Bruins and Sabres in 2015–2016, they each sold about the same number of seats to fans at their home games and are therefore equally popular.

Given the data and its distribution in Table A7.1, the AD's Maple Leafs and also MD's Devils, Islanders, Rangers, Flyers, and Capitals each played their home games in relatively large markets; the AD's Bruins, Red Wings, Panthers, Canadiens, and Lightning, in addition to the MD's Penguins in midsized markets; and the AD's Sabres and Senators plus MD's Hurricanes and Blue Jackets in small markets. Thus, 37.5% of the league's EC teams existed in MSAs with plenty of fans and television homes during the league's 2015–2016 season, and also 37.5% had home sites in less populated areas with fewer television homes, while another 25% performed within markets with below-average or inferior data.

According to rankings in the table — except for the EC's Devils, Islanders, and Rangers in the New York–Newark–Jersey City area and Capitals in the Washington–Arlington–Alexandria metropolis, and also Sabres in the Buffalo–Cheektowaga–Niagara area and Senators in Ottawa, the other teams' markets within and across divisions are each different demographically and roughly represent their economies and the sport's fan base.

For more about variables in Table A7.1 and their potential to be future hockey markets after the league's 2016–2017 season, the most populated places without an NHL team are such US MSAs as Riverside–San Bernardino–Ontario (4.48 million), St. Louis (2.81 million), Portland–Vancouver–Hillsboro (2.39 million), Orlando–Kissimmee–Sanford (2.38 million), San Antonio–New Braunfels (2.38 million), Sacramento–Roseville–Arden–Arcade (2.27 million), and Las Vegas–Henderson–Paradise (2.11 million). With respect to DMAs in the top thirty, those without a club — besides Houston, Texas and Seattle-Tacoma, Washington — are others like Orlando–Daytona Beach–Melbourne, Charlotte, Cleveland–Akron, Portland, Baltimore, Indianapolis, San Diego, Nashville, and Hartford–New Haven.[5]

If the league expands at a site in an area not hosting a current NHL team, a few of these places are viable markets. In addition, they are potential sites for any existing NHL clubs with outdated stadiums and who compete for local fans with other teams in Major League Baseball (MLB) and any in the National Basketball Association (NBA) and/or National Football League (NFL). Among the group, there has been speculation in the media about locating a new or existing franchise especially in Las Vegas, Nevada, or another one in Los Angeles, and also in smaller US metropolitan areas such as Kansas City, Missouri, or Milwaukee, Wisconsin.

Despite being homes of former NHL or WHA teams that folded or relocated in years from 1917 to 2000 or not admitted into the NHL for various reasons, the group includes such cities as Atlanta, Georgia; Baltimore, Maryland; Birmingham, Alabama; Cincinnati and Cleveland, Ohio; Hamilton, Ontario; Hartford, Connecticut; Indianapolis, Indiana; Kansas City, Missouri; and Oakland, California. In short, a number of places are potentially adequate sites to host an NHL expansion team or one that struggles to get local fans to attend its home games and/or earn enough money to operate effectively within a division of the EC.

Before discussing teams' performances in the next section of this chapter, the NHL Players Association (NHLPA) signed a Collective Bargaining Agreement (CBA) with the league on 12 January, 2013. This concluded a four-month lockout by owners of the league's clubs. The CBA sets the terms and conditions of employment of all professional hockey players playing in the league as well as the rights of the NHL and also its clubs and the NHLPA.[6]

The following are some general but interesting features of the Agreement:

- The CBA is a 10-year agreement, but both participants can choose to opt out after eight years. The NHL has the first opportunity to do so before 1 September, 2019. If it declines, the NHLPA can decide to opt out by 19 September, 2019. The 10-year deal expires September 15, 2022.
- Re-entry waivers have been eliminated with no more half-price discounts.
- By the time it expires in 2022, the NHL's minimum salary will be $750,000.
- Supplementary discipline that results in fines can increase to $10,000 for the first offense and up to $15,000 for each and every one after that infraction. Still, there is not even a slap on the wrist for offenses that do not warrant suspension. There will also be a neutral third party if a player chooses to appeal a suspension of six games or more.

- Beginning with the league's 2013–2014 season, teams had to schedule from six to eight preseason games.
- Random drug testing occurs during training periods, regular seasons, playoffs, and in off-seasons.
- Beginning with players' second contract, they are entitled to their own hotel room on the road.
- The new Christmas break is December 24–26. In seasons where December 26 is a Saturday, the break takes place December 23–25.
- Intermission lengths in games increase from 17 to 18 minutes and all between-periods activities are shortened from five to four minutes. This helps to improve the ice surface.
- If requested by the NHL, teams must participate in at least one international game during the time period of the CBA. As a result, the NHL Premiere or non-North American Games in Europe do not appear to be going anywhere.

Performances

During the league's 100-year history (1917–2017), the number of pre-EC/EC teams ranged from four in the 1921–1922 to 1923–1924 seasons to sixteen from 1972–1973 to 2016–2017. Because of differences in performances, some of their players were among all-time leaders in points, goals per game, and total games within the sport. These include, for example, such players as the Panthers' Jaromir Jagr, Red Wings' Gordie Howe, Hurricanes' Ron Francis, and Penguins' Mario Lemiuex in points; in goals per game, Islanders' Mike Bossy, Senator's Cy Denneny, Patricks'/Maple Leafs' Babe Dye, and Capitals Alex Ovechkin; and in total games, Flyers' Mark Recchi, Red Wings' Chris Chelios, Devils' Scott Stevens, and Bruins' Ray Bourque. A few coaches with outstanding careers, in part, with conference teams were the Canadiens' Scotty Bowman, Islanders' Al Arbour, Maple Leafs' Hap Day, Maple Leafs'/Sabres' Punch Imlach, and Red Wings' Tommy Ivan and Jack Adams.[7]

Points

Besides differences in the abilities of coaches and players, each team's total seasons in the league — as listed in Column 2 of Table A7.2 — partly influenced results. While the conference average was approximately 52 seasons per team, the AD's equaled 62 and MD's 42. As of 2015–2016, the Canadiens and Maple Leafs led the group of 16 teams each with 99 seasons followed by the Bruins and then Red Wings and Rangers. With the least number of seasons, however, were the Panthers at 14th, Hurricanes at 15th, and Blue Jackets at 16th.

Other than totals, deviation in seasons existed among the two group of clubs. Compared to 30 on average for the conference, the AD's and MD's were respectively 36 and 22 seasons. These differences in divisions occurred, in part, because the Bruins, Red Wings, Canadiens and Maple Leafs each played at least ninety years but the Hurricanes and Blue Jackets each less than 20.

Given the number and distribution of seasons by division, an important factor in ranking EC teams' performances is their total points through the leagues' 2015–2016 season. According to data in Column 3 of Table A7.2, the most successful in the conference have been the Canadiens, Bruins, and Red Wings while the fewest points belong to the Panthers, Hurricanes, and Blue Jackets. Relative to an overall mean score of 4,032 points, AD teams averaged 4,658 and the MD's 3,407.

Montreal scored more than 7,600 points because of such coaches — besides Scotty Bowman and Pat Burns — as Newsy Lalonde, Mario Tremblay, Toe Blake, and Jacques Martin, and also performances by centers' Henri Richard, Saku Koivu, and Guy Charboneau. Besides them, goalies Jacques Plante, Ken Dryden, and Patrick Roy, defensemen Doug Harvey, Emile Bouchard, and Guy Lapointe, and right wingers Boom Boom Geoffrion, Maurice Richard, and Dickie Moore had successful careers with the club. In fact, these players contributed to Canadiens' teams having many winning seasons and qualifying, in part, for 82 playoffs in 99 or approximately 83% of their years.

In addition to Montreal, Boston's NHL club also scored in excess of 7,000 points. While franchise presidents' Charles and Weston Adams and Walter Brown are in the sport's Hall of Fame, so are such players as goalies Tiny Thompson, Gerry Cheevers, and Bernie Parent, defensemen Ray Borque, Dit Clapper, and Bobby Orr, right wingers Bobby Bauer, Cam Neely, and Harry Oliver, and left wingers' John Bucyk, Woody Dumart, and Roy Conacher. Others whose uniform numbers by the Bruins were retired included centers' Phil Esposito and Mitt Schmidt, while head coaches Don

Cherry, Pat Burns, and Claude Julien won the Jack Adams Award for leading their teams in specific seasons.

Following Montreal and Boston, Detroit's NHL club was ranked third in points as of the league's 2015–2016 season. Its most prominent coaches, in part, have been Hall of Famers Jack Adams, Tommy Ivan, and Scotty Bowman, and such trophy winners as goalies Terry Sawchuk, Glen Hall, and Roger Crozier, centers Alex Delvecchio, Pavel Datsyuk, Sid Abel, and Steve Yzerman, right wingers Gordie Howe and Sergi Federov, and left wingers Ted Lindsay and Henrik Zetterberg.

Because of different problems including competition from various teams, the AD's Panthers, Senators, and Lightning and MD's Hurricanes and Blue Jackets each scored fewer than 2,000 points as of 2016 and as a result, they lost a majority of regular-season games despite making changes to improve their coaching staff and active roster of players. Following is specific information about each of them.

For examples of their performances prior to the league's 2016–2017 season, the Panthers won only one conference title but zero Stanley Cups, and none of the team's players earned a Selke, Norris, Vezina, or Hart Trophy; the Senators have just two Hall of Famers, retired uniform numbers of only three players and in 15 playoffs, won five titles but zero Stanley Cups; during 24 seasons, the Lightning appeared in nine playoffs, had one Hart Trophy winner but zero players getting a Selke, Norris, Vezina, or Calder Trophy; the Hurricanes won three division and two conference titles in nineteen seasons with no top coaches, while their players failed to perform well enough to earn a Masterton, Norris, Vezina, or Hart Trophy; and the Blue Jackets have zero titles, only one Hall of Famer, and one Vezina Trophy in its 16 years in the league. In short, these five clubs have underperformed within their division of the EC and relative to competitors across the NHL.

Statistically, the standard deviation is used to measure the variation or inequality in number of points between and within divisions of the EC. The widest variation in points occurred among teams in the AD (2,587) and least in the MD (1,646). Because of a relatively large difference in deviations between divisions, the highest and lowest within them indicated, for example, that the Canadiens had 5,862 more points than the Lightning in the AD while the Rangers' 6,388 points exceeded the Blue Jackets' by 5,210 in the MD. Thus, in evaluating and ranking their total points scored as of 2016,

AD teams have been the most unequal competitively among themselves and when compared to those in the other division of the conference.

Playoffs

The league's 2016 season was the third year in which the top three teams in each division qualified for the playoffs along with two wild cards in each conference, or a total of eight playoff teams each from the AD and MD. Regarding playoff brackets in each round, teams compete in a best-of-seven series following a 2-2-1-1-1 format. The team with home ice advantage plays at its arena for games one and two and if necessary, games five and seven, while the other team is at home for games three and four and, if necessary, game six.

In the First Round, the lower seeded wild card in the conference plays against the division winner with the best record, while the other wild card plays against the other division winner, and both wild cards are de facto number four seeds. The other series match the second and third place teams from the divisions. In the first two rounds, home ice advantage is awarded to the team with the better seed, and in the last two rounds, to the team that had the better regular season record.[8]

Based on their performances in NHL regular seasons from 1917–1918 to 2015–2016, the Canadiens ranked first with 82 playoffs, Bruins second with 69, Maple Leafs third with 65, Red Wings fourth with 64, and Rangers fifth with 58. In contrast to them, the Blue Jackets ranked 16th with two, Hurricanes and Panthers tied for fourteenth each with five, and Lightning thirteenth with nine. With respect to EC teams' total number of playoffs, AD clubs had the highest average with 42 or approximately 63% of the division' while MD clubs were, on average, in 25 or 37% of them. This reflects, in large part, differences in these teams' number of seasons in the league — Column 2 of Table A7.2 — which averaged 62 in the AD and 42 in the MD.

Regarding inequality between the most and least successful within each division of the EC, the AD's Canadiens have been in 77 more playoffs than the Panthers while the MD's Rangers competed in 56 more than the Blue Jackets. From a historical perspective, these results indicate greater difficulty in getting into the playoffs among teams in the MD despite outstanding performances by coaches and players of such clubs as the Penguins and

Capitals but also because of below-average regular-seasons especially of the Hurricanes and Blue Jackets.

Regarding the variation or spread within and across the two divisions, the conference mean was 25 playoffs with 30, on average, among AD teams and 17 for those in the MD. This suggests more equality or wider distribution in playoff appearances between the Red Wings and seven other teams in their division but less between the Rangers, Flyers, and their six opponents in the MD. Simply put, such typical clubs as the Bruins and Maple Leafs had a better opportunity to qualify for and perhaps advance in the playoffs than the majority of those in the MD.

Division titles

According to Column 5 of Table A7.2, the 16 EC clubs claimed 173 division titles during their years within the league. From most to least, those in the AD won 114 or approximately 66% of the total and MD teams 59 or about 34%. More specifically, the Canadiens ranked first in number of them as of 2016, Red Wings second, and Bruins third while the Hurricanes placed 13th, Panthers and Lightning tied for 14th, and Blue Jackets 16th.

With respect to the distribution of their division titles, the Canadiens won one in the 1910s, two in the 1920s, three each in the 1930s and 1950s, four in the 1940s, seven in the 1960s, six in the 1970s and 1980s, one in the 1990s, and another three from 2008 to 2015. While owned first by Ottawa sportsman J. Ambrose O'Brien and financed by magnate T.C. Hare, such outstanding head coaches — besides Scotty Bowman and Pat Burns — as Claude Ruel, Jacques Lemaire, Jean Perron, and Jacques Demers challenged their players to win enough regular-season games to lead their division.

Some of Montreal's productive players included Hall of Fame goalies Gump Worsley and Patrick Roy, defensemen Serge Savard and Larry Robinson, centers Jacques Plante and Roger Vachon, and wingers Bob Gainey and Steve Shutt. Besides the league's top coach Scotty Bowman in 1977 and 12 years later Pat Burns, most of these and other players won awards for being the best at their positions in games.

In winning division titles, the 1976–1977 Canadiens set new records in dominance as Steve Shutt scored 60 goals for left wingers. Helping to set Shutt up during games was Guy LaFleur who won the Hart Trophy by establishing a new franchise record of 1,936 points. Along with Shutt and LaFleur, the goalie combo of Ken Dryden and Bunny Larocque won the Vezina Trophy, and Larry Robinson took home the Norris Trophy while establishing an incredible all-time NHL best record of 60-8-12 with 132 points. In the playoffs, Montreal crushed the St. Louis Blues in four consecutive games outscoring them 19-3 to advance to the Prince of Wales final. In that conference's series, the Canadiens fought off a challenge from the Islanders in six games and in the Stanley Cup finals, they easily beat the Bruins in four straight as LaFleur was named the Conn Smythe Trophy winner. The victory gave the Canadiens their second consecutive championship.

As a group, the Hurricanes, Panthers, Lightning, and Blue Jackets have won seven division titles in 82 regular seasons through 2016. Respectively, Carolina is three-time titlists and Florida and Tampa Bay each twice while Columbus failed to win any titles in 16 seasons. In fact, these teams' most impressive seasons include the following: Hurricanes in 2005–2006 after finishing 52-22-8 in the regular season, scoring 112 points, and defeating the Edmonton Oilers for the Stanley Cup; Panthers in 2015–2016 with a 47-26-9 record and 103 points, and competing but losing in the Stanley Cup finals; Lightning in 2003–2004 after defeating the Calgary Flames and winning a Stanley Cup; and Blue Jackets in 2013–2014 with a 43-32-7 record and 93 points in the regular season, and getting a wild card berth but losing to the Penguins in the conference playoffs.

Regarding the deviation between divisions in winning titles, there has been less variation among teams in the MD than AD. While the Bruins, Red Wings, and Canadiens have won 93 or 81% of those in the AD, the Flyers dominate the MD with 16 or only 27% of the total. Thus, it has been more of a struggle for the Sabres and four other clubs to win their division than the majority of teams in the MD — except for the very dismal performance of the Blue Jackets.

Conference titles

The 16 EC teams in Table A7.2 won a total of 53 conference titles during their various seasons in the league. Of the two groups, AD clubs won 25 or 47% of them and those in the MD 28 or 53%. The most and least successful clubs have been, respectively, the Canadiens and Flyers and then Bruins and

Red Wings, but winning fewest the Maple Leafs and Blue Jackets with zero and Panthers, Senators, and Capitals each with one.

Since 1974–1975, the Canadiens won their conference four times in the 1970s, twice in the 1980s, and once in the 1990s; Flyers twice in the 1970s, three times in the 1980s, and once each in the 1990s and 2000s; Bruins twice each in the 1970s and 2000s, and once each in the 1980s and 1990s; and the Red Wings three times each in the 1990s and 2000s. Ranked behind these four teams are the Devils, Islanders, and Penguins each with five titles; Rangers three; Sabres, Lightning, and Hurricanes each with two; Panthers, Senators, and Capitals each with one; and Maple Leafs and Blue Jackets with zero.

While located in Boston for 92 seasons before 2016–2017, the Bruins, for example won their conference in 1977–1978, 1988, 1990, 2011, and 2013. When coached by Don Cherry, Terry O'Reilly, Mike Milbury, or Claude Julien, one or more of these clubs were led by centers Jean Ratelle, Ken Linesman, Craig Janney, and Brad Marchand, defensemen Brad Park, Ray Bourque, Greg Hawgood, and Zdeno Chara, and wingers Wayne Cashman, Bobby Schmautz, Cam Neely, and Milan Zucic. One of their best seasons, the Bruins set 37 individual and team NHL records in 1976–1977 and finished in first place for the first time in 30 years with a 57-14-7 record. Bobby Orr won his third straight Norris Trophy and second Hart Trophy. In the playoffs, however, the Bruins were defeated by the Canadiens in seven games.

Besides Boston, the Flyers had a great season in 1975–1976. After finishing 51-13-16 and scoring 118 points, Philadelphia sought its third straight Stanley Cup. Nevertheless, not even the scoring of Reggie Leach — who set an NHL record with nineteen goals to capture the Conn Smythe Trophy — kept the Flyers from being swept in four straight games by the Canadiens.

Based on a 62-13-7 record in 1995–1996, Detroit had one of the finest season's in NHL history winning a record 62 games on the way to claiming its second straight President's Trophy. In the playoffs, the Red Wings defeated the lame-duck Winnipeg Jets in six games. But in the second round, the club needed an overtime goal against the St. Louis Blues in Game seven to win the series. However, Detroit lost the first two games in the conference finals at home to the Colorado Avalanche and never recovered, thus falling to their opponent in six games.

From the league's 1974–1975 to 2015–2016 season, the Maple Leafs and Blue Jackets failed to win the EC title. Playing in five conference finals, Toronto had its best team in 2003–2004. The club's record was 45-24-10-3 and scored 103 points but lost to the Flyers in the second round. Regarding the Blue Jackets, they were competitive in 2013–2014. Although they posted a 43-32-7 record and scored 93 points in the regular season, the Pittsburgh Penguins defeated them in the playoffs.

Stanley cups

According to Column 7 in Table A7.2, the 16 EC teams won a total of 72 Stanley Cups as of 2016. Among divisions, AD clubs had victories in 54 or 75% of them and those in the MD 18 or 25%. While the most successful clubs have been the Canadiens followed by the Maple Leafs and Red Wings, five or approximately 31% of the group have failed to win a Stanley Cup.

With respect to being champions, some NHL players who won the league's Most Valuable Player (MVP) award — Hart Trophy — include the Canadiens' centers Howie Morenz three times and Jean Beliveau twice, rightwing Guy Lafleur twice, and 10 others each once; Maple Leafs' center Teeder Kennedy and defenseman Babe Pratt each once; and Red Wings' rightwing Gordie Howe six times and Sergei Fedorov once, and defenseman Ebbie Goodfellow once. Some of these players were also other trophy winners and/or in all-star games, and perhaps scoring leaders for their team.

Besides them, the Panthers, Senators, and Capitals each played but lost in their only Stanley Cup final. After missing the playoffs in its first two seasons, Florida jumped out of the gate quickly posting the best record in the EC before the all-star break in 1995–1996. Although the club cooled off a bit in the second half of the season, it finished in third place with a solid 41-31-10 record and earned its first playoff berth. Despite defeating the Bruins and then Penguins, the Panthers lost to the Avalanche in four games for the championship.

Winning the conference in five games led to a nine-day-break for the Senators before the start of the Stanley Cup finals against the Anaheim Ducks in 2007. This delay, however, blunted Ottawa's momentum as they allowed two third-period goals losing 3-2. In Game 2, the Senators continued to struggle as they managed just 16 shots on goal in a frustrating 1-0 loss.

After the series shifted to Ottawa, the Senators seemed rejuvenated by the home crowd as they beat the Ducks 5-2 in Game 3. However, the Ducks rebounded to win Game 4 and then next the series in five games.

A new era began for the Capitals as they started the 1997–1998 season with Coach Ron Wilson and playing at a brand new arena in downtown Washington in December. In their surroundings, the Capitals rebounded off their lost season finishing in third place with a 40-30-12 record. Despite wins over the Bruins and Senators in the playoffs, Washington was overmatched by the Red Wings who easily swept them in four games.

Especially important for the NHL's future, the Toronto Arenas tied the Canadiens for first place in the 1917–1918 regular season with each of them scoring 26 points and finishing 13-9-0. However, both teams benefited from default wins against the Montreal Wanderers — who withdrew from the league after fire destroyed their arena. After defeating the Canadiens for the NHL title, the Arenas faced the PCHA's champion Vancouver Millionaires for the Stanley Cup. The entire five-game series was played in Toronto with rules alternating between East six-man and West seven-man games. Although neither team was comfortable with the other's style, Toronto won the series in five games because, in part, of playing three of these games with six men.

Total performances

This result — or the total performance (TP) for each team — includes their division and conference titles plus number of Stanley Cups as listed in Columns 5–7 of Table A7.2. Among 298 TPs through the league's 2015–2016 season, AD clubs won 193 or 65% of them followed by the MD's 105 or 35%.

While the Canadiens ranked first with 66 TPs, Red Wings second with 46, and Bruins third with 40, the Blue Jackets had zero, Panthers three, and Senators and Lightning each had five. Other teams with at least 17 include the Maple Leafs, Devils, Flyers, and Penguins.

Regarding TPs for each division, AD teams averaged 24 and MD's 13. In fact, the largest gap within each group was between the Canadiens' 66 TPs and Panthers' five compared to the Flyers' 25 and Blue Jackets' zero. Also, the AD had a greater variation in TPs with a standard deviation of 23 versus the MD's seven. Consequently, more equality occurred among MD teams in winning titles and Stanley Cups because of the ability and knowledge of their coaches and players' experience and talent.

Considering only clubs' total points and number of playoffs combined as a measure of their performances, those with the most impressive results have been the Canadiens followed closely by the Bruins and then Red Wings, Maple Leafs, Rangers, Flyers, Penguins, Sabres, Islanders, and Capitals. In contrast to them, the Blue Jackets, Hurricanes, and Panthers had the worst-ranked numbers of the group as of 2016 compared to the Senators, Lightning, and Devils.

After sports experts researched and published the history of all NHL teams, some of these articles reported the most dominant and/or successful EC teams of all-time. Based on different metrics and hockey information from various sources, among the best of all-time — in chronological order — are the following clubs from the ED/EC.[9]

• The 1970 championship is considered Boston's most famous title, since it concluded with Bobby Orr's fabulous flying goal in overtime that gave the Bruins the title over the St. Louis Blues. However, the Bruins were a more mature and determined team in 1972 after being upset the year before by the Montreal Canadiens. Indeed, they played with an edge. The club was 54-13-11 during the regular season and finished with 119 points. Boston eliminated the Toronto Maple Leafs and St. Louis Blues in the first two rounds of the playoffs before defeating a powerful New York Rangers team in six games to win their second Stanley Cup in three years.

• Many hockey purists despise the Philadelphia Flyers' teams that won back-to-back Stanley Cup championships in 1974 and 1975. The Flyers used size, strength, and physical intimidation to bully their way into elite status and earned their nickname, "Broad Street Bullies". While they may not have been pure, the club played sensational hockey and had far more talent than given credit. The 1975 Flyers, for example, established a 51-18-11 record with 113 points. Bobby Clarke was their best player and spiritual leader, and joined in games by Bill Barber, Gary Dornhoefer, Moose Dupont, and the sensational Bernie Parent in goal. While the 1974 team scored a memorable triumph in the Stanley Cup finals, the 1975 Flyers were more confident and accomplished as they defeated the high-scoring and talented Buffalo Sabres in six games to win their second straight championship.

- The 1976–1977 Montreal Canadiens dominated the league from start to finish. They were a remarkable 60-8-12 during the regular season and led the league in scoring with 387 goals and also ranked first in fewest goals allowed with 171. The team defeated the St. Louis Blues in four straight games in the first round of the playoffs. The New York Islanders provided some opposition, pushing the Canadiens to six games before bowing out. Montreal then earned their twentieth Stanley Cup by sweeping a strong Boston Bruins team.

- The 1981–1982 New York Islanders were 54-16-10 under head coach Al Arbour, scoring 118 points and led by such players as Bryan Trottier, Mike Bossy, Denis Potvin, and Billy Smith. While the club was extended to five games by the Pittsburgh Penguins in their opening round best-of-five series, it subsequently defeated the neighboring New York Rangers in six games in the second round. The Islanders followed with four-game sweeps of the Quebec Nordiques and Vancouver Canucks to clinch their third straight championship. Bossy was sensational that season recording 64 goals and 83 assists, and basically unstoppable with the puck in the offensive zone.

- The 1997–1998 Detroit Red Wings won their second straight Stanley Cup championship when they swept an overmatched Washington Capitals team in four consecutive games. Detroit had actually been pushed by the Phoenix Coyotes, St. Louis Blues, and Dallas Stars in six-game series prior to the finals. However, once the Wings found their rhythm in the Stanley Cup finals, it was no contest. The club was led by such players as Steve Yzerman, Nicklas Lidstrom, and Brendan Shanahan, while head coach Scotty Bowman provided his team with the confidence and leadership that allowed it to look any opponent in the eye and win whenever challenged. Chris Osgood may not have been one of the all-time greats in net, but he was good enough and came up with big saves in key moments.

For various reasons such as lacking talented players, coaching problems, and/or both of them, some of the league's pre-EC/EC teams had terrible performances in their regular seasons. Several of these clubs were evaluated based on their ability to score points, deny goals, and win games. In chronological order, the following is five of the worst clubs in the pre-conference and conference's history as of the NHL's 2016 season.[10]

- The worst team that the New York Rangers ever put on the ice was during a season when World War II was still at the forefront of global news. The 1943–1944 Rangers got just 17 total points from their record of 6-39-5, getting outscored by 148 goals in that span. The first and last two months of the season were pitiful for the Rangers, with a combined record of 0-25-5 during the period of games. Bryan Hextall led all scorers for New York with 54 points, with nobody else being very close.

• Believe it or not, the 1972–1973 New York Islanders are the only team in franchise history to make the worst list, and it was their first year in the league. Gordie Howe turned down the head coaching job, and things did not get much better for the squad. The Islanders got blown out time and time again, scoring just 170 goals throughout the season while giving up 347. That minus-177 difference is one of the biggest ever in the sport's history. After scoring just 30 points on the regular season, the Islanders finished the season in the basement and 58 points out of a playoff spot.

• According to some experts of the sport, the worst team to ever play in the NHL was the Washington Capitals in their inaugural season of 1974–1975. While their record is on par with the Senators and Sharks from 1992–1993 at 8-67-5, it was the goal differential — and a 1-39-0 road record — that really represented their performance. The Capitals scored just 181 goals on the season while allowing an NHL record 446 of them. Their best goalie was Michel Belhumeur, who finished the year with a laughable 5.36 goals against average. The worst loss that the Capitals had was 12-1, and they actually pulled that off twice.

• You may know them as the Winnipeg Jets now, but they were once known as the Atlanta Thrashers and did not last in the city very long. The Thrashers played their first season in 1999–2000, with some lousy results. The Thrashers' final tally was a 14-57-7-4 record, with only five wins on the road. Atlanta only scored 170 goals during the season, with Andrew Brunette leading the way at 23. The club finished with 39 points, fifteen behind the fourth-place Lightning in the division, a team that had just 19 wins of their own.

• Another deplorable team was the 1992–1993 Ottawa Senators, who played in their first NHL season. The Senators had fewer wins than the Sharks that year with ten, but avoided breaking the record for most losses by having four ties and finishing with one loss less than San Jose. Perhaps the most embarrassing statistic that the Senators had that year was their 1-41-0 road record. The Senators were not as bad as the Sharks in terms of giving up goals — allowing 395 — but were even worse at scoring them with 202 on the season.

LEAGUE ECONOMICS

In this section, there are data and other information about the commercial and financial aspects of franchises in the EC and their significance from an economic perspective. Besides attendances at home and away games, anything else that affects teams' income, market value, and wealth is included in the analysis, quantified, and discussed. In other words, the NHL is an organization consisting of for-profit enterprises that operate to compete each season typically within a division and/or conference and seek in various ways to improve their performances in current and future games.

Franchise Financials

Forbes sports editors published financial data of EC franchises following their 2015–2016 season. As denoted in Columns 2–6 of Table A7.3, these amounts include, respectively, their estimated market value — which is based on the current stadium deal without deduction for debt — and also total revenue, gate receipts, operating income — earnings before interest, taxes, depreciation, and amortization (EBITDA) — and debt-to-value (D/V) percentages. For each of the two divisions, the information reveals the financial status and wealth of these teams both individually and relative to each other as a group. The following section identifies and highlights the data.

In Table A7.3, Column 2 is the estimated market value of each EC team, by division, as of 2016. Ranked from most to least, AD clubs averaged $605 million and MD's $536 million. While the Rangers were first at $1.25 billion, Canadiens second at $1.12 billion, and Maple Leafs third at $1.10 billion, least in value included the Hurricanes at $230 million, Panthers at $235 million, and Blue Jackets at $245 million. In comparison to the typical club's market value of $570 million, only seven or approximately 43% of the group actually exceeded that amount.[11]

Several factors caused differences in teams' market values. In no specific order, these were their history and success in the league, location in big, midsized or small markets, size of each's fan base, number of titles and championships, and such financial data as their revenue, operating income, and gate receipts. Based on these and other reasons, they ranged in value by more than $1 billion.

To compare their standard deviation or variation in market values, the highest within groups were AD teams ($364 million) and lowest among those in the MD ($336 million). This meant inequality or greater deviation in these EC franchise's values existed in 2015–2016 to a greater extent between the Canadiens and other AD teams than among clubs in the other division. Although these were only estimates, the amounts influence such things as the clubs' relative wealth, economic power in the league, and future price if offered for sale to potential investors. Interestingly, the market value of six teams fell below the conference's average deviation of $340 million.

Each team's revenue — net of stadium revenues used for debt payments — is displayed in Column 3 of Table A7. 3. While the Rangers had the highest at $219 million followed by the Canadiens' $202 million and Maple Leafs' $186 million, the three lowest-ranked were the Hurricanes' $99 million at 16th and Panthers' and Blue Jackets' $100 million each tied for 14th. The differences in amounts occurred for several reasons including their home attendances, range in ticket prices, points in games, and number of hockey fans in the area.

Because of various demographic and sport-specific factors, there were disparities in teams' revenue. While the conference's standard deviation equaled $38 million, MD teams had the highest variation in revenue at $41 million and then those in the AD at $36 million. The latter division's revenues had the smallest differences because similar amounts existed for the Sabres and Senators and also the Red Wings and Lightning. Besides win–loss records and points scored in the regular season, the deviations reflect the population and growth in population of their markets, popularity at home games, and per capita income and the type of jobs and standard of living of local households.

Each EC teams' 2015–2016 gate receipts — in millions of dollars — appear in Column 4 of Table A7.3. While the conference's average was $51 million, the Rangers had the most ($92 million) and then the Penguins ($85 million) and Canadiens ($76 million). In contrast to these amounts, the Blue Jackets ($29 million), Hurricanes ($22 million), and Panthers ($16 million) had the smallest gate receipts in the NHL that year.

The average dispersion or disparity in gate receipts was greatest among MD clubs ($26 million) compared to AD teams ($20 million). Because of the large gap in amounts between, for example, the Rangers and Hurricanes, the division's standard deviation exceeded that of the AD's Canadiens and Panthers, and any comparison of other teams' amounts. Simply put, the New York–Newark–Jersey City and Greater Montreal and Toronto metropolitan areas are large and more prosperous hockey markets relative to gate receipts than others except for the Penguins' MSA.

In Table A7.3, Column 5 contains the operating income or EBITDA of 16 EC teams as of their 2015–2016 season. For the group, it averaged $18 million. From most to least by division, AD clubs averaged $22 million and the MD's $15 million. Because of excessive payments for players' salaries and other types of expenses, the Panthers, Hurricanes, Blue Jackets, and Devils had negative EBITDA's while the Canadiens, Rangers, and Maple Leafs earned the most income by operating efficiently. For various reasons, the Sabres, Senators, Lightning, and Islanders were also marginally efficient along with some others within different areas of NHL markets.

While $30 million was the average deviation in operating income of these EC teams, the AD's equaled $33 million and MD's $27 million. The gap or variation between the most and least EBITDA within divisions occurred, respectively, for the Canadiens and Panthers and also Rangers and Hurricanes. In other words, their earnings varied because each of them operated differently by applying former and new business practices, strategies, and tactics of the sports industry.

In Table A7.3, Column 6 includes the D/V percentages of each EC franchise in 2016. On average, the conference's was 24% or in amount, approximately $136 million per team based on estimated market values. Among each group, the AD's averaged 17% and MD's 32%. Although four clubs had debt percentages of 0%, the D/V ratios exceeded 50% each for the Hurricanes, Devils, and Islanders.

As described for other variables in the table, the average standard deviations of D/V were unequal among divisions and franchises within divisions. MD teams, for example, had the greatest variation at 28% and then those in the AD at 18%. In order to reduce their ratios for financial reasons and operate more effectively, several teams needed to restructure themselves operationally as business enterprises in order to generate higher market values and/ or record less amount of debt in accounts on their balance sheet.

As reported in *Forbes* for being an important, necessary, and periodic payment from an operations perspective, players' expenses — including benefits and bonuses — were listed in the magazine for these 16 teams in 2016. For the conference, they totaled approximately $1.1 billion or $71.7 million per team. On average, the AD clubs' were $71 million and those in the MD $72 million. While the Rangers, Penguins, and Bruins ranked highest, seven or approximately 43% in the group paid less than $70 million in players' expenses. Given these amounts, only three of the 10 ranked highest plus lowest had an above-average or talented roster of players and won enough games in the regular season to qualify for the playoffs. Indeed, the other seven failed to be competitive and participate in the EC's post-season partly because of their relatively small or misallocated investment in players' salaries.

Players' expenses were different and also significantly deviated between the two EC divisions. From most to least in variation among the groups — as measured by their standard deviations — these included the MD's $7 million and then the AD's $4 million. Such amounts denote that the greatest disparity in payments occurred because of the Rangers' $82 million or Penguins' $81 million versus the Hurricanes' $63 million in the MD, whereas the range in players' expenses within the AD of the Bruins' $76 million, Red Wings' and Canadiens' each $75 million, and also Lightnings' $74 million differed less than $10 million compared to those of the others. Thus, not all EC teams with the greatest revenues and/or largest market values always compensated their players more than rivals within their division.

Arenas

As of the NHL's 2015–2016 season, the sixteen EC teams played their home games in venues that differed in age, construction cost and market value, and also in such other ways as location, capacity, and ownership. Based on various criteria including their amenities, concessions, and sightlines, they have been ranked from best to worst overall, most to least accessible, and highest to lowest in quality as facilities to entertain spectators at games. Given those comparisons, this section provides some data and other information regarding the facilities of the conference's clubs and discusses specific characteristics about them.[12]

Among EC teams' home sites within each division as of 2016, they ranged in age as follows: within the conference's AD, from the Maple Leafs'

18-year-old Air Canada Center to the Red Wings' 38-year-old Joe Louis Arena and within the MD, from the Islanders' 5-year-old Barclays Center to the Rangers' 49-year-old Madison Square Garden. Of EC teams' 16 venues, eight or 50% of them were financed privately and two or 12% publicly. Furthermore, the other six or 38% received funds from private sources and also a municipality and/or state government.

Their construction ranked from being relatively cheap to very expensive. From the least to most costly within the conference's AD, it was $57 million to erect 20,000-seat Joe Louis Arena in 1979 for the Red Wings compared to $199 million to build 19,200-seat BB&T Center in 1998 for the Panthers; and in the MD, from $123 million for 18,000-seat Madison Square Garden in 1968 for the Rangers — and NBA New York Knicks — to $845 million for 15,700-seat Barclays Center in 2012 for the Islanders.

The 16 stadiums' average cost for construction equaled $305 million, while the divisions' standard deviation or variation in amounts ranged from the AD's $175 million to the MD's $234 million. Thus, stadiums of the Bruins, Sabres, and the other six AD teams had less difference in their construction costs than the eight stadiums in the MD especially because of the Islanders' Barclays Center being relatively expensive at $845 million.

Regarding the most recent renovation of a current venue in the EC, the Lightning in conjunction with Hillsborough County spent at least $25 million to improve Amalie Arena. Fan-facing upgrades included a nearly complete reconstruction of the club level — with the addition of 140–160 loge seats at the north end of the arena — and new concession stands, rebuilt restrooms, and an expanded exterior deck on the northeast quadrant of the club level. Two club level lofts were increased in size, which offers group buyers the opportunity to invite at least eighty people to games and events and enjoy them in a private environment.[13]

Recently *Forbes* sports editors assigned economic values to stadiums of teams in the EC. From lowest to highest within divisions, respectively, amounts in the AD were $51 million for the Panthers' 19,200-seat BB&T Center in Miami to $282 million for the Maple Leafs' 18,800-seat Air Canada Centre in Toronto; and within the MD, from $41 million for the Hurricanes' 18,600-seat PNC Center in Raleigh to $394 million for the Rangers' renovated, 18,000-seat Madison Square Garden in New York.

While the 16 stadiums of EC teams had an average value of $156 million in 2016, those in the AD alone were $159 million and MD $153 million. In addition, the eight venues in the MD were more unequal in value because they had a larger standard deviation compared to those in the AD. Although the latter group of stadiums was worth more on average in 2016 than those in the MD, they also deviated less in age, construction cost, and economic value. Nevertheless, because of increasing real estate prices in urban areas and popularity of the sport in North America, most of these facilities will likely appreciate economically, particularly those within the largest and most populated markets and wealthiest metropolitan areas.

In various studies, NHL stadiums have been ranked by various ice hockey experts and sports journalists in the media with respect to their location and different attributes and problems. Although results vary according to each study's parameters, a few venues rank among the best while some others placed in the worst group. For example, the most attractive, entertaining, and well-structured facilities within the EC based on their name, aesthetics and experience for fans, include the Sabres' KeyBank Center (former First Niagara Center) and Bruins' TD Garden.[14]

As reported in the *Stadium Journey* as of mid-2016, the two best hockey buildings of EC teams were rated highest in the group based on these reasons:

> "First Niagara Center [now KeyBank Center] still has the look and feel of a new arena even though it's been open since 1996. It was built just blocks away from Buffalo's old Memorial Auditorium, a beloved sports barn that served the region for over half a century and was recently demolished. The arena, located at the foot of Main Street in Buffalo, is the anchor of the emerging Canalside and Cobblestone districts, which became the biggest attraction in downtown Buffalo."

For why Boston's arena ranked second in the conference, the editor provided these comments:

> "The Garden underwent a massive renovation project over the past two summers, which touched several areas of the venue. This comprehensive, $70 million arena-wide upgrade featured redesigned modern concourses and new concession offerings, comprehensive renovation of the Legends restaurant, the development of a new Pro Shop, and an upgraded technology infrastructure to support improved digital fan interactions well into the future."

In another study, two of the lowest-ranked EC facilities were the Hurricanes' PNC Arena (former RBC Center) and Panthers' BB&T Center. Among others in the conference, the former ranked 13th (26th in the NHL) and the latter 12th (25th in the league). The study's author evaluated each of them, respectively, as follows[15]:

"The Carolina Hurricanes are one of those teams that are located in a spot that is not considered to be a traditional hockey market. However, Raleigh has been fairly good to them, especially after helping them build the RBC Center [renamed PNC Arena] in 1999 for $158 million. The arena's colors really intensify the experience when you enter the concourse to an array of red, black and white — in addition to all the lighting around the arena. Though the concourse is easily the best part of the arena, the food is nothing to write home about. The big downside of the arena is the location — seven miles west of Raleigh. It is basically in the middle of nowhere (though extremely well-lit and easy to find). But it would be nicer to have something around the arena, as opposed to trekking back and forth to and from the city for a game."

Regarding why the BB&T Center ranked almost last in the conference and league, comments were as follows:

"When the BB&T Center [not BankAtlantic Center] opened for the 1998-99 NHL season, the Florida Panthers' attendance jumped almost 26 percent from the previous season, bringing in more than 750,000 fans and filling their stadium to 95 percent capacity. After BB&T paid $20 million over 10 years for the naming rights in 2005, the Panthers finally had a home to themselves, once the ABA's [American Basketball Association's] Florida Pit Bulls moved out. One of the best features of the arena is the concourse, which is lined with carpeting and keeps with the warm feeling of simply being in Florida. The design of the concessions in the concourse also keeps lines short and prevents them from jutting out into the middle of the hall, making walking and perusing through the arena an extremely easy task. The only problem with the BB&T Center [is] its location. It is squished between a mall and a swamp and is a hassle to get to — maybe an excuse why the Panthers can no longer sell out their arena."

Fan cost index

For several years, a Chicago-based company named Team Marketing Report (TMR) has prepared and published a Fan Cost Index (FCI) for the home games of teams in professional sports leagues. To attend a game for a typical family with two kids, an FCI includes the cost of four average-priced tickets, two cheapest-priced draft beers, four each lowest-priced soft drinks and hot dogs, parking for one vehicle, and two each game programs and least-expensive, adult-sized adjustable caps. Costs are determined by telephone calls with team representatives, venues, and concessionaires and from questions asked during interviews.[16]

In the NHL's 2014–2015 season (2015–2016 not available), the average FCI for a family to attend a regular season game of an EC team was $364. While Maple Leafs' home games each cost $572, the Panthers had the conference's lowest FCI at $255. Among divisions, the average from most to least was those of AD teams at $365 and MD's at $363. The order from ranking them first and then second occurred, in part, because FCIs of the Bruins, Canadiens, and Maple Leafs each exceeded $400, while those of such teams as the Blue Jackets, Devils, and Islanders were each below $325.

For specific items in TMR's 2014 FCI, the approximate range in amounts from most to least expensive — or first compared to sixteenth across the EC — were listed as follows: average ticket, Maple Leafs $113 to Panthers $33; average premium ticket, Rangers $332 to Panthers $57; beer, Rangers $10.50 to Penguins $5.25; soft drink, Bruins $5.75 to Penguins and Sabres each $3; hot dog, Rangers $6.50 to Senators $3.57; parking, Bruins $42 to Blue Jackets $7; program, Rangers $10 to Sabres $2; and for a cap, Rangers $30 to Islanders and Sabres each $15. Based on economics principles, these prices were set by teams and/or vendors to sell enough units to maximize revenue from their sales at home games in the stadiums.

From the NHL's 2010 to 2014 season, there were some significant increases but also relatively small, and even, decreases in FCIs of teams in the EC. For examples of these changes, the Hurricanes' FCI rose from $251 to $341 or approximately 36% but the Red Wings' from only $299 to $307 or about 2%, while the Senators' actually declined from $328 to $296 or 10%. Because of such things as inflation, number of — and amount spent by — families at games in arenas, and local economic conditions and other factors, the majority of teams and/or vendors raised their prices each year rather than keeping them constant or reducing amounts.

In evaluating year-to-year FCIs between, for example, the EC's 2013–2014 and 2014–2015 seasons, the Bruins' increased the most, in other words, from $444 to $509 or approximately 15%. Alternatively, fans' costs fell for home games of the Sabres, Red Wings, Panthers, Canadiens, Maple Leafs, and Islanders, but remained the same for those of the Islanders at $313. Thus, there were different payments for tickets and other things by families to attend conference teams' home games at their stadiums especially from 2010 to 2015.

The largest deviation or variation in FCIs in 2014–2015 occurred, on average, among AD clubs ($118) rather than those in the MD ($65). Of the highest and lowest in each division, the Maple Leafs' amount exceeded the Panthers' by $317 compared to $191 for the Rangers and Blue Jackets. These gaps in FCI's reflect differences in teams' pricing policies and other factors such as their attendances at home games, number of points scored, win–loss record, stadium capacity, and popularity in the local and regional sports market.

ORGANIZATION HIGHLIGHTS

Besides regular-season and post-season games, the EC and its franchises are involved in — and affected by — community events and also business-related and government affairs, news, and projects. Because these things and other topics influence the conference in different but perhaps important and historic ways, following are a few of them from the academic and popular literature.[17]

First, the NHL is expanding into the Las Vegas market. While the absence of a new franchise for Quebec City was disappointing to some hockey fans, this news about Las Vegas continues to reveal how expansion is a must for the modern sport league. Even more notable is highlighting the adoption of cities that were once thought unimaginable. This development appears to be all the rage and is really more about growth strategies and competition between sports than it is about the cities selected. The Vegas expansion helps the league grow as a team in Nevada, where gamblers congregate from all over the world. The end result is more global visibility. Further, in the US, where hockey has always been viewed behind the other big four professional sports, youth participation continues to grow. According to USA Hockey, more than 100,000 new players have signed up and became members of the organization since the 2005–2006 timespan.

Second, Quebec City is a potential expansion candidate. Media Company Quebecor, which owns Quebec City's new arena, made an expansion bid along with Vegas. Their bid was ultimately deferred, a result of the weakened Canadian dollar. Though the economy limited their chances in 2017, Quebec City has vied for an NHL return. If admitted, Quebec City would most likely join the AD, where they would rekindle their old rivalry with the Canadiens, who are only three hours away. If NHL hockey returns to Quebec City, there would likely be at least one team that switches divisions. While Las Vegas adds to the WC, Quebec City would give the EC seventeen teams. To balance the conferences, one team would need to move to the WC.

Third, the predictions for the 2016–2017 regular-season standings and 2017 Stanley Cup playoffs are in, and they denote some interesting results. According to 20 voters from NHL.com and NHL Network, the EC's Lightning is the odds-on favorite to win the Stanley Cup and also one-half of those polled have the Lightning-runner-up in 2015 — as the last team standing this season. The Pittsburgh Penguins, who won the Stanley Cup in 2016, were picked by two voters to repeat as champions. The Detroit Red Wings, in 1997 and 1998, are the most recent team to repeat.

Fourth, nine EC teams had capacity attendances at their home games in the league's 2015–2016 season. While the Canadiens, Maple Leafs, Bruins, and Penguins attendances at home actually exceeded 100%, the smallest relative to capacities in their arenas included the Hurricanes at 65% in Raleigh, Blue Jackets at 80% in Columbus, and Islanders at 86% in New York City. On the road, the leaders in filling their opponents' stadiums in away games were the Canadiens and Red Wings but least popular included the Devils, Lightning, and Sabres.

Fifth, regarding their performances as of mid-2016, the EC's Blue Jackets have never advanced past the first round of the post-season; Senators teams made the post-season five times in the past nine seasons but won only one series; the Panthers reached the post-season just four times since 1996; Washington has not reached the conference final since 1998; and the Sabres are currently on a five-year post-season-less streak.

Sixth, based on Stanley Cups and finals appearances, among the 10 greatest NHL franchises in one study are the EC's Canadiens, Red Wings,

Maple Leafs, Bruins, Rangers, Pirates (renamed Penguins), Islanders, and Devils. The other two are the WC's Chicago Blackhawks and Edmonton Oilers, ranked, respectively, fifth and sixth. However, according to their all-time performances in the EC as of 2016, the Flyers were sixth in number of points and playoffs, fourth in division titles, tied for first in conference titles, and ninth in Stanley Cups. Thus, Philadelphia has won more titles and Stanley Cups than five EC teams ranked in the top 10.

Seventh, in all-time points percentages of teams, the most successful EC coaches include the Bruins' Tom Johnson, Penguins' Dan Bylsma, Canadiens' Claude Ruel and Toe Blake, Senators' Pete Green, and Sabres'/Maple Leafs' Floyd Smith. Others in the group such as Scotty Bowman, Mike Babcock, Todd McLellan, and Bruce Boudreau coached some WC teams during one or more seasons. Ranked from first to last, Johnson had the highest percentage, winning 73.8% of his games while Smith's teams won 62.6%.

Eighth, ranking them based on asset management, draft history, and salary cap, the best general manager of an EC team as of 2016 was the Lightning's Steve Yzerman. Besides being responsible for building an enduring contender around Steven Stamkos and Victor Hedman, he has a superb draft record and shows businesslike efficiency in the trade market. But what sets him apart is having his assets all toe the line. In contrast to him, the Blue Jackets' David Clarkson ranked sixteenth in the conference and 30th in the NHL.

Ninth, given the willingness to spend money to improve his team, and based on the stability and capabilities of the franchise's front office and management, amenities at the team's venue, the club's culture and interactivity with fans and its record, Red Wings' Mike Ilitch (now deceased) was the league's best owner as of 2016. After purchasing the franchise in 1982 for $8 million, the Little Caesars Pizza magnate immediately pumped money into the organization and, under his ownership, brought in several impact players. Eventually the Red Wings became a perennial playoff team and, finally, brought Lord Stanley back to Hockeytown in 1997 — the first of four championships of the Ilitch era.

Tenth, according to criteria including Toronto's record, the worst NHL owner is Maple Leafs Sports & Entertainment (MLSE). Because of the dysfunctional relationship between MLSE's primary investor — the Ontario Teacher's Pension Plan and its principals' Richard Peddie and Larry

Tannenbaum — the club has not won a Stanley Cup since 1967 due to MLSE being too busy with its many sports properties and also breaking ground on too many real estate projects.

NOTES

1. For the history of the sport and its leagues, see such references as "History of North American Hockey" http://www.hockeyleaguehistory.com [cited 25 January 2017]; *National Hockey League Official Guide & Record Book 2016.* Chicago, IL: Triumph Books (2016); D'Arcy J (2016). *The NHL: 100 Years of On-Ice Action and Boardroom Battles.* Toronto, Canada: Anchor Canada; Jozsa FP Jr. (2010). "Hockey Business: NHL Franchises, Markets and Strategies," unpublished manuscript, Misenheimer, NC, Pfeiffer University.
2. Some online sources for information about the NHL and its teams and their players are http://www.nhl.com, http://www.hockey-reference.com, and http://www.sportsencyclopedia.com.
3. "History of NHL Relocation," http://www.puckreport.com [cited 5 January 2017] and Klein C, "From Six Teams to 31: History of NHL Expansion," http://www.nhl.com [cited 1 January 2017].
4. "Metropolitan Statistical Areas of the United States of America," https//en.wikipedia.org [cited 12 November 2016]; "Population Estimates 2015," http://www.census.gov [cited 12 November 2016]; "Annual Population Estimates by Census Metro Area." http://www.statcan.ca [cited 16 January 2017].
5. Besides the sources in Note 4 and various U.S. census data, see also "The 382 Metropolitan Statistical Areas of the United States of America," http://www.en.wikipedia.org [cited 12 October 2016].
6. "Collective Bargaining Agreement Between National Hockey League and National Hockey League Players' Association," http://www.nhl.com [cited 19 January 2017] and Leahy S, "'10' Interesting Highlights From the NHL's New CBA," http://www.sports.yahoo.com [cited 19 January 2017].
7. To research and learn players' all-time performances, for example, there is "NHL & WHA Career Leaders and Records for Points," http://hockeyreference.com [cited 20 January 2017] and "NHL Player & Team Records," http://www.statshockey.homestead.com [cited 20 January 2017].
8. See "Stanley Cup Playoffs Format, Qualification System," http://www.nhl.com [cited 21 January 2017] and "Playoff Formats," http://www.nhl.com [cited 3 February 2017].

9. Three references are Jason Key, "Greatest NHL Teams of All-Time," http://www.thehockeynews.com [cited 20 January 2017]; Bass A, "NHL: 50 Best Teams in History," http://www.bleacherreport.com [cited 22 January 2017]; Silverman S, "The NHL's 10 Greatest Stanley Cup Championship Teams of the Last 50 years," http://www.bleacherreport.com [cited 22 January 2017].

10. See, for example, "Top 15 Worst NHL Teams of All Time," http://www.thesportster.com [cited 20 January 2017] and Shannon M, "NHL History: The Ten Worst Teams of All Time," http://www.bleacherreport.com [cited 20 January 2017].

11. In addition to such readings as "2016 NHL Valuations," http://www.forbes.com [cited 1 February 2017], see also Ozanian M, Kurt Badenhausen and Christini Settimi, "The Business of Hockey," http://www.forbes.com [cited 3 November 2016]; "Rodney Fort's Sports Economics," http://sites.google.com [cited 24 January 2017]; "Ranking the Value of All 30 NHL Franchises," http://www.thesportster.com [cited 24 January 2017].

12. These venues are in "Present National Hockey League Arenas," http://www.hockey.ballparks.com [cited 25 January 2017] and "NHL Arenas," http://www.statshockey.homestead.com [cited 25 January 2017].

13. "Lightning Announce Two-Year Renovation Concepts for Amalie Arena," http://www.nhl.com [cited 23 January 2017] and also Levesque W, "Lightning, Hillsborough to Split $25 Million Cost for Amalie Arena Upgrades," http://www.tampabay.com [cited 23 January 2017].

14. Swaney P, "2016 NHL Arena Experience Rankings," http://www.scout.com [cited 24 January 2017].

15. Bass A, "Power Ranking the League's 30 Arenas," http://www.bleacherreport.com [cited 24 January 2017].

16. Greenberg J, "NHL Fan Cost Index 2014–15," http://www.teammarketing.com [cited 25 January 2017] and for other years of sports leagues and their teams, see *Idem*, "Rodney Fort's Sports Economics" and also "Fan Cost Index," http://www.teammarketingreport.com [cited 16 November 2016].

17. See such readings as Rick Burton and Norm O'Reilly, "Reading the Tea Leaves: Will Expansion Transcend Borders?" http://www.sportsbusinessdaily.com [cited 24 January 2017]; Zane Watson, "Examining Future NHL Expansion Scenarios," http://www.thesportsquotient.com [cited 24 January 2017]; "Predictions for 2016–17 Season," http://www.nhl.com [cited 24 January 2017]; "NHL Attendance Report — 2015–16," http://www.espn.com [cited 24 January 2017]; Eisenband J, "12 NHL Franchises That Have Never Won Stanley Cup," http://www.thepostgame.com [cited 24 January 2017]; Pogany B, "The 10 Greatest NHL Franchises," http://www.definitivedose.com [cited 25

January 2017]; Clinton J, "Top Ten Coaches by Points Percentage: Where Does Mike Babcock Sit?" http://www.thehockeynews.com [cited 25 January 2017]; Cuthbert J, "Ranking the 31 NHL General Managers," http://www.thescore. com [cited 25 January 2017]; "SI's Best & Worst Owners in NHL," http:// www.si.com [cited 25 January 2017].

Chapter 8

WESTERN CONFERENCE

HISTORY

Established during November 1917 in Montreal, Quebec, by several officials from the former National Hockey Association (NHA) — which folded because of a dispute between Toronto Blueshirts' owner Eddie Livingstone and executives in the organization — the National Hockey League (NHL) began its first season with four clubs. These were the Montreal Canadiens, Montreal Wanderers, Ottawa Senators, and Toronto Arenas. Although Quebec City held a franchise, it decided not to operate. At the time, the NHL competed for a Stanley Cup along with such professional leagues as the Pacific Coast Hockey Association (PCHA).[1]

During the next 25 years, the NHL changed with respect to its structure and also scheduling and playoff format. In 1924, the Boston Bruins became the first American club to join the league, and within three years, six of the 10 teams were based in the United States (US). Led by coaches Pete Green and Dave Gill, the Senators dominated the league in the 1920s with four Stanley Cup victories but had financial problems and folded in 1934.

From 1942 to 1967, the NHL consisted of six teams including the Canadiens and Bruins and also the Toronto Maple Leafs (previously nicknamed Arenas), Chicago Blackhawks, Detroit Red Wings, and New York Rangers. While Montreal and Detroit each won two championships during the 1930s, the Maple Leafs dominated the league with five Stanley Cups in the 1940s because of such players as Walter "Turk" Broda, Syl Apps, Ted Kennedy, and Max Bentley.

After the Maple Leafs, the Red Wings had great teams in early 1950s and then the powerful Canadiens won consecutive Stanley Cups from the league's 1955–1956 to 1959–1960 season. The 1960s began with Chicago's first Stanley Cup victory in 23 years, led by the brilliant play of Bobby Hull, Stan Mikita, and Glenn Hall. In addition, Toronto won the Stanley Cup three more times, and Montreal twice, before the league decided to expand for economic and sport-specific reasons.

To meet demand for the sport across the nation and the league's growing popularity, the NHL added six US-based teams in 1967. These were the California Seals, Los Angeles Kings, Minnesota North Stars, Philadelphia Flyers, Pittsburgh Penguins, and St. Louis Blues. Three years later, the Vancouver Canucks joined and then in 1972, the Atlanta Flames and New York Islanders. With the addition of the Kansas City Scouts and Washington Capitals in 1974, there were nine teams each in the Clarence Campbell Conference (CCC) and Prince of Wales Conference (PWC), with only three of them located in Canada.

Founded in 1971, the World Hockey Association (WHA) broke the NHL's monopoly in the sport. Recruiting and hiring players from the NHL, the WHA began with 12 teams and added two more before inflation, rising expenses, and dwindling crowds reduced it to seven in the 1978–1979 season. In 1979, the WHA folded causing the Winnipeg Jets and Edmonton Oilers to join the Smythe Division of the NHL's CCC while the Quebec Nordiques became a member of the PWC's Adams Division and Hartford Whalers the Norris Division.

Since the early-to-mid-1970s, the sport increasingly emphasized offensive play and scoring points. The Bruins' Phil Esposito, for example, set records for points and defenseman Bobby Orr won a scoring championship. Then in the 1980s, the Oilers' Wayne Gretzky established career milestones in points, goals, and assists.

During the early 1990s, the NHL expanded and thus increased in size to 26 teams including the Calgary Flames in the Smythe Division and Ottawa Senators in the Adams Division. Then in 1993, the league restructured organizationally. As a result, it created an Eastern Conference (EC), which consisted of an Atlantic and Northeast Division, and also added a Western Conference (WC), which had teams in a Central Division (CD) and Pacific Division (PD).

While two teams each became new members of the EC and WC in 1993, the Nordiques had financial trouble from playing in the league's smallest market. Consequently, they were sold in 1995 and relocated to Denver, Colorado, where they were renamed Colorado Avalanche and played in the WC's PD. One year later, the conference's Jets were sold to a group in Phoenix, Arizona, and after moving there, renamed Phoenix Coyotes and placed in the CD. These changes, in turn, left only six franchises based in Canada.

In the summer of 1997, the league announced that it would expand and put teams in four more American cities. With the addition of the Nashville Predators (1998), Atlanta Thrashers (1999), and the Minnesota Wild (2000) and Columbus Blue Jackets (2000), the NHL had increased to 30 teams — 15 each in the EC and WC. But then five years after the Thrashers moved from Atlanta, Georgia, to Manitoba, Canada, and were renamed Winnipeg Jets, NHL commissioner Gary Bettman announced that a new franchise based in Las Vegas, Nevada, and nicknamed Golden Knights, would join the league to play in the 2017–2018 season, bringing the total number of clubs to 31.[2]

Besides those historical but specific and unique changes from an operations perspective, other things contributed in expected and also uncertain ways to the popularity and/or success of the NHL and its continuous development in the sports world. This information is important to remember before identifying and discussing fourteen WC teams' markets and performances, evaluating their stadiums, explaining economics of the sport, and discussing organizational highlights especially related to the conference.

Among topics, for example, the spread of hockey and growing proficiency of players in Sweden, Finland, Czech Republic, Slovakia, and the US reflects the increasing number of these men on NHL teams, particularly Russian, Swedish, Finnish, and Czech stars who emerged in the 1990s. In fact, this has caused a significant decline in the recruitment of Canadian junior hockey players because of there being a large supply of competitive athletes from these other countries.

As of 2015, Canadians were approximately 50% of the league's players, a decrease of about 25% since 1990. Nevertheless, Canadians play crucial roles on some NHL teams. For example, the Blackhawks' Jonathan Toews led his club to victories in 2010, 2013, and 2015, while the Penguins' captain Sidney Crosby hoisted the Stanley Cup in 2009 and 2016.

Team owners enforced a lockout banning members of the NHL Players' Association (NHLPA) during late 2004. Because of players' resistance to a salary cap, the lockout lasted more than 300 days or from mid-September 2004 to mid-July 2005. The result, however, was implementation of a salary cap of $39 million — in US dollars — per team in the league's 2005–2006 season but also a major reduction in players' salaries. This was the first time a major North American sports league lost an entire season due to a labor dispute. The lockout also resulted in cancellation of the Stanley Cup playoffs for the second time in its history — the first was in 1919 due to an influenza epidemic.

When the 2005 collective bargaining agreement expired in 2012, teams and players found themselves again arguing about money. This time, the major issue was the percentage of hockey-related revenues that players received in a season. According to the existing contract, players collected 57% of all hockey-related revenues, but the NHL wanted to significantly reduce that percentage. After neither the players nor league owners budged, the resulting lockout cancelled 510 regular-season games, the NHL All-Star Game, and the 2013 Winter Classic between the Red Wings and Maple Leafs. On January 12, 2013, an agreement was finally reached between the two groups with players and owners equally sharing hockey-related revenues, among other terms.[3]

Although ice hockey has the smallest fan base and revenue and also least sponsorship of the four US major professional sports leagues, a 2004 study by the Stanford Graduate School of Business found that NHL fans in America were the most educated and affluent of the groups. Furthermore, the study reported that season-ticket sales were more prominent in the NHL than the other three leagues because of the financial ability of its fans to purchase them.

TEAMS

Markets

From 1917 to the early 1970s, several NHL franchises became "defunct" and folded their operations or moved to another city because of such things as disappointing attendances at their home games, financial and/or ownership problems, a better arena at the new site, or simply greater opportunities to increase revenue and profit elsewhere. The Montreal Wanders disbanded in 1918, Hamilton Tigers in 1925, Philadelphia Quakers in 1931, St. Louis Eagles in 1935, Montreal Maroons in 1938, and Brooklyn Americans in 1942. In addition to them, some clubs relocated to a different area for similar business and economic reasons. Specifically, these were the Quebec Bulldogs→Hamilton in 1920; Hamilton Tigers→New York in 1925; Pittsburgh Pirates→Philadelphia in 1930; and Ottawa Senators→St. Louis in 1934.[4]

After the league restructured from its franchises being in divisions and created a CCC and Prince of Wales Conference (PWC) each in 1974, and then nineteen years later adopting an EC and WC, more NHL teams transferred to other metropolitan areas in order to perform in modern arenas and also potentially earn additional operating income and perhaps profit from their games. These included the PWC's California Golden Seals→Cleveland and CCC's Kansas City Scouts→Colorado each in 1976; CCC's Atlanta Flames→Calgary in 1980; CCC's Colorado Rockies→New Jersey in 1982; CCC's Minnesota North Stars→Dallas in 1993; EC's Quebec Nordiques→Colorado in 1995; WC's Winnipeg Jets→Phoenix in 1996; EC's Hartford Whalers→Raleigh in 1997; and EC's Atlanta Thrashers→Winnipeg in 2011.[5]

In 1993, the 12 WC clubs existed in relatively large, midsized, and small cities. Geographically, they ranged north to south or stretched in other directions from Toronto and Winnipeg to Dallas in the CD and from Calgary and Vancouver to Los Angeles in the PD. Their metropolitan areas' populations were also different and within the two divisions ranked from most to least in (millions) as follows: in the CD were teams based in Chicago (8.2), Detroit (5.1), Dallas (4.0), Toronto (3.8), St. Louis (2.4), and Winnipeg (0.6); and in the PD, they included two in Anaheim/Los Angeles (14.5) and one each in San Jose (6.2), Vancouver (1.6), Edmonton (0.8), and Calgary (0.7). Although there were no CD clubs in areas west of St. Louis and east of Detroit in the US and Toronto in Canada, those in the PD had home sites in the US on or near the west coast and also in western Canada.[6]

During the NHL's 1993–1994 to 2015–2016 season, new WC teams began to play at home in such locations — with Metropolitan Statistical Area (MSA) populations in (millions) — as Anaheim (14.5), Minneapolis (2.9), Columbus (1.6), and Nashville (1.3). In addition, the Minnesota North Stars moved from Minneapolis (2.5) to Dallas (4.0), Nordiques from Quebec (0.4) to Denver (1.9), Jets from Winnipeg (0.6) to Phoenix (2.7), and Thrashers from Atlanta (5.3) to Winnipeg (0.7). Most relocations occurred, in part, because of changes in franchise owners, construction of a new or renovated stadium at the post-move site, and also because their post-move MSAs — Census Metropolitan Areas (CMAs) in Canada — contained more people including households with higher and increasing disposable and/or per capita incomes.

By 2000, Canadian teams were increasingly pressured to compete financially with clubs existing in American markets although the Montreal Canadiens and Toronto Maple Leafs were the only two that consistently played to sellout or near-sellout crowds. Meanwhile, the NHL's Canadian Assistance Programs offered aid only when teams demonstrated their viability to survive, and for most of them located in Canada, their viability was threatened by declining attendances.

In 1999, Ottawa Senators' owner Rod Bryden announced that unless Canada's federal government was willing to offer financial support, his club would be the next team sold to US investors. Responding to Bryden's strategy, the country's federal government considered offering aid to Canadian hockey teams at least until 2004. However, there was widespread criticism of the proposal, causing its retraction. Consequently, the Senators remained in Ottawa, and since 2005 their home attendances and those of other Canadian franchises have remained relatively steady during seasons.

To provide and examine some current but interesting and relevant data and facts about existing WC teams in order to examine the sizes and other elements of their markets, there is information about them in Table A8.1. Within the table, variables researched were each team's Metropolitan Statistical Area Population (MSAPOP) — or CMA in Canada — number of Designated Market Area Television Homes (DMATVH), and average attendances (AVGATT) relative to home games in the NHL's 2015–2016 season. These criteria were quantified, listed, and ranked in order to reveal the attributes of such competitors and rivals as the CD's Chicago Blackhawks and St. Louis Blues, and PD's Anaheim Ducks and Los Angeles Kings.

Based on data listed in Column 2 of Table A8.1, the typical WC team had a MSAPOP of 4.02 million. More specifically, CD teams' areas were ranked first in population at 4.06 million followed by those in the PD at

3.98 million. While the Blackhawks, Stars, and Ducks/Kings had the largest group of people within their markets, the three smallest included areas of the Flames, Oilers, and Jets because of such factors as their economic and historical development, growth, and prosperity. These differences demographically, in turn, affected and influenced each club's actual and potential ticket sales, revenue from games and other local/regional sources, and also estimated market value especially for those identical or similar in size within divisions like the CD's Avalanche and Blues but not Stars and Jets, and the PD's Ducks and Kings in addition to Flames and Oilers but not Coyotes and Canucks.

Besides averages for the league and by division, the variation or dispersion in MSAPOPs — including CMAs for those in Canada — was determined mathematically using the standard deviation. While it averaged 2.61 million people across the conference's 16 teams, the CD's ranked highest at 3.11 million followed by the PD's 2.26 million. In other words, the least equal in market population were areas of the Predators and their divisional rivals but most alike are those of PD teams particularly the Coyotes and Sharks but not, for example, the Ducks and Oilers. Because of such widespread variation in markets' MSAPOPs, teams' locations impacted them in various ways such as their attendances at home games, media coverage, travel costs, and other variables of these franchises.

In Table A8.1, Column 3 is the estimated number of television homes in each team's designated market area (DMATVH) in years' 2016–2017. While it averaged 1.78 million across the conference, the CD teams' on average equaled 1.74 million television homes and those in the PD 1.82 million. Similar to but not exactly like the distribution of the MSAPOPs, the largest number of homes with televisions for these clubs is in the Chicago and then Los Angeles, Dallas, San Jose, and Phoenix DMAs, while the fewest existed in Calgary, Edmonton, and Winnipeg.

As explained before for the MSAPOP, the standard deviation of television homes in teams' areas denotes differences across the conference and also between and within divisions. While the variation was 0.92 or 920,000 television homes among the group of markets in the WC, CD clubs on average had the largest number at 1.03 or 1,030,000, and the PD 0.87 or 870,000. Within divisions, for example, the difference between the number of television homes in Calgary and Edmonton was about the same, for example, as between Phoenix and Vancouver. Also interesting, the CD's Avalanche and Wild besides the Predators and Blues were similar with respect to this characteristic of their market. This, however, does not mean more or fewer fans actually watched these teams' games on television at home or other places.

In Table A8.1, Column 4 lists the average attendance of each WC team while playing games in its home venue during the league's 2015–2016 season. For this statistic, the Blackhawks ranked first at the 19,700-seat United Center in Chicago, Illinois, Wild second at 18,500-seat Xcel Energy Center in Minneapolis, and Flames third at 19,200-seat Scotiabank Saddledome in Calgary. In contrast to them, teams' with the smallest attendances at home were the Ducks at 17,100-seat Honda Center in Anaheim, Jets at 15,200-seat MTS Centre in Winnipeg, and Coyotes at 17,100-seat Gila River Arena in Glendale, Arizona.

While the conference's attendance was 17,640 per game, CD teams averaged 18,250 fans and those in the PD about 17,020. Ranked first and second within their division, respectively, games of the CD's Stars and Blues were more popular, for example, than those of the Avalanche and Predators. In addition, the Ducks and Coyotes had the lowest-ranked combined attendances in the conference and not the CD's Predators and Jets or PD's Oilers and Sharks. In fact, such things as these teams' total points, ticket prices, advertising promotions and marketing campaigns, number of superstar goalies and other players, and even the weather affected in some way their Sunday and other night attendances at home games.

Regarding the deviation in teams' average attendances in the league's 2015–2016 season, it was 2,040 people per game for the conference, but from most to least by division it was as follows: 2,130 spectators in the CD and 1,890 in the PD. This suggests that clubs had greater variation in number of fans at their games, in part, because of sellouts at the Blackhawks' United Center, Wild's Xcel Energy Center, Kings' Staples Center in Los Angeles and Flames' Scotiabank Saddledome in Calgary, near sellouts at the Stars' American Airlines Center in Dallas and Oilers' Rogers Place in Edmonton, but not at the Coyotes' Gila River Arena in Glendale, Predators' Bridgestone Arena in Nashville, and Sharks' SAP Center at San Jose.

For various reasons including competitiveness and ability to entertain fans and also capacity of their stadiums, very small differences in attendances between them occurred, for example, at the Stars' American Airlines Center, Blues' Scottrade Center, Kings' Staples Center, and Canucks' Rogers Arena.

Although the Stars and Blues each won more regular-season games and scored more points than the Kings and Canucks in 2015–2016, individually they sold about the same number of seats to fans at their home games.

Given the data and its distribution in Table A8.1, the CD's Blackhawks and Stars and PD's Ducks and Kings each played their home games in relatively large markets; the CD's Avalanche, Wild, and Blues and PD's Coyotes, Sharks, and Canucks in midsized markets; and the CD's Predators and Jets and PD's Flames and Oilers in small markets. Thus, approximately 28–29% of the league's WC teams existed in MSAs with plenty of fans and television homes during the league's 2015–2016 season and also 43% had home sites in less populated areas with fewer television homes while another 28–29% performed within markets with below-average data.

According to rankings in the table — except for the WC's Blackhawks in the Chicago–Naperville–Elgin MSA, Ducks and Kings each in the Los Angeles–Long Beach–Anaheim area, and the Jets in Manitoba Province and Flames and Oilers each in Alberta Province — the other teams' markets within and across divisions are each different demographically and roughly represent their economies and the sport's fan base. Similar results also occurred for some teams within the league's EC.

For more about variables in Table A8.1 and their potential to be future hockey markets after the league's 2016–2017 season, some populated places without an NHL team are such MSAs as Houston–The Woodlands–Sugar Land (6.65 million), Riverside–San Bernardino–Ontario (4.48 million), Orlando–Kissimmee–Sanford (2.38 million), San Antonio–New Braunfels (2.38 million), Sacramento–Roseville–Arden–Arcade (2.27 million), and Las Vegas–Henderson–Paradise (2.11) in the US, and possibly Quebec (0.7), Hamilton (0.7), and Kitchener–Cambridge–Waterloo (0.7) in Canada. With respect to DMAs in the top 30, those without a club — besides Houston and Seattle–Tacoma in the US — are others like Orlando–Daytona Beach–Melbourne, Charlotte, Cleveland–Akron, Portland, Baltimore, Indianapolis, San Diego, Nashville, and Hartford–New Haven.

If the league expands at a site in an area not hosting a current NHL team, a few of these places — especially Las Vegas — might be profitable markets. In addition, some are potential sites for any existing NHL clubs with inferior stadiums and who compete for local fans with other teams in Major League Baseball (MLB) and any in the National Basketball Association

(NBA) and/or National Football League (NFL). Among the group, there has been speculation in the media about locating a new or existing club especially somewhere in New York or another one in Los Angeles, and also in smaller US metropolitan areas such as Kansas City, Missouri, or Milwaukee, Wisconsin.

Despite being homes of former NHL or WHA teams that folded in years from 1917 to 2000 or were not admitted into the NHL, the group includes such cities as Atlanta, Georgia; Baltimore, Maryland; Birmingham, Alabama; Cincinnati and Cleveland, Ohio; Hamilton, Ontario, Canada; Hartford, Connecticut; Indianapolis, Indiana; Kansas City, Missouri; and Oakland, California. In short, a number of cities are potentially adequate sites to host an NHL expansion team or one that struggles to get local fans to attend its home games and/or earn enough money to operate effectively within a division of the WC.

Before discussing teams' performances in the next section of this chapter, the NHL and NHLPA signed a Collective Bargaining Agreement (CBA) that covers the period of 16 September, 2012 to 15 September, 2022. Commencing on the day prior to the start of the regular season and concluding with each respective club's last NHL game in a league year, the active roster includes all players on a club's reserve list who are signed to an approved and registered Standard Players Contract (SPC), who are not on the injured reserve list, injured non-roster, designated non-roster, or loaned. A player on a conditioning loan is included on a club's active roster. During training camp, a player shall be deemed to be on the club's active roster only if he had been on it after the trade deadline in the preceding season on other than an emergency recall basis.[7]

Other important and also interesting information within the CBA, there is a maximum of 23 players on each club's active roster at any one time, provided that on the date of each season's trade deadline, a club's active roster may be increased to any number of players the club determines to be appropriate. In addition, clubs are not permitted to loan players where the result of a loan or loans would reduce the club's active roster below eighteen skaters and two goaltenders. However, clubs will not be required to recall players to maintain the minimum skaters and goaltenders on days they do not play an NHL game, provided that the deficiency below those thresholds is a result of an injury that caused the removal of such disabled player from the active roster. Except in an emergency, there shall be no reduction of the required minimum playing rosters of the clubs, below eighteen skaters and two goaltenders.

Performances

During the league's 100-year history, the number of pre-WC/WC teams ranged from one (Chicago Black Hawks) in the 1926–1927 season to 15 from 2000–2001 to 2012–2013. Because of differences in performances, some of their players were among all-time leaders in points, goals per game, and total games within the sport. These include, for example, such players as the Oilers' Wayne Gretzky, Avalanche's Joe Sakic, Blackhawks' Stan Mikita, Ducks' Teemu Selanne, and Sharks' Joe Thornton in points; in goals per game, Flames'/Blues'/Stars' Brett Hull, Blues' Peter Stastny, and Canuck's Cam Neely; and in total games, Coyotes' Shane Doan, Stars' Mike Modano, Sharks' Patrick Marleau, Jets' Teppo Numminen, and Flames' Jerome Iginla. A few coaches with outstanding careers, in part, with conference teams were the Blues' Bob Berry, Oilers' Glen Sather, Kings' Pat Quinn, Kings' Ron Wilson, Blackhawks' Rudy Pilous, Avalanche's Bob Hartley, and Wild's Jacques Lemaire.[8]

Points

Besides differences in abilities of coaches and the talents of players, their total seasons in the league — as listed in Column 2 of Table A8.2 — partly influenced results. While the conference average was approximately 32, CD teams' averaged 31 and PD's 33. As of 2015–2016, the Blackhawks led the group of 14 teams with 90 seasons followed by the Blues and Kings each with 49, and then the Canucks, Oilers, and Flames. With the least number of seasons were the Predators ranked 12th, Wild 13th, and Jets 14th.

Other than totals, deviations in seasons existed among the two groups of clubs. Compared to 21 on average for the conference, the CD's and PD's were respectively 28 and 11. These differences in divisions occurred, in part, because of the Blackhawks' large number of seasons and the Jets' five and Wild's 16 while the Ducks, Coyotes, and Sharks each played from 20 to 25 seasons and the Flames 36 and Oilers 37. For these reasons, PD clubs had more equality or smaller variation in seasons played than those in the CD.

Given the number and distribution of seasons by division, an important factor in ranking WC teams' performances is their total points through the league's 2015–2016 season. According to data in Column 3 of Table A8.2, the most successful in the conference have been the Blackhawks, Blues, and Kings while the fewest points scored belong to the Predators, Wild, and Jets. Relative to an overall mean score of 2,617 points for the conference, CD teams averaged 2,520 and the PD's 2,714.

Chicago scored more than 6,200 points because of such coaches — besides Hall of Famers' Tommy Gorman and Rudy Pilous — as Clem Loughlin, Billy Reay, Orval Tessier, Mike Keenan and Denis Savard, and also centers' Dick Irvin, Max Bentley, and Phil Esposito. Besides them, goalies Hugh Lehman, Chuck Gardiner, Ed Belfour, Glen Hall, and Tony Esposito, defensemen Arthur Coulter, Bill Gadsby, Earl Siebert, and Bobby Orr, and left wingers Bobby Hull, Ted Lindsay, Bert Olmstead, and Michel Goulet each had successful careers in their seasons with the club. In fact, these players contributed to Blackhawks (nicknamed Black Hawks before 1986–1987) teams having many winning seasons and qualifying, in part, for 61 playoffs in 90 or approximately 67% of their years.[9]

In addition to Chicago, St. Louis's clubs scored in excess of 4,000 points. While coaches' Scotty Bowman, Al Arbour, and Emile Francis are in the Hall of Fame, so are such players as goalies' Grant Fuhr and Jacques Plante, defensemen' Doug Harvey, Guy LaPointe, Al MacInnis, and Chris Pronger, centers' Bernie Federko, Doug Gilmour, and Adam Oates, right wingers' Glen Anderson, Brett Hull, and Joe Mullen, and left winger Brendan Shanahan. Others whose numbers were retired by the team included defensemen' Bob Gassoff and Barclay Prager and also left winger Brian Sutter, while top coaches Red Berenson, Joe Quenneville, and Ken Hitchcock won the Jack Adams Award for leading their teams in specific seasons.

Following Chicago and St. Louis, the Kings ranked third in points as of the league's 2015–2016 season. Their most prominent coaches, in part, included Hall of Famers Pat Quinn and Roger Neilson, and such trophy winners as defensemen Rob Blake and Drew Doughty, centers Butch Goring, Bob Bourne, Marcel Dionne, and Anze Kopitar, and left wingers Luc Robitaille and Dave Taylor. In addition, goalie Jonathan Quick and right wing Justin Williams won Most Valuable Player (MVP) awards in playoffs.

Because of various problems including competition from various teams in their conference, the CD's Avalanche, Wild, Predators, and Jets, and PD's Ducks and Coyotes each scored fewer than 2,000 points and lost the majority of their regular-season games despite making changes to improve the coaching staff and active roster of players. Following is specific information about each of them.

For examples of their performances during various years, the Avalanche won two each conference titles and Stanley Cups in 21 seasons, yet none of the team's players earned a Masterton, Selke, Norris, or Vezina Trophy; the 16-year-old Wild have zero Hall of Famers, retired uniform numbers of two players, and in seven playoffs won zero conference titles; during 18 seasons, the Predators appeared in nine playoffs and had one Masterton Trophy winner but zero of its players received a Lady Pyng, Selke, Norris, Vezina, Calder, or Hart Trophy; the Jets had no trophy winners or top coaches in five seasons while in its only playoff, they were swept by Anaheim; although the Ducks won two conference titles and one Stanley Cup, the club's players have only four trophies while their coaches earned zero top awards in 23 years; and in 20 seasons, the Coyotes appeared in eight playoffs but have won only one division title and no conference titles. In short, these six clubs have underperformed within their division of the WC and bad as or worse than any competitors in the EC.

Statistically, the standard deviation is used to measure the variation or inequality in number of points between and within divisions of the WC. The widest variation in points occurred among teams in the CD (1,990) and least for those in the PD (845). Because of a relatively large difference in deviations between divisions, the highest and lowest within them indicated, for example, that the Blackhawks had 5,836 more points than the Jets in the CD while the Kings' 3,779 points exceeded the Coyotes' by 2,180 in the PD. Thus, in evaluating and ranking their scoring results, CD teams have been the most unequal competitively among themselves and when compared to those in the other division of the conference.

Playoffs

The league's 2015 season was the third consecutive year in which the top three teams in each division qualified for the playoffs along with two wild cards in each conference, or a total of eight playoff teams from the AD and MD. Regarding playoff brackets in each round, teams competed in a best-of-seven series following a 2-2-1-1-1 format. The team with home ice advantage played at home for games one and two and if necessary, games five and seven, while the other team performed at home for games three and four and, if necessary, game six.[10]

In the First Round, the lower seeded wild card in the conference played against the division winner with the best record, while the other wild card played against the other division winner, and both wild cards were de facto number four seeds. The other series matched the second and third place teams from the divisions. In the first two rounds, home ice advantage was awarded to the team with the better seed and in the last two rounds, to the team that had the better regular season record.

Based on their performances in NHL regular seasons from 1917–2018 to 2015–2016, the Blackhawks ranked first with 61 playoffs, Blues second with 40, Kings third with 29, Canucks fourth with 27, and Flames fifth with 21. In contrast to them, the Jets ranked 14th with one, Wild 13th with seven, and Coyotes 12th with eight.

With respect to these WC teams' total number of playoffs, CD clubs averaged 20 or approximately 51% of the group and the PD's nineteen or about 49%. Although almost equal in playoffs as reflected in Column 4 of Table A8.2, there were marginal differences in these teams' number of seasons per division — which averaged 31 in the CD and 33 in the PD — and also because of 10,341 points scored by the Blackhawks plus Blues compared to 7,328 by the Kings and Canucks combined.

Regarding inequality between the most and least successful teams within each division of the WC, the CD's Blackhawks were in sixty more playoffs than the Jets, while the PD's Kings competed in 21 more than the Coyotes. From a historical perspective, these results indicate greater difficulty in getting into the playoffs among teams in the PD because of similar performances by coaches and players of such clubs as the Flames and Oilers but also inferior regular-seasons especially of the CD's Wild and Predators along with the Jets.

Regarding the variation or spread within and across the two divisions, the conference average was 15 playoffs, with 21 among CD teams and seven within the PD. This suggests more equality in playoff appearances between the Ducks and six other teams in their division but not between the Blackhawks, Blues, and their five opponents in the CD. Simply put, typically such clubs as the Flames, Oilers, Kings, and Canucks had a better opportunity to qualify for and perhaps advance in the playoffs than most of those in the CD.

Division titles

According to Column 5 of Table A8.2, the 14 WC clubs accumulated 70 division titles during their years in the league. From most to least, those in the PD won 36 or approximately 51% of the total and CD teams 34 or 49%. More specifically, the Blackhawks ranked first in number of them as of 2016, Canucks second, and the Avalanche and Blues tied for third, while the Coyotes and Kings tied for 11th and Predators and Jets for 13th.

With respect to the distribution of their division titles, the Blackhawks won one in the 1960s, seven in the 1970s, three each in the 1980s and 1990s, and two in the 2000s. Initially owned by military veteran Frederick McLaughlin and currently by the Wirtz Corporation, such outstanding head coaches — besides Billy Reay, Tommy Gorman, and Joe Quenneville — as Keith Magnuson, Bob Murdoch, Lorne Molleken, and Trent Yawney challenged their players to win enough regular-season games to lead other teams in their division.

Some productive Chicago players included Hall of Fame goalies Frank Brimsek and Dominik Hasek, defensemen Pierre Pilote and Allan Stanley, centers Duncan McKay and Clint Smith, and wingers George Kay and Duke Keats. Besides 1983 top coach Orval Tessier, most of these and other players won awards for being the best at their positions.

In winning division titles, the 2009–2010 Blackhawks set new records in dominance as right wing Patrick Kane scored 88 points and three other players at least 66. Helping to pace the 52-22-8 Blackhawks — who had led the NHL in attendance — was their one-two punch of Kane and Jonathan Toews. Both players had a strong season with 30 and 25 goals, respectively, to lead a balanced offensive attack featuring six players scoring 20 or more goals. This did not include Duncan Keith who won the Norris Trophy as the best defensive player in the league while posting an impressive 55 assists. After sweeping the Sharks in the playoffs, the club defeated the Flyers to win the Stanley Cup. Captain Toews held the Conn Smyth Trophy as his 22 assists earned him playoff MVP honors.

As a group, the Wild, Coyotes, Kings, Predators, and Jets have won a total of four division titles in 108 regular seasons through 2016. Respectively, the Wild are two-time titlists and Coyotes and Kings each once, while Nashville failed to win any titles in 18 seasons and Jets in five.

In fact, these five teams' most impressive seasons include the following: Wild in 2006–2007 by finishing 46-26-8 in the regular season, scoring 104 points, and reaching the playoffs for just the second time in franchise history but overmatched and losing to the eventual Stanley Cup champion Ducks in five games; Coyotes reached the playoffs in 2009–2010 for the first time in eight years with a franchise record of 50-25-7, but despite their best season since joining the NHL, the organization still lost money and struggled with the lowest attendance in the NHL as its future in Phoenix remained in doubt; Kings won Stanley Cups in 2012 and 2014 but also after finishing 42-17-21 and scoring 105 points in 1974–1975; Predators in the 2006–2007 season when they had a 51-23-8 record and 110 points but unable to recover in the playoffs after losing games and finding themselves in a three-to-one hole against the Sharks; and the Jets' best season was in 2014–2015 with a 43-26-13 record and 99 points but then swept by the Ducks in the playoffs.

Regarding deviations between divisions in winning division titles, there has been less variation or dispersion among teams in the PD than CD. While the Blackhawks, Avalanche, and Blues won 34 or 77% of those in the CD, the Sharks and Canucks have the most in the PD with only 17 or 47% of the division's total. Thus, it has been more of a struggle for the Predators and two other clubs to win their division than the majority of teams in the PD — except for the Coyotes and also Kings.

Conference titles

The 14 WC teams in Table A8.2 won a total of 27 conference titles during their multiple seasons in the league. Of the two groups, CD clubs won eight or approximately 30% of them and the PD 19 or 70%. Regarding these titles, the most and least successful clubs have been, respectively, the Oilers and Blackhawks and then equally the Flames, Kings, and Canucks, and with zero of them the Wild, Predators, Blues, Jets, and Coyotes.

Since 1974–1975, the Oilers won their conference five times in the 1980s and once each in the 1990s and 2000s; Blackhawks (after 1973) once in the 1990s and three times in the 2000s; Flames twice in the 1980s and once in the 2000s; Kings once in the 1990s and twice in the 2000s; and Canucks once each in the 1980s, 1990s, and 2000s. Ranked behind these four teams in victories are the Avalanche, Stars, and Ducks each with two titles and Sharks one.

While they have been located in Edmonton for 37 seasons or since 1979, the Oilers, for example, won their conference in 1983–1985, 1987–1988, 1990, and 2006. When coached by Glen Sather, John Muckler, Ted Green, or Craig MacTavish, one or more of these clubs were led by centers Wayne Gretzky and Mark Messier, defensemen Paul Coffey and Chris Pronger, and wingers Glen Anderson and Jari Kurri.

In one of their impressive seasons, the Oilers set several individual and team NHL records in 1982–1983 by finishing in first place of the Smythe Division with a record of 47-21-12 and scoring 119 points. Gretzky continued to dominate, as he won his fourth straight Hart Trophy and third straight scoring title with 71 goals. In addition, "The Great One" was recognized as the 1982 Sportsman of the Year by Sports Illustrated. An amazing accomplishment considering the magazine's lackluster hockey coverage, and that many Americans could not find Edmonton on the map. However, the New York Islanders swept the Oilers in the Stanley Cup finals by holding them to just six goals in four games.

While located in Chicago for ninety seasons before 2016–2017, the Blackhawks, for example won their conference in 1992, 2010, 2013, and 2015. When coached by Darryl Sutter or Joel Quenneville, one or more of these four clubs were led by players at various positions such as Chris Chelios, Ed Belfour, Patrick Kane, Jonathan Toews, Brent Seabrook, Dave Bolland, Duncan Keith, and Corey Crawford. In one of their best seasons, Chicago set individual and team NHL records in 2009–2010 (52-22-8 record and 112 points). They had not won a Stanley Cup since 1961 and faced the Philadelphia Flyers, who qualified for the playoffs on the last day of the season, and overcame a three-game deficit to reach the finals. After defeating the Flyers, the city of Chicago joined in as the Blackhawks were Stanley Cup champions. Before winning it, Captain Jonathan Toews held the Conn Smyth Trophy and earned playoff MVP honors.

Besides NHL teams in Edmonton and Chicago, the Flames had a great season in 1988–1989. Calgary, who took advantage of the Oilers trading Gretzky to the Kings, captured its second straight President's Trophy with a solid 54-17-9 record and scoring 117 points as right wing Lanny McDonald was playing his final season and seeking the Stanley Cup that had eluded him throughout his stellar 16-year career. After defeating the Canadiens to win the championship, the Flames became the first road team to win it at the Montreal Forum as defenseman Al MacInnis claimed the Conn Smythe trophy while an emotional McDonald embraced the Stanley Cup as he finally captured the ultimate prize.

Although scoring only 105 points, the Kings had one of their finest seasons historically in 1974–1975 although not winning a Stanley Cup. With realignment of the league, the Kings were placed in the Norris Division within the Prince of Wales Conference. Despite playing in a division with the Canadiens, the Kings put together a strong season posting the third best record overall while finishing in second place with a 42-17-21 record. However, in the playoffs, the Kings got a cold dose of reality being beaten by the Toronto Maple Leafs in a three game series. Nevertheless, Coach Bob Pulford won the Jack Adams award for his leadership of the team.

As the Canucks celebrated their 40th anniversary in 2011, some felt it could be a dream season at the newly renamed Rogers Arena. Vancouver, who already was one of the top teams in the WC, had a big offseason from landing terrific two-way forward Manny Malhotra and also Dan Hamhuis, a defenseman aimed at making the Canucks a tougher team. They finished the 2010–2011 season with a 54-19-9 record, the best mark in franchise history and won the President's Trophy for the best record in the NHL for the first time in franchise history. However, as the playoffs began, the Canucks learned they would be without one of their key players, as Manny Mahlotra suffered a severe eye injury against the Colorado Avalanche. As a result, the Bruins defeated them in the Stanley Cup finals and to make matters worse, a riot erupted in the City of Vancouver, which added a black eye to the tear-filled eyes of hockey fans in British Columbia.

Stanley Cups

According to Column 7 in Table A8.2, the 14 WC teams won a total of 18 Stanley Cups as of 2016. Each division, in fact, claimed nine or 50% of them. While the most successful clubs have been the Blackhawks and Oilers followed by the Avalanche and Kings, seven or 50% of the group have failed to win a Stanley Cup.

With respect to being champions, some players who won the MVP award in the Stanley Cup playoffs — Conn Smythe Trophy — include the Blackhawks' Duncan Keith, Patrick Kane, and Jonathan Toews each once; Oilers' Bill Ranford and Mark Messier each once and Wayne Gretzky twice; and Avalanche's Joe Sakic and Patrick Roy each once; and the Kings' Justin Williams and Jonathan Quick each once. Some of these players were also other trophy winners and/or performed in all-star games, and perhaps scoring leaders for their team.

San Jose and Vancouver each lost their games in Stanley Cup finals. In 2016, the Sharks faced Pittsburgh with the championship on the line. The Penguins eventually added an empty net goal to win the Stanley Cup with a 3-1 win in Game 6. The Sharks, however, had nothing to be ashamed about as Logan Couture led all scorers with 30 points in the postseason highlighted by 20 assists, while team captain Joe Pavelski led the way with 14 goals.

The Canucks, meanwhile, competed in Stanley Cup finals during 1982, 1994, and 2011. Facing the two time defending champion New York Islanders in 1982, the Canucks had a chance to steal Game 1 on the road, as they went into overtime tied 5-5. However, just a little over a minute left in the first overtime, the clock struck midnight on the Canucks Cinderella season as Mike Bossy scored to give the Islanders a 6-5 win and sweep the series in four games.

Then in 1994 against the Rangers, the Canucks threw everything they could at goalie Mike Richter. However, they were unable to get the tying goal as New York barely hung on to win the Cup. Sadly fans in Vancouver, who partied like they won the Cup a few days earlier, rioted giving the city an unneeded black eye and tarnishing a great Canucks run. And then in 2011, the Bruins had a three-game lead that sucked life out of the Canucks. After Brad Marchand added an empty net goal, Boston claimed the Stanley Cup. Making matter worse, a riot erupted in Vancouver.

Total performances

This result — or the total performance (TP) for each team — includes their division and conference titles plus number of Stanley Cups as listed in Columns 5–7 of Table A8.2. Among 125 TPs through the league's 2015–2016 season, PD clubs won 64 or 51% of them followed by the CD's 61 or 49%.

While the Blackhawks ranked first with 26 in TPs, Oilers second with 18, and Avalanche and Canucks tied for third each with 13, the Predators and Jets had zero, Coyotes one, and the Wild two. Other teams with at least ten TPs during their seasons in the WC included the Stars and Flames.

Regarding TPs for the divisions, PD teams averaged nine and the CD's eight. In fact, the largest gap within them existed between the Blackhawks' 26 TPs and Predators and Jets with zero compared to the Oilers' eighteen and Coyotes' one. Furthermore, the CD had a greater variation or spread in TPs with a standard deviation of nine TPs versus the PD's seven. Consequently, more equality occurred among PD teams in winning titles plus Stanley Cups because of such things as their competitiveness in regular seasons and post-seasons of the conference, success of divisional rivals, and teams' coaches and players' talents.

When considering only their total points scored and number of playoffs combined as a measure of these 14 teams' performances, those with the most impressive results have been the Blackhawks followed closely by the Blues and then Kings, Canucks, Flames, Oilers, Stars and Sharks, and Avalanche and Ducks. In contrast to them, the Wild, Predators, Jets, and Coyotes had the worst-ranked numbers of the group as of 2016.

After sports experts researched and published the history of all NHL teams, some of these articles reported the most dominant and/or successful WD/WC teams of all-time. Based on different metrics and hockey information from various sources, among the best — in chronological order — are the following clubs.[11]

• As a team, the 1983–1984 Edmonton Oilers scored an NHL record 446 goals. At even strength, they were tops with an even strength for/against of 1.46. At home, the Oilers were 31-5-4 and on the road, were no slouch. At 26-13-1, they had the best road record of any Stanley Cup Champion since the 1977–1978 Montreal Canadiens. Edmonton had Hall of Fame talent at all positions, arguably the greatest player of all time at his peak, and perhaps the second best offensive defenseman of all time in Paul Coffey. Led by Hall of Famer Wayne Gretzky, the team won the Stanley Cup in five games.

• What separated the 1986–1987 Oilers from other teams in history was their offense. It simply was among the greatest of all time in the league. Wayne Gretzky, Jari Kurri, Mark Messier, and Glenn Anderson scored numerous goals. On defense, Paul Coffey was making people think he was the second coming of Bobby Orr with his offensive rushes. What separates this group from other Oilers teams — except in 1983–1984 — was their ability to play timely defense when needed. For example, in Game 7 — the decisive period of the Stanley Cup finals — they only gave up two shots on goal. This team was fantastic offensively and also good enough defensively.

• The 1988–89 Flames finished the regular season 54-17-9 with 117 points, and tops in the NHL. The team won its division and conference each by 26 points and the President's Trophy by two points over the Canadiens. Joe Mullen, who led the team in scoring with 51 goals and 110 points, broke the NHL record for points by an American player. As a team, the Flames finished second in the league in goals, goals against and power play (PP) percentage, first in penalty kill (PK) percentage and also strength for/against, and had an outstanding home record of 32-4-4 — which was best of any Stanley Cup Champion since the late 1950s.

• Led by Hall of Famers Joe Sakic and Patrick Roy, the 1995–1996 Colorado Avalanche team was one of the greatest in the NHL of all time and yet, flew under the radar for most of its season. What sets this team apart and allows them to rank with the greatest was their leadership, talent, and incredible even strength play. At even strength, the Avalanche posted a 1.49 even strength efficiency, which is the 11th best mark all time of 43 Stanley Cup champions. Even strength play is widely regarded as the statistic that most indicates Stanley Cup success, and this team was phenomenal.

• Statistically, the 2000–2001 Avalanche team was very strong. They were fourth in both goals for and against and had the third best PP in the league. While their PK did not rank well at 19th, percentage-wise they were competitive. Another positive for this team was the performances of their young players. Relied on heavily that year, Alex Tanguay and Milan Hejduk stepped up in a big way contributing 27 and 41 goals, respectively. Colorado got almost a full year out of their $10 million man Peter Forsberg and in 73 games, he contributed 27 goals and 89 points. Their offense, however, started with Joe Sakic. He tallied fifty-four goals, 118 points, and won the Hart

Trophy. In total, the club had five players tally 24 or more goals, giving them one of the deepest attacks in the NHL. This Avalanche team won the Stanley Cup and thus remembered as one of the greatest of all time.

For various reasons such as lacking talented players, coaching problems and/or both of them, some American Division and WD/WC teams had terrible performances in their regular seasons. Several of these clubs were evaluated based on their ability to score points, deny goals, and win games. In chronological order, the following is a list of a few of the worst clubs in the pre-conference and conference's history as of its 2016 season.[12]

• We must go way back to see another Chicago Black Hawks season (1928–1929), in what was only their third year in the league. There were only five teams in the American Division at this time in the NHL, and the Black Hawks were so bad that they finished behind the 9-27-8 Pittsburgh Pirates. Chicago's final record of 7-29-8 was not even the saddest part. Unfortunately, they finished with just 33 goals and 22 points in their 44 game schedule, and Ty Arbour was their leading assist man with only four on the season.

• There might be a Chicago Blackhawks dynasty these days, but the team had a long stretch of futility. They make the worst list quite a few times, especially when the team's nickname was Black Hawks. For example, in the 1950–1951 season — when able to somehow be worse from their last place finish the year before — they finished with a record of 13-47-10 in 70 games. Roy Conacher led the team with just 50 points while it got off to a good start at 7-3-2 in the league's regular season before completely falling apart. The Boston Bruins made the playoffs that year with just 62 points, but the Black Hawks still finished 26 points out.

• In just their third year in the league (1969), the Los Angeles Kings had their most pathetic season in franchise history. The team was completely anemic on offense, and its coach fired just 24 games into the season. The Kings scored only 168 goals in 76 games, and their road record was miserable at 2-30-6. At one point, the Kings played 17 games in which they did not secure a win. It was a huge regression after reaching the playoffs in their first two seasons as a team. This was especially bad, however, because all the expansion teams of 1967 were plucked into the same division. This meant the Kings heavily fell behind their fellow expansion teams.

• If there is one thing to learn from listing the worst NHL clubs of all-time, expansion ice hockey teams had it pretty rough at least historically. While in their second season (1980–1981), the Winnipeg Jets had three different coaches and totaled just nine wins to go against 57 losses and 14 ties, and at one point, starting the season 1-25-7. The club seemed to not want to play at the arena most nights and would eventually move to Phoenix before Winnipeg welcomed a franchise from Atlanta.

• The San Jose Sharks did not stand much of a chance when they debuted in the league's 1991–1992 season. Perhaps the most embarrassing part of their season was finishing 3-35-2 on the road and being outscored by 140 goals. The team had a final record of 17-58-5, and Pat Falloon was their highest scorer with just 59 points. The Sharks were able to somehow give up 10 or more goals on three separate occasions during the season, with their worst loss coming 11-1 against Detroit.

• In their 1992–1993 season, the Sharks made history by breaking futility records. They finished 11-71-2 with just 24 points. Their 71 losses are a record for most in a season, and they also set the record for most consecutive losses with 17. The team got thrashed repeatedly, scoring just 218 goals on the season and surrendering 414 — most in the league. Thankfully for San Jose, they would not be the worst team of all time, let alone that season, because there was one other team equally bad. The EC's Ottawa Senators won only 10 games, lost 70, tied four, and also scored just 24 points.

LEAGUE ECONOMICS

In this section, there are data and other information about the commercial and financial aspects of franchises in the WC and their significance from an economic perspective. Besides attendances at home and away games, anything else that affects teams' income, market value, and wealth is included in the analysis, quantified, and discussed. In other words, the NHL is an organization consisting of for-profit enterprises that operate to compete each season typically within a division and/or conference and seek in various ways to improve their performances in current and future games.[13]

Franchise Financials

Based on financial data published in *Forbes*, in Column 2 of Table A8.3 is the estimated market value of each WC team, by division, as of 2016.

Ranked from most to least, PD clubs averaged $468 million and the CD's $443 million. While the Blackhawks were first at $925 million, Canucks second at $700 million, and Kings third at $600 million, the least in value included the Coyotes' $240 million, Predators' $270 million, and Blues' $310 million. In comparison to the typical club's market value of $456 million within the conference, only four or approximately 28% of the group actually exceeded that amount.[14]

Several factors caused differences in teams' market values. In no specific order, these were their history, tradition, and success in the league, being located in a big, midsized, or small market, size of each's fan base, number of titles and championships, and such financial data as their revenue, operating income, and gate receipts. Based on these and other reasons, they ranged in value by more than $684 million.

To compare their standard deviation or variation in market values, the highest within groups were CD teams ($224 million) but lowest among those in the PD ($147 million). This means inequality or variation in these WC franchise's values existed in 2015–2016 to a greater extent between the Blackhawks and other CD teams than among clubs in the other division. Although these were only estimates, the differences in amounts influenced such things as the clubs' relative wealth, economic power in the league, and future price if offered for sale to potential investors. Interestingly, the market value of each NHL franchise exceeded the conference's average deviation of $182 million.

Each team's revenue — net of stadium revenues used for debt payments — is displayed in Column 3 of Table A8.3. While the Blackhawks had the highest at $173 million followed by the Canucks' $146 million and Stars' $144 million, the three lowest-ranked in revenue were the Coyotes' $101 million at 14th, Jets' $112 million at 13th, and Avalanche's $115 at 12th. The differences in amounts occurred for several reasons including their home attendances, range in ticket prices and points in regular-season games, and also number of hockey fans in the area and their commitment to the sport.

Because of various demographic, socio-economic, and sport-specific factors, there were disparities in teams' revenue. While the conference's standard deviation equaled $18 million, CD teams had the highest variation in revenue at $21 million and then the PD's at $16 million. The latter division's revenues had the smallest differences because the same amounts existed for the Ducks and Flames and also similar amounts for the Kings, Sharks, and Canucks. Besides win–loss records in the regular season, the deviations reflect population size and the growth in population of their markets, popularity among fans at home games, and per capita income and the employment and type of jobs of local households.

Each WC teams' 2015–2016 gate receipts — in millions of dollars — appear in Column 4 of Table A8.3. While the conference's average was $48 million, the Blackhawks had the most ($74 million) and then the Sharks ($63 million) and Canucks ($62 million). In contrast to these amounts, the Coyotes ($20 million), Avalanche ($33 million), and Predators ($38 million) had the smallest gate receipts of franchises in the NHL that year.

The average dispersion or disparity in gate receipts was greatest among PD clubs ($14 million) compared to CD teams ($13 million). Because of the large gap in amounts between, for example, the Sharks and Coyotes, the division's standard deviation exceeded that of the CD's Blackhawks and Avalanche, and any comparison of other teams' amounts. Simply put, the Chicago–Naperville–Elgin, San Francisco–Oakland–Heyward, and Vancouver metropolitan areas are lucrative and more prosperous hockey markets relative to teams' gate receipts than surprisingly the Los Angeles–Long Beach–Anaheim and Dallas–Fort Worth–Arlington MSAs.

In Table A8.3, Column 5 contains the operating income or EBITDA of WC teams as of their 2015–2016 season. For the group of 14, it averaged $10 million. From most to least by division, CD clubs averaged $11 million in operating income and the PD's $8 million. Because of excessive payments for players' salaries and other types of expenses, the Predators, Ducks, Coyotes, and Kings had negative EBITDA's while the Blackhawks, Canucks, and Stars earned the most income by operating efficiently. For various reasons, the CD's Avalanche, Wild and Blues, and PD's Sharks were marginally efficient or not greatly inefficient operationally along with some others within different areas of NHL markets.

While $12 million was the average deviation in operating income of these WC teams, the CD's equaled $12 million and PD's $13 million. The gap or variation between the most and least EBITDA of teams within divisions occurred, respectively, for the Blackhawks and Predators ($36.6 million), and Canucks and Coyotes ($37.6 million). In other words, their earnings varied because each of them operated differently by applying former and new business practices, strategies, and tactics of the sports industry.

Sixth column of Table A8.3 includes the debt-to-value (D/V) percentage of each WC franchise in 2016. On average, the conference's was 20% or in amount, approximately $91 million per team based on their estimated market values. Among each group, CD's clubs averaged 21% and those in the PD 19%. Although two in the group had debt percentages of 0%, the D/V ratios exceeded 25% each for the Stars, Wild, Predators, Jets, and Coyotes.

As described for other variables in the table, the average standard deviations of D/V were unequal among divisions and franchises within divisions. PD teams, for example, had the greatest variation at 17% and then those in the AD at 15%. In order to reduce their D/V ratios for financial reasons and operate more effectively, several teams needed to restructure themselves or reform internally as businesses in order to generate higher market values and/or reduce the amount of debt in accounts on their balance sheet.

As reported in *Forbes* for being an important, necessary, and periodic payment from an operations perspective, players' expenses — including benefits and bonuses — have been reported for these 14 teams in 2016. For the league, they totaled approximately $991 million or $70 million per team. On average, CD clubs' expenses totaled $71 million and the PD's $70 million. While the Blackhawks, Kings, and Sharks ranked highest, six or 42% in the conference paid less than $70 million in players' expenses. Given these amounts, only one (Ducks) of the latter group had an above-average or talented roster of players and won enough games in the regular season to qualify for the playoffs. Indeed, the other five failed to be competitive enough to participate in the conference's post-season partly because of their relatively small or misallocated investment in players' salaries.[15]

Players' expenses were different and also slightly deviated among teams within the two WC divisions. From most to least in variation among the groups — as measured by their standard deviations — these included the PD's $7 million and then the CD's $6 million. Such amounts denote that the greatest disparity in payments occurred partly because of the Kings' $80 million versus Coyotes' $60 million, whereas the range in players' expenses within the CD of the Blackhawks' $82 million, Wild's and Blues' each $74 million, and the Stars' and Predators' each $71 million differed less than $20 million when compared to expenses of others. Thus, not all WC teams with the greatest revenues and/or largest market values always compensated their players more than rivals within their division.

Arenas

As of the NHL's 2015–2016 season, the 14 WC teams played their home games in venues that differed in age, construction cost and market value, and also in such other ways as location, capacity, and ownership. Based on various criteria including their amenities, concessions, and sightlines, they have been ranked from best to worst overall, most to least accessible, and highest to lowest in quality as facilities to entertain spectators at games. Given those comparisons, this section provides some data and other information regarding the facilities of the conference's clubs and discusses specific characteristics about them.[16]

Among WC teams' home venues within each division as of 2016, they ranged in age as follows: within the conference's CD, from the Jets' 13-year-old MTS Center to the Blackhawks' 23-year-old United Center and also Blues' Scottrade Center, and within the PD, from the Oilers' new Rogers Place to the Flames' 34-year-old Scotiabank Saddledome. Of WC teams' 14 facilities, three or 21% of them were financed privately and seven or 50% publicly. Furthermore, the other four or 29% received funds from private sources and also a municipality and/or state or province.

Their construction ranked from being relatively cheap to very expensive. From the least to most costly within the conference's CD, it was $134 million to erect 15,200-seat MTS Centre in 2004 for the Jets in Winnipeg compared to $420 million to build 18,500-seat American Airlines Center in 2001 for the Stars in Dallas; and in the PD, from $110 million to construct 18,800-seat Rogers Arena in 1995 for the Canucks in Vancouver to $375 million to build 18,200-seat Staples Center in 1999 for the Kings in Los Angeles.

The 14 stadiums' average cost for construction equaled $205 million, while the divisions' standard deviation or variation in amounts ranged from the CD's $98 million to the PD's $112 million. Thus, stadiums of the Avalanche, Jets, and other five CD teams had smaller differences in their construction costs than the seven stadiums in the PD especially because of the Kings' Staples Center being relatively expensive at $375 million and also Oilers' Rogers Place at $363 million.

Regarding plans to renovate a current venue of a team in the WC as of January 2017, city leaders and St. Louis Blues executives seek taxpayer subsidies to pay for a $138 million renovation of the Scottrade Center. The city's $67.5 million contribution — from current sales taxes generated at Scottrade as well as a new 1% sales tax on Scottrade Center ticket sales, concessions and other retail — would fund new seating and a scoreboard, sound system and lighting upgrades, renovated locker rooms and concessions stands, and new administrative offices. The Blues' owners intend to contribute $50 million during the next 20–30 years for additional improvements beyond the other renovations and request state contributions for the project to be $6 million in annual installments. Team chairman Tom Stillman said the stadium generates $14 million total in sales tax annually, with about $6 million allocated to the city and $8 million to the state.[17]

Recently *Forbes* sports editors assigned economic values to stadiums of teams in the WC. From lowest to highest within divisions, respectively, amounts in the CD were $77 million for the Predators' 17,100-seat Bridgestone Arena in Nashville to $315 million for the Blackhawks' 19,700-seat United Center in Chicago; and within the PD, from $54 million for the Coyotes' 17,100-seat Gila River Arena in Glendale to $208 million for the Canucks' 18,800-seat Rogers Arena in Vancouver.[18]

While the 14 stadiums of WC teams had an average economic value of $135 million, those in the CD are worth $132 million and PD $138 million. In addition, the seven venues in the CD were more unequal or ranged in value because they had a larger standard deviation compared to those in the PD. Although the latter group of stadiums was worth more on average in 2016 than those in the CD, they also deviated more in age and construction cost but not in value. Nevertheless, because of increasing real estate prices in urban areas and popularity of the sport in North America, most of these facilities will likely appreciate economically particularly those within the largest and most populated markets and wealthiest metropolitan areas.

In various studies, NHL stadiums have been ranked by various ice hockey experts and sports journalists in the media with respect to their location and also different attributes, characteristics, and problems. Although results differed according to each study's parameters, a few venues ranked among the best in the conference while some others placed in the worst group. For example, the most attractive, entertaining, and well-structured facilities within the WC based on their name, aesthetics, and experience for fans include the Jets' MTS Centre and Wild's Xcel Energy Center.

As reported in the *Stadium Journey* as of mid-2016, the two best hockey buildings of WC teams were rated highest based on these reasons[19]:

"For the second straight season, the MTS Centre in Winnipeg takes our top spot as the best arena experience in the NHL. Fans are loud and proud in Winnipeg, and they savor having an NHL team after the 15 year absence that concluded in 2011. The remarkable atmosphere begins right from the arrival of the Jets on the ice, with the fans giving them a loud round of applause followed by the first Go! Jets! Go! chant prior to the singing of the anthems. The energy continues during the anthem(s) when the building does the 'True North' shout out during O Canada. This started in the first season the Jets were back as an acknowledgement and thank you to True North Sports and Entertainment who purchased the team and brought them to Winnipeg."

For why Minnesota's hockey arena ranked second in the conference, the editor provided these comments:

"Minneapolis/St Paul combines as a great sports town, and it's no surprise that the State of Hockey's NHL franchise provides an excellent arena experience. The 'X,' as it's referred to, has hosted 18,000+ rabid hockey fans every game night since its opening, and the experience of enjoying a game there still has not lost its luster. Sixteen years later, the Xcel Energy Center remains one of the premier arenas to enjoy an NHL game."

In the same study, two of the lowest-ranked EC facilities were the Canucks' Rogers Arena and Ducks' Honda Center. Among others in the conference, the former ranked 12th (27th in the NHL) and the latter 14th (30th in the league). The study's author evaluated each of them, respectively, as follows:

"Rogers Arena is a fun place for all different types of fans to take in a Canucks game. The Canucks have had some good teams in past years and this is a great place to watch a game of hockey. If you are willing to open up your wallet a bit, you will get a great game to go along with a fun atmosphere. The food is good, but it doesn't come cheap."

Regarding why the Honda Center ranked last in the conference and league, the comments were interesting:

"Rising from the Southern California landscape stands an arena, situated adjacent to the Angels' MLB stadium. The Honda Center, still referred to as 'The Pond' by Ducks loyalists, is an arena of contrasts. On the outside, the building looks modern and clean-cut. Inside, the floors and stairways of the arena's concourses are marble. In the bowl, the seats are small but comfortable, and the suites look like a melding of the exterior and the halls. However, a green ceiling mixed with an unfinished look seems out of place, and it seems to draw the eye's attention away from the action on the ice. For the third straight year, the Ducks take the last spot on our list."

Fan cost index

In the league's 2014 season, the average Fan Cost Index (FCI) for a family to attend a regular season game of a WC team was $358. While Blackhawks' home games each cost $463, the Stars had the conference's lowest FCI at $263. Among divisions, the average from most to least was PD teams at $361 and those in the CD $355. The order from ranking them first and then second occurred, in part, because FCIs of the Canucks, Oilers, and Kings each exceeded $380 while those of such teams as the Avalanche, Stars, and Blues were each below $330.[20]

For specific items in Team Marketing Report's 2014 FCI, the approximate range in amounts from most to least expensive — or first compared to 14th across the WC — were listed as follows: average ticket, Canucks $84 to Stars $37; average premium ticket, Canucks $202 to Wild $100; beer, Wild and Coyotes each $9.50 to Stars $6; soft drink, Blackhawks $5.75 to Predators $3.50; hot dog, Blackhawks $6.25 to Flames $3.61; parking, Canucks $26.77 to Wild, Predators, Coyotes, and Avalanche each $10; program, the Blackhawks, Sharks, and Stars each $5 to Blues $1; and for a cap, Blackhawks $25 to Jets $13.38. Based on economics principles, these prices were set by teams and/or vendors to sell enough units to maximize revenue from their sales at home games in the stadiums.

From the NHL's 2010–2011 to 2014–2015 season, there were some significant increases but also relatively small and even decreases in FCIs of teams in the WC. For examples of these changes, the Canucks' FCI rose from

$357 to $456 or approximately 28% but the Ducks' from only $284 to $288 or about 2%, while the Flames' actually declined from $366 to $352 or 4%. Because of inflation, number of — and amount spent by — families at games in arenas, local economic conditions and other factors, the majority of teams and/or vendors raised their prices each year rather than keeping them constant or reducing amounts.

In evaluating year-to-year FCIs between, for example, the WC's 2013–2014 and 2014–2015 seasons, the Avalanche's increased the most, in other words, from $266 to $295 or approximately 11%. Alternatively, fans' costs fell at home games of the Jets, Flames, and Canucks but remained the same for those of the Stars at $263. Thus, there were different payments for tickets and other things by families to attend the conference teams' home games at their stadiums especially from 2010 to 2015.

The largest deviation or variation in FCIs in 2014–2015 occurred among CD clubs ($69) than those in the PD ($56). Of the highest and lowest in each division, the Blackhawks' amount exceeded the Stars' by $200 compared to $168 between the Canucks and Ducks. These gaps in FCI's reflect differences in teams' pricing policies and other factors such as their attendances at home games, number of points scored, win–loss record, stadium capacity, and popularity and respect in the local and regional sports market.

ORGANIZATION HIGHLIGHTS

Besides regular-season and post-season games, the WC and its franchises are involved in — and affected by — community events and also business-related and government affairs, news, and projects. Because these things and other topics influence the conference in different but perhaps important and historic ways, following are a few of them from the academic and popular literature.[21]

First, among the greatest WC franchises of all-time, a study ranked the Oilers first, Avalanche second, and Ducks third. Edmonton established its place in the study by winning an incredible amount of games, while being in the league for only 37 seasons. Besides the first two Presidents' trophies, they have collected five Stanley Cups and won seven conference championships and their division six times. The greatest player in league history — Wayne

Gretzky — is a major part of the Oilers' impressive ranking. Alternatively, the Predators have the least successful history of all NHL franchises.

Second, based on the willingness to spend money to improve its team, stability and capabilities of the front office and management, amenities at the team's venue, the club's culture and interactivity with fans, and success or failure on the ice, Silicon Valley Sports & Entertainment (SVS&E) — renamed Sharks Sports and Entertainment in 2011 — was one of the best owners of a WC team. SVS&E presided over the most sustained period of success in the organization's history and a consistent threat for that elusive first Stanley Cup. Because of their all-time record and also attendance and financial problems, the league's worst franchise owner is Nashville's Predators Holdings LLC.

Third, given their history with their current organization in the WC as of 2017, among the top general managers of teams are the Blackhawks' Stan Bowman and Ducks' Bob Murray. Stan is excellent with the salary cap, made the right trades to create space to extend key players, and did an outstanding job finding value in the draft. One of the best traders in the league, Bob has assembled an ascending group of defensemen to help provide balance to a forward unit that includes some top players in the league.

Fourth, in a survey of each NHL team's front office, the Predators placed first (third in the league) and Stars second (sixth overall) among those only in the WC. Besides adding a number one center and defenseman in the span of a few months while getting rid of a horrible contract, Nashville has arguably one of the best top four defense groups for less than $20 million. Although thin at center, Dallas's front office made mistakes but the decision-making process has been mostly on point.

Fifth, among those that discontinued operations, the Montreal Maroons were the only team to win more than 50% of their games while playing 14 seasons in the NHL. Within the group, the Philadelphia Quakers had the lowest winning percentage at 0.136 and then the Montreal Wanderers and Quebec Bulldogs each at 0.167. The Quakers folded because of financial problems during the Great Depression, Wanderers lacked enough skilled players due to World War I, and the Bulldogs were sold to another company.

Sixth, the last five Stanley Cup champions — as of August 2016 — were WC teams and eight of the last 10 winners also came from the conference. Since 1999, the league's championship was awarded to a WC team ten times and to one in the EC just seven times. The last stint of real dominance by the EC came at the beginning of the 2000s when its teams won the Cup in 2002–2004 and 2006 by respectively the Red Wings, Devils, Lightning, and Hurricanes while a lockout occurred in 2005.

Seventh, the arenas/stadiums of WC teams, on average, were younger and less expensive to build, and had a lower economic value than those of EC clubs as of 2016. In age, they ranged from the Oilers' Rogers Place to the Rangers' Madison Square Garden (MSG); in construction costs, from the Red Wings' Joe Louis Arena to the Islanders' Barclays Center; and in value, from the Coyotes' Gila River Arena to the Rangers' MSG.

Eighth, fans paid less on average to attend home games of teams in the WC's CD and PD than those of clubs in the EC's Atlantic Division and Metropolitan Division in the league's 2014–2015 season. Based on their FCIs, the cost per game exceeded $500 for Maple Leafs and Bruins home games in the EC and at least $400 to see the Blackhawks, Canucks, and Jets play at their arenas in the WC.

Ninth, the Blackhawks, Jets, and Oilers had the largest attendances in 2015–2016 among WC teams at their road games while the Coyotes, Canucks, and Stars attracted the fewest people away from home. For home plus away games, the Blackhawks, Wild, and Flames led their conference in attendance while the Coyotes and then Jets and Ducks finished at the bottom.

Tenth, named after the US military academy's West Point Black Knights and assigned to the league's WC, the Vegas Golden Knights will play at home in the 17,500-seat, multipurpose T-Mobile Arena in Paradise, Nevada. Fidelity National Financial and Black Knight Financial Services' Chairman of the Board William P. Foley II is the lead investor in Black Knight Sports & Entertainment — the consortium awarded an expansion franchise by the NHL. Prior to becoming the Golden Knights' lead owner, Foley was reportedly interested in acquiring the NFL Jacksonville Jaguars.

NOTES

1. For historical information about the sport and its professional leagues and their teams and players, see "National Hockey League (NHL)," http://www.thecanadi-anencyclopedia.ca [cited 27 January 2017] and Dan Diamond, *The Official*

Encyclopedia of the National Hockey League. Kingston, NY: Total Sports Publishing (2000).

2. "History of NHL Relocation," http://www.puckreport.com [cited 5 January 2017] and the *National Hockey League Official Guide & Record Book 2016.* Chicago, IL: Triumph Books (2016).

3. Two sources are "Collective Bargaining Agreement," http://www.nhlpa.com [cited 3 February 2017] and "Collective Bargaining Agreement Between National Hockey League and National Hockey League Players' Association," http://www.nhl.com [cited 19 January 2017].

4. "Defunct NHL Teams," http://www.infoplease.com [cited 19 January 2017] and "Defunct Teams Histories," http://www.sportsencyclopedia.com [cited 15 January 2017].

5. See Jozsa FP Jr. (2010). "Hockey Business: NHL Franchises, Markets and Strategies," unpublished manuscript, Misenheimer, NC, Pfeiffer University.

6. The reference is *The Statesman's Year-Book: 1992–93.* London: Palgrave Macmillan Press (1993).

7. *Idem*, "Collective Bargaining Agreement Between National Hockey League and National Hockey League Players' Association."

8. "NHL & WHA Career Leaders and Records for Points," http://www.hockey-reference.com [cited 20 January 2017].

9. For specific data on the performances of teams and their coaches and players, see such websites as http://www.nhl.com, http://www.sportsencyclopedia.com, and http://www.hockey-reference.com.

10. "Playoff Formats," http://www.nhl.com [cited 3 February 2017] and "Stanley Cup Playoffs Format, Qualification System," http://www.nhl.com [cited 21 January 2017].

11. Key J, "Greatest NHL Teams of All-Time," http://www.thehockeynews.com [cited 20 January 2017]; Bass A, "NHL: 50 Best Teams in History," http://www.bleacherreport.com [cited 22 January 2017]; Silverman S, "The NHL's 10 Greatest Stanley Cup Championship Teams of the Last 50 Years," http://www.bleacherreport.com [cited 22 January 2017]; Prashanth Iyer, "Top 15 NHL Teams of All Time," http://www.hookedonhockeymagazine.com [cited 1 February 2017].

12. Three sources are "Top 15 Worst NHL Teams of All Time," http://www.thesportster.com [cited 20 January 2017]; Shannon M, "NHL History: The Ten Worst Teams of All Time," http://www.bleacherreport.com [cited 20 January 2017]; Jeff Eisenband, "12 NHL Franchises That Have Never Won Stanley Cup," http://www.thepostgame.com [cited 24 January 2017].

13. Sports economics is thoroughly covered, for example, in Quirk J and Fort RD (1992). *Pay Dirt: The Business of Professional Team Sports.* Princeton, NJ: Princeton University Press (1992) and history of the league in D'Arcy Jenish, *The NHL: 100 Years of On-Ice Action and Boardroom Battles.* Toronto, Canada: Anchor Canada (2016).

14. Please read "2016 NHL Valuations," http://www.forbes.com [cited 1 February 2017] and Mike Ozanian, Kurt Badenhausen, and Christini Settimi, "The Business of Hockey," http://www.forbes.com [cited 3 November 2016].

15. *Idem.*

16. See "Present National Hockey League Arenas," http://www.hockey.ballparks.com [cited 25 January 2017]; "NHL Arenas," http://www.statshockey.homestead.com [cited 25 January 2017]; Alan Bass, "Power Ranking the League's 30 Arenas," http://www.bleacherreport.com [cited 24 January 2017].

17. Faulk M and Addo K, "City, Business Leaders Want $138 Million in Renovations for Scottrade Center," http://www.stltoday.com [cited 2 February 2017].

18. *Idem*, "2016 NHL Valuations" and "The Business of Hockey."

19. Swaney P, "2016 NHL Arena Experience Rankings," http://www.scout.com [cited 24 January 2017].

20. "Rodney Fort's Sports Economics," http://sites.google.com [cited 24 January 2017] and Greenberg J, "NHL Fan Cost Index 2014–15," http://www.teammarketing.com [cited 25 January 2017].

21. Zimmer D, "NHL Power Rankings: Every Franchises Statistically Ranked All-Time," http://www.fansided.com [cited 3 February 2017]; "SI's Best and Worst Owners in the NHL," http://www.si.com [cited 25 January 2017]; Simmons J, "NHL Power Rankings: General Managers," http://www.sportsnet.ca [cited 3 February 2017]; Luszczyszyn D, "How Much Confidence Does Each NHL Fan Base Have in Their Front Office? A Ranking of All 30 Teams," http://www.thehockeynews.com [cited 3 February 2017]; "Defunct NHL Teams," http://www.infoplease.com [cited 19 January 2017]; Eric Roberts, "The West Has Become the NHL's Elite Conference," http://www.thehockeywriters.com [cited 3 February 2017]; "NHL Fan Cost Index," http://www.teammarketing.com [cited 2 February 2017]; "NHL Attendance Report — 2015–16," http://www.espn.com [cited 24 January 2017]; "William P. Foley II," http://www.bkfs.com [cited 3 February 2017].

CONCLUSION

MAJOR LEAGUE BASEBALL

For this sport, the National League (NL) formed in 1876 and 25 years later, the American League (AL). In 1994, each league reorganized into an East Division (ED), Central Division (CD), and West Division (WD). Table 1 contains such variables as market data, team performances, and financial data of each division in Major League Baseball (MLB). Following are results of comparing this information about the two leagues.

On average, AL teams are based in more-populated markets (MSAPOP) with a larger number of television homes (DMATVH) than those in the NL. Because of the New York area and its size and location, each league's ED ranks ahead of other teams' markets within the CD and WD. Besides New York, the Chicago, Los Angeles–Anaheim, and San Francisco–Oakland areas also host two each MLB teams. According to these variables' standard deviation — which measures variation or dispersion — NL teams' areas have greater deviation in their MSAPOP and DMATVH and thus more widely spread market data.

In average attendance (AVGATT) of teams within divisions, the NL's WD ranked first primarily because the Los Angeles Dodgers and San Francisco Giants were competitive, popular, and successful during MLB's 2016 season. Alternatively, the AL's CD was sixth among the group due to relatively small home attendances of the Chicago White Sox, Cleveland Indians, and Minnesota Twins.

Table 1: MLB, American League and National League.

	American League			National League		
	ED	**CD**	**WD**	**ED**	**CD**	**WD**
Market Data						
MSAPOP	7.36	4.30	7.09	8.81	3.68	5.73
DMATVH	3.13	1.89	2.98	3.37	1.51	2.50
AVGATT	31.77	25.69	29.18	27.09	32.53	34.70
Team Performances						
Seasons	352	452	194	276	542	209
World Series	40	13	5	7	24	9
Pennants	62	30	9	19	58	19
Divisions	43	38	35	38	39	34
Playoffs	95	57	41	46	80	45
TP	145	81	49	64	121	62
Financial Data						
Value	1,650	955	1,118	1,207	1,311	1,485
Revenue	317	248	267	266	271	308
GR	115	65	67	71	91	89
OI	14.8	21.3	30.6	20.8	36.3	11.0
D/V	7.8	12.0	9.2	16.4	11.8	12.0
PE	165	134	137	133	132	179

Note: Abbreviated is Metropolitan Statistical Area Population (MSAPOP) in millions; Designated Market Area Television Homes (DMATVH) in millions; Average Attendance (AVGATT) in thousands; teams' Total Performances (TP), which include number of division titles, pennants, and World Series; Gate Receipts (GR) in millions; Operating Income (OI) in millions; Debt-to-Value (D/V) in percent; and Players Expenses (PE) in millions. Value and Revenue are each in millions.

Source: *Official Major League Baseball Fact Book* 2005 Edition (St. Louis, MO: Sporting News, 2005); websites' http://www.sportsencyclopedia.com, http://www.baseball-reference.com, http://www.mlb.com; Kurt Badenhausen, Michael Ozanian, and Christina Settimi, "The Business of Baseball", http://www.forbes.com [cited 1 October 2016].

Similar to deviations for the MSAPOP and DMATVH, the NL's divisions had more variation in attendances relative to those in the AL. This was really apparent, for example, between the ED's Washington Nationals and Miami Marlins, CD's St. Louis Cardinals and Cincinnati Reds, and the WD's Dodgers and Arizona Diamondbacks.

With respect to team performances in Table 1, NL divisions collectively lead in average seasons but so do the AL's in number and proportion of World Series, pennants, division titles, playoffs, and total performances (TP) — their total World Series plus pennants, and division titles. The ED's New York Yankees and then Boston Red Sox have each played at least 114 years and dominate others in both groups by qualifying for and winning championships in postseasons.

For worst performances among baseball divisions, the NL's WD mostly ranked fourth or fifth and the AL's WD fifth or sixth. More specifically, the former division's Arizona Diamondbacks, Colorado Rockies and San Diego Padres, and the latter division's Houston Astros, Seattle Mariners, and Texas Rangers have each performed below expectations during their years in MLB especially in winning pennants and World Series. Simply put, these clubs have been inconsistent because they failed to sign enough talented players and hire smart, experienced managers to continuously excel in regular seasons and then in playoffs. Furthermore, there is too much competition for them from such rivals in their division as respectively the Dodgers and Giants, and Los Angeles Angels of Anaheim and Oakland Athletics.

With respect to financial data in the table, the NL's three divisions combined have a higher average market value and more revenue, gate receipts, operating income, debt-to-value (D/V) ratios, and player's expenses than those in the AL. The results between the leagues are different, in part, because of there being a few more midsized- but less small-market clubs in the NL and their history, financial success, and fan base.

While AL teams' ballparks are older, on average, they did not cost as much to build and also were less valuable in 2016 than those of NL clubs. Among the six divisions in MLB, ballparks ranked from 6-year-old Marlins Park in Miami to 106-year-old Fenway Park in Boston; in construction costs, from less than $1 million each for Fenway Park and Chicago's Wrigley Field to $688 million for Citi Field in New York; and in economic value, from $89 million for Marlins Park to $593 for New York's Yankee Stadium.

To attend games at these venues in baseball's 2016 season, the fan cost index for families ranged from $132 per game at Chase Field in Glendale, Arizona to $360 at Fenway Park. On average, families paid $224 to attend an AL game and $213 to view any in the NL. While the Red Sox, Yankees, and Cubs home games each cost more than $300, fans paid less than $200 each for those of eleven other clubs.

NATIONAL BASKETBALL ASSOCIATION

The 12-year-old National Basketball League and 3-year-old Basketball Association of America merged in 1949 and became the National Basketball Association (NBA). Then in 1976, the American Basketball Association folded and four of its teams joined the NBA. Twenty-nine years later, the NBA changed its structure by expanding from two to three divisions each in the Eastern Conference (EC) and Western Conference (WC). Table 2 contains market data, team performances, and financial data about each conference and their divisions.

As a group the EC's divisions and their teams exist, on average, in larger metropolitan areas with more television homes than those in the WC. That is because the Nets and Knicks are based in the New York area, Bulls in Chicago, and others in such big markets as Toronto, Philadelphia, Miami, and Washington. While the Atlantic Division (AD) ranks first in MSAPOP and DMATVH, the Northwest Division (NWD) is sixth since it includes teams in such small-to-midsized markets as Oklahoma City and Salt Lake City.

Although the WC's Pacific Division (PD) ranked first in average attendance and Southwest Division (SWD) third, the EC had two teams whose home games each exceeded 20,000 and another three at least 19,000. Thus, the conferences' per-game attendances were about the same.

Regarding team performances in Table 2, the EC's 15 teams collectively had the highest number of seasons and playoffs and also won more division and conference titles and championships than all clubs combined in the WC. Among six divisions in the NBA, the AD was first in TPs, CD third, and the Southeast Division (SED) fifth. Although the Lakers had the most TPs with 57, the conference's Portland Timberwolves, Los Angeles Clippers, Sacramento Kings, Memphis Grizzlies, and New Orleans Hornets/Pelicans each had fewer than three. Based on these results, the EC has been the superior conference in team performances.

With respect to financial data in the table, the average value of franchises in each conference equaled $1.22 billion with their revenue at $172 million. As a group, however, WC clubs' had the highest average operating income, gate receipts and players expenses, but not debt-to-value (D/V) percent. Financially, the differences in amounts between conferences occurred partly because data for the WC's PD ranked first or second due to the recent success of the Golden State Warriors.

Table 2: NBA, Eastern and Western Conference.

	Eastern Conference			Western Conference		
	AD	**CD**	**SD**	**ND**	**PD**	**SD**
Market Data						
MSAPOP	7.42	3.89	4.52	2.24	4.96	3.74
DMATVH	3.12	1.75	1.85	1.22	2.24	1.47
AVGATT	17.58	18.17	17.85	17.02	18.42	18.01
Team Performances						
Seasons	218	243	158	158	212	150
W%	0.496	0.495	0.469	0.516	0.489	0.523
Playoffs	139	138	88	95	112	101
Division	50	42	25	26	42	30
Conference	18	17	10	6	23	12
Championship	21	11	4	1	13	8
TP	89	70	39	33	78	50
Financial Data						
Value	1,576	1,153	947	875	1,705	1,096
Revenue	199	167	150	149	195	174
OI	39	27	13	18	47	31
GR	63	38	37	34	59	47
D/V	11	17	17	9	11	12
PE	80	78	78	77	81	82

Note: Abbreviated is Metropolitan Statistical Area Population (MSAPOP) in millions; Designated Market Area Television Homes (DMATVH) in millions; Average Attendance (AVGATT) in thousands; winning percentage (W%); teams' Total Performances (TP), which include number of division and conference titles and championships; Gate Receipts (GR) in millions; Operating Income (OI) in millions; Debt-to-Value (D/V) in percent; and Players Expenses (PE) in millions. Value and Revenue are each in millions.

Source: *Official National Basketball Association Guide 2015–16*. New York, NY: NBA Properties (2015); websites' http://www.basketball-reference.com, http://www.nba.com, and http://www.sportsencyclopedia.com; Badenhausen K, M Ozanian and C Settimi, "The Business of Basketball", http://www.forbes.com [cited 27 June 2016].

In comparing arenas in each conference as of the NBA's 2015–2016 season, those of teams in the WC are older and less valuable, on average, but also did not cost as much to build. In addition, the majority of them are privately owned in the EC and publicly in the WC. This data suggests that some venues in each conference are obsolete and need to be replaced and others renovated such as the Warriors' 51-year-old Oracle Arena and Kings' 29-year-old Sleep Train Arena, and the Milwaukee Bucks' 29-year-old BMO Harris Bradley Center and the Cleveland Cavaliers' 23-year-old Quicken Loans Arena.

For families to attend teams' games in the association's 2015 season, the EC's average fan cost index was greater than the WC's partly because each home game of the New York Knicks, Chicago Bulls, Miami Heat, Boston Celtics, and Brooklyn Nets exceeded $400. But in the SWD, it was less than $300 per-game to watch and root for the Dallas Mavericks, Memphis Grizzlies, and New Orleans Hornets/Pelicans at their arenas. Given their history, popularity and performances in their division and conference during the season, and in order to generate revenue, these and the other 22 teams in the NBA had different prices for such things as non-premium and premium tickets, beer, soft drinks, parking, programs, and caps.

NATIONAL FOOTBALL LEAGUE

Established in Canton, Ohio in 1920, the American Professional Football Association changed its name to National Football League (NFL) in 1922. From 1933 to 1949, the league consisted of an Eastern Division and Western Division and since 1950, an American Conference (AFC) and National Football Conference (NFC). After the American Football League folded in 1969, ten of its teams joined the NFL's AFC. Beginning in the 2002 season, the AFC and NFC each included an ED, ND, South Division (SD), and WD. Table 3 contains market data, team performances, and financial data for clubs in these divisions as of the league's 2015 season.

With respect to market data, NFC teams as a group led those in the AFC in average metropolitan populations (MSAPOP) and number of television homes (DMATVH). In fact, the AFC's ND, SD, and WD ranked sixth to eighth among the eight divisions for both variables because of such relatively midsized-to-small-market teams in Buffalo, Cincinnati, Indianapolis,

Table 3: NFL, American and National Football Conference.

	American Football Conference				National Football Conference			
	ED	ND	SD	WD	ED	ND	SD	WD
Market Data								
MSAPOP	5.51	2.33	2.97	2.62	7.33	4.41	3.09	5.99
DMATVH	2.09	1.15	1.30	1.21	2.94	1.87	1.53	1.54
AVGATT	69.74	65.06	65.99	65.42	79.80	66.53	69.37	71.80
Team Performances								
Seasons	184	166	85	171	309	327	160	184
Wins	364	295	166	337	563	601	267	346
Win%	0.512	0.461	0.479	0.507	0.515	0.520	0.436	0.497
Division	39	34	19	40	71	70	22	45
Conference	17	12	3	12	27	21	5	14
Championships								
NFL	0	0	0	0	9	21	0	1
SB	6	8	1	5	12	5	2	6
TP	62	54	23	57	119	117	29	66
Financial Data								
Value	2,506	2,018	2,181	2,113	3,187	2,225	1,937	2,537
Revenue	407	357	359	343	499	350	349	372
OI	99	71	90	62	163	80	68	95
GR	71	58	55	55	85	57	58	59
D/V	15	9	5	7	9	12	14	15
PE	192	182	170	184	188	167	182	170

Note: Abbreviated is Metropolitan Statistical Area Population (MSAPOP) in millions; Designated Market Area Television Homes (DMATVH) in millions; Average Attendance (AVGATT) in thousands; winning percentage (W%); teams' Total Performances (TP), which include number of division and conference titles and championships; National Football League (NFL); Super Bowl (SB); Gate Receipts (GR) in millions; Operating Income (OI) in millions; Debt-to-Value (D/V) in percent; and Players Expenses (PE) in millions. Value and Revenue are each in millions.

Source: 2014 Official NFL Record & Fact Book. New York, NY: National Football League (2014); websites' http://www.nfl.com, http://www.sportsencyclopedia.com, and http://www.football-reference.com; "Sports Money: 2016 NFL Valuations", http://www.forbes.com [cited 1 January 2017].

Jacksonville, and Nashville. Furthermore, more NFC teams were based in large and large to midsized areas besides New York such as in Chicago, Los Angeles, and Dallas.

Among divisions, the average attendances of AFC teams at their home games were less than those in the NFC by more than 5,000 per game. While the Oakland Raiders and San Diego Chargers had the smallest attendances in the NFL, the Cowboys ranked first with 92,000 at each of their games in Dallas, Texas but only five AFC teams had attendances greater than 71,000. Besides these teams' competitiveness and popularity, the differences in attendances reflect their market size and other demographic and sport-specific factors.

In their performances as of early 2016, NFC teams combined played more seasons than those in the AFC. Moreover, the former group of clubs had a higher average number of wins and winning percentage, and also more total division and conference titles, championships, and TPs. The most successful in performances have been the Green Bay Packers and New York Giants followed by the Cowboys and Pittsburgh Steelers while the worst of them includes the AFC's Cleveland Browns, New York Jets, Jacksonville Jaguars, and Houston Texans. These results, in large part, were caused by differences in number of seasons of the 10 former AFL clubs within divisions of their NFL conference.

The NFC's franchises, on average, were more valuable in 2016 than those in the AFC because of larger attendances and revenue, operating income, and gate receipts earned from their home games and other operations. As denoted in Table 3, the NFC's ED ranked first financially because of millions generated by the Dallas Cowboys, New York Giants, Philadelphia Eagles, and Washington Redskins in comparison to much smaller amounts by teams in other divisions of both conferences except for the AFC's New England Patriots. Interestingly, for various reasons, AFC clubs as a group had a smaller average D/V ratio yet their higher players expenses were comparable to the NFC's.

Regarding other topics in the NFL, stadiums of teams in both conferences were approximately 23-years-old on average but those in the NFC cost more to build and had greater economic value in 2016. In addition, individuals and groups of investors joined taxpayers to provide funds to construct the majority of these venues.

According to a recent fan cost index (FCI), the average was $522 for a family to attend an NFC game in the league's 2015 season. The amounts ranged from the Tampa Bay Buccaneers' $418 to the Chicago Bears' $685. In comparison, the index equaled $481 for each AFC game with the Jacksonville Jaguars lowest at $367 and New England Patriots highest at $652. These amounts included various prices for tickets, beer, soft drinks, hot dogs, parking, and caps. Because the sport and NFL games are popular in America, teams typically operate at a profit especially those in the biggest and most lucrative markets.

NATIONAL HOCKEY LEAGUE

Then the National Hockey Association stopped operating during World War II, seven elite teams from Canada formed the National Hockey League (NHL). The league was split into the American and Canadian Divisions during the 1926 to 1937 seasons, ED and WD from 1967 to 1974, and then into the Clarence Campbell Conference and Prince of Wales Conference until being renamed EC and WC in 1993. Twenty years later the EC was divided into the AD and Metropolitan Division (MD), and the WC into the CD and PD. Table 4 contains market data, team performances, and financial data for the two conferences by division as of early 2016.

As a group, EC teams on average had the largest metropolitan area populations (MSAPOP) and number of television homes (DMATVH) and also the highest attendances at their home games as of the league's 2015 season. While large-market clubs within the conference exist in the New York, Washington, Miami, Philadelphia, and Toronto areas, several small-market teams have their home sites in territories within the WC.

Besides the EC's demographic advantages, the average attendances at Detroit Red Wings' and Montreal Canadiens' home games, for example, exceeded those of 13 WC teams but not games of the CD's Blackhawks in Chicago. In other words, EC clubs tended to locate in larger and more populated markets than those in the WC. Thus, the Red Wings, Canadiens, and their rivals have higher attendances at their games particularly when playing others in the AD and MD.

In their historical performances, AD clubs ranked first and the MD's second in average seasons and points scored, and also in total playoffs,

Table 4: NHL, Eastern and Western Conference.

	Eastern Conference		Western Conference	
	AD	MD	CD	PD
Market Data				
MSAPOP	3.82	4.74	4.06	3.98
DMATVH	1.72	1.99	1.74	1.82
AVGATT	18.79	16.22	18.25	17.02
Team Performances				
Seasons	497	343	222	236
Points	37,226	27,260	17,640	18,998
Playoffs	338	203	145	135
Division	114	59	34	36
Conference	25	28	8	19
SC	54	18	9	9
TP	193	105	61	64
Financial Data				
Value	605	536	443	468
Revenue	144	141	132	127
GR	49	53	48	48
OI	22	15	11	8
D/V	17	32	21	19
PE	71	72	71	70

Note: Abbreviated is Metropolitan Statistical Area Population (MSAPOP) in millions; Designated Market Area Television Homes (DMATVH) in millions; Average Attendance (AVGATT) in thousands; Stanley Cup (Scup); teams' Total Performances (TP), which include number of division and conference titles and Stanley Cups; Gate Receipts (GR) in millions; Operating Income (OI) in millions; Debt-to-Value (D/V) in percent; and Players Expenses (PE) in millions. Value and Revenue are each in millions.

Source: "Annual Population Estimates by Census Metro Area", http://www.statcan.gc.ca [cited 16 January 2017]; "Population of Census Metropolitan Areas 2015", http://www.statcan. gc.ca [cited 27 January 2017]; "North American Television Market Ranking 2015–16," http://www.statcan.gc.ca [cited 27 January 2017]; "NHL Teams & Other Hockey Teams", http://www.hockey.reference.com [cited 16 January 2017] and "NHL Teams", http://www. sportsencyclopedia.com [cited 16 January 2017]; Ozanian M, K Badenhausen and C Settimi, "The Business of Hockey", http://www.forbes.com [cited 3 November 2016]; "2016 NHL Valuations", http://www.forbes.com [cited 1 February 2017].

division titles, and number of Stanley Cups and TPs. Within the conference, the most and least successful of them have been, respectively, the Montreal Canadiens, Detroit Red Wings and Boston Bruins, as opposed to the Columbus Blue Jackets, Florida Panthers, and Ottawa Senators.

Among those in the WC, the Nashville Predators, Winnipeg Jets, and Arizona Coyotes have performed below-expectations because of inferior players on their rosters and coaching problems. Consequently, there are significant differences between the conferences when comparing the achievements of their clubs, in part, because teams in the EC's divisions averaged 52 seasons in the league as of 2016 and the WC's only 32.

From a financial perspective, EC franchises combined were more valuable in 2016 than all those in the WC because of differences in their total revenue, gate receipts, and operating income. The Canadiens, Toronto Maple Leafs and New York Rangers, for example, were each worth more than $1 billion while ten clubs within the WC had market values below $500 million.

Regarding other information in Table 4, EC teams also had the highest average D/V percent and players expenses compared to the WC's. In short, the data denotes the economics of these franchises by division and as businesses whose objective is to maximize profit in their operations during each season.

On average as of 2016, the sixteen arenas of EC teams were older, more expensive to build, and had a higher economic value compared to those in the WC. Among divisions within conferences, AD stadiums ranked first in age at 22 years and in value at $159 million while the MD's cost $305 million to erect.

To attend EC and WC teams' games during the league's 2014–2015 season, the FCI for families was, respectively, $364 and $358. While those of the Bruins and Maple Leafs each cost more than $500, families paid less than $300 to root for such clubs as the Buffalo Sabres, Florida Panthers, and New York Islanders in the EC, and Colorado Avalanche, Dallas Stars, and Anaheim Ducks in the WC.

To summarize results of my research, Table 5 reveals the distribution of financial information for MLB's leagues and NBA, NFL, and NHL conferences as of 2016. First, the most and least valuable group of professional sports organizations — with the highest and lowest average revenue and operating income — are, respectively, teams in football's NFC and ice

Table 5: Professional Sports Organizations, Average Amounts, 2016.

Financial Data	Value	Revenue	GR	OI	D/V	PE
Major League Baseball						
American League	1,241	277	82	22	9	145
National League	1,334	281	83	22	13	148
National Basketball Association						
Eastern Conference	1,225	172	46	26	15	78
Western Conference	1,225	172	47	32	10	80
National Football League						
American Football Conference	2,204	366	59	80	9	182
National Football Conference	2,471	392	64	101	12	176
National Hockey League						
Eastern Conference	570	142	51	18	24	71
Western Conference	455	129	48	9	20	70

Note: Value is teams' estimated market value in millions. Revenue is in millions. Abbreviations are Gate Receipts (GR) in millions, Operating Income (OI) in millions, Debt-to-Value (D/V) in percentages, and Players Expenses (PE) in millions.

Source: See Tables A1.1–A8.3 in the appendix.

hockey's WC. Second, because of baseball's 162-game schedule in regular seasons, AL and NL teams have the largest average gate receipts. Third, the NHL's conferences rank first and second with the two highest D/V ratios. Fourth, MLB's leagues and the other sports' conferences each spend similar amounts on players' expenses. Fifth, MLB's NL, NBA's WC, NFL's NFC, and the NHL's EC are financially the most successful organizations within their sport.

APPENDIX: TABLES

Table A1.1: MLB, American League Teams Market Data, selected years.

Team	MSAPOP (R)	DMATVH (R)	AVGATT (R)
East Division			
Baltimore Orioles	2.79 (13)	1.11 (14)	26.81 (10)
Boston Red Sox	4.77 (7)	2.42 (8)	36.48 (4)
New York Yankees	20.18 (1)	7.34 (1)	37.81 (2)
Tampa Bay Rays	2.97 (12)	1.90 (9)	15.87 (15)
Toronto Blue Jays	6.10 (6)	2.90 (4)	41.88 (1)
Central Division			
Chicago White Sox	9.55 (3)	3.46 (3)	21.82 (12)
Cleveland Indians	2.06 (15)	1.49 (13)	19.65 (13)
Detroit Tigers	4.30 (9)	1.85 (10)	31.17 (7)
Kansas City Royals	2.08 (14)	0.91 (15)	31.57 (6)
Minnesota Twins	3.52 (11)	1.74 (12)	24.24 (11)
West Division			
Houston Astros	6.65 (5)	2.45 (7)	28.47 (8)
LA Angels of Anaheim	13.34 (2)	5.47 (2)	37.23 (3)
Oakland Athletics	4.65 (8)	2.48 (6)	18.78 (14)

(Continued)

Table A1.1: *(Continued)*

Team	MSAPOP (R)	DMATVH (R)	AVGATT (R)
Seattle Mariners	3.73 (10)	1.80 (11)	27.99 (9)
Texas Rangers	7.10 (4)	2.71 (5)	33.46 (5)

Note: Abbreviations are Major League Baseball (MLB), Metropolitan Statistical Area Population (MSAPOP) in 2015, Designated Market Area Television Homes (DMATVH) in 2016–2017, Average Attendance (AVGATT) at home games in 2016, Rank (R) among AL teams, and Los Angeles (LA). MSAPOP and DMATVH are each estimates in millions and AVGATT in thousands.

Source: "Metropolitan Statistical Areas of the United States of America", https// en.wikipedia.org [cited 12 November 2016]; "Population Estimates 2015", http://www. census.gov [cited 12 November 2016]; "Local Television Market Universe Estimates", http://www.rtdna.org [cited 12 November 2016]; "Annual Population Estimates by Census Metro Area", http://www.statcan.gc.ca [cited 16 January 2017]; "Population of Census Metropolitan Areas 2015", http://www.statcan.gc.ca [cited 27 January 2017]; "North American Television Market Ranking 2015–2016", http://www.statcan.gc.ca [cited 27 January 2017]; "MLB Attendance Report — 2016", http://www.espn.com [cited 12 November 2016].

Table A1.2: MLB, American League Team Performances, selected years.

Team	Seasons	World Series	Pennants	Divisions	TP
East Division					
Baltimore Orioles	63	3	6	9	18
Boston Red Sox	116	8	13	8	29
New York Yankees	114	27	40	18	85
Tampa Bay Rays	19	0	1	2	3
Toronto Blue Jays	40	2	2	6	10
Central Division					
Chicago White Sox	116	3	6	5	14
Cleveland Indians	116	2	6	8	16
Detroit Tigers	116	4	11	7	22
Kansas City Royals	48	2	4	8	14
Minnesota Twins	56	2	3	10	15
West Division					
Houston Astros	4	0	0	0	0
LA Angels of Anaheim	56	1	1	9	11
Oakland Athletics	49	4	6	16	26
Seattle Mariners	40	0	0	3	3
Texas Rangers	45	0	2	7	9

Note: MLB is Major League Baseball. Selected years are 1901–2016. TP is total team performances. LA is Los Angeles. Seasons are teams' total number of MLB regular seasons in the AL and include years when teams had other nicknames such as the Boston Americans (1901–1907), New York Highlanders (1903–1912), Tampa Bay Devil Rays (1998–2007), Cleveland Blues (1901)/Cleveland Broncos (1902)/Cleveland Naps (1903–1914), and Los Angeles/California/Anaheim Angels (1961–2004). Division titles exclude 1994 when a players' strike ended the season on August 12. Besides playoffs, the number of World Series, Pennants, and Divisions won are these teams' TPs.

Source: "Teams", http//www.baseball-reference.com [cited 3 November 2016]; "Teams", http://www.sportsencyclopedia.com [cited 3 November 2016]; "Division Series Summary", http//www.mlb.com [cited 3 November 2016]; *Official Major League Baseball Fact Book 2005* Edition (St. Louis, MO: Sporting News, 2005).

Table A1.3: MLB, American League Teams Financial Data, 2015.

Team	Value	Revenue	Gate Receipts	OI	D/V
East Division					
Baltimore Orioles	1,000	239	53	8.8	18
Boston Red Sox	2,300	398	176	43.2	0
New York Yankees	3,400	516	259	13.0	0
Tampa Bay Rays	650	193	29	8.2	21
Toronto Blue Jays	900	241	59	1.2	0
Central Division					
Chicago White Sox	1,050	240	46	20.2	7
Cleveland Indians	800	220	30	18.0	9
Detroit Tigers	1,150	268	79	11.0	15
Kansas City Royals	865	273	99	39.0	7
Minnesota Twins	910	240	73	18.5	22
West Division					
Houston Astros	1,100	270	73	66.6	25
LA Angels of Anaheim	1,340	312	90	41.7	0
Oakland Athletics	725	208	38	32.7	8
Seattle Mariners	1,200	271	64	16.8	0
Texas Rangers	1,225	275	71	(4.7)	13

Note: MLB is Major League Baseball LA is Los Angeles. Amounts are in millions of dollars except for Debt-to-Value (D/V), which is a percent. Data was calculated in March 2015. Value is based on the current stadium deal (unless new stadium is pending) without deduction for debt (other than stadium debt). Revenue is for teams' 2015 season. Gate Receipts include club seats. Operating Income (OI) is earnings before interest, taxes, depreciation, and amortization for teams' 2015 season. D/V includes stadium debts.

Source: Ozanian M, K Badenhausen and C Settimi, "The Business of Baseball", http://www.forbes.com [cited 3 November 2016].

Table A2.1: MLB, National League Teams Market Data, selected years.

Team	MSAPOP (R)	DMATV (R)	AVGATT (R)
East Division			
Atlanta Braves	5.71 (7)	2.41 (7)	24.94 (12)
Miami Marlins	6.01 (6)	1.69 (9)	21.40 (15)
New York Mets	20.18 (1)	7.34 (1)	34.87 (5)
Philadelphia Phillies	6.06 (5)	2.94 (4)	23.64 (13)
Washington Nationals	6.09 (4)	2.47 (6)	30.64 (7)
Central Division			
Chicago Cubs	9.55 (3)	3.46 (3)	39.90 (4)
Cincinnati Reds	2.15 (14)	0.84 (15)	23.38 (14)
Milwaukee Brewers	1.57 (15)	0.89 (14)	28.75 (9)
Pittsburgh Pirates	2.35 (13)	1.16 (12)	28.11 (10)
St. Louis Cardinals	2.81 (12)	1.21 (11)	42.52 (2)
West Division			
Arizona Diamondbacks	4.57 (9)	1.89 (8)	25.13 (11)
Colorado Rockies	2.81 (11)	1.63 (10)	32.12 (6)
Los Angeles Dodgers	13.34 (2)	5.47 (2)	45.71 (1)
San Diego Padres	3.29 (10)	1.06 (13)	29.02 (8)
San Francisco Giants	4.65 (8)	2.48 (5)	41.54 (3)

Note: Abbreviations are Major League Baseball (MLB), Metropolitan Statistical Area Population (MSAPOP) in 2015, Designated Market Area Television Homes (DMATVH) in 2016–2017, Average Attendance (AVGATT) at home games in 2016, and Rank (R) among NL teams. MSAPOP and DMATVH are each estimates in millions and AVGATT in thousands. Despite similar populations, Denver actually ranked 11th and St. Louis 12th in their MSAPOP.

Source: "Metropolitan Statistical Areas of the United States of America", https// en.wikipedia.org [cited 12 November 2016]; "Population Estimates 2015", http://www. census.gov [cited 12 November 2016]; "Local Television Market Universe Estimates", http://www.rtdna.org [cited 12 November 2016]; "MLB Attendance Report — 2016", http://www.espn.com [cited 12 November 2016].

Table A2.2: MLB, National League Teams Performances, selected years.

Team	Seasons	World Series	Pennants	Divisions	TP
East Division					
Atlanta Braves	51	1	5	17	23
Miami Marlins	24	2	2	0	4
New York Mets	55	2	5	6	13
Philadelphia Phillies	134	2	7	12	21
Washington Nationals	12	0	0	3	3
Central Division					
Chicago Cubs	141	3	17	6	26
Cincinnati Reds	127	5	9	11	25
Milwaukee Brewers	19	0	0	1	1
Pittsburgh Pirates	130	5	9	8	22
St. Louis Cardinals	125	11	23	13	47
West Division					
Arizona Diamondbacks	19	1	1	5	7
Colorado Rockies	24	0	1	0	1
Los Angeles Dodgers	59	5	9	15	29
San Diego Padres	48	0	2	5	7
San Francisco Giants	59	3	6	9	18

Note: MLB is Major League Baseball. Selected years are 1876–2016. TP is total team performances. Seasons are teams' total number of MLB regular seasons in the NL and include years when teams had other nicknames such as the Florida Marlins (1993–2011), Philadelphia Quakers (1883–1889), Chicago White Stockings (1876–1889)/Chicago Colts (1890–1897)/Chicago Orphans (1898–1902), Pittsburgh Alleghenys (1887–1890), and St. Louis Browns (1892–1898)/St. Louis Perfectos (1899). Division titles exclude 1994 when a players' strike ended the season on August 12. The number of World Series, Pennants, and Divisions won are these teams' TPs.

Source: "Teams", http//www.baseball-reference.com [cited 3 November 2016]; "Teams", http://www.sportsencyclopedia.com [cited 3 November 2016]; "Division Series Summary", http//www.mlb.com [cited 3 November 2016].

Table A2.3: MLB, National League Teams Financial Data, 2015.

Team	Value	Revenue	Gate Receipts	OI	D/V
East Division					
Atlanta Braves	1,175	266	49	27.8	0
Miami Marlins	675	199	36	15.8	31
New York Mets	1,650	313	104	46.8	18
Philadelphia Phillies	1,235	263	72	(8.9)	7
Washington Nationals	1,300	293	97	22.5	26
Central Division					
Chicago Cubs	2,200	340	144	50.8	19
Cincinnati Reds	905	237	63	9.0	8
Milwaukee Brewers	875	234	64	27.0	6
Pittsburgh Pirates	975	244	58	35.3	10
St. Louis Cardinals	1,600	300	129	59.8	16
West Division					
Arizona Diamondbacks	925	223	44	17.4	15
Colorado Rockies	860	227	54	5.5	7
Los Angeles Dodgers	2,500	438	130	(73.2)	16
San Diego Padres	890	244	48	32.9	20
San Francisco Giants	2,250	409	172	72.6	2

Note: MLB is Major League Baseball. Amounts are in millions of dollars except for Debt-to-Value (D/V), which is a percent. Data was calculated in March 2015. Value is based on the current stadium deal (unless new stadium is pending) without deduction for debt (other than stadium debt). Revenue is for teams' 2015 season. Gate Receipts include club seats. Operating Income (OI) is earnings before interest, taxes, depreciation, and amortization for teams' 2015 season. D/V includes stadium debts.

Source: Ozanian M, K Badenhausen and C Settimi, "The Business of Baseball", http://www.forbes.com [cited 3 November 2016].

Table A3.1:   NBA, Eastern Conference Teams Market Data, selected years.

Team	MSAPOP (R)	DMATV (R)	AVGATT (R)
Atlantic Division			
Boston Celtics	4.77 (9)	2.42 (7)	18.27 (6)
Brooklyn Nets	10.09 (1t)	3.67 (1t)	15.12 (14)
New York Knicks	10.09 (1t)	3.67 (1t)	19.81 (4)
Philadelphia 76ers	6.06 (6)	2.94 (4)	14.88 (15)
Toronto Raptors	6.10 (4)	2.90 (5)	19.82 (3)
Central Division			
Chicago Bulls	9.55 (3)	3.46 (3)	21.82 (1)
Cleveland Cavaliers	2.06 (13)	1.49 (11)	20.56 (2)
Detroit Pistons	4.30 (10)	1.85 (8)	16.51 (12)
Indiana Pacers	1.98 (14)	1.08 (13)	16.84 (10)
Milwaukee Bucks	1.57 (15)	0.89 (14)	15.16 (13)
Southeast Division			
Atlanta Hawks	5.71 (8)	2.41 (7)	16.83 (11)
Charlotte Hornets	2.42 (11)	1.18 (12)	17.48 (9)
Miami Heat	6.01 (7)	1.69 (9)	19.74 (5)
Orlando Magic	2.38 (12)	1.51 (10)	17.54 (8)
Washington Wizards	6.09 (5)	2.47 (5)	17.69 (7)

Note: Abbreviations are National Basketball Association (NBA), Metropolitan Statistical Area Population (MSAPOP) in 2015, Designated Market Area Television Homes (DMATVH) in 2016–2017, Average Attendance (AVGATT) at home games in the 2015–2016 NBA season, Rank (R) among Eastern Conference teams, and a tie (t) in rank. MSAPOP and DMATVH are each estimates in millions and AVGATT in thousands. Since the Nets and Knicks share the New York–Newark–Jersey City sports market and to avoid double counting, their MSAPOP and DMATV are each one-half of the actual number as indicated in columns two and three.

Source: "Metropolitan Statistical Areas of the United States of America", https://en.wikipedia.org [cited 12 November 2016]; "Population Estimates 2015", http://www.census.gov [cited 12 November 2016]; "Local Television Market Universe Estimates", http://www.rtdna.org [cited 12 November 2016]; "NBA Attendance Report — 2016", http://www.proxy.espn.com [cited 5 December 2016].

Table A3.2: NBA, Eastern Conference Team Performances, selected years.

Teams	Seasons	W%	Titles			
			Playoffs	Division	Conference	Championship
Atlantic Division						
Boston Celtics	70	0.588	53	30	9	17
Brooklyn Nets	4	0.463	3	0	0	0
New York Knicks	70	0.493	42	8	4	2
Philadelphia 76ers	53	0.501	33	8	5	2
Toronto Raptors	21	0.438	8	4	0	0
Central Division						
Chicago Bulls	50	0.522	34	9	6	6
Cleveland Cavaliers	46	0.464	20	5	3	1
Detroit Pistons	59	0.485	33	9	5	3
Indiana Pacers	40	0.497	23	6	1	0
Milwaukee Bucks	48	0.510	28	13	2	1
Southeast Division						
Atlanta Hawks	48	0.502	32	5	0	0
Charlotte Bobcats/ Hornets	12	0.386	3	0	0	0
Miami Heat	28	0.520	19	12	5	3
Orlando Magic	27	0.490	14	5	2	0
Washington Wizards	43	0.448	20	3	3	1

Note: Teams are listed alphabetically by division as of their 2015–2016 or simply 2015 season. Seasons include the Basketball Association of America (BAA) 1946–1948 and National Basketball Association (NBA) 1949–2015 seasons. The W% is win–loss or winning percent. The table excludes BAA and NBA teams at their previous sites: New York Nets (1977) and New Jersey Nets (1978–2012); Syracuse Nationals (1950–1963); Fort Wayne Pistons (1949–1957); Tri-Cities Blackhawks (1950–1951), Milwaukee Hawks (1952–1955), and St. Louis Hawks (1956–1968); Chicago Packers (1962), Chicago Zephyrs (1963), and Baltimore Bullets (1964–1973). The Charlotte Bobcats were renamed Hornets in the NBA's 2014–2015 season.

Source: "NBA and ABA Team Index", http://www.basketball-reference.com [cited 1 December 2016] and "Historical Moments", http://www.sportsecyclopedia.com [cited 25 June 2016].

Table A3.3: NBA, Eastern Conference Teams Financial Data, 2015.

Teams	Value	Revenue	OI	GR	D/V	PE
Atlantic Division						
Boston Celtics	2,100	181	57	56	8	69
Brooklyn Nets	1,100	220	–5	63	15	99
New York Knicks	3,000	307	108	128	0	88
Philadelphia 76ers	700	124	13	21	21	60
Toronto Raptors	980	163	23	48	12	87
Central Division						
Chicago Bulls	2,300	228	67	72	2	87
Cleveland Cavaliers	1,100	191	24	52	18	87
Detroit Pistons	850	154	16	22	22	71
Indiana Pacers	840	138	19	20	18	75
Milwaukee Bucks	675	126	11	24	26	71
Southeast Division						
Atlanta Hawks	825	142	7	30	30	67
Charlotte Hornets	750	142	3	24	20	82
Miami Heat	1,300	180	20	67	7	89
Orlando Magic	900	143	35	34	17	66
Washington Wizards	960	146	2	31	14	89

Note: NBA is National Basketball Association. Teams are listed alphabetically by Division. Value is based on the current stadium deal (unless new stadium is pending) without deduction for debt (other than annual stadium debt). Revenue is net of stadium revenues used for debt payments. Operating Income (OI) is earnings before intetest, taxes, depreciation, and amortization. Gate receipts include income from club seats. Debt-to-Value (D/V) is percent and includes ballpark debts. Players Expenses (PE) contains benefits and bonuses. Value, Revenue, OI, GR, and PE are each in millions of US dollars.

Source: Badenhausen K, Ozanian M, and Settimi C, "The Business of Basketball", http://www.forbes.com [cited 27 June 2016].

Table A4.1: NBA, Western Conference Teams Market Data, selected years.

Team	MSAPOP (R)	DMATV (R)	AVGATT (R)
Northwest Division			
Denver Nuggets	2.81 (8)	1.63 (8)	14.09 (15)
Minnesota Timberwolves	3.52 (7)	1.74 (7)	14.17 (14)
Oklahoma City Thunder	1.35 (12)	0.72 (13)	18.20 (8)
Portland Trail Blazers	2.38 (9)	1.14 (10)	19.36 (3)
Utah Jazz	1.17 (15)	0.89 (12)	19.30 (4)
Pacific Division			
Golden State Warriors	4.65 (5)	2.48 (4)	19.59 (2)
Los Angeles Clippers	6.67 (2t)	2.73 (1t)	19.19 (5)
Los Angeles Lakers	6.67 (2t)	2.73 (1t)	18.99 (6)
Phoenix Suns	4.57 (6)	1.89 (6)	17.10 (11)
Sacramento Kings	2.27 (11)	1.37 (9)	17.25 (10)
Southwest Division			
Dallas Mavericks	7.10 (1)	2.71 (3)	20.14 (1)
Houston Rockets	6.65 (4)	2.45 (5)	17.98 (9)
Memphis Grizzlies	1.34 (13)	0.63 (15)	16.69 (13)
New Orleans Pelicans	1.26 (14)	0.64 (14)	16.79 (12)
San Antonio Spurs	2.38 (10)	0.93 (11)	18.44 (7)

Note: Abbreviations are National Basketball Association (NBA), Metropolitan Statistical Area Population (MSAPOP) in 2015, Designated Market Area Television Homes (DMATVH) in 2016–2017, Average Attendance (AVGATT) at home games in the 2015–2016 NBA season, Rank (R) among Western Conference teams, and tie (t). MSAPOP and DMATVH are each estimates in millions and AVGATT in thousands. Since the Clippers and Lakers share the Los Angeles–Long Beach–Anaheim sports market and to avoid double counting, their MSAPOP and DMATV are each one-half of the actual number as indicated in columns two and three.

Source: "Metropolitan Statistical Areas of the United States of America", https://en.wikipedia.org [cited 12 November 2016]; "Population Estimates 2015", http://www.census.gov [cited 12 November 2016]; "Local Television Market Universe Estimates", http://www.rtdna.org [cited 12 November 2016]; "NBA Attendance Report — 2016", http://www.proxy.espn.com [cited 5 December 2016].

Table A4.2:   NBA, Western Conference Team Performances, selected years.

| Teams | Seasons | W% | Titles | | |
			Playoffs	Division	Conference	Championship
Northwest Division						
Denver Nuggets	40	0.484	24	7	0	0
Minnesota Timberwolves	27	0.391	8	1	0	0
Oklahoma City Thunder	8	0.616	6	5	1	0
Portland Trail Blazers	46	0.535	32	5	3	1
Utah Jazz	37	0.554	25	8	2	0
Pacific Division						
Golden State Warriors	45	0.467	15	4	3	2
Los Angeles Clippers	32	0.398	9	2	0	0
Los Angeles Lakers	56	0.613	49	28	18	11
Phoenix Suns	48	0.546	29	6	2	0
Sacramento Kings	31	0.424	10	2	0	0
Southwest Division						
Dallas Mavericks	36	0.510	21	3	2	1
Houston Rockets	45	0.531	29	5	4	2
Memphis Grizzlies	15	0.488	9	0	0	0
NO Hornets/Pelicans	14	0.466	6	1	0	0
San Antonio Spurs	40	0.621	36	21	6	5

Note: NBA is National Basketball Association. Teams are listed alphabetically by division as of their 2015–2016 or simply 2015 season. NO is New Orleans. Seasons include the Basketball Association of America (BAA) 1946–1948 and National Basketball Association (NBA) 1949–2015 seasons. The W% is win–loss or winning percent. The table excludes BAA and NBA teams at their previous sites: Philadelphia Warriors (1949–1957) and San Francisco Warriors (1963–1971); San Diego Rockets (1968–1971); Buffalo Braves (1971–1978) and San Diego Clippers (1979–1984); Minneapolis Lakers (1949–1960); Vancouver Grizzlies (1996–2001); Seattle Supersonics (1968–2008); Rochester Royals (1949–1957), Cincinnati Royals (1958–1972), Kansas City-Omaha Kings (1973–1975), and Kansas City Kings (1976–1985); and New Orleans Jazz (1975–1979).

Source: "NBA and ABA Team Index", http://www.basketball-reference.com [cited 1 December 2016] and "Historical Moments", http://www.sportsecyclopedia.com [cited 25 June 2016].

Table A4.3: NBA, Western Conference Teams Financial Data, 2015.

Teams	Value	Revenue	OI	GR	D/V	PE
Northwest Division						
Denver Nuggets	855	140	26	26	0	64
Minnesota Timberwolves	720	146	15	19	14	76
Oklahoma City Thunder	950	157	20	48	15	87
Portland Trail Blazers	975	157	4	42	11	94
Utah Jazz	875	146	27	36	9	67
Pacific Division						
Golden State Warriors	1,900	201	57	77	13	80
Los Angeles Clippers	2,000	176	20	59	0	92
Los Angeles Lakers	2,700	304	133	98	1	76
Phoenix Suns	1,000	154	21	35	18	76
Sacramento Kings	925	141	4	29	25	81
Southwest Division						
Dallas Mavericks	1,400	177	24	45	8	90
Houston Rockets	1,500	237	74	75	7	85
Memphis Grizzlies	780	147	10	27	22	81
New Orleans Pelicans	650	142	19	30	19	80
San Antonio Spurs	1,150	170	31	59	7	76

Note: NBA is National Basketball Association. Teams are listed alphabetically by Division. Value is based on the current stadium deal (unless new stadium is pending) without deduction for debt (other than annual stadium debt). Revenue is net of stadium revenues used for debt payments. Operating Income (OI) is earnings before interest, taxes, depreciation, and amortization. Gate receipts include income from club seats. Debt-to-Value (D/V) is percent and includes arena debts. Players Expenses (PE) contain benefits and bonuses. Value, Revenue, OI, GR, and PE are each in millions of US dollars.

Source: Badenhausen K, M Ozanian, and C Settimi, "The Business of Basketball", http://www.forbes.com [cited 27 June 2016].

Table A5.1: NFL, American Football Conference Teams Market Data, selected years.

Team	MSAPOP (R)	DMATV (R)	AVGATT (R)
East Division			
Buffalo Bills	1.13 (16)	0.59 (16)	68.50 (6)
Miami Dolphins	6.01 (3)	1.69 (4)	65.51 (9)
New England Patriots	4.77 (4)	2.42 (3)	66.82 (7)
New York Jets	10.09 (1)	3.67 (1)	78.16 (1)
North Division			
Baltimore Ravens	2.79 (7)	1.11 (9)	71.10 (5)
Cincinnati Bengals	2.15 (10)	0.86 (14)	60.51 (14)
Cleveland Browns	2.06 (12)	1.49 (6)	64.31 (12)
Pittsburgh Steelers	2.35 (8)	1.16 (8)	64.32 (11)
South Division			
Houston Texans	6.65 (2)	2.45 (2)	71.86 (4)
Indianapolis Colts	1.98 (13)	1.08 (10)	65.54 (8)
Jacksonville Jaguars	1.44 (15)	0.68 (15)	61.91 (13)
Tennessee Titans	1.83 (14)	1.01 (12)	64.65 (10)
West Division			
Denver Broncos	2.81 (6)	1.63 (5)	76.77 (2)
Kansas City Chiefs	2.08 (11)	0.91 (13)	73.32 (3)
Oakland Raiders	2.32 (9)	1.24 (7)	54.58 (16)
San Diego Chargers	3.29 (5)	1.06 (11)	57.02 (15)

Note: Teams are listed in alphabetical order by division as of their 2015 season. Abbreviations are the National Football League (NFL), American Football Conference (AFC), Metropolitan Statistical Area Population (MSAPOP) in 2015, Designated Market Area Television Homes (DMATVH) in 2016–2017, Average Attendance (AVGATT) at teams' home games as of early 2016, and Rank (R) among AFC teams. MSAPOP and DMATVH are each estimates in millions and AVGATT in thousands. Since the AFC Jets and National Football Conference (NFC) Giants share the New York–Newark–Jersey City sports market, the AFC Raiders and NFC 49ers share the San Francisco–Oakland–Hayward sports market, and to avoid double counting, their MSAPOP and DMATV are each one-half of the actual number as indicated in Columns 2 and 3.

Source: "Metropolitan Statistical Areas of the United States of America", https://en.wikipedia.org [cited 12 November 2016]; "Population Estimates 2015", http://www.census.gov [cited 12 November 2016]; "Local Television Market Universe Estimates", http://www.rtdna.org [cited 12 November 2016]; "NFL Attendance — 2015", http://www.espn.com [cited 21 December 2016].

Table A5.2: NFL, American Football Conference Team Performances, selected years.

Teams	Seasons	Wins	Win%	Titles Division	Titles Conference	Championships NFL	Championships Super Bowl
East Division							
Buffalo Bills	46	328	0.462	7	4	0	0
Miami Dolphins	46	414	0.581	13	5	0	2
New England Patriots	46	399	0.560	17	8	0	4
New York Jets	46	318	0.446	2	0	0	0
North Division							
Baltimore Ravens	20	173	0.540	4	2	0	2
Cincinnati Bengals	46	332	0.466	9	2	0	0
Cleveland Browns	17	87	0.321	0	0	0	0
Pittsburgh Steelers	83	590	0.517	21	8	0	6
South Division							
Houston Texans	14	97	0.433	3	0	0	0
Indianapolis Colts	32	271	0.531	11	2	0	1
Jacksonville Jaguars	21	152	0.452	2	0	0	0
Tennessee Titans	18	145	0.503	3	1	0	0
West Division							
Denver Broncos	46	417	0.585	15	8	0	3
Kansas City Chiefs	46	348	0.488	6	0	0	0
Oakland Raiders	33	249	0.486	9	3	0	2
San Diego Chargers	46	335	0.471	10	1	0	0

Note: Teams are listed in alphabetical order by division as of their 2015 season. Abbreviations are the National Football League (NFL), American Football Conference (AFC), and win percentage (Win%). Except for the Pittsburgh Steelers (1933–2014), the total period for other teams is from the league's 1970 through 2015 season. Seasons, Wins, Win%, Titles, and Championships exclude performances of any teams while playing in the All American Football Conference (1946–1949) and American Football League (1960–1969). The column NFL is number of championships before 1966. Performance data includes the Boston Patriots (1970) followed by the New England Patriots (1971–2014), Tennessee Titans (1998–2014) in Nashville, and Oakland Raiders (1970–1981 plus 1995–2014). It excludes the Baltimore Colts (1953–1983), Cleveland Browns' other franchises (1946–1995), Tennessee Oilers in Memphis (1997), Houston Oilers (1960–1996), and Los Angeles Raiders (1982–1994).

Source: "NFL Links", http://www.sportsecyclopdia.com [cited 22 December 2016] and "Teams", http://www.football-reference.com [cited 1 December 2016].

Table A5.3: NFL, American Football Conference Teams Financial Data, 2016.

Franchises	Value	Revenue	OI	GR	D/V	PE
East Division						
Buffalo Bills	1,500	326	26	50	13	206
Miami Dolphins	2,375	359	58	58	19	189
New England Patriots	3,400	523	212	99	6	182
New York Jets	2,750	423	102	77	22	192
North Division						
Baltimore Ravens	2,300	378	103	68	12	169
Cincinnati Bengals	1,675	329	60	48	6	185
Cleveland Browns	1,850	347	53	54	11	182
Pittsburgh Steelers	2,250	376	68	63	9	195
South Division						
Houston Texans	2,600	416	129	64	7	182
Indianapolis Colts	2,175	336	68	54	3	178
Jacksonville Jaguars	1,950	344	92	54	4	152
Tennessee Titans	2,000	342	73	48	8	169
West Division						
Denver Broncos	2,400	387	82	71	5	188
Kansas City Chiefs	1,875	340	62	55	4	182
Oakland Raiders	2,100	301	46	40	14	169
San Diego Chargers	2,080	344	59	54	7	199

Note: Abbreviations are the National Football League (NFL) and American Football Conference (AFC). Franchises are listed in alphabetical order, by division, as of the league's 2015 season. Amounts are in millions of dollars. Value of a team is based on the current stadium deal (unless new stadium is pending) without deduction for debt (other than stadium debt). Revenue is net of stadium revenues used for debt payments. Operating Income (OI) is earnings before interest, taxes, depreciation, and amortization Gate Receipts (GR) include revenue from club seats. Debt-to-Value (D/V) includes stadium debts.

Source: Badenhausen K, Ozanian MK, and Settimi C, "Sports Money: 2016 NFL Valuations", http://www.forbes.com [cited 22 December 2016].

Table A6.1: NFL, National Football Conference Teams Market Data, selected years.

Team	MSAPOP (R)	DMATV (R)	AVGATT (R)
East Division			
Dallas Cowboys	7.10 (4)	2.71 (5)	92.53 (1)
New York Giants	10.09 (2)	3.67 (2)	78.78 (3)
Philadelphia Eagles	6.06 (6)	2.94 (4)	69.59 (10)
Washington Redskins	6.09 (5)	2.47 (6)	78.30 (4)
North Division			
Chicago Bears	9.55 (3)	3.46 (3)	60.36 (16)
Detroit Lions	4.30 (9)	1.85 (10)	60.79 (14)
Green Bay Packers	0.3 (16)	0.43 (16)	78.21 (5)
Minnesota Vikings	3.52 (11)	1.74 (12)	66.78 (12)
South Division			
Atlanta Falcons	5.71 (7)	2.41 (7)	69.99 (9)
Carolina Panthers	2.42 (13)	1.18 (14)	73.79 (6)
New Orleans Saints	1.26 (15)	0.64 (15)	73.10 (7)
Tampa Bay Buccaneers	2.97 (12)	1.90 (8)	60.62 (15)
West Division			
Arizona Cardinals	4.57 (8)	1.89 (9)	64.83 (13)
Los Angeles Rams	13.34 (1)	5.47 (1)	83.16 (2)
San Francisco 49ers	2.32 (14)	1.24 (13)	70.17 (8)
Seattle Seahawks	3.73 (10)	1.80 (11)	69.07 (11)

Note: Teams are listed in alphabetical order by division as of their 2015 season. Abbreviations are the National Football League (NFL), National Football Conference (NFC), Metropolitan Statistical Area Population (MSAPOP) in 2015, Designated Market Area Television Homes (DMATVH) in 2016–2017, Average Attendance (AVGATT) at home games in the 2016–2017 NFL season, and Rank (R) among NFC teams. MSAPOP and DMATVH are each estimates in millions and AVGATT in thousands. Since the American Football Conference (AFC) Jets and NFC Giants share the New York–Newark–Jersey City sports market, the AFC Raiders and NFC 49ers share the San Francisco–Oakland–Hayward sports market, and to avoid double counting, their MSAPOP and DMATV are each one-half of the actual number as indicated in Columns 2 and 3.

Source: "Metropolitan Statistical Areas of the United States of America", https://en.wikipedia.org [cited 12 November 2016]; "Population Estimates 2015", http://www.census.gov [cited 12 November 2016]; "Local Television Market Universe Estimates", http://www.rtdna.org [cited 12 November 2016]; "NFL Attendance — 2016", http://www.espn.com [cited 2 January 2017].

Table A6.2: NFL, National Football Conference Team Performances, selected years.

Teams	Seasons	Wins	Win%	Titles Division	Titles Conference	Championships NFL	Championships Super Bowl
East Division							
Dallas Cowboys	56	480	0.564	22	8	0	5
New York Giants	91	673	0.528	24	11	4	4
Philadelphia Eagles	83	548	0.474	13	3	3	0
Washington Redskins	79	554	0.497	12	5	2	3
North Division							
Chicago Bears	95	731	0.551	20	4	8	1
Detroit Lions	82	507	0.441	8	4	4	0
Green Bay Packers	95	720	0.552	23	9	9	4
Minnesota Vikings	55	449	0.536	19	4	0	0
South Division							
Atlanta Falcons	50	330	0.429	3	1	0	0
Carolina Panthers	21	166	0.494	11	2	0	0
New Orleans Saints	49	331	0.439	2	1	0	1
Tampa Bay Buccaneers	40	241	0.383	3	1	0	1
West Division							
Arizona Cardinals	28	184	0.411	15	1	0	0
Los Angeles Rams	50	368	0.542	14	2	1	0
San Francisco 49ers	66	520	0.536	9	6	0	5
Seattle Seahawks	40	315	0.502	10	3	0	1

Note: Teams are listed in alphabetical order by division as of their 2015 season. Abbreviations are the National Football Conference (NFC), National Football League (NFL), Super Bowl (SB), and win percentage (Win%). The column NFL is number of championships before 1966. Performance data includes the Chicago Staleys (1921) and Green Bay Packers (1921) while in the American Professional Football Association (renamed National Football League in 1922), Dallas Cowboys in the Western Conference (1960), Phoenix Cardinals (1988–1993), Los Angeles Rams in the Western Division/Western Conference/ NFC (1946–1994 and 2016), and the Seattle Seahawks while in the AFC (1976–2001) and NFC (2002–2014). It excludes the Boston Braves (1932), Boston Redskins (1933–1936), Chicago Cardinals (1921–1959) and St. Louis Cardinals (1960–1987), Cleveland Rams (1937–1945), St. Louis Rams (1995–2015), Decatur Staleys (1920), Portsmouth Spartans (1930–1933), and San Francisco 49ers (1946–1949) while in the All American Football Conference.

Source: "NFL Links", http://www.sportsencyclopedia.com [cited 22 December 2016] and "Teams", http://www.football-reference.com [cited 1 December 2016].

Table A6.3: NFL, National Football Conference Teams Financial Data, 2016.

Franchises	Value	Revenue	OI	GR	D/V	PE
East Division						
Dallas Cowboys	4,200	700	300	98	5	190
New York Giants	3,100	444	133	96	16	182
Philadelphia Eagles	2,500	407	105	69	8	188
Washington Redskins	2,950	447	115	80	8	193
North Division						
Chicago Bears	2,700	385	104	67	4	173
Detroit Lions	1,650	321	64	51	16	151
Green Bay Packers	2,350	391	101	65	5	177
Minnesota Vikings	2,200	306	51	46	23	168
South Division						
Atlanta Falcons	2,125	336	69	56	40	171
Carolina Panthers	2,075	362	53	67	3	195
New Orleans Saints	1,750	358	77	62	4	191
Tampa Bay Buccaneers	1,800	341	75	49	10	171
West Division						
Arizona Cardinals	2,025	348	95	56	7	168
Los Angeles Rams	2,900	317	67	43	31	161
San Francisco 49ers	3,000	446	154	76	18	157
Seattle Seahawks	2,225	377	67	62	7	197

Note: Abbreviations are the National Football League (NFL) and National Football Conference (NFC). Franchises are listed in alphabetical order, by division, as of the league's 2015 season. Amounts are in millions of dollars. Value of a team is based on the current stadium deal (unless new stadium is pending) without deduction for debt (other than stadium debt). Revenue is net of stadium revenues used for debt payments. Gate Receipts (GR) include revenue from club seats. Operating Income (OI) is earnings before interest, taxes, depreciation, and amortization. Player Expenses (PE) includes benefits and bonuses. Debt-to-Value (D/V) includes stadium debts.

Source: Badenhausen K, Ozanian MK, and Settimi C, "Sports Money: 2016 NFL Valuations", http://www.forbes.com [cited 22 December 2016] and Mike Ozanian, "The NFL's Most Valuable Teams 2016", http://www.forbes.com [cited 4 January 2017].

Table A7.1: NHL, Eastern Conference Teams Market Data, selected years

Team	MSAPOP (R)	DMATVH (R)	AVGATT (R)
Atlantic Division			
Boston Bruins	4.77 (8)	2.42 (7)	18.77 (6)
Buffalo Sabres	1.13 (16)	0.59 (15)	18.59 (7)
Detroit Red Wings	4.30 (9)	1.85 (9)	20.02 (2)
Florida Panthers	6.01 (7)	1.69 (11)	15.38 (12)
Montreal Canadiens	4.02 (10)	1.83 (10)	21.28 (1)
Ottawa Senators	1.31 (14)	0.58 (16)	18.08 (10)
Tampa Bay Lightning	2.97 (11)	1.90 (8)	19.09 (5)
Toronto Maple Leafs	6.05 (6)	2.90 (2)	19.15 (4)
Metropolitan Division			
Carolina Hurricanes	1.27 (15)	1.15 (13)	12.20 (16)
Columbus Blue Jackets	2.02 (13)	0.92 (14)	14.66 (14)
New Jersey Devils	6.72 (1t)	2.45 (4t)	15.07 (13)
New York Islanders	6.72 (1t)	2.45 (4t)	13.62 (15)
New York Rangers	6.72 (1t)	2.45 (4t)	18.00 (11)
Philadelphia Flyers	6.06 (5)	2.94 (1)	19.22 (3)
Pittsburgh Penguins	2.35 (12)	1.16 (12)	18.55 (8)
Washington Capitals	6.09 (4)	2.47 (3)	18.51 (9)

Note: Teams are in alphabetical order by division. Abbreviations are National Hockey League (NHL), Metropolitan Statistical Area Population (MSAPOP) in 2015, Designated Market Area Television Homes (DMATVH) in 2016–2017, Average Attendance (AVGATT) at home games in 2016, Rank (R) among EC teams, and tie (t). MSAPOP and DMATVH are each estimates in millions and AVGATT in thousands per game. Since the Devils, Islanders, and Rangers share the New York–Newark–Jersey City MSA professional ice hockey market, their MSAPOP and DMATVH are each one-third of the total for these variables.

Source: "Metropolitan Statistical Areas of the United States of America", https://en.wikipedia.org [cited 12 November 2016]; "Population Estimates 2015", http://www.census.gov [cited 12 November 2016]; "Annual Population Estimates by Census Metro Area", http://www.statcan.gc.ca [cited 16 January 2017]; "Local Television Market Universe Estimates", http://www.rtdna.org [cited 12 November 2016]; "NHL Attendance Report — 2015–2016", http://www.espn.com [cited 24 January 2017].

Table A7.2: NHL, Eastern Conference Team Performances, selected years.

Team	Seasons	Points	Playoffs	Titles Division	Titles Conference	Titles Stanley Cups
Atlantic Division						
Boston Bruins	92	7,028	69	28	6	6
Buffalo Sabres	46	3,906	29	6	2	0
Detroit Red Wings	90	6,705	64	29	6	11
Florida Panthers	23	1,756	5	2	1	0
Montreal Canadiens	99	7,618	82	36	7	23
Ottawa Senators	24	1,932	15	4	1	0
Tampa Bay Lightning	24	1,774	9	2	2	1
Toronto Maple Leafs	99	6,547	65	7	0	13
Metropolitan Division						
Carolina Hurricanes	19	1,533	5	3	2	1
Columbus Blue Jackets	16	1,178	2	0	0	0
New Jersey Devils	34	2,869	21	9	5	3
New York Islanders	44	3,501	24	6	5	4
New York Rangers	90	6,388	58	8	3	4
Philadelphia Flyers	49	4,433	38	16	7	2
Pittsburgh Penguins	49	3,923	30	8	5	4
Washington Capitals	42	3,435	25	9	1	0

Note: NHL is National Hockey League. Data includes the league's 1917–1918 to 2015–2016 seasons. New Jersey Devils' results exclude those of the Kansas City Scouts (1974–1976) and Colorado Rockies (1976–1982), and Carolina Hurricanes' of the Hartford Whalers (1979–1997). Besides the Clarence Campbell Conference and Prince of Wales Conference from the NHL's 1974–1975 to 1992–1993 season, the Eastern Conference and Western Conference have each existed since the 1993–1994 season.

Source: "NHL Teams & Other Hockey Teams", http://www.hockey.reference.com [cited 16 January 2017] and "NHL Teams", http://www.sportsencyclopedia.com [cited 16 January 2017].

Table A7.3:   NHL, Eastern Conference Teams Financial Data, 2015.

Team	Value	Revenue	Gate Receipts	OI	D/V
Atlantic Division					
Boston Bruins	800	169	69	33.5	0
Buffalo Sabres	300	116	40	1.1	27
Detroit Red Wings	625	137	44	6.1	0
Florida Panthers	235	100	16	−15.4	49
Montreal Canadiens	1,120	202	76	76.9	19
Ottawa Senators	355	118	36	6.3	32
Tampa Bay Lightning	305	127	42	3.0	0
Toronto Maple Leafs	1,100	186	72	68.0	10
Metropolitan Division					
Carolina Hurricanes	230	99	22	−15.0	54
Columbus Blue Jackets	245	100	29	−2.4	31
New Jersey Devils	320	126	32	−0.9	81
New York Islanders	385	114	40	2.7	52
New York Rangers	1,250	219	92	74.5	0
Philadelphia Flyers	720	160	65	24.7	0
Pittsburgh Penguins	570	178	85	25.7	20
Washington Capitals	575	136	63	11.7	23

Note: NHL is the National Hockey League. Amounts are in millions of dollars except for Debt/Value (D/V), which is a percent. Calculated in March 2015, Value is teams estimated market value and based on the current stadium deal (unless new stadium is pending) without deduction for debt (other than stadium debt). Revenue is for teams' 2015 season. Gate Receipts include club seats. Operating Income (OI) is earnings before interest, taxes, depreciation, and amortization for teams' 2015 season. D/V includes stadium debts.

Source: Ozanian M, K Badenhausen and C Settimi, "The Business of Hockey", http://www.forbes.com [cited 3 November 2016] and "2016 NHL Valuations", http://www.forbes.com [cited 1 February 2017].

Table A8.1: NHL, Western Conference Teams Market Data, selected years.

Team	MSAPOP (R)	DMATVH (R)	AVGATT (R)
Central Division			
Chicago Blackhawks	9.55 (1)	3.46 (1)	21.85 (1)
Colorado Avalanche	2.81 (8t)	1.63 (8)	17.03 (8)
Dallas Stars	7.10 (2)	2.71 (4)	18.37 (6)
Minnesota Wild	3.52 (7)	1.74 (7)	19.82 (2)
Nashville Predators	1.83 (11)	1.01 (11)	16.97 (9)
St. Louis Blues	2.81 (8t)	1.21 (10)	18.45 (4)
Winnipeg Jets	0.80 (14)	0.43 (14)	15.29 (13)
Pacific Division			
Anaheim Ducks	6.67 (3t)	2.73 (2t)	16.33 (12)
Arizona Coyotes	4.57 (6)	1.89 (6)	13.43 (14)
Calgary Flames	1.44 (12)	0.72 (12)	19.14 (3)
Edmonton Oilers	1.36 (13)	0.71 (13)	16.84 (10)
Los Angeles Kings	6.67 (3t)	2.73 (2t)	18.27 (7)
San Jose Sharks	4.65 (5)	2.48 (5)	16.74 (11)
Vancouver Canucks	2.50 (10)	1.50 (9)	18.43 (5)

Note: Teams are in alphabetical order by division. Abbreviations are National Hockey League (NHL), Metropolitan Statistical Area Population (MSAPOP) in 2015, Designated Market Area Television Homes (DMATVH) in 2016–2017, Average Attendance (AVGATT) at home games in 2016, Rank (R) among EC teams, and tie (t). MSAPOP and DMATVH are each estimates in millions and AVGATT in thousands per game. Since the Ducks and Kings share the Los Angeles–Long Beach–Anaheim MSA, their MSAPOP and DMATVH are each one-half of the total numbers. The Shark's DMATVH is San Francisco–Oakland–San Jose.

Source: "Metropolitan Statistical Areas of the United States of America", https://en.wikipedia.org [cited 12 November 2016]; "Population Estimates 2015", http://www.census.gov [cited 12 November 2016]; "Annual Population Estimates by Census Metro Area", http://www.statcan.gc.ca [cited 16 January 2017]; "Population of Census Metropolitan Areas 2015," http://www.statcan.gc.ca [cited 27 January 2017]; "North American Television Market Ranking 2015–2016," http://www.statcan.gc.ca [cited 27 January 2017]; "Local Television Market Universe Estimates", http://www.rtdna.org [cited 12 November 2016]; "NHL Attendance Report — 2015–16", http://www.espn.com [cited 24 January 2017].

Table A8.2:   NHL, Western Conference Team Performances, selected years.

Team	Seasons	Points	Playoffs	Titles Division	Conference	Stanley Cups
Central Division						
Chicago Blackhawks	90	6,280	61	16	4	6
Colorado Avalanche	21	1,878	13	9	2	2
Dallas Stars	23	2,097	14	8	2	1
Minnesota Wild	16	1,352	7	2	0	0
Nashville Predators	18	1,528	9	0	0	0
St. Louis Blues	49	4,061	40	9	0	0
Winnipeg Jets	5	444	1	0	0	0
Pacific Division						
Anaheim Ducks	23	1,934	12	5	2	1
Arizona Coyotes	20	1,599	8	1	0	0
Calgary Flames	36	3,047	21	6	3	1
Edmonton Oilers	37	3,014	20	6	7	5
Los Angeles Kings	49	3,779	29	1	3	2
San Jose Sharks	25	2,076	18	7	1	0
Vancouver Canucks	46	3,549	27	10	3	0

Note: NHL is National Hockey League. Data includes the league's 1917–1918 to 2015–2016 seasons. Colorado Avalanche's results exclude those of the Quebec Nordiques (1979–1995); Dallas Stars' of the Minnesota North Stars (1967–1993); Winnipeg Jets' of the Atlanta Thrashers (1999–2011); Arizona Coyotes' of the Winnipeg Jets (1979–1996); and the Calgary Flames' of the Atlanta Flames (1972–1980). The Anaheim Ducks' includes the Mighty Ducks of Anaheim (1993–2006), and the Arizona Coyotes' of the Phoenix Coyotes (1996–2014). Besides the Clarence Campbell Conference and Prince of Wales Conference from the NHL's 1974–1975 to 1992–1993 season, the Eastern Conference and Western Conference have each existed since the 1993–1994 season.

Source: "NHL Teams & Other Hockey Teams", http://www.hockey.reference.com [cited 16 January 2017] and "NHL Teams", http://www.sportsencyclopedia.com [cited 16 January 2017].

Table A8.3: NHL, Western Conference Teams Financial Data, 2015.

Team	Value	Revenue	Gate Receipts	OI	D/V
Central Division					
Chicago Blackhawks	925	173	74	34.4	0
Colorado Avalanche	360	115	33	6.3	0
Dallas Stars	500	144	43	20.9	29
Minnesota Wild	400	136	55	5.6	28
Nashville Predators	270	116	38	−2.2	31
St. Louis Blues	310	129	49	3.2	21
Winnipeg Jets	340	112	45	11.4	38
Pacific Division					
Anaheim Ducks	415	121	40	−1.2	15
Arizona Coyotes	240	101	20	−8.0	57
Calgary Flames	410	121	53	18.0	7
Edmonton Oilers	445	117	54	15.4	21
Los Angeles Kings	600	142	46	−0.4	12
San Jose Sharks	470	141	63	7.1	11
Vancouver Canucks	700	146	62	29.6	11

Note: NHL is National Hockey League. Amounts are in millions of dollars except for Debt/Value (D/V), which is a percent. Calculated in March 2015, Value is based on the current stadium deal (unless new stadium is pending) without deduction for debt (other than stadium debt). Revenue is for teams' 2015 season. Gate Receipts include club seats. Operating Income (OI) is earnings before interest, taxes, depreciation, and amortization for teams' 2015 season. D/V includes stadium debts.

Source: Ozanian M, Badenhausen K and Settimi C, "The Business of Hockey", http:// www.forbes.com [cited 3 November 2016] and "2016 NHL Valuations", http://www. forbes.com [cited 1 February 2017].

BIBLIOGRAPHY

ARTICLES

Alexandra, B. (2017). The NHL's goal: Get younger fans. *Wall Street Journal*, R6.

Andrew, B. (2015). The NFL's least optimistic fan bases. *Wall Street Journal*, D6.

Ben B, and A. Zimbalist (2014). Quantifying efficiencies in the baseball players market. *Eastern Economic Journal*, 40(Fall), 488–498.

Brian, C. (2015). The CEO who gets to hand out world series rings. *Wall Street Journal*, R4.

Eliot, B. (2016). When the new ballpark is already too old. *Wall Street Journal*, A3.

Eric, F. (2011). Realignment will test interleague's popularity. *Sports Business Journal*, 6.

Images: MLB All-Star Game Moments. *Daily Herald* (2015), 1.

Jason, G. (2016) My dream life in the NFL...accounting. *Wall Street Journal*, D6.

Kevin, C. (2014). The league that runs everything. *Wall Street Journal*, B8.

Matthew, F. (2015). NFL's money machine never blinks. *Wall Street Journal*, B1–B2.

Matthew, F. and H. Karp. (2017). A football double feature in L.A. *Wall Street Journal*, A12.

Rankings of U.S. Standard Metropolitan Statistical Areas. *World Almanac & Book of Facts* (1972), 154–155.

Rick, R. (2014). Putting a price tag on the panthers. *Charlotte Observer*, 2D.

Sarah E, N. (2016). MLB in league with riot games. *Wall Street Journal*, B3.

Smith, CM. (2015). A calculus of color: The integration of baseball's American league. *Choice*, 53, 283.

BOOKS

Dan, D. (2000). *The Official Encyclopedia of the National Hockey League.* Kingston, NY: Total Sports Publishing.

D'Arcy, J. (2016). *The NHL: 100 Years of On-Ice Action and Boardroom Battles.* Toronto, Canada: Anchor Canada.

Jozsa, FP, Jr. (1999). and John J. Guthrie Jr. *Relocating Teams and Expanding Leagues in Professional Sports: How the Major Leagues Respond to Market Conditions.* Westport, CT: Quorum Books.

Jozsa, FP, Jr. (2006). *Baseball, Inc.: The National Pastime as Big Business.* Jefferson, NC: McFarland.

Jozsa, FP, Jr. (2008). *Baseball in Crisis: Spiraling Costs, Bad Behavior, Uncertain Future.* Jefferson, NC: McFarland.

Jozsa, FP, Jr. (2009). *Major League Baseball Expansions and Relocations: A History, 1876–2008.* Jefferson, NC: McFarland.

Jozsa, FP, Jr. (2010). *Football Fortunes: The Business, Organization and Strategy of the NFL.* Jefferson, NC: McFarland.

Jozsa, FP, Jr. (2011). *The National Basketball Association: Business, Organization and Strategy.* Hackensack, NJ: World Scientific.

Jozsa, FP, Jr. (2014). *National Football League Strategies: Business Expansions, Relocations, and Mergers.* New York, NY: Springer.

Jozsa, FP, Jr. (2015). *National Basketball Association Strategies: Business Expansions, Relocations, and Mergers.* New York, NY: Springer.

Jozsa, FP, Jr. (2016). *American League Franchises: Team Performances Inspire Business Success.* New York, NY: Springer.

Jozsa, FP, Jr. (2016). *Major League Baseball Organizations: Team Performances and Financial Consequences.* Lanham, MD: Lexington Books.

Jozsa, FP, Jr. (2016). *National Football League Franchises: Team Performances, Financial Consequences.* Lanham, MD: Lexington.

Jozsa, FP, Jr. (2016). *National League Franchises: Team Performances Inspire Business Success.* New York, NY: Springer.

Kirchberg, C. (2007). *Hoop Love: A History of the National Basketball Association.* Jefferson, NC: McFarland.

Quirk, J. and RD. Fort (1992). *Pay Dirt: The Business of Professional Team Sports.* Princeton, NJ: Princeton University Press.

Surdam, DG. (2012). *The Rise of the National Basketball Association.* Urbana, IL: University of Illinois Press.

The Statesman's Year-Book: 1992–93. London: Palgrave Macmillan Press.

DISSERTATIONS AND THESES

Jozsa, FP, Jr. (1977). An economic analysis of franchise relocation and league expansions in professional team sports, 1950–1976. Ph.D. diss., Georgia State University.

INTERNET SOURCES

Aldridge, D. NBA, NBAP reach tentative seven-year CBA agreement. http://www.nba.com [cited 15 December 2016].

Alsher, J. The ten best NBA teams of all-time. http://www.cheatsheet.com [cited 2 December 2016].

Annual population estimates by census metro area. http://www.statcan.ca [cited 16 January 2017].

Anzilotti, E. How the NBA's progressivism is helping it thrive. http://www.theatlantic.com [cited 13 December 2016].

Arthur, K. What the NFL will look like in 2018. http://www.sportsonearth.com [cited 14 January 2017].

Badenhausen, K, MK. Ozanian, and C Settimi. Sports money: 2016 NFL valuations. http://www.forbes.com [cited 22 December 2016].

Badenhausen, K, M Ozanian, and C Settimi. The business of baseball. http://www.forbes.com [cited 1 October 2016].

Badenhausen, K, M Ozanian, and C Settimi. The business of basketball. http://www.forbes.com [cited 27 June 2016].

Baseball-reference all-star game index. http://www.baseball-reference.com [cited 1 November 2016].

Baseball roster history. http://www.baseball-almanac.com [cited 8 November 2016].

Bass, A. NHL: 50 best teams in history. http://www.bleacherreport.com [cited 22 January 2017].

Bass, A. Power ranking the league's 30 arenas. http://www.bleacherreport.com [cited 24 January 2017].

Brown, M. With 2016 season half over, TV ratings for MLB shows RSNs rulings in prime time. http://www.forbes.com [cited 21 November 2016].

Burton, R, and N O'Reilly. Reading the tea leaves: Will expansion transcend borders?" http://www.sportsbusinessdaily.com [cited 24 January 2017].

CBA 101" http://www.nba.com [cited 8 December 2016].

Chase, C. The AFC north has been the NFL's best division in past decade. http://www.ftwusatoday.com [cited 2 January 2017].

Chase, C. Ranking the best and worst NFL stadium, from No. 1 (Lambeau) to 31 Soldier). http://www.ftwusatoday.com [cited 31 December 2016].

Clinton, J. Top ten coaches by points percentage: Where does Mike Babcock sit?" http://www.thehockeynews.com [cited 25 January 2017].

Colangelo, M. Alternating American League, National League coverage favors fox over turner this year. http://www.thefieldsofgreen.com [cited 2 December 2016].

Collective bargaining agreement. http://www.nhlpa.com [cited 3 February 2017].

Collective bargaining agreement between National Hockey League and National Hockey League Players' Association. http://www.nhl.com [cited 19 January 2017].

Commissioners of Major League Baseball, and American League Presidents and National League Presidents. http://www.baseball-almanac.com [cited 24 November 2016].

Complete team list. http://www.databaseball.com [cited 6 November 2016].

Cuthbert, J. Ranking the 31 NHL general managers. http://www.thescore.com [cited 25 January 2017].

Dahlgren, L. Power rankings: NBA arenas. http://www.fansided.com [cited 11 December 2016].

Dallas Cowboys dominating NFL TV ratings. http://www.upi.com [cited 14 January 2017].

Defunct AL teams. http://www.sportsencyclopedia.com [cited 6 November 2016].

Defunct baseball teams. http://www.sportsencyclopedia.com [cited 24 November 2016].

Defunct NHL teams. http://www.infoplease.com [cited 19 January 2017].

Defunct NL franchises. http://www.sportsencyclopedia.com [cited 6 November 2016].

Defunct teams histories. http://www.sportsencyclopedia.com [cited 15 January 2017].

Determining the best Major League Baseball team ever from 1902–2005. http://www.baseball-almanac.com [cited 27 November 2016].

Diamond, J. Why a National League designated hitter is inevitable. http://www.wsj.com [cited 2 December 2016].

Diaz, A. The 25 worst NFL teams of all time. http://www.complex.com [cited 29 December 2016].

DiRocco, M. Shad Khan: Jaguars moving to St. Louis isn't a possibility. http://www.espn.com [cited 2 January 2017].

Division series summary. http://www.mlb.com [cited 3 November 2016].

Doleiden, Z. George Halas Trophy: 5 fast facts you need to know. http://www.heavy.com [cited 15 January 2017].

Dragon, T. Buffalo bills evaluating potential new stadium options. http://www.nfl.com [cited 2 January 2017].

Edwards, C. Estimated TV revenues for all 30 MLB teams. http://www.fangraphs. com [cited 2 December 2016].

Eisenband, J. 12 NHL franchises that have never won Stanley cup. http://www. thepostgame.com [cited 24 January 2017].

Exner, R. NBA's Western Conference tops East for sixteenth time in seventeen seasons, but separation much tighter in 2015–16. http://www.cleveland.com [cited 20 December 2016].

Fan cost index. http://www.teammarketingreport.com [cited 16 November 2016].

Faulk, M, and K Addo. City, business leaders want $138 million in renovations for scottrade center. http://www.stltoday.com [cited 2 February 2017].

Fromal, A. Each NBA franchise's worst team ever. http://www.bleacerreport.com [cited 10 December 2016].

George Halas Award. http://www.profootballwriters.org [cited 15 January 2017].

Gonos, D. Top ten media markets without an NBA team. http://www.sportsgrid. com [cited 12 December 2016].

Greenberg, J. NHL fan cost index 2014–15. http://www.teammarketing.com [cited 25 January 2017].

Heisler, M. Heisler: From bad to worse to vivek: Top ten worst owners in NBA. http://www.dailynews.com [cited 12 December 2016].

Hill, J. NBA: 5 arenas that need to be torn down right now. http://www.fansided. com [cited 12 December 2016].

Hill, J. NBA owners power ranking: Who is the best owner in basketball? http:// www.fansided.com [cited 12 December 2016].

Historical moments. http://www.sportsencyclopedia.com [cited 25 June 2016].

History of NHL relocation. http://www.puckreport.com [cited 5 January 2017].

History of North American Hockey. http://www.hockeyleaguehistory.com [cited 25 January 2017].

Iyer, Prashanth. Top 15 NHL teams of all time. http://www.hookedonhockeymaga zine.com [cited 1 February 2017].

Key, J. Greatest NHL teams of all-time. http://www.thehockeynews.com [cited 20 January 2017].

Khan, A. Top ten richest NBA owners. http://www.thesportster.com [cited 12 December 2016].

Klein, C. From six teams to 31: History of NHL expansion. http://www.nhl.com [cited 1 January 2017].

Leahy, S. 10 Interesting highlights from the NHL's new CBA. http://www.sport. yahoo.com [cited 19 January 2017].

Levesque, W. Lightning, Hillsborough to split $25 Million cost for Amalie Arena Upgrades. http://www.tampabay.com [cited 23 January 2017].

Liebman, R. Schedule changes since 1876. http://www.research.sabr.org [cited 7 November 2016].

Lightning announce two-year renovation concepts for Amalie Arena. http://www.nhl.com [cited 23 January 2017].

List of major league baseball principal owners. http://www.baseball-reference.com [cited 23 November 2016].

Local television market universe estimates. http://www.rtdna.org [cited 12 November 2016].

Luszczyszyn, D. How much confidence does each NHL fan base have in their front office? A ranking of all 30 teams. http://www.thehockeynews.com [cited 3 February 2017].

Mather, V. A brief history of the single-elimination wild-card game. http://www.nytimes.com [cited 6 November 2016].

Median household income in the past 12 Months by 25 most populous metropolitan areas. http://www.census.gov [cited 18 November 2016].

Metropolitan statistical areas of the United States of America. https://en.wikipedia.org [cited 12 November 2016].

MLB all-star game history. http://www.espn.com [cited 1 November 2016].

MLB attendance report — 2016. http://www.espn.com [cited 12 November 2016].

MLB links. http://www.sportsencyclopedia.com [cited 23 November 2016].

Morosi, J.P. Which locations make the most sense for MLB expansion? http://www.foxsports.com [cited 18 November 2016].

Muret, D. Ranking all NFL stadiums. http://www.sportingnews.com [cited 10 January 2017].

National Hockey League (NHL). http://www.thecanadianencyclopedia.ca [cited 27 January 2017].

National League Presidents. http://www.sportsencyclopedia.com [cited 24 November 2016].

NBA all-star game results. http://www.nba.com [cited 12 December 2016].

NBA and ABA team index. http://www.basketball-reference.com [cited 1 December 2016].

NBA arenas. http://www.hoopsonline.com [cited 11 December 2016].

NBA attendance report — 2016. http://www.proxy.espn.com [cited 5 December 2016].

NBA championships: Winners by conference. http://www.landofbasketball.com [cited 12 December 2016].

NBA collective bargaining agreement. http://www.npba.com [cited 8 December 2016].

NBA front-office rankings: 2015. http://www.espn.com [cited 13 December 2016].

NBA history — MVP. http://www.espn.com [cited 2 December 2016].

NBA most valuable player recipients. http://www.basketball.realgm.com [cited 2 December 2016].

NBA playoffs history. http://www.nba.com [cited 15 December 2016].

NBA salaries. http://www.hoopshype.com [cited 20 December 2016].

NFL attendance — 2015. http://www.espn.com [cited 21 December 2016].

NFL attendance — 2016. http://www.espn.com [cited 2 January 2017].

NFL collective bargaining agreement. http://www.nfllabor.com [cited 24 December 2016].

NFL links. http://www.sportsecyclopdia.com [cited 22 December 2016].

NFL stadium comparisons. http://www.stadiumsofprofootall.com [cited 25 December 2016].

NHL arenas. http://www.statshockey.homestead.com [cited 25 January 2017].

NHL attendance report — 2015–16. http://www.espn.com [cited 24 January 2017].

NHL & WHA career leaders and records for points. http://www.hockey-reference.com [cited 20 January 2017].

NHL fan cost index. http://www.teammarketing.com [cited 2 February 2017].

NHL player & team records. http://www.statshockey.homestead.com [cited 20 January 2017].

NHL teams. http://www.sportsencyclopedia.com [cited 16 January 2017].

NHL teams & other hockey teams. http://www.hockey.reference.com [cited 16 January 2017].

North American television market ranking 2015–16. http://www.statcan.gc.ca [cited 27 January 2017].

Oakland Mayor announces framework for stadium agreement. http://www.espn.com [cited 2 January 2017].

Other 0–7 starts in American League history. http://www.startribune.com [cited 18 November 2016].

Ourand, J. ESPN wants all games of eastern finals. http://www.sportsbusinessjournal.com [cited 13 December 2013].

Ozanian, M. The NFL's most valuable teams 2016. http://www.forbes.com [cited 4 January 2017].

Ozanian, M. 2016 NFL valuations. http://www.forbes.com [cited 1 December 2016].

Ozanian, M, K Badenhausen, and C Settimi. The business of baseball. http://www.forbes.com [cited 3 November 2016].

Ozanian, M, K Badenhausen, and C Settimi. The business of hockey. http://www.forbes.com [cited 3 November 2016].

Paine, N. The best NFL teams of all time, according to Elo. http://www.fivethirtyeight.com [cited 23 December 2016].

Picking the best team ever for all 32 NFL franchises. http://www.espn.com [cited 23 December 2016].

Players union to fund health insurance for NBA retirees. http://www.nba.com [cited 13 December 2016].

Playoff formats. http://www.nhl.com [cited 3 February 2017].

Pogany, B. The 10 greatest NHL franchises. http://www.definitivedose.com [cited 25 January 2017].

Population estimates 2015. http://www.census.gov [cited 12 November 2016].

Population of census metropolitan areas 2015. http://www.statcan.gc.ca [cited 27 January 2017].

Predictions for 2016–17 season. http://www.nhl.com [cited 24 January 2017].

Present national basketball association arenas. http://www.basketball.ballparks.com [cited 11 December 2016].

Present national hockey league arenas. http://www.hockey.ballparks.com [cited 25 January 2017].

Ranking the value of all 30 NHL franchises. http://www.thesportster.com [cited 24 January 2017].

Ratto, R. The 'Raiders Stadium Deal' that isn't a stadium deal at all. http://www.csnbayarea.com [cited 1 January 2017].

Reed, R. Fly the 'W' for cubs business strategy. http://www.chicagotribune.com [cited 3 December 2016].

Roberts, E. The west has become the NHL's elite conference. http://www.thehockey writers.com [cited 3 February 2017].

Rod Fort's sports business data. http://sites.google.com [cited 1 November 2016].

Rodney Fort's sports economics. http://sites.google.com [cited 24 January 2017].

Rymer, Z. Which is baseball's superior overall league, the AL or the NL? http://www.bleacherreport.com [cited 18 November 2016].

Schaal, E. 5 worst teams of the modern era. http://www.cheatsheet.com [cited 10 November 2016].

Schaal, E. 8 greatest MLB teams of all time. http://www.cheatsheet.com [cited 10 November 2016].

Selbe, N. The 10 greatest MLB teams seasons in history. http://www.mlb-teamspointafter.com [cited 27 November 2016].

Shannon, M. NHL history: The ten worst teams of all time. http://www.bleacher report.com [cited 20 January 2017].

Silver, N. Which MLB teams overperform in popularity? http://www.fivethirtyeight.com [cited 2 December 2016].

Silver, N, and R Fischer-Baum. How we calculate NBA Elo ratings. http://www.fivethirtyeight.com [cited 5 December 2016].

Silverman, S. The NHL's 10 greatest Stanley cup championship teams of the last 50 years. http://www.bleacherreport.com [cited 22 January 2017].

Simmons, J. NHL power rankings: General managers. http://www.sportsnet.ca [cited 3 February 2017].

SI's best & worst owners in NHL. http://www.si.com [cited 25 January 2017].

Smith, MD. Las Vegas would be the NFL's fifth-smallest media market. http://www.profootballtalknbcsports.com [cited 2 January 2017].

Spedden, Z. Financial details emerge on guaranteed rate field. http://www.ballparkdigest.com [cited 18 November 2016].

Sports money: 2016 NFL valuations. http://www.forbes.com [cited 1 January 2017].

Standard deviation calculator. http://www.easycalculation.com [cited 3 January 2017].

Stanley cup playoffs format, qualification system. http://www.nhl.com [cited 21 January 2017].

Swaney, P. 2015 NFL stadium experience rankings. http://www.scout.com [cited 31 December 2016].

Swaney, P. 2016 NHL arena experience rankings. http://www.scout.com [cited 24 January 2017].

Team encyclopedias and records. http://www.pro-football-reference.com [cited 1 December 2016].

Team marketing report — MLB 2016. http://www.teammarketing.com [cited 25 January 2016].

Team marketing report — NBA 2015–16. http://www.teammarketing.com [cited 12 December 2016].

Team marketing report — NFL 2016. http://www.teammarketing.com [cited 15 January 2017].

Teams. http://www.baseball-reference.com [cited 3 November 2016].

Teams. http://www.football-reference.com [cited 1 December 2016].

Teams. http://www.sportsencyclopedia.com [cited 3 November 2016].

10 worst records in NBA history. http://www.cheatsheet.com [cited 12 December 2016].

The 382 metropolitan statistical areas of the United States of America. http://www.en.wikipedia.org [cited 12 October 2016].

The Naismith Memorial Basketball Hall of Fame. http://www.hoophall.com [cited 1 December 2016].

The ten worst Major League Baseball seasons ever. http://www.writing.jmpressely.net [cited 24 November 2016].

This day in history: The NBA is born. http://www.history.com [cited 14 December 2016].

Top 15 worst NHL teams of all time. http://www.thesportster.com [cited 20 January 2017].

Top U.S. metropolitan areas by population, 1790–2010. http://www.peakbagger. com [cited 5 December 2016].

Tour every NFL stadium. http://www.espn.com [cited 25 December 2016].

2016 NFL attendance data. http://www.pro-football-reference.com [cited 6 January 2017].

2016 NHL valuations. http://www.forbes.com [cited 1 February 2017].

Watson, Z. Examining future NHL expansion scenarios. http://www.thesportsquo tient.com [cited 24 January 2017].

Which is baseball's Superior Overall League, the AL or the NL? http://www.bleach erreport.com [cited 18 November 2016].

Which locations make the most sense for MLB expansion? http://www.foxsports. com [cited 18 November 2016].

William PF, II. http://www.bkfs.com [cited 3 February 2017].

Williams, E. Failed stadium vote leaves little time to mull options. http://www.espn. com [cited 2 January 2017].

Wolf, D. 10 reasons why the AFC is better than the NFC since 2000. http://www. bleacherreport.com [cited 2 January 2017].

Worst NFL teams of all time. http://www.espn.com [cited 29 December 2016].

Zegers, C. About the NBA playoffs. http://www.basketball.about.com [cited 13 December 2016].

Zierlein, L. 2017 NFL draft order and needs for every team. http://www.nfl.com [cited 2 January 2017].

Zimmer, D. All 32 NFL franchises statistically ranked in all-time greatness. http:// www.nflspinzone.com [cited 14 January 2017].

Zimmer, D. NHL power rankings: Every franchise statistically ranked all-time. http://www.fansided.com [cited 3 February 2017].

Zuckerman, M. Ranking all 30 MLB ballparks. http://www.csnmidatlantic.com [cited 17 November 2016].

MEDIA GUIDES

National Hockey League Official Guide & Record Book 2016. Chicago, IL: Triumph Books (2016).

Official Major League Baseball Fact Book, 2005 Edition. St. Louis, MO: Sporting News (2005).

Official National Basketball Association Guide 2015–16. New York, NY: NBA Properties (2015).

2014 Official NFL Record & Fact Book. New York, NY: National Football League (2014).

UNPUBLISHED MANUSCRIPT

Jozsa, FP, Jr. (2010). Hockey business: NHL franchises, markets and strategies. Unpublished manuscript, Misenheimer, NC: Pfeiffer University.

INDEX

Printed in the United States
By Bookmasters